Islam without Fear

Islam WITHOUT FEAR

EGYPT *and the* NEW ISLAMISTS

RAYMOND WILLIAM BAKER

HARVARD UNIVERSITY PRESS
CAMBRIDGE, MASSACHUSETTS, AND LONDON, ENGLAND 2003

Printed in the United States of America

Library of Congress Cataloging-in-Publication Data

Baker, Raymond William, 1942–
Islam without fear : Egypt and the new Islamists / Raymond William Baker.
p. cm.
Includes bibliographical references and index.
ISBN 0-674-01203-8 (alk. paper)
1. Egypt—Politics and government—1981–
2. Islam and politics—Egypt.
3. Religious awakening—Egypt.
4. Secularism—Egypt. I. Title.
DT107.87.B347 2003
962.05′5—dc21 2003051081

Designed by Gwen Nefsky Frankfeldt

For Elaine, Sarah, Dorian, Madalyn, and Pamela,
who shared this voyage of knowing and loving

Contents

O mankind! We created you from a single (pair) of a male and a female, and made you into nations and tribes, that ye may know each other (not that ye may despise each other). Verily the most honored of you in the sight of God is (he who is) the most righteous of you. And God has full knowledge and is well acquainted (with all things).

—Quran, Surah: 49:13

Introduction

This book tells the story of a group of centrist Islamist intellectuals who call themselves the "New Islamist Trend." They think of their intellectual school as an outgrowth of the centrist Islamic mainstream, or *Wassatteyya.* The group is driven by a positive, mainstream vision which they affirm in thought and practice, rather than by defensive fears. Rooted in Egypt, the New Islamists address with considerable influence the broader Arab Islamic world. Their work poses the central question addressed in this book: whether an Islamic project of the center, speaking for an Islam without fear, can address effectively the demands of our global age.

The New Islamists first formulated the manifesto of their group in the early 1980s and circulated it widely among intellectuals. Because of adverse political conditions, however, the manifesto was not published until 1991 by its primary author, Kamal Abul Magd, an internationally known constitutional lawyer. The book, entitled *A Contemporary Islamic Vision,* immediately elicited widespread discussion. However, the most productive critique came somewhat later in 1994 from Sayyid Yassine, a highly respected public intellectual, director of the Al Ahram Center for Political and Strategic Studies, and an influential critic of the Islamic trend. The lively debate that ensued on the pages of the *al Ahram* newspaper between Yassine and Abul Magd introduces the major themes of this book.

Yassine begins with the important acknowledgment that the New Islamists, unlike other groups, "do not claim the role of spokespersons of Islam." Instead, he comments approvingly, they "deliberately present their ideas as simply one available view, subject to public discussion." Yassine then launches his critique by saying that he finds nothing that is "new" and little that is distinctively "Islamic" in the manifesto. He advances three of the most telling arguments typically made against Islamist moderates, charging them with passive complicity in the violence of the extremists, totalizing and unrealistic ideological claims, and failure to respond in creative and novel ways to Egypt's pressing national needs. In a dismissive move characteristic of secular critics, he asks: "Wouldn't it be more worthy for the statement writers to highlight the criminal, extremist violence disguised by Islam and condemn it clearly and categorically?" In response, Abul Magd defends the statement as "a cry for salvation" and expresses regret that Yassine has failed to respond to the substance of this moderate program in favor of yet another attack on the extremists. However, recognizing that Yassine has stated a widespread criticism of the centrist Islamic project, mounted by critics in Egypt and abroad, Abul Magd seizes the moment to offer a spirited defense. "Yassine knows perfectly well," Abul Magd argues, "that I spent, together with the other authors of this statement, more than thirty years condemning violence and warning of its implications loudly and vigorously, while refuting the claims of the violent groups." The electric exchange between the two writers sets in sharp relief the core issues of the struggle for Islam, waged by secular Muslims, moderate Islamists, and violent extremists. This debate in *al Ahram* immediately captured the attention of Egypt's political class.[1]

Given Islam's remarkable global importance, the debate deserves an even wider audience. In the second half of the twentieth century, the world witnessed a "return of religion" to challenge the secularization that had everywhere seemed an inevitable dimension of modernization. In Arab countries, this global phenomenon took the form of an "Islamic Awakening" that was advanced by varied Islamist currents, groups, and movements.[2] These Islamist forces ranged from quietists who focused on individual belief and ritual to extremists who sought to remake their societies along religious lines with the use of violence. In the Arab Islamic world the *Wassatteyya,* a broad centrist current, took shape between these extremes. This moderate Islamic mainstream eschewed the passivity of the religious quietists and called for the transformation of society along Islamic grounds. However, they categorically rejected violent methods as incompatible with the goals they sought. Their notions of both ends and means embodied the core values of Islam, notably justice. The transformation they envisioned as both process and goal must be consonant with these higher purposes at all stages. Rooted in the nineteenth-century work of such pioneers of renewal as Muhammad Abduh, this Islamic mainstream achieved its most enduring expression in the Muslim Brothers organization, founded in Egypt in 1928 by Hassan al Banna. The Brotherhood drew its mass strength from the middle class, especially its lower strata. By midcentury the Muslim Brothers had attracted approximately a million adherents to their project of Islamic renewal as an antidote to decline. However, a clash with the Free Officer Movement of Gamal Abdul Nasser that seized power in 1952 led to the Brotherhood's repression by the mid-fifties and almost total eclipse for several decades. In the early 1980s, however, Anwar al Sadat released the Brothers from Egypt's jails and encouraged their activities in a circumscribed way as a counterbalance to his rivals on the left. Despite these manipulative intentions, it would be a mistake to see the return of the Muslim Brothers as simply the outcome of government maneuvers. The unexpected successes of the Brothers since their 1980s reemergence owes a great deal more to the genuine appeal of their broad orientation toward Islamic renewal. The rebirth of the movement was a central chapter in the larger story of a worldwide reassertion of religion. While a marginal and violent minority of the Brothers took the extremist path during the years of repression, the mainstream, moderate current secured a recognized place in public and civic life with a conscious strategy of accommodation with the government and a program of peaceful social change. The resilience of the centrist Muslim Brothers provided testimony to the continued relevance of Islamic renewal as a way to come to grips with the contemporary world.

The Brotherhood was the movement out of which the New Islamist Trend emerged as an independent critical force, shaped as much by reaction to the shortcomings and failures as by the successes of the Muslim Brothers. Nevertheless, the New Islamist Trend owed a great deal to the organizational and intellectual work of the Brotherhood and, in particular, to the inspiration of Hassan al Banna.

Today, more than two decades since Egypt's New Islamists first cohered as an intellectual school, it is possible to take the measure of their work. The task is an important one. Egypt plays a role of unique importance in the Arab Islamic world. Because it is the most modernized of the Arab states, with a cosmopolitan image shaped for international tourism, Egypt's deeply rooted Islamic identity and character are often obscured. In fact, Egypt has been a seedbed for a wide range of both extremist and moderate interpretations of Islam that have inspired movements with effects far beyond its borders. However, it is reform Islam that has the deepest roots in Egypt's extremely complex culture and history. There is no better place to assess the struggle within Islam that sets the Islamic mainstream against violent extremists. In the wake of September 11, questions have emerged with new urgency that can perhaps best be addressed from this critical Egyptian vantage point: What are the prospects of reform Islam today? Is Islamic moderation on key cultural, social, and political questions possible? What is the shape of the future that centrist Islam promises? The New

Islamists have given clear and compelling answers to all of these questions on both theoretical and practical planes. For the most part, however, language barriers and cultural differences have meant that these important aspects of mainstream Islam that flow from New Islamist interpretations have been largely ignored in the West.

Like other great religious traditions, Islam can be grasped in the most meaningful way through the human interpretations of the divine message that in turn inform belief and behavior. Religion is in this sense a lived interpretation, and it is people who make that possible. The central figures of the New Islamist School who appear in the following pages bring the possibilities of centrist Islam to life. Egypt's New Islamists include individuals whose writings are known throughout the Arab world and the larger Islamic circle. Yusuf al Qaradawy, for example, is frequently identified as perhaps the most influential Islamic scholar in the Islamic world today. Fahmy Huwaidy has undoubtedly the clearest and best-known journalistic voice for Islamist perspectives heard today throughout the Arab world. Many regard the late Shaikh Muhammad al Ghazzaly as one of the best-loved religious figures of twentieth-century Islam. As a school of centrist thinkers, the New Islamists represent a major intellectual force in Egypt, the Arab Islamic world, and beyond.

There are no sound scholarly reasons for the critical gap in the Western understanding of Islam for which they speak; the historical record is there to be surveyed and assessed. The New Islamists have done more than raise speculative questions. In the impressive body of their scholarly work and the record of their active roles in public life, these remarkable and diverse individuals—lawyers, a judge and historian, a journalist, and several major religious scholars—have produced a reformist elaboration of the role of the arts and education in Islam; the character of Islamic community and the ways in which it should be regulated; gender relations; the status and rights of non-Muslims; the nature of Islamic banking and economics; the relationship of state and society; and Islam's global role. All of these issues are addressed in a recognizable and understandable social context. Precisely because these Islamic scholars have maintained an organic relationship to their society as individuals and as a group, their work can be situated in the modern history of Egypt and the Middle East. Non-specialists as well as specialists can appreciate the character and importance of their contributions.

Each of this book's three sections on the New Islamist vision for culture, society, and politics opens with an introductory piece—a commentary from the abundant cultural critique, satirical and insightful, that is standard fare for Egypt's intellectuals, including the New Islamists. In very human terms, these brief commentaries set major themes for the analysis that follows, often displaying the humor that Egyptians characteristically use to deal with the trying circumstances of their personal and national lives. The section on the cultural realm of education, treated in Chapter 1, and the arts, discussed in Chapter 2, opens with a satirical piece that makes an imaginative link between the diversionary excesses of popular culture, represented by Egypt's most famous belly dancer, and the defensive and ineffectual ruling establishment. The chapters on society—Chapter 3, dealing with community, and Chapter 4, on the economy—are introduced by a review of an essay that lampoons the distortions of Islamist extremists of all kinds who divert attention from the national agenda to secondary issues, like exaggerated Islamic dress, and in the process mask the humane face that the New Islamists seek to reveal. Finally, an assessment of a brief satirical essay, very much in touch with the popular mood and New Islamist political judgments, introduces Chapter 5, on politics, and Chapter 6, on foreign policy. The essay captures the sense of profound disillusionment that Egyptians feel with the emptiness of nearly all aspects of political and civic life, thereby opening an important space for mainstream Islam as understood by the New Islamists to articulate alternatives outside of politics and beyond civil society.

Kamal Abul Magd concluded his exchange with Sayyid Yassine by pointing to the history of the New Islamists' accomplishments: their numerous publications on fundamental issues of culture, society, politics, and the economy, and their active interventions in public life on behalf of their principles. There is no better introduction to that recent history than the events of the Cairo Book Fair of 1992, to which I now turn.

The crowds gather early and soon fill the large hall, spilling out onto the pavilion to occupy the surrounding spaces of the newly opened fairground in greater Cairo. The occasion is the 1992 Book Fair, the twenty-fourth in a tradition that always makes the Cairo opening an important cultural event, and occasionally something more.[3] The presence of Shaikh Muhammad al Ghazzaly, one of Egypt's renowned religious leaders and the best known of the New Islamists to ordinary Egyptians, guarantees that large numbers of people will come. When Shaikh Ghazzaly led the prayers on the occasion of the great Islamic celebrations, as many as a quarter of a million people from all walks of life would gather in the public squares of Cairo.

This day, however, Shaikh Ghazzaly will not lead prayers. In the featured event of the Fair, Ghazzaly, as a centrist Islamist, is to debate the question of an Islamic versus a secular state with one of the most prominent of Egypt's secularists, the writer Farag Foda.[4] With Ghazzaly to represent the

The late Shaikh Muhammad al Ghazzaly, regarded as one of the leading twentieth-century scholars of Islam. (photograph courtesy of Muhammad Abdul Qudus)

Islamist trend, but very much in his shadow, stands the head of the Muslim Brothers, Mamun al Hudaiby.[5]

From the moment the printed program for the 1992 Fair appears in the newspaper *al Ahram,* the attention of the political class focuses on the dialogue between the Islamists and the secularists. Intellectuals throughout the country immediately grasp the significance of the event: the Book Fair debate gives a tangible, contemporary expression to the competing claims of two national projects that have vied for the soul of Egypt for over a century. Shaikh Muhammad al Ghazzaly embodies the belief of Egypt's Islamist centrists that only a state reformed on the foundations of Islam can provide Egyptians with an authentic yet modern and democratic political community. Farag Foda represents the secularist principle that a "religious" state could not provide the kind of government required by the conditions of the late twentieth century.

Outside the hall young men, many bearded, predominate in the crowd. As the numbers swell, the uniformed police become more assertive, guiding the newcomers to ever-wider circles around the building, while keeping the approaches to the hall clear. The crowd accepts this direction. The word spreads that Shaikh Ghazzaly is already inside. Periodically, the police-escorted cars of dignitaries make their way slowly to the entrances, and the young men guess the names of a distinguished intellectual, a celebrity, or a high government official. The crowds react most when Farag Foda arrives. He is recognized immediately, having made himself a public figure very clearly identified with an assertive secularism, pronounced in the most uncompromising terms. With his usual dramatic flair, Farag Foda arrives only when the crowds are in place. He makes his way confidently through the front entrance, accompanied by his elegantly dressed family.

Strange shadows cast themselves over the event, not yet recognized as ominous but felt with some uneasiness on that winter day. When small groups of bearded young men begin to cluster in animated circles, it is not immediately clear that they are simply assembling for group prayers. At the same time, an unannounced but easily recognized presence threatens to stifle the promised national dialogue. The uniformed police are not alone in representing the regime on the Book Fair grounds. As the crowds grow, the secret police make their presence felt. Toughs dressed in street clothes, armed with clubs not so subtly concealed in their clothing, periodically emerge, at one point ringing the main entrance. Directions to the swollen crowd take the form of menacing pushes and prods. The bearded young men grow sullen. They begin the rhythmic chanting of "God is Great, God is Great," at times associated with militant actions. The stage appears set for confrontation. Shaikh Ghazzaly then intervenes over the loudspeaker system, stating firmly that he dislikes such exclamations. He immediately announces the beginning of the noontime prayer. The young men drop the chants and begin to prepare for the communal prayer, while the secret police slowly blend back into the crowd. Dialogue, with prayer as prelude, preempts violence.

For three hours, the debate over an Islamic versus a secular order proceeds without a single incident. Ghazzaly speaks first, while the potential for violence still hangs in the air. He begins by reviewing the history of Western incursions and depredations that goes to the heart of the story of the West in the Islamic world. Ghazzaly reminds his audience that Egyptians won the hundred-year battle against the violent usurpations of the colonizers. But they did so, he cautions, at disabling costs to themselves and their precious Islamic heritage. "We were left," Ghazzaly unsparingly intones, "with deformed personalities" and "far from our heritage." Their confidence shattered, too many Egyptians sought to adopt the ways of the conquerors. Such an embrace of the secularism of the West, Ghazzaly warns, eroded the sense of identity and belonging that Islam affords. Egyptians will find success in the modern world "only by renewing our connection to Islam and by ridding ourselves of educational, legislative, and intellectual colonialism." To this end, Ghazzaly holds out the promise of the Islamic state and rejects the notion of imitating the secular regimes of the West.

Do Western societies really offer models worthy of blind imitation? Ghazzaly refuses to overlook the flaws of even the most powerful of the secular societies of the West, citing in particular the moral laxity, criminal violence, and double standards of American society. Why, he asks, do Americans tolerate the collapse of moral values and ravages of poverty reflected in so many violent crimes in their cities? Responding to the familiar attacks in the West that equate Islam with obscurantism, he states that "Islamic government is not against reason because such government will perform its duties according to the Holy Quran and to reason." Ghazzaly distinguishes sharply between an "Islamic" and a "religious" state and refuses the identification between the two. He adds that centrist Islamists want to renew the roots of community in Islam, which had established a powerful civilization fourteen centuries ago, because such is "the demand of the nation, and failing to realize it will mean denial of the people's will."

With a deft gesture to the enormous prestige of Ghazzaly, Farag Foda prefaces his remarks with an admonition to those assembled that interruptions and outbursts from the floor signal a lack of confidence in those on the podium who represent their point of view. Foda then quickly advances the basic premises of his case. He insists first that his remarks in no way bear on the religious commitments of Muslims. What he does question is rulership in the name of Islam, identifying this claim as one of "competing visions, disparate judgments, and disagreement." He then establishes the flawed character, both historically and in current circumstances, of self-described Islamic governments and movements. Foda quotes Ghazzaly himself in a 1987 interview in *Rose al Yusuf* magazine, where the latter wrote that only in the era of the immediate successors of Muhammad was true Islamic *Sharia* [the provisions from Quran and *Sunnah* to regulate human behavior] applied. Otherwise, violent power politics marked the successive eras of the Islamic nation.

Asking his listeners to bear these statements in mind, Foda argues that if true Islamic *Sharia* was applied only during the times of the first caliphs, then clearly history bears witness against the Islamist position that relies in the first instance on the application of *Sharia* to provide for just Islamic rule. He points to Iran and Sudan as states whose attempts to create religious states based on *Sharia* have degenerated into massive repression and bloodshed. Since the Islamists have neither detailed programs nor compelling policies to address the problems of the country, Foda states, "Egypt should never put its destiny in the hands of those who have only slogans and illusions, negated by history and by the harsh realities of neighboring countries." Foda points to the rash of violent crimes committed under Islamic banners, linking them to the precedent set by the "secret society" of the Muslim Brothers in the 1930s and 1940s. He also warns against the threat to national unity posed by the idea of a religious state. Foda categorically rejects the idea that the Christian minority should ever experience the injustice of being governed by the religion of the majority; he insists instead on national cohesion grounded in a non-religious principle of citizenship. He cites the outbreaks of violence with the Sadat assassination and the Gulf War as dangerous tims when both sides to these conflicts justified their position in Islamic terms. Foda warns that religious faith should be preserved from the corruption of the political realm. He concludes with a call to continue the dialogue.[6]

Shaikh Ghazzaly focuses his response on the issue of *Sharia*, clarifying his point that, although *Sharia* was fully applied only by the rightly guided caliphs, even its imperfect implementation during the Ummayyad, Abbasid, and Ottoman eras of Islamic history secured the impressive advances in civilization made during these periods. Ghazzaly establishes the link between *Sharia* and the broad Islamic civilizational heritage rather than the narrow political order or some misleading notion of religious law. For Ghazzaly and the New Islamists the distinction between an Islamic state and a religious one is critical, though all too often obscured by the secularists. Islam as a civilization is inclusive and tolerant, far from the closed and rigid ideas that the notion of a religious state invokes. Ghazzaly concludes his references to Islamic history with the reminder that the West, in its own drive to progress, drew on the heritage of those Islamic civilizations in learning and especially in science, including medicine, to secure its own advance.

Thus the debate, with these notable disagreements over the idea of an Islamic versus a religious state and over the character and role of *Sharia*, comes to an end. As one reporter at the Book Fair puts it, the debate is important because "an audience used to hearing only one point of view, today was able to hear two opinions." He adds that "by the end of the debate the tension and the inclination toward violence had disappeared, showing that the present generation sorely needs real dialogue and not the monologue that has prevailed for more than ten years."[7]

The exchanges between Shaikh Ghazzaly and Farag Foda dominated media coverage of the 1992 Book Fair. Just as important, however, was the seminar given by Kamal Abul Magd where he formally introduced the manifesto of the New Islamist School, *A Contemporary Islamic Vision.* The manifesto defined the moral and intellectual space from which Ghazzaly had argued for the Islamic, rather than religious, state. Written in 1980 and circulated at that time to a hundred and fifty Islamic and other intellectuals for discussion, the manifesto was first published only in 1991 and then again in 1992 to coincide with the Book Fair. The core group of new Islamists, including the Islamic scholar Yusuf al Qaradawy, the journalist Fahmy Huwaidy, the lawyer and specialist on *Sharia* Muhammad Selim al Awa, and the judge and historian Tareq al Bishry, in addition to Ghazzaly and Abul Magd, had all contributed ideas that were integrated into its major themes.

Although political conditions did not allow publication of the statement in 1980, the decade of the eighties was supportive in other ways of the promise of the Islamic centrists in Egypt. Looking back over those years in January 1990, Fahmy Huwaidy, the spokesperson for the New Islamists in *al Ahram,* pointed especially to victories in electoral politics and to the strong presence of the New Islamists in professional associations. Huwaidy tempered these grounds for optimism, however, with worry over lack of discipline and proper education in the growing Islamic body in Egypt and elsewhere. He warned against the use of Islamic symbols in un-Islamic ways, which confused those within the movement and alarmed those outside. Huwaidy linked the anarchic growth of the Islamic body to the failure of Arab regimes to make a decisive civilizational choice, leaving Arab societies divided between a Westernizing elite and masses deeply attached to Islam. Huwaidy also drew attention to potentially hostile ideological writings in the West, noting that influential Western intellectuals were announcing the global triumph of the Western liberal idea, while hinting in ominous ways that the Islamic world might be a recalcitrant exception and therefore a target. This ideological stance, Huwaidy cautioned, might well translate into hostile actions, whether by external forces or by the political regimes linked to them.[8]

Despite these cautionary notes, the New Islamist School hoped to build on the gains for centrist Islam registered in the 1980s. They moved decisively at the Book Fair of 1992 into the public space now open to them, asserting a new claim to intellectual leadership for which the careful work of the eighties had prepared them. The featured presence of the New Islamists at the Book Fair seems to confirm the more optimistic strands in Huwaidy's analysis.

In his seminar remarks at the Book Fair, Abul Magd advanced the claim that those who focus on the militant Islamic trends inevitably underestimate the growing appeal of the Islamic centrist mainstream, or

Kamal Abul Magd, Professor of Law at Cairo University and an international legal authority, admired and respected as an Islamist thinker. (photograph courtesy of *al Ahram* newspaper)

Wassatteyya, with which the New Islamists identified. The strength of the *Wassetteyya,* in Abul Magd's view, flows from its secure grounding in a comprehensive and substantive understanding of the higher purposes of Islam. Abul Magd stressed that, although the "angry trends" of political Islam dominate headlines, the *Wassatteyya* is winning supporters all over the Arab Islamic world who look to this centrist trend to lead a real renaissance based on Islam, rightly understood. The *Wassatteyya,* in their view, provides the inspiration for their contemporary vision of Islamic reform and renewal, inclusive and open to the world.[9]

For the New Islamists, the 1992 Book Fair was more than an opportunity to debate the secularists; it was an exemplary forum through which the "mind" or intellectual leadership of the moderate Islamic trend and representatives of the "body," made up of large and diverse groups of Islamist youth, could be brought together. As intellectuals with a strong attachment to the Islamic renewal, the New Islamists put forward a vision that relies on a rational interpretation of both the sacred texts, the Quran and the *Sunnah,* and also *fiqh* ["understandings" of Quran and *Sunnah*], which addresses a wide variety of religious and social issues in the Islamic tradition. At the same time, their thinking and public interventions are shaped by a deep concern for the plight of modern Egyptians and Muslims, in areas related not only to their beliefs and religion, but also to their social, political, cultural, economic, and psychological well-being. They regard the prospect of progress for the peoples of the Arab Islamic world as linked integrally to both an understanding of Islamic ideas, spirit, and way of life, and a clear, rational knowledge of the modern world and the prerequisites for survival and success within it.[10]

A hallmark of this intellectual school is belief in Islam as a civilization that entails commitment to constructive social action. The New Islamists feel strongly that it is the duty of all Islamist leaders, thinkers, and activists to face the challenge of progress with creative solutions that embody Islamic values and principles. They insist that moderate approaches to the problems challenging contemporary Islamic societies do not necessitate the overthrow of existing institutions. Many of the laws in Egypt, for example, do not contradict *Sharia* in the judgment of the New Islamists. Moreover, the New Islamists insist that those areas where changes are needed should be approached thoughtfully and gradually, so as to avoid creating even greater havoc in society. They see worthwhile, practical activity as the correct path to spiritual and worldly salvation, even if the results are sometimes flawed or incomplete. The New Islamists call for a healthy, vibrant Islamic body which, in its own activities, will help create an open environment of tolerance, understanding, and dialogue that yields a fuller understanding of both Islam and the modern world.

The New Islamists believe that a body engaged in such constructive social activity requires a capable intellectual leadership to provide *tarshid* [guidance]. From the platform of the Book Fair, this group made their bid for such a leadership role. Their qualifications combine strong and diverse theoretical and scholarly abilities, exemplified by the Islamic scholar Yusuf al Qaradawy and by the lawyers Kamal Abul Magd and Selim al Awa; powerful intellectual and personal magnetism, personified by the late Shaikh Muhammad al Ghazzaly; and prominent career positions like that of the journalist Fahmy Huwaidy, with his influential weekly column in *al Ahram,* and the judge and historian Tareq al Bishry, the First Deputy President of the Council of State, who enjoys deep respect from all political and intellectual trends. Their "school" attracts numerous colleagues, collaborators, students, and activists, notably among the youth who seek an Islamic alternative to the extremists. Though reaching out to others, these central figures rely on one another to define the essential thrust of the New Islamist School. Their shared focus is an impressive interpretive project that rethinks the values and purposes of their heritage and strives to translate it into constructive reform. They are connected by long-standing personal relations, durable intellectual connections tangibly expressed by common references and mutual citations, and joint interventions in public life, often in conditions of controversy and at times of danger. All of these key New Islamist figures have registered achievements as researchers and writers. All are recognized public figures with access to a variety of civic platforms. They constitute a group widely regarded as untarnished by the questionable political practices of either the opposition or the regime. Their faces are seasoned though still impressively fresh. They are stepping into a widely acknowledged leadership void in Egyptian society.

The constituency to which the New Islamists appeal are those within the broad Islamic Awakening and society as a whole who have a deep commitment to Islam and to its reintegration into public life through moderate, peaceful means. This New Islamist leadership believes that there is "a strong moderate heart" to the centrist Islamic movement, which arose from the Awakening and is growing stronger every day, and that on this centrist foundation can be built a more promising future both for the Islamic movement and for Egypt. Neither these scholars and intellectuals nor the centrist Islamic movement of which they are a part have appeared out of nowhere or overnight. Moreover, neither can be adequately understood as a secondary symptom of some more basic factor, whether the confrontation with the West or the 1967 defeat, as many insist. Rather, they stem from the *Wassatteyya* tradition of centrist Islamic reform with deep roots in Egyptian history, which affords them a durable presence in contemporary Egyptian society. Anchored in the higher purposes of Islam, the *Wassatteyya* has been enriched by the intellectual legacy of Muhammad Abduh and Gamal Eddine al Afghany, the great nineteenth-century reformers, and by certain elements of the complex and contradictory legacy of social activism of Hassan al Banna, the founder of the Muslim Brothers, one of the most successful twentieth-century Islamist mass movements. The *Wassatteyya* views the world from an angle of vision in which Islam is not only a system of religious beliefs but also an intellectual and cultural reservoir, an instructive experience of political, economic, and social history, and a moral and practical guide for the improvement of life. Both the pioneers and the contemporary leaders of the *Wassatteyya* have struggled to harmonize Islamic values and current realities, a task they recognize as possible only in strong, independent, and dynamic societies. This broad understanding of the origins and character of the *Wassatteyya* tradition means that the New Islamists have a twofold task: to bring a deeper and more rational understanding of Islam to followers, and to effect the necessary changes in various social and political structures that impede the realization of a strong and independent Islamic society built on such understanding.[11]

The New Islamists feel compelled to advance their vision and call to action because of the vague and inaccurate terms in which calls for the "Islamic solution" are generally framed, more often than not by those who know little of the ways in which an Islamic direction can be specified and the means appropriate to its contemporary implementation. While buoyed by the signs from around the world of a religious renewal in which Muslims play a prominent part, the New Islamists are distressed by the distortions to which Islam has been subjected by those who rely on speculations and assumptions, often inspired by fear rather than confidence in the faith's enduring values and higher purposes. Too often, in their view, movements and regimes have sullied the Islamic call and fueled hostile reactions to the faith. It is time, they conclude, to advance a New Islamist vision.

To this end, the New Islamists present their thought as derived from Islamic principles, and they address their message in the first instance to the people of Egypt and the larger Islamic world. Yet they also strive with openness and flexibility to interpret the Islamic heritage in ways responsive to a new time in human history, when "the barriers between peoples are falling and distances are shrinking." They welcome the opportunities of the global age. They seek in their work to make the Islamic renewal part of this new era, seeing it as a time of great promise "when states, peoples, and cultures around the world are searching for common intellectual ground and shared interests and seeking civilizational rapprochement and cultural cooperation for the sake of values like justice, peace, freedom, and respect for human rights."[12]

part I

Culture

With exaggerated seriousness, the prominent Islamist columnist Ahmed Bahgat reports in *al Ahram* of August 13, 1995, on "breaking news" from the art world. He structures his article as a conversation between two intellectuals, one of whom opens the dialogue with the announcement that Egypt's most famous belly dancer "recently bought an armored car!"

His friend confesses that he has fallen so far behind in cultural developments that he missed the announcement, opening the way to an explanation of Fifi Abdu's cultural prominence. After all, she is most likely "the highest paid belly dancer in the entire Middle East!" More subtly, this astute observer conveys that Fifi keeps her focus clear, never, for example, giving even a hint of a serious thought on political issues. The excited raconteur goes on to report that even though Fifi was unfazed by the several-million-pound price tag for her vehicle, the purchase was not easy. There is, it seems, a long waiting list of high government officials in need of protection as they move through the city.

But why, exactly, the naive listener asks, does a belly dancer have such a need? Fifi is indeed an unlikely target of terrorists, his friend explains. Much more likely is the prospect of a political future. Given the record of official performance in the cultural and educational spheres, Fifi Abdu clearly has all the qualifications for a government post. All that was lacking was an armored car. Don't be surprised, the sophisticate concludes, to "find dear Fifi a minister in the next cabinet!"

chapter 1

Reforming Education

Egyptian audiences are enthralled on March 28, 1994, when the government arranges for the interview of a "repentant terrorist" on national television. Government propaganda has made the terrorist character a stereotype: Egyptians already know who the terrorist is and what he *really* thinks. The repentant terrorist's role will be to verify in his own words the official view of terrorism as a particularly evil form of criminality that arises from Islamist sources. His confession will confirm the necessity for sweeping repression of the Islamic wave in a government campaign of "drying the springs," that is, eradicating the religious roots of extremism. The regime rejects the distinction between violent extremists and moderates, choosing to ignore all evidence that distorted militant views of Islam can be corrected by reliable centrist understandings of the faith. It also refuses the notion that the roots of terrorism lie in the despair caused by the failure of policies for economic and social development that leave even educated youth without real prospects. The interview with the repentant terrorist is staged to confirm the official view that an irrational, evil force has suddenly arisen to strike the state and its citizens. Such absolute evil must be crushed by any and all means. In fact, calling this media event an "interview" is not quite right. The notion of an "exhibition" would better capture the intent.

On the surface, the government effort goes well. Extremism is given a face, and the young man has a carefully controlled opportunity to tell "his story." Quite unexpectedly, however, the television medium carries an excess of meaning that creates an opportunity, for the attentive public at least, to see more in that face than is intended and to hear more in that voice than can be spoken. The entrancement with the public performance fixes attention just long enough for second thoughts to take shape about where criminal responsibility actually lies.

Adel Abdul Baqi, age 33, was born and raised in Fayyum, a poor and neglected province, or governorate, that was a known breeding ground for violent Islamist extremists.[1] He entered the world of the violent militants in 1977. Abdul Baqi then spent more than sixteen years with various groups before his arrest, moving from one governorate to another, proselytizing and recruiting young people. In his "confession" Abdul Baqi confirms the official representation of the extremists, pronouncing them "a band of thieves, criminals, and mercenaries who use religion simply as a cover." With the authority of an insider, he extends the indictment to all the major extremist groups, portraying an Islamist underworld that glorifies a widespread immorality and criminality. Abdul Baqi describes members of the major extremist groups like Jihad and Islamic Group as having "no religion or values," while those of another, Takfir wal Higra, are "a gang of immoral people who commit adultery and prostitution under the cover of Islam."

The intimate vignettes from his life underground and the personal impressions of well-known figures enliven the indictments, making the interview a useful sensation. Abdul Baqi recounts how he first made contact with the extremists while exercising at a youth sports club attached to a mosque. He mentions Omar Abdul Rahman, later imprisoned for terrorism in the United States. Abdul Baqi describes him as "a dissolute, power-hungry preacher" who headed a "charitable" organization attached to the same mosque. Drawn into these extremist circles, Abdul Baqi eventually emerged as something of an intellectual leader among the young men who gathered around extremist shaikhs like Abdul Rahman. While claiming never to bear arms himself, he describes his role as the brain behind a series of spectacular robberies directed against both Muslims and non-Muslims to secure funding for the extremists.[2]

Yet, for all the usefulness of the interview, Adel Abdul Baqi's confession tells more about himself and his passage into the underground than the government wants. The television interviewers formally control the interview, and they dutifully frame their questions from a security perspective. Abdul Baqi provides the expected confirmations. Still, the television interview carries an added meaning that subtly disturbs the representation of a terrorist that the regime hopes to project. The undercurrent of Abdul Baqi's story, for those able to listen, is an account of Egypt's "lost generation" and the way society, beginning with its educational system, failed them.

As a personality, Abdul Baqi almost immediately eclipses the two television interviewers. Speaking a polished yet unpretentious Arabic, drawing without strain on the classical language of the Quran, the "terrorist" quickly reveals himself as an excellent speaker of obvious intelligence, personal dignity, even charisma. However dissolute his final destination, Abdul Baqi establishes that his journey began as the genuine religious quest of a deeply devout 17-year-old. Asked how he joined the movement, Abdul Baqi describes himself as from a religious family in Fayyum, where he was "an excellent student and a very good reader."[3] Intellectual development, however, came not from the overcrowded and neglected public schools he attended, but from the informal reading and discussion circles that emerged out of the mosques. Abdul Baqi left school without finishing his education, despite his obvious intellectual gifts. Eager to improve his understanding of Islam, he avidly read the books provided by the young men who frequented the mosques.

Abdul Baqi began his education in extremism by reading well-known texts of radical Islamist thinkers that made sense for him of the conditions of poverty and depression that he saw all around him in Fayyum. One book by the Pakistani Islamist Abul Ala al Maududi, founder of the Islamic Association, had a particularly powerful effect. In *Four Terms* Maududi argues that existing conditions in so-called Islamic societies contradict the vision of society revealed in the Quran. Maududi urges true Muslims to assume responsibility for correcting existing evils, by force if necessary, and for giving society a genuine Islamic character. Abdul Baqi explains how he learned from Maududi that the use of force to achieve this end is legitimated by a *hadith* [sayings of the Prophet that illuminate his thoughts and actions, accompanied by their sources]. The *hadith* reports that the Prophet called on believers to use the sword to defend the faith.

Abdul Baqi turned next to *Landmarks on the Way*, the most important radical text by Sayyid Qutb, the Egyptian Muslim Brother leader. Qutb wrote the book after his experience in prison, where he was tortured and eventually hanged. His work persuaded Abdul Baqi of the relevance of Maududi's message to Egypt. Qutb argues that since Egypt's current rulers are not real Muslims, the overthrow of the regime by true believers is Islamically approved. Abdul Baqi explains how these general commitments are elaborated and deepened by the concepts of *takfir* [declaring Muslims to be unbelievers] and *istihlal* [considering that which is religiously forbidden to be acceptable], which are common currency in the extremist circles that he enters. The notion of *takfir* is understood to mean that the regime and even the entire society in Egypt are un-Islamic, while the notion of *istihlal* carries the implication that, in such conditions of unbelief, true Muslims have the right to appropriate the wealth of non-Muslims (both those who falsely claimed to be believers and Christians) and give it back to the true owners, the real Muslims who join the extremist underground. Behavior that under normal conditions would be *haram* [religiously forbidden] becomes *halal* [religiously permitted] under the conditions of *jahilliyya* [an un-Islamic, atheist or pagan era] in which Egyptians find themselves. This reasoning justifies the crimes Abdul Baqi commits to support his group.

Abdul Baqi's personal account of his education into terrorism subverts the simplistic notion advanced by the government and overtly seconded by Abdul Baqi himself that the extremists are common criminals who cynically adopted a religious cover for their crimes. It makes the contrary point that there is a religious impulse and an intellectual dimension in the conversion to violent extremism, and provides insight into the process by which conditions of desperation facilitate the turn to force when a plausible explanation is provided. Abdul Baqi also explains how, through their criminal activities, the extremist groups have garnered resources with which they can provide housing and even enable marriages for their members. Thus, a young man who works with the extremists can almost overnight find himself employed, with a modest home, and a family. Of course, the crimes remain crimes and the violence, however justified, remains violence. Nevertheless, motivations do matter if the resort to violence is to be understood.

The implications of a more complex understanding of the formation of a terrorist become even clearer in Abdul Baqi's account of the process of "redemption" that leads to his confession and dramatic disavowal of extremism. (Later official reports of the interview, including a very detailed Arabic transcript released by the Middle East News Agency, omit these apparently unwelcome details.) The ascent from corruption and criminality, as Abdul Baqi tells the story, parallels the descent. He convincingly recalls the deep and principled thinking about issues of faith and society and the part of religious scholars as guides. However, the important writings are no longer those of Maududi and Qutb.

Shaikh Muhammad al Ghazzaly, perhaps the best known of the New Islamists, emerges as the key figure in Abdul Baqi's account of his rejection of extremist thought. Rethinking begins under the impact of Ghazzaly's book *Fiqh of the Prophet's Biography,* where Abdul Baqi finds a striking account of a critical incident in the Prophet Muhammad's life. Preparing for the flight from a hostile Mecca to a safe refuge in Medina where he would strengthen the community of Muslims, the Prophet arranges to leave Aly Ibn Abu Taleb behind. The decision surprises Abdul Baqi, who knows that Ibn Abu Taleb was one of the most important followers of the Prophet. Abdul Baqi asks himself: "How could he possibly leave him behind at so critical a moment?" Ghazzaly explains that Ibn Abu Taleb's mission was to return the properties that members of the Quraish tribe of Mecca had entrusted to the Prophet—an account that directly challenges the extremist notions of *takfir* and *istihlal.* Abdul Baqi describes what this story meant to him:

> I knew the Quraish as unbelievers who had done such great harm to the Prophet that he had been forced to flee. Yet he still returned their wealth. I went through other books and confirmed that the incident really happened in this way. At that point, I was certain that what we were doing was just outright theft.

Ghazzaly has prepared the way for Abdul Baqi's redemption.

A second book by Ghazzaly, *The Prophet's Sunnah between the People of Fiqh and the People of Hadith,* drove the wedge deeper between Abdul Baqi and his co-conspirators. Abdul Baqi reports that Ghazzaly's account of the role of women in Islamic society made him realize how far extremist thinking deviated from sound Islamic teachings.[4] To illustrate, he recounts how one female member of the extremist group was persuaded to divorce her first husband because he was judged to be an unbeliever, and then her second husband because he sent their son to the "schools of the atheist regime." The woman, Abdul Baqi continues, was then obliged to marry yet a third member of the group, all this without legal documents, because the extremists do not believe in the legal system. Abdul Baqi concludes starkly: "These *takfir*-style perceptions made the situation of women little better than prostitution." Ghazzaly's views on women in the Islamic community convinced him that this could not be Islam.

At the conclusion of the interview, Abdul Baqi is asked how others could be rescued from the grip of the extremists. He replies that there are really two kinds of underground extremists. The first are thoughtful believers in the righteousness of their actions, however mistaken they might be; the second are simply opportunists motivated by power and greed. This second group can be reached only by force. The first type, however, can be reasoned with and persuaded, if the proper approach is made. "We found no one to correct our ideas," explains Abdul Baqi, "so we stuck to our false beliefs." "Talk to us," he adds, commenting that the officially arranged dialogues do not work because they degenerate into either lectures by officials or debates in which the parties fail to listen to each other. "Real dialogue is imperative," he concludes.

In the wake of the interview, the press reports that the government is planning to assemble religious figures to discuss the distorted thinking of the terrorists that Abdul Baqi had exposed. Those discussions, too, will be televised. Shaikh Muhammad al Ghazzaly is not included among those invited to participate.

The government did dispatch special "caravans" of official *ulama* [Islamic scholars] to Upper Egypt ostensibly to combat the influence of extremist *amirs* [leaders of Islamic groups], publicizing these staged episodes of religious education in the media. The indicators that such efforts would be ineffective mattered little. They were merely "Islamic" cover for a policy of attacking the Islamic wave generally, making the mainstream as much a target as the extremists. The real energy and resources of the regime went into this indiscriminate campaign of repression. The government's far-reaching policy of "drying the springs" aimed to eliminate all independent sources of religiousness in society with the rationalization that they fed extremism. The security forces were given free reign to crush the extremist groups. Violent government assaults on extremist strongholds, massive arrests, and systematic torture of those caught up in the massive sweeps became the weapons of choice against the Islamists. By the late 1990s, these violent methods did end the deadly assaults by the violent Islamist groups, either killing their members or driving them deeper underground or into exile. The broader ideological campaign of "drying the springs" also had the effect of dampening the surface signs of the broad Islamic revival.

The New Islamists spoke out strongly and consistently against extremist violence, condemning it in Islamic terms.[5] Moreover, they welcomed the containment of the terrorist campaign that was achieved by the end of the 1990s. However, they also pointed out that repression, even when apparently successful, did nothing to remedy the root causes that drove young people to such desperate means in the first place, or to discredit the distorted ideas that rationalized their behavior. They also could not ignore the terrible costs of that success in the suffering of innocent people caught up in the net the security forces indiscriminately cast. The New Islamists warned that this wave of violent repression, especially the brutal torture in camps and prisons scrupulously documented by Egyptian and international human rights groups, would produce yet another generation of terrorists, twisted in mind and body by the abuses they suffered. How durable, they asked, would the respite from violence prove to be if underlying causes continued to fester and large numbers of young people were irrevocably alienated from society?

In the broadest terms, the New Islamists believed that the only lasting solution for violent extremism lay in renewing the national struggle against poverty and for justice and progress in order to rekindle genuine faith and a sense of hope. They argued that educational reform must be the engine of any such national platform. By "education," Egyptians traditionally mean not only *talim* [formal schooling] but also *tarbeyya* [proper upbringing], that is, the moral, cultural, and social formation of children. While the first takes place primarily in the schools, the field for the second extends to the broader civic arena and the public and private institutions that complement the school and the family in shaping the character and behavior of young people. The New Islamists' emphasis on education emphatically included *tarbeyya.* "The question of culture and *tarbeyya,*" the manifesto of the New Islamists declared, "must be the principal cornerstone of Islamic reform."[6] Successful cases of development around the world, as Fahmy Huwaidy put it, "had everywhere begun by education . . . a change in the curriculum and the schools."[7] The New Islamists called for a national commitment to education as the first and essential step in developing the country and lifting people from the sense of desperation that feeds Islamist extremisms—indeed extremisms of all kinds. Only a coherent and compelling national vision could give the reform effort a sense of direction and engender the broad political support necessary for its realization.[8] Egypt lacked such a vision, they argued, drawing attention to the state's neglect of education in the post-Nasser years, a neglect only exacerbated by a chaotic record of piecemeal government "campaigns" and administrative reshuffling. Repeated failures and diminished hopes left Egypt's young people exposed to disruptive pressures and forces, not least the dangers of entrapment in violent extremism.

The New Islamists' priority of educational reform has a twofold focus. On the one hand, they strive to develop a realistic critique of the deteriorating conditions in education and the inadequacy of the government's response. On the other hand, they outline their own centrist Islamist vision of comprehensive reform and indicate how progress can be made toward its realization. Their assessment begins with a survey of the devastating impact of the lack of resources for public education. More precisely, the New Islamists deplore the piecemeal and shallow quality of government efforts. Key questions, they allege, are left unanswered. In what ways should the educational system serve the shared goals of the national community? How can education be made the engine of national development? What do students need to learn to define their own place as productive citizens in a distinctive Egyptian community, and Egypt's place in the larger world? These unanswered questions point to the damaging consequences of the absence of a comprehensive vision for educational reform.

The New Islamist School aims to show how that void in the educational sphere can be filled. Going beyond critique, they propose a qualitative reform of education that emphasizes values and purposes drawn from an inclusive centrist understanding of Egypt's Islamic heritage as it has been developed by Muslims and non-Muslims in the service of the national community. While recognizing that meaningful reform cannot be achieved without a commitment of resources, they also argue that real reform must rest on secure intellectual foundations that foster a broadly shared sense of national identity and purpose. Reform, they insist, is not only about resources but also about creative intelligence and inventiveness within the constraints of Egypt's current circumstances and cultural inheritance.

The Crisis in Education: New Islamist *Fiqh* (Understanding) of Reality

"When a catastrophe is received indifferently as ordinary news," commented Fahmy Huwaidy, "we know we are facing a true disaster."[9] In the fall of 1997, the press reported that three young girls from poor families attempted suicide in order to escape the intolerable conditions in their school. Their parents could not afford both the school fees and the private lessons urged on them by their teacher. The primary students preferred death to the isolation and certain failure that they saw ahead of them. In the disturbing particulars of the story, Huwaidy saw the grave deterioration of national education in Egypt. In the lack of a strong public reaction to the incident, he read the widespread despair of repairing the generalized breakdown in education.

As Egypt prepared for the twenty-first century, a host of problems besieged education at all levels. It was clear that the advances in education and other social services brought about earlier by the Nasser revolution were being systematically hollowed out. In the heady years of the fifties and sixties, Free Officer rule made education free not only in the primary and secondary years but virtually so at the university level as well. The main beneficiaries were lower-middle and middle-class urban families, who appeared to chart a course for social mobility that others would be able to follow. During this period the numbers of elementary and secondary schoolchildren doubled, while the increases at the university level were even more dramatic. In addition, university graduates were guaranteed jobs in the public sector, making their degrees a passport to an improved life. The political economy to sustain these reforms rested in part on the appropriation of assets from privileged strata, including foreigners, Egyptianized urban minorities, and large landowners. It was supported as well by Nasser's aggressive and profitable investment in foreign policy, which won foreign assistance from both superpowers in a bipolar world.

Sadat reversed course. Responding to the signs of Soviet decline, he shifted from a tilt toward the Soviet Union and a socialist orientation to the ascendant United States and a more open economy. This reorientation resulted in less attention to the social needs of Egypt's poorer classes and a reassertion of privilege. For a time, however, windfall profits from external sources, notably oil, Suez Canal revenues, worker remittances, and tourism, delayed these consequences. These revenues allowed the Sadat government to preserve a scaled-down version of the entitlements and some of the social mobility of the Nasser years. High annual growth rates of about 9 percent on average sustained optimism for about a decade from the late seventies into the eighties. However, the expansion came to an end with the adverse economic developments triggered by the collapse of world oil prices in 1984. Growth rates fell to about 2 percent, as external pressures for economic restructuring and retrenchment mounted. Strong pressures also grew for cutbacks in subsidies and social services, including education.

In the 1980s and 1990s the regime did manage to resist the most draconian measures urged by the International Monetary Fund (IMF) as part of its structural adjustment policies. The government only partially accommodated these international pressures by allowing the actual cost and value of the various subsidies and supports to erode. The bread loaves became smaller, and the wait for government jobs longer. For education, investment slowed in absolute amounts and declined as a percentage of the budgets. Classes grew larger, teachers' salaries shrank in buying power, and buildings were no longer maintained. To sustain even diminished entitlements, the regime borrowed heavily from abroad.

In response to the periodic collapses and crises that the erosions of support precipitated, the government would routinely announce expanded budgets for education. However, the economic resources and ideological commitment to sustain higher levels of support to public education simply were not there. As in other social spheres, the regime quietly withdrew. As government benefits eroded, the regime encouraged "private" solutions to what had been seen as public responsibilities.[10] Conditions worsened in the public schools; in some of the poorer urban districts, multiple sessions meant that students attended school as little as three or four hours per day. Those with the means to do so fled from the public schools to the growing private sector, for education of very uneven quality.

For the most part, official government reports glossed over the terrible deficiencies in public education that resulted, with one notable exception. Writing in February 2001, Fahmy Huwaidy brought to public attention a suppressed Ministry of Education survey completed in 1996 of 3,000 schools at all levels in twenty governorates.[11] Because of its critical nature, the report was never circulated and its chief author suffered administrative discipline that ended his career. The report paints a devastating picture of the decay of public education, highlighting in particular the adverse effect of private tutorial lessons, which are described as virtually a "parallel education system." The inadequacies of public education drove desperate parents into the hands of education entrepreneurs over whom it was virtually impossible to exercise any real supervision.

The statistics make clear the reasons for the flight from the schools. The Ministry of Education report found that 77 percent of the primary schools surveyed had two sessions a day, with some schools in Cairo, Giza, and Qalubeyya operating with three shifts. Only one of the primary schools surveyed had an equipped playground, and 75 percent of the schools had no rooms set aside for extracurricular activities of any kind. A full 80 percent of the primary schools did not contain adequate libraries. The classrooms in 40 percent were in poor shape, while another 20 percent should not have been in use at all. A shocking 10 percent of the school buildings were declared dangerous and unfit overall. The evaluators also learned that 95 percent of the primary schools had no teacher rooms and that an additional 5 percent had rooms with no chairs, desks, or cupboards. Conditions in the middle schools were roughly the same, while the secondary schools were in even worse shape. The report noted that the number of secondary pupils in a class often rose above 50, while many of the buildings had not yet been repaired from the damages inflicted by the 1992 earthquake. The typical secondary-school classroom suffered from cracked blackboards, broken windows, and an inadequate number of desks and chairs. When "libraries" could be found, they invariably contained no books. Although there were rooms designated as science or computer labs, they were rarely equipped in even a minimally adequate way. The report also noted that overall cleanliness in the schools was miserable, including 70 percent with bathrooms in such poor condition that "they were a source of pollution and disease." Huwaidy concludes that the report clearly shows that "the destiny and future of the nation" were at risk.[12]

Developments in higher education reveal an equally disturbing pattern of neglect, although the same kind of thorough and reliable documentation is not available. The deterioration shows up clearly enough, however, in the declining quality of university graduates. Two notorious cases stand out in the 1990s. Qualifying examinations for the Foreign Ministry, traditionally a bastion for the well-connected and well-educated, exposed the ill-preparedness of even the most privileged of Egypt's youth. Similarly, very desirable openings for radio and television announcers went unfilled because of the poor preparation of the hoards of university graduates seeking the positions.[13]

The Sadat regime had recklessly continued the expansion of higher education of the Nasser years by creating seven regional universities. In the decade from 1975 to 1985, the number of university graduates increased almost threefold. The financial demands of the new universities meant that inadequate resources were stretched even further. Undeniably, the regional universities enabled more students to gain access to the university. In many of the less well supported academic programs, however, it is hard to call their diminished experience "education." Although higher standards have been preserved in the premier faculties of the most important universities, conditions in the lesser faculties in universities in Cairo and Alexandria, and much more generally at the various provincial universities, are unacceptably low. Huwaidy concluded a review of the overall conditions in the national universities with the comment of one faculty member who said, "We are not professors and this is not a university."[14]

With these ill-considered expansions, the acceptance rate of students accelerated greatly. For a while, the Sadatist dreams of peace and prosperity for an Egypt linked to the West and the world market kept optimism alive. However, in the end Sadat brought economic prosperity for only a narrow band of the privileged and only a cold peace with Israel, which, even so, cost him his life.[15] External sources of income dried up. Egypt's young people found themselves marooned in underfinanced and overextended universities, with poorly equipped laboratories and overcrowded lecture halls. The vast majority of the graduates received devalued certificates, and their optimism vanished when it became clear that no meaningful employment awaited them outside the university gates. The last decades of the twentieth century saw the emergence of an army of "educated proletarians" who drove taxis and served tables, while they waited ten years or more for assignment to a low-paying public-sector job. The government spoke vaguely of opportunities in the private sector, a situation really only open to those with the foreign-language and social skills of the well-born and well-connected. The majority of new graduates dreamed of escape though immigration to the West, while the thoughts of some turned to revenge on the society that had betrayed their dreams. Many found in the Islamic renewal that grew in strength on all university campuses in those years the only vestiges of hope in a dismal landscape of broken promises. On the fringes of the Islamic wave, the extremists of political Islam aggressively recruited the educated unemployed and disillusioned into their ranks.

The disarray in education is reflected in the endless reshuffling that characterized the administration of education during the 1990s. The personalization of policies that has been the rule in the Egyptian government compounds these difficulties. Each new minister of education takes office with grand announcements of a new policy that he sets about immediately to implement, with scant regard for the work of the previous minister. When his term ends, often abruptly, his successor in turn typically starts from scratch with an entirely new agenda in precisely the same way. Occasionally there were bright spots, marked by an infusion of funding or talk of how computers would save the day. But the overall pattern in education was one of continued decline.

The weakness and neglect of the educational system created a vacuum into which all kinds of disruptive forces moved—anomic social pressures, antisocial forces, and various groups with competing political agendas. These outside intruders ranged from American education experts, brought in at the upper levels, to Islamist extremists who crowded in from below. In the final decade of the century, the educational system found itself besieged on all sides. In the spring of 1993, for example, bizarre instances of the mass fainting of young girls in schools spread throughout almost a dozen governorates and eventually involved hundreds of pupils. Doctors could find no medical reasons for the incidents and concluded that they were apparently triggered by anxiety.[16] In overcrowded and poverty-stricken urban systems, violence and crime found their way into the schools at an accelerated rate in the nineties, judging from press reports and periodic studies. True, Egypt continued to have crime rates of which America could only dream in its poor urban neighborhoods. Nevertheless, the nineties did bring a growing number of reports of student violence and drug trafficking, from which the country had once seemed immune. These signs of social distress were not confined to the poor. Among middle- and upper-class high school and college students, reports of drug use increased and various kinds of cult activities were uncovered. The press also reported an increase in antisocial behavior among the children of privilege that had become increasingly obnoxious and even dangerous.[17] Reports from the private-sector schools that cater to the wealthy indicate that this kind of behavior, and worse, has indeed found its way into the classroom.[18]

The evident difficulties in education also invited more structured interventions from organized social forces and groups. On the basis of press reports, Fahmy Huwaidy signaled that a unit of American education experts was incorporated directly into the Ministry of Education and at one point seemed to be influencing the content of the required curriculum for the public schools.[19] Huwaidy complained that the proposed curricular reforms would diminish attention to Arab Islamic history, while increasing attention to the Pharaonic period. In particular, proposed changes would delete all references to conflicts with Jewish tribes during the era of the

Prophet. Huwaidy remarked that Egypt's peace treaty with Israel appeared to be behind these revisions. Does that mean, he asked, that Egypt's good relations with the British and French necessitate excising references to European imperialism as well? Huwaidy's main point, however, was that Islamic culture is one of the stable features of national identity, representing an inclusive cultural framework to which historically Muslims, Christians, and Jews all contributed. Huwaidy described any weakening of this sense of belonging to the Islamic world as threatening.[20] It is impossible to gauge accurately the extent of the influence American consultants actually exercised on these proposed changes. However, the incident does indicate just how permeable education had become.

Islamic militants made the same point by their successful intrusions into the educational process on the grassroots level. The dearth of educational materials created an opening for teachers with strong religious views to import religious teaching materials, notably audio cassettes, directly into their classrooms. Confiscations of these materials revealed that some of the extreme and dangerous *amirs* and shaikhs secured direct access in this way to a captive audience of young people.

The New Islamists joined other critics in urging that these dangerous intrusions of extremist ideas be halted. However, they also warned against an indiscriminate purge.[21] These cautionary warnings went unheeded, and the Minister of Education launched a national campaign to remove from the teaching profession all those who fostered extremist ideas.[22] The teachers were charged with "spreading the thought of terrorism," based on security investigation, parental and student complaints, and media reporting. It is impossible to know exactly how many teachers were fired, transferred, or otherwise affected. The official figure, clearly understated, was 2,000 by 1998.[23] As feared, the indiscriminate character of the government crackdown extended beyond the militants to a broad purge of all teachers who had Islamist leanings, damaging further an already wounded educational system.

In the end, however, neither the American consultants nor the penetration by militant Islamists proved to be the most durable of the disruptive influences on education. The press spotlighting of the role of the foreigners was enough to undermine the influence of the American consultants, while the government's policy of repression did curtail the militants, though at considerable cost. Market forces proved far more durable in impact. As the state slowly lowered the levels of its support for public education, market forces of various kinds moved in with powerful and largely unregulated effects. The patterns of market influence emerged slowly in the decade of the eighties, achieving notable impact in the nineties. Although the market intrusion did not derive from any conscious official design, this did not make the outcomes any less significant.

The market affected public education most decisively through the system of private tutoring. Private lessons had a generalized effect from kindergarten through university, effectively destroying the commitment to free public education as parents sought desperately to offset the adverse impact on their children of the deterioration of public education. Families from all social classes were drawn into the competition for the best teachers and bore the burdens of the soaring costs of supplementing regular classroom instruction. However, the impact went deepest in the public sphere and was inevitably most harmful to the poor. The fees for lessons created an informal system of charges that inevitably favored the better-off students who were still trapped in the public schools. The escalation of the problem followed directly from the fact that teachers' salaries in the public schools did not keep pace with inflation and no longer provided a living wage.[24]

From the New Islamist perspective, the corrupting influence of private lessons so undermined the role of education in proper upbringing that schools became, in their view, more commercial than educational establishments.[25] Fahmy Huwaidy remarked bitterly on the "absence of *tarbeyya* in schools" and the fact that "the teacher is no longer a role model. What we read in newspapers convinces us that schools are no longer *tarbeyya* institutions; indeed, with private lessons, they are no longer educational institutions either."[26]

An aggressive new "for-profit" model of private education established itself at all levels of education and for all social classes from the lower-middle class upward. By the year 2000 more than 5,000 private schools were operating, under very loose regulation by the Ministry of Education.[27] At the primary and secondary levels, Islamic and Westernized variations of the basic model competed. The Islamic schools all too often emphasized the most external and superficial aspects of an Islamic orientation, such as a focus on dress rather than any serious attempt to inculcate values. Private schools with relatively modest fees first appeared in urban areas in the 1970s, and lower-middle and middle-class families responded to the government neglect of public education by turning to these alternatives. Generally, facilities were minimal and instruction only marginally better than in the public schools. However, for growing numbers of families the margin did make a difference. Even in these modest versions of the for-profit elementary and secondary schools, whether Westernized or Islamic, the message came through that English and computers were now important. Both subjects were neglected in the public schools and were part of the appeal of the private institutions. Typically, for about the equivalent of three hundred dollars a year, families of modest means could enter this lowest tier of private education.

Meanwhile, the same market forces registered their transformative effects at the upper end of the socioeconomic scale with a vengeance. Many of the elite who rode the dominant nationalist wave before the revolution had been educated in private English- and French-language schools, established by the colonial powers. These exclusive private schools had created a dualism in cultural life that set apart the Westernized elite, with their command of foreign languages and familiarity with Western life-styles, from those educated in Arabic. Starting in the boom years of the 1970s, a new tier of private secondary schools emerged that eclipsed the older language schools and catered to the socially mobile who profited from the windfalls in remittances, oil, tourism, and Suez Canal revenues. The process accelerated in the period following the Gulf War of 1991, when large numbers of Egyptians returned from the Gulf. Although Egyptians of modest means lost everything in the invasion, a group of the very prosperous whose children had attended private schools in Kuwait had sent their new wealth abroad. Their return to Egypt heightened the demand for more exclusive private education. These new secondary schools built campuses, extravagant by Egyptian standards, in the suburbs of Cairo, and they typically featured foreign teachers, instruction in English, and the latest computer technologies. The fees charged at times exceeded ten thousand dollars a year. In fact, the total fees in the most elaborate schools were not much different from the cost of a private elite education in the United States.[28]

At the university level, private education in Egypt has a highly successful prototype in the American University in Cairo (AUC). Founded in 1919, AUC provides a model of *non-profit* private education. The powerful market forces unleashed in the eighties and nineties, however, resolved the national debate over private higher education in an aggressively *for-profit* direction instead. The opening of four private universities in the second half of the nineties did little to improve the general picture. The essential motives of these ventures seem to be more profit than education: their facilities are modest, and the faculties are mainly overworked adjuncts drawn from the national universities. First reports indicate that overall educational standards are, in fact, considerably lower than at the national universities.[29]

Not surprisingly, students at the university level experience a generalized sense of disorientation and divorce from the national community that compounds the material hardships they confront. The New Islamists point out that in Egypt, as in much of the Arab world, fundamental social questions such as the role of religion in public life or the cultural character of the national community remain unresolved.[30] Issues of national identity and direction remain matters of great confusion. University students thus face adulthood and its responsibilities without even tentative answers to basic social questions. The uncertainties extend from religious and historical matters to a whole range of social and even university issues. Fahmy Huwaidy cites the following revealing letter from a university student in the education faculty, who writes:

> Nothing is clear: Sometimes we read that the *neqab* [face-veil] for a woman is a religious duty, other times we are told that it is just a heresy. Some say dancing and music are *haram,* others say they are *halal.* We read our history with stories of the greatness of Muslim conquerors, and then we encounter other writers who claim that Islamic history is but a series of disasters. Some speak of the Caliphate proudly, and others say it was a nightmare that should never be revived. More seriously, even for our own time we do not understand whether the Islamic investment companies have served the national economy or not; whether the members of the organization "Egypt's Revolution" [an underground Nasserist armed group] were criminals or not; and whether the sale of San Stephano Hotel [a widely cited example of the privatization of public assets] is in the national economic interest or not. Are the Americans our friends or our enemies? Is Gamal Abdul Nasser a national leader or a corrupt dictator who deceived people and whose era was a dismal page in Egyptian history? We don't know whether private lessons are something positive or a kind of bribery.

It is little wonder, Huwaidy concludes, that students are "frustrated and disoriented." They are truly faced with an "Age of Confusion."[31]

University education in Egypt fails to provide students with the means to address the fundamental concerns these confusions raise. In order to do so, students must have knowledge of the broader social and political forces that shape their life chances. They also require access to public forums in which the imprecise and controversial impact of these forces can be debated and discussed. They need above all larger frameworks of understanding within which to make sense of the confusing signals they receive and the freedom to explore them. For the most part, they get none of these things as part of their higher education.

The material conditions of the majority of students at the national universities do provide some insight into the causes of these failures. Hamed Ammar, one of Egypt's leading education specialists, concludes that "the simple truth is that many students in the national universities quite simply cannot afford to buy the newspapers and magazines they would need to follow national events."[32] These deprivations provide only part of the explanation, however. Newspapers and magazines can be shared. They are available in libraries. If students had a strong sense of connection to national issues and a desire to know what is going on, they would find such means to inform themselves. More important than these material deprivations are the harsh restrictions on intellectual freedoms, justified as part of the official war on terrorism. They seriously hamper university life and deny students the opportunity to debate issues and experiment with a variety of ideas and theories of the world. Students have very few opportunities to test what ideas might mean when translated into social action, even within the university setting.

Consistently and often with great eloquence, the New Islamists argue that the absence of freedoms makes real university education impossible. They believe that the educational experience of youth defines the kinds of contributions they will be prepared to make to national political, social, and cultural life. Young people silenced by fears of official repression, preoccupied solely with unmet material needs, or driven to extremism are not easily transformed into productive citizens.[33] As Kamal Abul Magd puts it, young people should enjoy a wide latitude to "disagree, cry out, hold conferences and participate in everything, and we should not be upset by all this."[34] To underscore the point, Abul Magd reports: "I feel pessimistic if a year passes without student demonstrations because I take it as a sign that their spirits are withering and dying."[35] He recounts how on one occasion he was told by a university guard to avoid the main gate because "the Islamist students are demonstrating. I said to him, 'Have we become afraid of our sons and daughters? Open the door. We should talk to them. They are innocent, simple, and honest. Some of the students may be impulsive, but they are loyal and we should encourage this loyalty and not destroy it.'" Abul Magd concludes by asking, "Do we really want youth who just say 'amen'? This will be the beginning of our national political death."[36]

The government, in contrast, clearly wanted precisely that compliant silence on university campuses, enforced by the system of emergency laws.[37] The security forces have responded consistently with repression to even peaceful student demonstrations. This systematic silencing of youth greatly alarms the New Islamists because it prevents young people from developing a sense of connection to larger national purposes. The young people of today, Kamal Abul Magd writes, are "prevented from dreaming, grieving, and acting for the future. In Egypt, they are completely separated from national action."[38] Public life, the New Islamists believe, should engage youth and provide them with a meaningful and compelling sense of collective purpose.[39] Earlier generations of young Egyptians who came of age in the fifties, sixties, and even into the seventies, noted Kamal Abul Magd, felt they were a part of the larger dramas of their times. In contrast, young people in Egypt today find themselves preoccupied in crippling ways with personal needs they cannot hope to meet. Kamal Abul Magd describes their fate:

> What you find in today's youth regrettably is a cluster of vague dissatisfactions and depressing mundane worries such as standing in lines at government stores to find necessities at a price they can afford, all the while suffering from a sense of hopelessness about finding jobs, a place to live in order to marry, and feeling constantly the massive gap between available income and basic needs.[40]

Abul Magd explains that as a result, the awareness of young people today "is not the same as was present in our consciousness as a response to the 1967 crisis or the 1973 crossing of the Canal. All such national issues became a great part of our consciousness, whether to inspire feelings of grief and pain or a sense of victory and optimism for the future. All such national feelings are absent in the youth of today."[41] Today's youth, writes Fahmy Huwaidy, suffer "from the absence of such a national project."[42]

There were some signs in the late nineties that the government was at last responding to the deplorable overall decline in education. Writing in 1997, Dr. Hamed Ammar, a respected independent specialist in education, argued that despite the deep-seated problems of long-term vision and immediate administration, some progress could be detected, at least in quantitative terms of resource allocation. He noted that some 6,500 new schools were built as part of renewed attention to education in the 1990s, although he cautioned that an additional 1,500 a year would be needed until the year 2007 to assure adequate facilities. At the same time, figures for those registered in primary, middle, and secondary schools rose from 52 percent in 1980 to 69 percent in 1994, an impressive statistic for an underdeveloped country. University registration increased from 16 to 17 percent during the same period and rose only one more percentage point to 18 percent in 1996. During the ten years beginning in 1986, illiteracy improved from a staggering 49.6 percent to a still-dismal 38.6 percent in 1996.[43]

The first years of the new century brought further signs that the crisis in education was at last receiving official attention. Ambitious plans were announced to continue the process of repairing schools and building new ones. Emphasis was placed on the importance of science and computer labs as well recreational facilities in primary, middle, and secondary schools. There were even efforts to curb the worst abuses of private tutoring by arranging group study sessions after school hours at more affordable rates. At the university level, teaching effectiveness programs, expanded use of information technologies, and greater efforts to assist the poorer students through scholarships and other subsidies were announced.[44] In the end, however, the government's record of grand but unrealized plans and policy reversals, punctuated by purges of teachers and the periodic jailing of activist students, made optimism difficult. The pattern of official responses seemed to represent more a patchwork of reactions to the worst abuses than the kind of well-formulated and long-term programs of comprehensive reform that the New Islamists believed were needed.

Cultural Crisis and Educational Reform: New Islamist *Tarshid* (Guidance)

The New Islamists identify the cause of the debacle in education as the underlying cultural crisis that stems from failure to resolve fundamental issues of national identity and direction. Only when the cultural crisis has been resolved, they argue, will the required national educational reform become possible. According to the New Islamists, the deep-seated paralysis over issues of national identity and purpose has roots that reach back to the nineteenth century. It originates in the historical conflicts among Egyptians about how best to deal with the colonial onslaught that, more than any other factor, shaped the context for Egypt's emergence as a modern state. Two powerful and competing currents arose in the late nineteenth century about how to face the violent imperialist assault: the first found inspiration for resistance in Islam, while the second turned to Westernized nationalism. Each current projected a quite different sense of the character of the nation and the direction Egypt should take. The two trends competed for the soul of Egypt, without decisive resolution.

By the mid-twentieth century, the nationalists had taken charge of the national agenda, with the Islamists represented by the Muslim Brothers as the most powerful Islamist alternative. The Free Officers' military coup in 1952 represented the triumph of Westernized nationalism. However, the 1967 defeat signaled the end of that dominance and the reassertion of the Islamist alternative. The disabling ambivalence of national identity and purpose persisted. As theorists, the New Islamists aim to address these unresolved ambivalences and ambiguities, seeking to find commonalties and to develop strategies to overcome rigid divisions and fixed polarities that have led to impasse. Their goal is to synthesize nationalist and Islamist positions, with the aim of providing inclusive intellectual and cultural foundations for the rebuilding of the educational system.

The historical and theoretical studies of Tareq al Bishry, the master historian of the New Islamist School, model this creative style of rethinking.

Tareq al Bishry, a distinguished member of the judiciary (retired) and a renowned historian. (photograph courtesy of *al Ahram* newspaper)

The entire corpus of his historical work can be read as offering a consensual view of Egyptian history that transcends the debilitating dualities that survive as scars from the colonial situation.[45] His general argument makes two separate and distinct points. Bishry suggests that the colonial experience shattered the Egyptian sense of sharing a comprehensive national vision. He argues further that, underlying the apparent opposition between the Westernized nationalist and Islamic wings of the national resistance, certain important common denominators can be identified, which he summarizes as the struggle for independence and for reform. It is possible, he suggests, to imagine two outcomes of the clash of the two orientations: one of the two competing trends might overwhelm the other and provide a single galvanizing sense of national purpose, or, through a complex social and intellectual process, a reintegration of the two competing orientations might take place. Bishry, along with his colleagues in the New Islamist

School, advocates the second outcome as the preferred alternative. The New Islamists write about the various dimensions of the cultural crisis with the aim of both exploring and enhancing that possibility. They seek to highlight shared historical dimensions of the national struggles and to posit dreams for the future that all Egyptians can hold in common.

Tareq al Bishry's work on the defining national struggles of the nineteenth century exemplifies the kinds of pathways the New Islamists seek to open up to other trends in their efforts to build a new centrist consensus. The conviction that the common ground on which a new cultural synthesis can be created can no longer exclude the Islamic mainstream drives Bishry's writing. He emphasizes, for example, the centrality of the Islamist contribution to the national awakening from the outset. He also argues strongly that the Westernized nationalist experience has effectively exhausted its potential to lead the nation alone. The national interest, in his view, now demands realization of the submerged promise of the Islamic mainstream as a critical partner in the long-term task of rebuilding, beginning with educational reform.

By the late twentieth century, Egypt had tried every variation of the Westernized nationalist formula. As a result, the various nationalist regimes had presided over a "strange pattern of social change," as Kamal Abul Magd put it, "that had brought 180-degree shifts in political and ideological orientation roughly each decade from mid-century on." When the Nasserist regime came to power, Egypt had an underdeveloped capitalist economic system, with heavy reliance on external power. The movement away from that system began slowly after the Free Officers' coup led by Gamal Abdul Nasser. It accelerated with the nationalizations of foreign property that followed in the wake of the British, French, and Israeli aggression against Egypt in 1956. With the deeper nationalization decrees of 1962 and 1963, the regime created a socialist system based on central planning and state ownership of the principal means of production. The socialist experiment lasted roughly ten years until the 1973 war. After the war, Anwar al Sadat reversed course and opened Egypt once again to the capitalist influences and structures dictated by the world market. He also promised a political liberalization, although by the end of his rule the shallowness of that commitment was clear. The subsequent decades of the eighties and nineties were characterized by a continuation of this basic Sadatist strategy of an economic open door and a surface liberalization. Kamal Abul Magd pointed out that each of these orientations required quite different legal, political, and moral value systems to sustain them. The skills and knowledge requirements of each system of social organization also differed markedly. As Abul Magd explained, corrupt or even criminal maneuvering under one system often became "smart behavior" under its successor.[46]

The New Islamists read the phenomenon of terrorism as the most dangerous symptom of the historical failure of Westernized nationalism. More precisely, they viewed terrorism as a phenomenon that grew up in the void created by the collapse of the regime's ideology into incoherence at a time when the material conditions of ordinary Egyptians were deteriorating. Terrorism's prospects were enhanced, they argued, by the repression of the moderate Islamist alternative. Without a sense that either the regime's ideology or a credible Islamist alternative could lift the nation from chaos, dreams of national development and personal betterment died. It was the collapse of hope, according to the New Islamists, that gave rise to extremism, exacerbated by the deterioration of material conditions for the mass of Egyptians. For many, the national project of the regime had been the repository of dreams. Others looked to the renewal of the mainstream Islamic movement, notably the Muslim Brothers. When both these routes appeared blocked, the terrorists found ready recruits for their small but deadly army.

In the mid-1990s, the competition between Westernized nationalist and Islamist social trends found unproductive expression in the dominance of public discourse by extreme secularists, who welcomed the Westernization, and Islamist extremists, who denounced it. The government appeared to encourage these diversionary "cultural wars." The exaggerated statements by Islamist extremists were taken to represent Islamist views generally. They were used to discredit the broad Islamic wave and to rally support from the secular left for the government assault on all Islamists. The New Islamists believed that this government repression was driven by its fear that the broad and moderate *Wassatteyya* might just provide the sense of direction and purpose that the regime could no longer deliver. In effect, the regime understood moderate Islam as its most serious opposition. Instead of turning to the Islamist moderates as allies against extremism, the regime sought aggressively to dry up all the Islamist sources for engagement in public life. Quite deliberately, this policy blurred the distinction between moderate and extremist Islamists. The highly publicized outbursts of the violent extremists provided a useful rationale for attacking the moderates as well. The policy of "drying the springs" allowed the regime to criminalize Islamist action for peaceful social change almost as insistently as violent opposition.

The New Islamists never questioned the government position that the extremists must be disarmed. Nor did they fail to appreciate that the process of taking away their weapons would necessitate the use of force. However, they did reject the notion that extremism as a social and intellectual phenomenon could be effectively countered with these security means. "The security authorities addressed the problem according to their jurisdiction only," explained Fahmy Huwaidy, "because the underlying social crises are the responsibility of political and civil institutions which were absent."[47] In short, the very factors that produced the "repentant terrorist" remained in place to draw successive waves of young people to the path that Abdul Baqi had taken. In particular, the New Islamists judged that the failures of Egypt's educational system represented no less than the abandonment of a lost generation.[48]

The best hope for Egypt's future, the New Islamists believed, lay in the renewal of Islam rightly understood, the Islam of the *Wassatteyya.* For this task of cultural rebuilding and educational reform, the New Islamists were well served by the *Wassatteyya* tradition. From mainstream Islam, and in particular the work of Muhammad Abduh, the New Islamists took the critical notion of the priority of culture in the struggle for autonomy, the commitment to educational reform as the first step to cultural rebuilding, and the belief that Islam rightly understood and democracy within an Islamic civilizational framework would provide the twin engines of the long-term process of cultural and social transformation. Understood in this deep sense, the New Islamist call for educational reform was the vehicle to reopen the profound debate about the nature of the modern Egyptian state and the identity of the Egyptians whom it would represent. The New Islamist vision had nothing to do with any backward-looking yearning for an earlier, more perfect age. It was also far more ambitious than the subversive plan sometimes attributed to it, to create a "parallel Islamic society." These misleading formulations were the projected imaginings of Western critics and the displaced fears of Egyptian opponents of extremist Islamist activism. The centrist vision of the New Islamists was in fact far more daring, more comprehensive, and more radical than these imaginings and fears. It responded to the basic questions first raised at the end of the nineteenth century about the character of the state and the identity of the people, the purposes for which state power should be used, the state's obligations to its citizens, and what it meant to be citizens and not subjects.[49] The New Islamists' broad thinking about education and activist interventions on behalf of educational reform represented the heart of their vision. Their collective *ijtihad* [effort of interpretation of the sacred texts] of education contained, in compressed form, the essentials of their hopes for the future, elaborated in more specialized treatments of culture, community, and politics by this school of centrist Islamist intellectuals and public figures.[50]

The New Islamists asserted the priority of culture over politics as a means of addressing the cultural crisis. They did so out of a conviction that the regime and the political arena it commanded were inadequate to the task—that the corruption and undemocratic character of the political arena made it an unpromising area for action. Although they did support efforts of mainstream Islamists to engage in party political activity, their attitude toward likely success in the political arena was guarded optimism at best. Even more emphatically, the New Islamists rejected outright any resort to violence to achieve political or other ends.

For the New Islamists, Islam represents a civilizational choice with implications that go far beyond the political realm. They juxtapose a comprehensive vision of Islam as a civilization to the much narrower conceptions of the advocates of political Islam. In the public arena where politics generally dominates, the New Islamists emphasize culture, the cultivation of knowledge, and the strengthening of values, rather than power and the control of administrative structures, as the primary instruments of social protection and transformation. This cultural emphasis gives them an inherently gradualist, long-term, and flexible perspective.

The Islamic mainstream made cultural autonomy along with openness to the world the twin pillars of its strategy of renewal. Standing resolutely in this tradition, Muhammad al Ghazzaly insisted that Egyptians must face the wounding implications of the Western colonization at the deepest cultural levels. In a 1992 article that appeared in *al Shaab,* Ghazzaly argued that "the West imposed itself by overwhelming force, attacking our most sacred beliefs and our characteristics as an Islamic culture. Colonization started with the military invasion of our land, full of hatred for our religion, our language, and our civilization and all its material and moral potentials." He continued: "Then the colonizers systematically transformed our people into consumers rather than producers, making them a wagon annexed to a Western engine pulling them where it wishes with or without their consent." Ghazzaly insists that Egyptians must face the fact that this history had more the character of rape than dialogue.[51]

Ghazzaly's most important point, however, is that the process of Western cultural disruption continued unabated, particularly in its invidious cultural dimensions. The cultural invasion faced today, Ghazzaly adds, still depends as it did historically on the West's military and political superiority. It uses the adverse balance of power to keep Egypt weak by supporting its enemies and imposing unequal exchanges in all dimensions of the interactions. "The West," Ghazzaly notes, "will send us weapons but will manage the supply of ammunition and spare parts on its own terms." Ghazzaly makes it clear that "the cultural invasion is shrewder than the military invasion. The cultural invasion is the erasure of the distinctive identity and the deliberate deformation of the nation's features." In these conditions, the most intimate elements of the culture, notably religion and language, are subject to great dangers of weakening and erosion.[52]

For Egyptians and other Muslims, the loss of Arabic would have dire consequences. Arabic, Ghazzaly reminds his readers, is the language of divine inspiration for Muslims and the language chosen by God to deliver His message in full clarity to humanity. The universalism of the message is reflected in the fact that Islam relies on Arabic. The Arab in the end is the person who speaks Arabic, and in the history of the Islamic world, non-Arabs who mastered the language became some of its most important teachers and scholars.[53] Ghazzaly considers the weakening of Arabic a major thrust of the cultural assault on Islamic civilization.[54] For those to whom the charge sounds exaggerated, he cites the example of Mahgreb and his own direct experience of the near loss of Arabic to French in Algeria. How, Ghazzaly asks, can we tolerate a situation where some of our educated people are "fluent in foreign languages, but if they were to speak Arabic we would hear a strange mumbling"?[55] "If Arabic dies," Ghazzaly wrote on one occasion, "the Quran will be put in museums, and our national heritage and literature will be lost."[56]

This insistent New Islamist emphasis on the symbolic cultural realm rather than the arena of administrative power makes them critics of all those who look first to the political kingdom. They do not believe that the government, despite its political power and impressive security resources, can create the new future for which Egyptians yearn. It is instructive that the New Islamists devote little attention to the grand solutions put forward by the regime. For example, they barely mention the Tushka development scheme, which the government touts as a worthy successor to the socialism and Pan-Arabism of Nasser or the Open Door of Sadat. Likewise, the New Islamists rarely take seriously the platforms and projects put forward by the official political opposition, regarding them as too divorced from people to have any real life. In the New Islamist view, these greatly diminished dreams of the regime or its domesticated political opposition merely register the extent of the depletion of a Westernized nationalist vision that can no longer provide either enlightenment or energy.

In sharp contrast, the New Islamists vigorously challenge the pretensions of political Islam, in particular its tendency to overemphasize politics. More pointedly, the New Islamists criticize the inclination of political Islam to exaggerate what could be accomplished if Islamists held political power and used that ruling power to implement political and legal restructuring from above. Yusuf al Qaradawy sums up the New Islamist position by arguing that "regulations alone never create societies. Societies are established on education and knowledge, and only then come laws that can act as a protection and shield." Education that gives the child "a contemporary and comprehensive Islamic upbringing," not politics and certainly not slogans about what can be achieved with political means, should be the essential element of the Islamic civilizational project.[57]

The New *Fiqh* of Education: *Tarshid* and National Consensus

As public figures, the New Islamists are determined to do more than produce a deep historical assessment of Egypt's cultural crisis. Driven by a strong sense of national responsibility, they respond to an activist impulse to turn these insights into a new national consensus with comprehensive educational reform as the nation's first priority.

For the New Islamists, as we have seen, reform requires nothing less than reconstruction of national identity and of the corollary sense of national purpose. The challenge of reforming education emerged from this analysis as an essential part of that larger task. The educational system built on the foundations of Westernized nationalism could no longer provide guidance as to what youth must know, understand, and value in order to belong to the nation. Goals could not be defined for education precisely because they could no longer be expressed in the logic and vocabulary of an imitative nationalism that had run its course.

By attributing the failed education system to the underlying cultural crisis that had paralyzed the nation, the New Islamists reopened the debate about the shape and character of the national political community held in abeyance since the 1952 revolution. Attention to these fundamental issues had first been delayed by the priority given to the struggle for independence, and the questions had remained obscured by the seemingly endless conflict with Israel. More recently, the deadly duel between government security forces and violent extremists again meant their postponement.

The New Islamists refused to accept a repressive regime and an extremist Islamist opposition as the only alternatives available to Egyptians. For the long term, they believed that Egypt deserved and was capable of more than this choice between two competing authoritarian solutions. They imagined a third way that looked to a broad and inclusive moderate center built on civilizational grounds. The rethinking of Egypt's heritage and the coalescing of moderate social forces around a civilizational identity and broad national consensus would require new definitions and understandings of the character of the nation and its place in the world, which could then be built into the educational experience of young Egyptians.

In clear and direct language, Huwaidy spoke for the New Islamist School to outline their strategy for meeting these challenges. The New Islamists did not view educational reform as a narrow policy problem to be dealt with by specialists. Rather, they regarded the remaking of education as an imperative for all Egyptians. The New Islamists saw their role in this process of cultural remaking as one of *tarshid* [guidance], a concept central to the *Wassatteyya* tradition. They sought to exercise *tarshid* in two distinct but related ways. Working within the Islamic wave, they strove to achieve a balance between a rationalizing "mind" and a vibrant but disciplined "body" that would enable the Islamic mainstream to play a constructive role in forging a new national consensus around educational reform. As public figures, they also spoke from their platform as leaders of the rationalized Islamic Awakening to advance the broader national interest. They aimed to help guide moderate social forces from all trends to an intellectual and cultural coalescence, out of which a national consensus on identity and direction could be realized. They believed that such a consensus must be achieved as the basis for a comprehensive remaking of national education. The New Islamists juxtaposed their complex notion of *tarshid* to the government's repressive "drying the springs" campaign. More precisely, they offered their "educational solution" as an alternative to the "security solution" of the regime.

The New Islamist understanding of the cultural crisis enabled them to transcend more conventional formulations that cast it in stark "secular versus Islamic" terms. The rigidity of these categories was reinforced by the tendency to identify the regime with the secular outcome and the Islamist extremists with the Islamic alternative. This artificial polarization, the New Islamists believed, had degraded national debate to the level of secondary questions, like the individual religious beliefs of a novelist or a scholar, and reduced the struggle for a better future to the choice between torture in the government jails or the bombings and kidnappings of the Islamist extremists. The New Islamists struggled to prepare for a creative center between these extremes, seeking to return to the fundamental issues first opened in the nineteenth century about the nature of the modern Egyptian state, its civilizational character, its obligations to its citizens, and its place in the world.

The New Islamists understand that only a gradual and long-term social process can accomplish the kind of cultural transformation they envision. Their scholarship contributes to that goal with its synthesizing, theoretical thrust that seeks to build a centrist national project. They aim to find points of connection and areas of agreement between the major competing trends on which future cooperation can be built. To that end, they clarify the enlightened positions of the Islamic *Wassatteyya* on core social, cultural, and political issues in ways that would enable the centrist Islamists to be a full partner in an emerging national consensus. The essential elements of this consensus, they believe, must be built into the education of the young.

In their manifesto, written in 1980, the New Islamists urge first that "the new generation be protected against the duality on which our cultural and educational life was based." They understand the artificial division between Westernizers and defenders of the heritage as the most destructive of the legacies of the colonial experience, one that must be overcome before the nation can move forward. In their work, the New Islamists address as well the questions of Islam and Arabism, Muslims and non-Muslims, with the same eye to finding shared understandings and common ground. Moreover, the New Islamist manifesto harshly condemns the neglect of rationality and science that derives from profoundly mistaken ideas that they conflict with Islam. Finally, the New Islamists celebrate creativity in general and the arts in particular for their critical educational role in forming a humane and tolerant sensibility that cultivates the inventiveness of the human spirit and responds to the harmony and beauty of God's universe. They will not tolerate the ignorant misreadings of Islam that banish music, dance, and artistic expression generally from the Islamic community.[58] They stand just as firmly against rote memorization and the divorce of learning from living, not just in religious studies but in all fields of learning.

The New Islamist call for educational reform erected on inclusive civilizational foundations is content-rich, cultivating a sense of belonging to the Arab Islamic world, and value-centered, emphasizing reason, inclusiveness, and creative thinking. In their view, the content of the curriculum at all levels should foster the development of a secure sense of identity and belonging. It must be characterized by attention to the Arabic language that all Egyptians share, familiarity with the common history of the larger Islamic world of which Egypt is a part, and appreciation for the distinctive identity of Egyptians as a tolerant and moderate people comprising both Muslims and Christians. The New Islamists emphasize these special features of Egyptian culture, religions, language, and history as essential components of education to create not only an educated citizen ready to function in the modern world, but also one with a sense of belonging and pride in Egypt's unique civilization. The link to the past would be selective, yet capable of the broadest possible sharing, while the bridge to the future would be inclusive, flexible, and open to the world. The resulting sense of connectivity would be built from adaptable and broad values and purposes, rather than rigid models and frozen institutions. Its strength would lie in generative possibilities for the future rather than imitative reproduction of fixed forms from the past.

The Islamic framework for educational reform advanced by the New Islamists gives pride of place to the values essential to build a strong community, such as hard work, cooperation, honesty, and respect for others. They charge all members of the community to make their heritage an active part of their lives in order to keep it alive for future generations. Young Egyptians who thus acquire a strong sense of where they come from and who they are can then be helped to engage the larger world by studying English, computer technology, and whatever else a global age requires. They should be expected to study and make their contributions to all the modern human and natural sciences. Whatever the subject matter, the New Islamists stress the importance of critical and imaginative thinking over rote memorization, pointedly emphasizing the importance of the arts and active participation in public life as two essential elements of a rich educational experience for young people.

Islamic civilization, in common with the cultures built on all the world's great religious traditions, provides the enduring values to support these educational emphases. The New Islamists understand Islamic civilization as one that inspires learning, instills confidence in human reason as a guide to understanding not only revelation but also the world, and embraces human differences as a positive dimension of the experience ordained for humankind. Egyptians will need the confidence that such a civilizational identity inspires to overcome the obstacles posed by their current circumstances. The New Islamists underestimate neither the debilitating effects of poverty nor weakness in the face of dominant Western power. They understand how the hard issues of economics, politics, and world affairs press with particular force on a people whose society is underdeveloped. Still, they argue that Egyptians must act within these constraints to take advantage of any and all opportunities open to them rather than waste time and energy blaming others for their condition. Egypt's inability to move forward, they believe, cannot be fully explained by these external factors. It has causes deeper than the inadequacies of its system of rule, its poverty, and its standing in the world order. Although they recognize the importance of each of these factors in creating powerful structural and institutional obstacles, they still insist that there remains a margin for creative, collective initiatives in major national policy areas that Egyptians have been unable to exploit. Only from a vantage point of confidence in their civilization can Egyptians hope to achieve a comprehensive understanding of their situation and draw the strength to act together to improve it.

As scholars, the New Islamists have focused their energies on creating the intellectual foundations for such a synthesis on civilizational grounds. Their innovative intellectual work on issues of culture and education, understood in broad terms, has given a persuasive form to the civilizational project for which they speak.

With an eye for commonalities of thought with other trends, the New Islamists have clarified critical historical questions like the role of Islam and Westernized nationalism in national resistance. They have produced a body of original work on such foundational issues as culture, language, and identity. They have rectified mistaken ideas about reason and science in an Islamic cultural context, and have clarified contemporary social questions relevant to national education like the relationship of Muslims and Christians in Egyptian national identity. In short, through their scholarship on education and culture, they have brought the Islamist civilizational project into the twenty-first century. Taken as a whole, the work of the New Islamists provides a powerful centrist treatment of the critical historical and analytical questions of identity and belonging, history and shared experience, and common destiny that might serve as the basis for educational reform. For a new generation, they have provided persuasive answers to the questions: Who are we? Where have we been? What kind of future can we hope to make? The New Islamists have not given definitive or closed answers to these critical questions; rather, they have offered tentative though compelling understandings, always subject to extension and revision.

Almost as important as the findings of their scholarly work has been the New Islamists' role as a school of Islamic intellectuals in exemplifying the educated Islamic mind in a deep social sense. Their enlightened and moderate method of engaging controversial educational and cultural issues makes its own contribution, distinct from their substantive commentaries. For the Islamic wave, they have shown how the mind or intellect can provide *tarshid* to the often unruly Islamic body to make it a productive partner in reforming the national and global society of which it is a part. For the nation, they have indicated the shape of a broad and moderate cultural synthesis and how the *Wassatteyya* might be one of the moderate forces contributing to it.

The New Islamists' treatment of Islam's relationship to Arabism and to non-Muslims has been marked by a characteristic inclusive approach. They articulate an accommodating notion of Islamic civilizational identity that takes for granted a multiplicity of human identifications deriving from geography, history, or religious affiliations. Egyptians, in their view, are by geography Arabs who share a history with the larger Arab world but also a nation with each other. Most Egyptians are Muslims, though numerous others no less Egyptian are Christians. As Egyptians they share not only a past but also "mutual aspirations and pains," as Yusuf al Qaradawy put it. "We have our distinctive Egyptian problems that we must cooperate to solve."[59]

As Egyptians reflect on the ways in which their Arabic language, their rich and varied history, and their deep Islamic and Christian religious traditions have shaped their identity, the New Islamists emphasize that there is no fixed formula for bringing these elements into an identity that will make sense of the present and speak to the future. Only a flexible approach to the inherited dimensions of identity that depends on reason and focuses on essentials can hope to accomplish that end. The commitment to reason lies at the heart of the New Islamist civilizational project, as their collective work on Islam and rationalism makes clear.

The issue of Islam and rationalism raised by the New Islamist School has interest and importance not only to Islamists but also to all major political and ideological trends. The New Islamists argue pointedly that Islam and rationalism are fully compatible, and that human reason plays a critical part in understanding revelation as well as human responsibility for the betterment of humankind and the earth. Reason has an even larger place in those vast areas of human endeavor where no clear revelation exists. From these abstract questions, however, the New Islamists quickly return to their first priority, the cultural remaking of Egypt. They aim to help their students become active and creative participants in the continuing effort to use knowledge and faith to build a better community. It is to that overriding end that they give sustained attention to clarifying the role of reason in human affairs.

No issue of Islamic community, whether the role of religion, the sense of belonging, or the value of living with an appreciation of difference, can be addressed without an understanding of how, in their view, Islam defines the role that reason plays in a human community that has received a divine message. The heart of the New Islamist position on this crucial issue lies in a fully engaged commitment to recognize and remove unnecessary barriers that impede the exercise of reason and limit its scope. They do not approach the question primarily as an abstract one of theology, but rather as a principled and pragmatic dimension of the task given to humankind to "build the world." This task of building is the essential human responsibility for which, in their view, each generation is charged to prepare the next. It is inconceivable without the wide scope for human reason that Islam, rightly understood, provides. Consequently, the New Islamists regard the treatment of reason and its role in human affairs as the cornerstone of their new *fiqh* ["understandings" of Quran and *Sunnah*] of education.

The very first verse of the Quran proclaims:

> Read!—In the name of thy Lord and Cherisher who created man . . . Read! And thy Lord is most bountiful—He who taught (the use of) the pen—Taught man that which he knew not.[60]

The New Islamists understand that opening verse to mean that God wanted to begin the era of rationality, of education and science, and that he was calling Muslims to play a role as leaders in its realization. In 1996, Yusuf al Qaradawy chose this theme for the inaugural lecture of a symposium named for his colleague and friend, Shaikh Muhammad al Ghazzaly, who died in 1994. Qaradawy spoke of the historic glories of the balanced and distinguished Islamic civilization which, from its great centers of learning in Cairo, Baghdad, and Cordoba, provided enlightenment for the entire world. All the most advanced sciences of the day, Qaradawy said, found expression in the world's preeminent language of science and learning, Arabic. Qaradawy related how Ghazzaly was deeply saddened that the Islamic community, the leading light for science and learning for a thousand years, had become backward and ignorant. But what most angered Ghazzaly was the blame placed on Islam for this backwardness. How could such an argument be sustained, he wondered, when Islam had proven itself to be the vehicle that brought science and enlightenment to the world? In Islam there was never a conflict between science and faith. "For us," pronounced Qaradawy, "science is religion and religion is science." The Quran enjoins man to be independent in thought and to rely on reason in efforts to better the human condition. For the Muslim, "thinking for an hour is better than praying for a whole year." The world is the mosque of the Muslim, and the best job is the one that meets the needs of people, whatever those needs might be at a particular time and place. While noting that there were important political and economic reasons for the decline of the great Islamic civilization, Qaradawy stated that the first cause was the failure of the educational system, which does not encourage creative and independent thinking. Second in importance was the absence of freedom in Egypt and in so much of the Islamic world. The man who is not free, Qaradawy remarked, will be dull and dependent. Finally, there must be faith and values for the confidence they give that "will be critical for attacking the backwardness from which we suffer." Qaradawy concluded: "Our nation should feel that it has a message which is different from others in the East and West." Only then will Egyptians really be able to "engage today's technological battles successfully."[61]

The New Islamists thus write for the long term. Their intellectual work aims to prepare the way for the moderate politics of tomorrow. As public figures, however, the New Islamists also respond to the immediate needs of the moment. They are unwilling simply to abandon the current generation of youth. Whenever possible, the New Islamists speak and act in the interest of Egypt's neglected young people, especially those trapped in the deteriorating public schools. Their commentaries on existing conditions and their insistent calls for some form of action to ameliorate these conditions are neither detached nor dispassionate. The New Islamists make it known that the crisis is immediate, and young lives are at risk. They often set aside their historical and theoretical researches to respond to some young person in need.

Muhammad al Ghazzaly, for one, has used his celebrated weekly newspaper column, "This Is Our Religion," to share hundreds of such stories with his readers. In one column in *al Shaab* in the summer of 1994, he wrote about a girl who entered his office, seeming very agitated. "She said to me: 'Please, hear my complaint and help me!'" The girl first told him that she had been a university student for three years and had completed most of her courses with the grade of "excellent." During those years her mother used to take care of the girl and her brothers, who passed their courses mostly with just fair grades. Everything was going well, she reported, until her mother fell ill and was confined to bed. Her brothers then decided that their sister should take their mother's place and take care of them and the house, arguing that this was her religious duty. "I suggested that we all share the housework when we come home from the university," the girl reported, "but they refused, saying 'you are a woman and you alone have the duty to serve!'"

Shaikh Ghazzaly asked, "What is it that you want from me?" She replied: "Write to them and tell them that we must cooperate. Mention that the Prophet himself was at his people's service, and that he did things at home that some men are ashamed to do now. It is unfair," the girl concluded, "that I should do all the housework alone when I'm successful in my education, serving them when they are beneath my level." Shaikh Ghazzaly needed to hear no more. He got out a piece of paper "and wrote a speech about Aisha, the mother of believers, and I gave it to her for her brothers to read!"

A man who had observed this interchange asked the Shaikh: "Why did you act in this way? Doesn't God say 'that the man is not like the woman'? The young woman should take care of her brothers, leave the university, and stay at home!" Shaikh Ghazzaly explained that the Quranic verse cited should not be read out of context; it is part of a speech by the wife of Omran, the mother of the Mary who was to bear the Christ child. The woman was pregnant and was expecting a male child who would be able to take a man's place in leading people in their prayers and religious ceremonies. When the baby came and was a girl (Mary), she expressed regret to God for not fulfilling her expectations and said: "God, I have borne a girl and God knows that the man is not like the woman. I called her Mary and I pray that she and her descendants will be kept from evil." By providing the full context of the verse, Ghazzaly made it clear that the phrase could not possibly have meant the denigration of women.

The man responded that, however that may be, "the male is more honorable than the female," and he continued to criticize Shaikh Ghazzaly for encouraging the girl to put her own education above what he saw as her responsibility as a woman to serve her brothers. Angered, Ghazzaly interrupted his interlocutor and asked him bluntly: "Do you mean that you are better [in God's eyes] than Mary? Pharaoh's woman [who rescued Moses] is more faithful than you are even though you are a man and she was the wife of a tyrant destined for hell, for you are ignorant of the facts of the world and of religion."[62]

With their eyes on the world as much as on the texts of their faith, the New Islamists have exercised their *tarshid* of the Islamic movement to protect the right to education when the ignorant and uninformed threatened it. They have sought to contain and counter those distortions by Islamist extremists that polarized the national community. They have struggled unrelentingly, as this image of Muhammad al Ghazzaly at work suggests, to deepen the understanding among Islamists of the inclusive implications of the higher purposes of Islam. They have tried consistently to make their own interventions serve as anticipations of the value and character of the longer-term civilizational project that they believe has a place for all Egyptians.

At the same time, the New Islamists have devoted their collective energies to the demanding task of thinking through the Islamic civilizational framework for comprehensive reform. This long-term project requires clarification of general Islamic purposes and principles of education, and, more important, it demands that commonalities between their moderate Islamic stance and the positions of others in the mainstream of national life be identified and strengthened. The search for common ground, the New Islamists believe, must begin with the riches of Egypt's history and culture that belong to all Egyptians.

No iron curtain separated these two sets of efforts. The opportunity to make a difference in the life chances of a young girl might well help the long-term effort to rethink the educational dimensions of the Islamic heritage in ways that could make it a central part of the thinking of the political mainstream in Egypt. Broader ideas of historic commonalities and shared dreams might well lend coherence to otherwise disparate interventions. Only a comprehensive vision would respond to the nation's deeper educational needs. Meanwhile, there was a "lost generation" that needed to be heard.

The New Islamists are public figures and not public officials. They cannot formulate and execute official policies in education or other areas of public policy. However, they can present their views through writings and other forms of public presentation to influence those who make educational policy now or might do so in the future. Given their stature as intellectuals with national and international reputations, the New Islamists are able to address wide audiences both within Egypt and in the larger Arab Islamic sphere. It nevertheless remains true that the most significant audience for their writing about the cultural crisis and education remains the Islamic Awakening, with which they are in constant interaction. They speak and act as proponents of the rationalization of the Islamic wave and as advocates for the general increase in the scope for reason in social life. The response evoked by their call for educational reform as the linchpin of national revival, not least from younger generations of Islamist activists, provides a particularly important measure of their weight in public life.

From the late 1960s on, two broad avenues of Islamist activity coexisted. On the one hand, various radical movements attracted young people into the dark paths of violent, anti-regime politics. The "repentant terrorist" took this course. In contrast, centrist Islamists such as the New Islamists charted a path of democratic participation in social life, whenever and wherever openings occurred. Despite some initial advances in democratization by the government in the years immediately following Sadat's assassination, opportunities for real participation in the political arena remained very circumscribed. The process of liberalizing the official political system slowed and then suffered a reversal by the end of the century. At various times, the institutions of civil society and an expanded private sector, including multinational companies and international banking, provided what appeared to be a promising alternative sphere within which advancement was possible. The New Islamists directed the attention of the young to these openings that provided somewhat more promising sites for the development of experience in moderation. Evidence, some anecdotal but some more systematic, indicates that the New Islamist message of rationalization did reach young people who were responding to the broad Islamic movement and did encourage them to seek out these new channels. The New Islamists took assertive positions, for example, against those in the Islamic wave who condemned working in banks or the new information technology fields as *haram* [religiously forbidden]. In opposition to these retrograde views, they encouraged youthful Islamist activists to move into global finance and international communications.[63] They also supported their work in the professional syndicates and encouraged them to seek leadership roles through democratic channels, appearing themselves in the new forums that the Islamic presence in the syndicates helped to create. The New Islamists encouraged young people to seek the best education they could find to prepare themselves to make a contribution to their nation as perhaps the best way to serve the faith. Even when faced with the repressive policy of "drying the springs," the New Islamists continued to provide young people with signposts to moderation.

Young people did hear the message. The story of Abdul Baqi, the "repentant terrorist," told in the official media carried the unintended message that moderate Islamist thinking had played the central role in his reeducation. While it is impossible to know just how typical his experience is, the broad publicity given to the event made it an important one and certainly signaled the possible consequences when serious, independent Islamist scholars reached the younger generation.

No less surprising, but much more indicative of the depth of the inroads of centrist Islamist thinking into the minds of an entire generation, was the 1996 announcement of the party program of the middle generation of Islamists, whose experience had included work in the professional associations and who sought to enter the political arena. The party platform of the Wassat Party bore the unmistakable moderate imprint of New Islamist thinking, all the more striking in that it came in the midst of a government policy of "breaking arms" in order to repress the Islamists across the board.[64]

Before moving to these social and political arenas, I turn next to the arts, another important aspect of the cultural realm. The New Islamist School stands firmly against the cultural nihilism and prohibition of the arts by the most extreme elements of political Islam. Through educational reform, the New Islamists aim to achieve an inclusive, orienting sense of identity and belonging. In their view, the arts will enhance that identity by strengthening an Islamic cultural formation that teaches the young to appreciate creativity and be moved by beauty. These too, they insist, represent skills and sensibilities that young people will need to build Islamic community.

chapter 2

Embracing the Arts

It is a "crime against Islam," thundered Shaikh Muhammad al Ghazzaly, reacting to the assassination attempt against Naguib Mahfuz, Nobel Laureate in literature. From the hospital bedside of the seriously wounded novelist, Ghazzaly denounced the fanatic who tried to murder Mahfuz in the fall of 1994.[1] Few other voices in Egypt could offer as authoritative a condemnation of the Islamist extremists who for years had put Mahfuz's life at risk with charges of apostasy. Decades earlier, Ghazzaly had recommended against the publication of Mahfuz's controversial novel *Children of Gebelaawi* as part of a panel of religious scholars representing al Azhar, the oldest and most respected mosque-university in Egypt. Distressed that his novel could be misread as inappropriate for an Islamic society, Mahfuz accepted the ruling and resisted all attempts in subsequent years to publish the work.[2] However, when the deadly attack on Mahfuz took place, Ghazzaly put aside his long-standing disagreements with the novelist and rallied to his side. He expressed the horror of the *Wassatteyya* at such a criminal assault on a writer.

In 1988 when the Nobel Prize was announced, extremists had renewed their attacks on Mahfuz. Shaikh Omar Abdul Rahman, a leader of the Jihad group who was later tried and convicted of violent crimes in the United States, pronounced outright that Naguib Mahfuz was an apostate. In the spring of 1989 Abdul Rahman issued a *fatwa* [religious opinion] condemning Mahfuz and inviting his assassination. "Islamically, Salman Rushdie as well as Naguib Mahfuz are apostates. Had we killed Mahfuz when he wrote his novel *Children of Gebelaawi*," he added ominously, "his death would have been an example to Salman Rushdie and the like."[3] At the same time, Abdul Rahman denounced leading moderate Islamists, naming Ghazzaly in particular, as "religious scholars of the regime" who failed to protect Egyptians from figures like Mahfuz.[4]

These charges by the militants did not dampen the excitement that the Nobel award brought in Egypt. Because many of Mahfuz's novels and short stories had been made into films, his work was widely known and appreciated. For a people who deserved recognition as more than an emblem of overpopulation and problems of development, or simply the subjects of a corrupt and inefficient government, the international acclaim for an Egyptian author led to a national jubilation all too rarely experienced in the eighties and nineties.

Mahfuz himself chose to pay as little attention as possible to both the celebrations and the threats. With characteristic simplicity, Egypt's preeminent novelist quietly deflected the flood of personal attention into more productive public channels, while ignoring the extremist warnings. He refused to allow either celebrity or fear to force a change in his modest way of living, very much in touch with the city of Cairo and its people. A substantial portion of the prize money was unobtrusively donated to the poor. The novelist preserved a modest public presence through a brief weekly column in *al Ahram*, where he addressed the most pressing issues of public life. When Mahfuz was asked to comment on the threatening *fatwa* of the extremist Omar Abdul Rahman, he wrote that his daily life would remain unchanged. "The power of the pen is stronger than that of the gun and the dagger," he said, "and random shots can never assassinate bold pens." Refusing security, the novelist added that he would not live "trembling in fear, with my hands shaking." "How," asked Mahfuz with a touch of the gentle humility for which he is renowned, "could I possibly impose on a security guard my habit of a walk through central Cairo at 4 a.m.?"[5]

The assassin's knife thus finds an easy target when the attack comes in 1994. Waiting outside his apartment with the car windows rolled down and accompanied only by a personal friend, Naguib Mahfuz is heading for his weekly literary meeting when the criminal thrusts a knife into his neck. "It was as if a ferocious inhuman beast was attacking me with uncontrollable hatred, despite my old age and inability to defend myself." By jamming his entire upper body into the car, the assassin blocks Mahfuz from escaping his blows and prevents his victim from seeing his face clearly.[6] Somehow, Mahfuz survives. He is rushed to a nearby hospital and fights his way to recovery as the nation struggles to make sense of this terrible crime.

Shaikh Ghazzaly acts immediately. Rushing to Mahfuz's hospital room, he issues his ringing condemnation that dramatizes the difference between criticism and violence, a distinction so crucial to the Islamic *Wassatteyya*. Mahfuz's Nobel award rekindled the memory of Ghazzaly's role in blocking publication of *Children of Gebelaawi.* For some thirty years, the al Azhar ban on that one work remained unchallenged, although Mahfuz went on to establish a commanding presence as an intellectual figure. However much Ghazzaly came to appreciate the larger corpus of Mahfuz's work, he never changed his opinion of the novel which the Nobel Committee subsequently chose to single out for special praise.[7]

During the visit to the hospital, Ghazzaly and Mahfuz exchange respectful greetings. However, when the subject of Ghazzaly's part in the decision not to publish the novel is raised, Ghazzaly makes it clear that he has not revised his opinion.[8] In fact, Ghazzaly's critical reserve toward Mahfuz has heightened in recent years, when Mahfuz became identified with the opening to Israel.[9] When the award was announced, other critics of Mahfuz raised awkward questions about a possible political motive in the Nobel committee selection, linked to the writer's well-known support for the American-backed negotiations between Israel and the Palestinians. Fahmy Huwaidy, among others, intimated that Mahfuz's celebrated literary salon had become a place where Egyptian intellectuals made quiet contact with Israeli researchers working in Egypt.[10] Mahfuz, for his part, made known his view that the peace with Israel would provide the opportunity to "get to know the others, to read their works, to listen to them."[11] In contrast, Ghazzaly stood with the overwhelming majority of intellectuals across the political spectrum who set themselves firmly against any such effort to move beyond a "cold peace" with an Israel that persisted in its illegal settlement of the occupied Palestinian territories.

At the moment of extreme danger, however, the venerable Shaikh Ghazzaly sweeps all his reservations about Mahfuz aside. In the wake of the stab wounds that Mahfuz has just barely survived, Ghazzaly does not hesitate to defy the threats of the extremists, question the religious and intellectual credentials of their leaders, and offer his own physical and moral presence to support the wounded novelist. Ordinary Egyptians cannot fail to notice the extraordinary steps that Ghazzaly takes to signal that his earlier criticisms of Mahfuz in no way provide justification for such criminal violence.[12] Ghazzaly directly castigates the shadowy Shaikh Omar Abdul Rahman, identified by the assailants as the "spiritual guide" who provided the Islamic rationale for the violent attacks on Mahfuz. He dismisses Abdul Rahman as a figure whose importance has been exaggerated by the media. "He is a simple Imam of a mosque of limited intellectual ability," pronounces Ghazzaly, "who has no weight as a religious scholar." On Islamic grounds, he directly challenges Abdul Rahman's dangerous distortions of the faith. Ghazzaly refuses both the condemnation of Mahfuz as an apostate and the resort to violence against the writer.[13]

Ghazzaly and the New Islamists understand the attack on Mahfuz not simply as an assault on the man and his views but as a more generalized attack on the arts. As a school, they reject the extremists who denigrate the arts, affirming the view of the *Wassatteyya* that the Islamic heritage is extraordinarily rich in the arts, with its own distinctive and honored traditions of poetry, calligraphy, and a wide range of artistic expressions.[14] The New Islamists contest and hold up for contempt the notorious and ignorant pronouncements on the arts by extremists like Abdul Rahman that make dancing a form of adultery and condemn singing generally, while declaring the voice of a woman, in particular, a source of shame to be hidden.[15] Ghazzaly forthrightly denies that Islam condemns artistic expression, whether literature, dance, music, or song. The New Islamists stand against all violent extremist actions that attempt to impose on society the distorted views of the militants, whether the burning of video clubs or attacks on theaters or university student musical concerts,[16] and they continue to oppose Abdul Rahman and other such extremist thinkers in Egypt and elsewhere in the Islamic world.

Kamal Abul Magd is out of the country when the attack against Mahfuz occurs. Given the precariousness of the novelist's condition, it is several weeks before a mutual friend, the journalist and writer Muhammad al Salmawy who acts as Mahfuz's spokesman, can arrange for Abul Magd to see Mahfuz. By then, or so it seems, all of the big questions concerning the assassination attempt have been discussed. That impression proves misleading, however, and the conversation, later recorded and published by Abul Magd himself under a special arrangement, provides one of the most moving and revealing exchanges to take place in the aftermath of the attempt on Mahfuz's life.[17]

Abul Magd and a small circle of literary figures gather in Mahfuz's small apartment. After the greetings and polite inquiries about Mahfuz's recovery, Kamal Abul Magd fills a lull in the conversation by asking Mahfuz about a comment that he sent to a recent a*l Ahram* symposium, "Toward an Arab Civilizational Project." Mahfuz made the succinct point that "any Arab project must be based on Islam and science." To Abul Magd and his other guests, Mahfuz explains that this sentiment has informed all of his literary production. Then, unexpectedly, he turns to a deeper consideration of the controversies that swirled around *Children of Gebelaawi* and prompted the assassination attempt. Mahfuz says that although all of his work, including the controversial *Children of Gebelaawi,* expresses a deep Islamic faith, literature cannot be read as an analytical essay, with the views of particular characters taken as the personal opinions of the author. To do so, he concludes, would inevitably generate misunderstandings:

> I'd like to say that even *Children of Gebelaawi,* which was misunderstood by some people, did not deviate from this vision. The novel makes the point that the people who abandon religion, represented by Gebelaawi, and think they can rely only on science (represented by Arafa) and organize their life (represented by the lane) with it alone, discover that science without religion becomes a tool of evil and leads to the dictatorship of the ruler. It deprives them of their freedom, so they begin again to search for Gebelaawi. The problem with this work from the beginning was that I wrote it as a novel and it was read by some as a book. A novel is a literary form that mixes reality and symbols. It is inevitably both real and imaginative.[18]

Kamal Abul Magd immediately embraces Mahfuz's critical distinction between a novel as a creative and imaginative work and a book as an exposition of the author's own ideas. As a school, the New Islamists share a general conception that worthwhile art should express the cherished values of a society, and that in an Islamic community these values will be Islamic. However, the judgments of the New Islamists on the relationship of a particular work of art to such values might vary,[19] and such differences of opinion have become a normal part of their interactions. Thus, it should come as no surprise that Kamal Abul Magd takes pointed issue with the influential negative reading of *Children of Gebelaawi* by his friend Shaikh Muhammad al Ghazzaly. With the same calm and reasonable tone that marks his exchanges with Egypt's leading secular intellectuals, Abul Magd goes immediately to the heart of the difference of interpretation, noting that it is important to understand that all the imaginative symbols employed in a novel do not necessarily represent the author's "own opinions of realities." Abul Magd then offers his own interpretation of the work, which stands unambiguously with Mahfuz and in sharp but respectful opposition to Ghazzaly:

> What remains in my mind to this very moment as the opinion the author wishes to convey through this symbolic story is the clear declaration of the need of the lane, which symbolizes human society, for religion and religious values expressed by an abstract symbol, Gebelaawi. The people of the lane thought otherwise. They were infatuated by Arafa, the symbol of science, who is completely devoid of the values needed to guide the people of the lane.[20]

Abul Magd notes that all those assembled on this particular occasion in Mahfuz's apartment consider themselves part of his reading public. They all belong to a generation that found in his work something between photography and literature that captured and clarified their social experience.[21] "In your description of Cairo and its residents, you provide an accurate picture full of color and detail." The reader, continues Abul Magd, "can almost hear the voices of the people, see their faces, and follow their movements through the streets, lanes, mosques, and cafés. One sometimes feels directly involved in the relationships you describe. How many times," he asks, "did some of us first get acquainted with the districts and streets of Cairo through your descriptions of them?"

More pointedly, he says that he understands in Mahfuz's old and new writings his attitude toward Islam and Egyptian society. Abul Magd feels that Mahfuz's sentiments and his manner of expressing them "represent the approach of our generation and the generation of our fathers in understanding Islam. *We were used, as they were, to breathe Islam and live with it quietly and comfortably, without overwhelming our gatherings and the gatherings of others with too much talk about it.*"[22] Abul Magd recognizes that Mahfuz, even in his most misunderstood work, speaks for the values of an Islam that was lived in quiet and comfortable ways at a time when the message was all too often shouted and misunderstood.

Abul Magd concludes by suggesting that Mahfuz record his own clarification of the meaning of *Children of Gebelaawi*, "so that the people would hear this clear-cut explanation which is not open to misinterpretation, and in this way learn of your intentions through your words, instead of through the commentaries of others." The suggestion is made that the entire discussion be recorded for a televised symposium. Mahfuz demurs, explaining that he is too weak to undertake such a project. Then, with an expression of compete confidence in Abul Magd, he suggests that Abul Magd undertake the task of writing an article that summarizes the conversations.

Kamal Abul Magd agrees, and the account of the dialogue appears soon after in *al Ahram*. Abul Magd offers the article as an authoritative record of Mahfuz's thinking, explicitly approved by him in the presence of three distinguished guests. He considers his article as a testimony "that I hope would free Naguib Mahfuz's writings of the misunderstandings of some people who quickly jump to accusations and forget that Islam itself has warned of such judgments of the aims of others." Abul Magd expresses the further hope that "it might also free his writings too of the ugly inventions of some writers who insist on reading what's in their own minds in Naguib Mahfuz's writings. They read what they wish to find and give themselves the authority that no one should have over anyone else, let alone a writer of Naguib Mahfuz's stature in literature, life experience, and unique, God-given talent."

The attack on Naguib Mahfuz did not come out of nowhere. In the course of the official investigation, Mahfuz himself offered a compelling explanation of the forces that led to the assault. Asked by investigators if he recognized his assailant, Mahfuz replied that he did not. However, he qualified his response with the stunning observation that, although he did not recognize him, "I know who he is." His face bore the marks of poverty and ignorance, Mahfuz explained. His spirit was crippled by the loss of opportunities and even dreams. His attempted revolt against these conditions had only subjected him to the *amirs* [leaders] of the extremist groups, who explained his terrible situation with distorted ideas of Islam, including a blanket condemnation of the arts. Mahfuz noted that the young man who attempted to murder him had not even read his novel; he was acting on orders from the *amir* of his group. Mahfuz understood that he was caught in the cross-fire between the violent elements that hijacked the idealism of Egypt's youth and the regime that had failed to save them. For Mahfuz, the young man who had tried to kill him was only a representative of "the lost generation" of Egyptian youth. Sadly, Mahfuz commented, "today's youth are all like my assassin. A whole generation that has been ignored and neglected."[23]

Art itself, as well as ideas about art, comes out of specific social conditions. It can be read as an expression of those particular conditions and the feelings they generate, even as it speaks in subtle and complex ways to the general human condition. The extremists' attacks on the arts flourished in a barren social and political landscape. When set against a background of poverty, misery, and loss of hope, the ideas of the violent groups made a certain perverse sense. Like Mahfuz, the New Islamists understood the origins of this extremist *anti-aesthetic* of deprivation and despair, seeing the complex link between art and context, between aesthetic consciousness and social conditions. The government's failure to project a coherent cultural identity and national project that expressed it created an intellectual and moral void that made material deprivations worse. In settings of poverty and lack of hope, attacks on the arts, and on beauty itself, in a perverse way compensate for the inability to overcome such misery.

The New Islamists argue that an Islamic community without art is unimaginable. Speaking for the *Wassatteyya*, they elaborate in their writings an *aesthetic of belonging*. Shaikh Muhammad al Ghazzaly has pronounced the artistic cultivation of beauty in Islamic civilization as something that, along with appreciation for the splendors of God's creations in the universe, only "sick persons" could reject.[24] In the New Islamist view, an Islamic society would be permeated by the values and purposes of Islam. The art that sprang from such a soil would both draw inspiration from and further cultivate a sense of belonging to the Islamic world. Further, the God-given talents of artists would provide refined and cultivated ways to express core Islamic values and thereby enhance the chances to realize them. Artists, explains Kamal Abul Magd, have an honored place in Islamic society; their special talents come from God, and their gifts refine and enrich human experience:

> Who is the artist? He is a person to whom God has granted a special gift, capability, and talent that allow him to receive things with an extraordinary sensitivity. He expresses himself with an accuracy and richness not granted to others. Whether a poet, writer, or painter, the artist sees in the rhythm of things louder voices and clearer expressions that he is able to capture in a special, unique way. . . . It is unimaginable that Islam would be against this.[25]

Abul Magd reminds Muslims that one way to worship is to praise the manifold gifts of God. Who could worship better than the artist? he asks, "with his refined sensitivity and developed imagination that responds to the beautiful over the ugly." Muslims, confused by the militant attacks on the arts, are reassured that "there is no convincing evidence in Islam that would forbid art, song, and music . . . and one should not feel he is doing wrong by listening to music, singing, or admiring the arts."[26] Meeting the militants confidently on the grounds of faith, Abul Magd argues: "To pay tribute to God is the best way of worshipping in all religions. However, this can never take place without genuinely feeling the real gifts of God. How can one feel those gifts without differentiating between beauty and ugliness?"[27] He concludes with an uncompromising warning to the militants that "those who prohibit the arts can never themselves feel the gifts of God."[28]

Despite the New Islamists' emphatic embrace of the arts, they have done so in ways that distance them from the extreme secularists almost as strongly as from the violent Islamist groups. The secularists championed abstract and unlimited freedom of expression as the answer to the extremist assault on the arts. Like the dominant thinking in the West, secular opinion spoke of art as having a universal language, for all times and places, that could tolerate no limits on its freedom of expression. From this vantage point of an *aesthetic of abstract rights,* the secularists regarded Islamist extremist views as atavistic and retrograde. However, they found the ideas of the New Islamist moderates on the arts almost as disturbing. The secularists were unwilling to accept the New Islamist conception that the arts originated from and belonged to a community whose fundamental values should be respected. They refused any notion of the social and cultural grounding of the arts that suggested that the creative process might be bound or limited in some way by these factors.

The New Islamists in turn rejected these extreme secular views as wrongheaded and detrimental to public well-being. In their view, the danger arose from the secularist refusal to recognize the importance of setting limits to protect the foundations of society. The secular call for absolute freedom, the New Islamists feared, might enable all kinds of excesses, and the exaggerations that would inevitably flow from such views might provide fuel for the violent Islamist radicals and their blanket condemnation of the arts and attacks on artists.

For these reasons, the New Islamists challenged directly the secularist refusal to recognize the importance of limits. No society, they claimed, is without a foundation of shared cultural and civic values. In addition, all societies place boundaries and limits on activities and behaviors, including those in the aesthetic realm that threaten to undermine those fundamentals. For the New Islamists, the starting point of the discussion of values had to be Egypt's belonging to the Arab and Islamic world by history and by culture. Within the framework of those broad affiliations, Egyptians in their view share two sets of values that must be defended. The first set of "basic values comes from religion, which in Egypt," as Fahmy Huwaidy points out, "means Islam *and* Christianity." The second comes from society, which embodies its national values in documents, the most important of which is the constitution. "The fundamentals of religion," Huwaidy elaborates, "are determined by categorically clear texts, while supreme interests determine the fundamentals of society." This formulation means, in his view, that "the fundamentals of religion are invariable, while those of society are relative, changing from stage to stage in the life of the nation."[29]

Huwaidy argued that these critical determinations of the character of the fundamentals should not be considered matters of individual interpretation or opinion. Rather, they express historical and cultural realities that find expression as the consciousness of the society. To those secularists who consider this call to protect basic values as rigid and backward, Huwaidy countered that progress in an Islamic society could not mean abandoning all ethical and moral obligations that flow from a shared history and culture.[30] Responding to critics who regard the protection of such values as an infringement on freedom, including creative freedom of expression, he noted simply that freedom and responsibility everywhere go together. Nowhere, he argued, are freedoms absolute. The freedoms protected by law are always and everywhere the freedoms that protect the basic values of the society.[31]

For many secularists, such limitations were intolerable. The extreme secularist notion of complete freedom of expression denied all such claims of cultural limitations. It also made it extremely difficult to recognize standards of aesthetic worth. Issues of quality, like questions of cultural appropriateness, became matters of individual taste rather than social standards. The New Islamists saw two sets of dangers in the aesthetic of abstract rights embraced by the extreme secularists. By placing no limits on expression, such an approach invited such dangerous excesses as pornography or blasphemy. Moreover, the New Islamists felt, Egypt, as a small and vulnerable country, faced serious threats to its culture from outside pressures, especially Western.

The New Islamist aesthetic of belonging occupied a strong and independent middle position that set them apart from both Islamist and secular extremists. Throughout the contentious years of the 1980s and 1990s, the New Islamists took an active part in the public debates and discussions about the arts, advocating and defending their centrist views. In addition, they continued their scholarly work to develop more fully their *Wassatteyya* understanding of the arts in Islamic society. Muhammad al Ghazzaly and Yusuf al Qaradawy provided the most vigorous and systematic grounding in the Quran and *Sunnah* [all the deeds and words of the Prophet] of the New Islamist aesthetic of belonging. The work of these two writers is most important for its authoritative documentation of New Islamist views on the arts according to the sacred texts as understood in the light of contemporary circumstances. They have also contributed to a deeper understanding of the importance of the arts for the Islamic Awakening in our global age. The principles elaborated by Ghazzaly and Qaradawy represent a consensus position of the New Islamist thinkers and public figures, all of whom helped to explain and develop the implications of the aesthetic of belonging in both theoretical and practical ways.

Addressing directly those extremists who condemn all art, Yusuf al Qaradawy pronounced unequivocally that no sound justification for the view that the arts are *haram* [religiously forbidden] can be found in the Quran or *Sunnah*.[32] The extremists' views depend on unconfirmed *hadith* [a report of the words and deeds of the Prophet] or misreading and misunderstandings of the sacred texts, added Muhammad al Ghazzaly. Both scholars point to abundant evidence in the Quran and *Sunnah* that Islam, on the contrary, embraces the arts. Ghazzaly and Qaradawy elaborate the argument that the artist has an important place in the Islamic community. The charge from God that Man act as his regent on Earth requires that Man use his capacity to respond to the beauty of God's creations to inspire his own work of building the Earth. The *Sunnah* provides vivid examples of the Prophet's approval of the arts, including poetry, singing, and dancing, to provide edification and enjoyment, both of which are enjoined for

Man by God.[33] Why, in these troubled times, asked Ghazzaly, would Muslims turn against a powerful instrument like the arts which has the capacity to uplift souls and rally people to renew their threatened community? Rather than condemning the arts, Ghazzaly sought to enlist artists to serve the Islamic community.[34]

Ghazzaly also clarified the essential premise of New Islamist thinking that saw the arts as one among many powerful instruments given to Man by God. Like other means available to human beings, it has the potential to serve the highest aims or to be misused. Ghazzaly rejected the idea put forward by the *amirs* that singing is *haram,* and in particular he objected strongly to the further notion advanced by many Islamists, both conservative and extremist, that a woman's voice is *haram* and should not be heard. On the other hand, Ghazzaly also refused to countenance the secularists' view that all lyrics set to music were appropriate for an Islamic society. Ghazzaly explained that singing, like the other arts, is an instrument to convey meaning. It might be used to communicate what is *halal* or what is *haram.* As he described it, "singing is just a form of speech. What is good of it is permissible and vice versa." Addressing the Islamists, Ghazzaly made the point that "instead of saying that Islam forbids singing, we have the task of sorting out words and meanings."[35] Responding to the secularists, he explained that there could be no blanket approval of all meanings transmitted by the arts under a general slogan of freedom of creation. Some meanings might well be unacceptable, others neutral in their effects, and still others perfectly attuned to an Islamic society and even effective instruments for its betterment. What matters is what meanings are being communicated and in what ways.[36]

Muhammad al Ghazzaly also made it clear that the New Islamist aesthetic of belonging did not refer only to the past and to the art forms of Islam's golden ages. Clearly, these treasures were to be savored and passed on to each new generation. The creative achievements of Islamic civilization would heighten the sense of identity and belonging to a community that had distinguished itself. However, Ghazzaly also provided the theoretical basis for resisting any rigid imposition of an Islamic canon, especially for literature but for the arts more generally. Creativity is an essential part of human nature, and one of its most valued qualities. It should not be stifled by imitation of rigidly imposed models. To make this point, Ghazzaly told the story of a prize of a piece of gold that the Prophet bestowed on a poet. The poet that Prophet Muhammad chose to honor had composed a piece in praise of God, but in a unique way unfamiliar to the professional poets of the day. Ghazzaly explained that the Prophet knowingly rewarded a work of a kind that others could not imitate because it came out of a heart filled with thanks to God and expressed itself in novel ways that did not contradict the essentials of Islam.[37]

While acknowledging that Islamic civilization has produced great works of art that enrich the cultural resources of the Islamic community, the New Islamists temper this respect for past cultural achievements with a distaste for imitation. Each generation, they caution, must be open to the distinctive creative possibilities of its own time. Yusuf al Qaradawy has emphasized with particular effect the vital contemporary role of the arts, including the new arts of the Information Age, for the Islamic Awakening, paying particular attention to the creative possibilities of the new information technologies. While attentive to the tasks of rethinking the Islamic heritage and supportive of those who work to that end, he also understands the ways in which new art forms such as computer graphics and Web site design can be powerful instruments to serve the ends of Islamic renewal.

Controversies over cultural and intellectual issues defined the turbulent decades of the 1980s and 1990s in Egypt. They can be usefully illuminated in terms of these competing aesthetics as they were played out in the public arena. More often than not, the New Islamists found their centrist aesthetic of belonging under attack from all sides. The Islamist extremists denounced the New Islamist defense of the arts as un-Islamic from the vantage point of their anti-aesthetic of deprivation and despair, while the secularists decried their arguments on behalf of boundaries to creative expression as anti-art from their viewpoint of an aesthetic of absolute rights. Meanwhile, the government for its own repressive purposes supported this secular misrepresentation of the New Islamist position as just another version of Islamic extremism.

Throughout these cultural wars, the New Islamists maintained that debate and discussion were the Islamic way to resolve such conflicts over the arts and their role in society. Their preferred venues were university, arts, or civic forums. In the absence of resolution in these locations, they urged that such matters be left to the courts. At times, they turned to the legal arena as a forum where their own centrist views, otherwise overshadowed by the shouting of extremists of all kinds, might at least get an airing. Just as frequently, the courts simply represented a way to calm the situation by deferral so that a distracted public might address other more pressing questions.

An incident from the 1980s is particularly helpful in highlighting these efforts of the New Islamists to speak for the *Wassatteyya* in projecting and defending a centrist Islamist position on the arts. The case involved a lawsuit by Mustafa Shakaa, a distinguished Islamist professor of literature who had close ties to the New Islamist circles. It reveals what the New Islamist aesthetic of belonging meant in practice and how such views contrasted with the positions on the arts of Islamic extremists, radical secularists, and the government.

The "Ramadan Riddles" and the Courts

Mustafa Shakaa phrased the charges of the lawsuit he lodged in 1988 with great care. His legal action pointedly targeted the popular but controversial "Ramadan Riddles" television program. Shakaa charged the program, in timing, content, and social impact, with undermining the Islamic values of Egyptian society, while failing to display any redeeming artistic value.[38] He brought the case against the state-run television monopoly, avoiding even the hint of a generalized condemnation of the arts, so often described by the regime as the position of the Islamist wave. In doing so, he made the point that public moneys should not be used to support programming that contradicted Islamic values.

As a professor of literature and former Dean of the Faculty of Arts at Ain Shams University in Cairo, Shakaa took for granted that the arts had a rightful place in Islamic society. The insistence on the close relationship between the arts and the values of society came naturally to Shakaa, the author of a prize-winning study, *Literature and the Development of Islamic Civilization,* which argues that literature and art are linked organically with the major issues of society.[39] Shakaa describes with "admiration" how Arabic literature developed by interacting with the needs and concerns of the people, including their need for entertainment.[40] Humorous literary forms, for example, arose early and became an important part of the literary heritage. Shakaa also celebrates the confident opening of Islamic civilization to the arts of other cultures,[41] and describes the ways in which poetic models from southern France left their distinctive mark on certain forms of Arabic poetry and songs in Spain under Islamic rule, forms that in turn influenced both Turkish and Persian poetry.[42]

Shakaa's impeccable scholarship and the cultured and cosmopolitan sensibility it reveals make it hard to equate his suit against the "Ramadan Riddles" with the cultural nihilism of the Islamist extremists. Shakaa's work showed that Egyptians have a tradition of openness to the world. However, he made the equally important point that the Islamic world has a rich heritage that can inform and guide the discriminations that should shape the future of its culture. Egyptians, he argued, must be educated to make qualitative distinctions about both indigenous and imported art forms, particularly those that dominate the public media.

Working from these premises, Shakaa's suit claimed that there should be a positive relationship between artistic expression and core Islamic values. Shakaa refrained from targeting individuals, questioning their beliefs, or asking for their punishment. He focused instead on a call to correct the negative social effects of the powerful national media of television, radio, and the official press, all of which are supported by public funds in Egypt. Shakaa claimed no personal injury in his suit. Rather, he based his case on alleged damage to the public interest from this program, in keeping with the Islamic concept of *hisbeh* [the principle that legal action in defense of the public interest may be taken, even though the individual making the charge has not personally suffered injury or harm].

The "Riddles" are now something of an Egyptian "tradition" during the month of Ramadan, when Muslims fast each day from sunrise to sunset. The program is aired in that critical period just after the fast is broken, when Egyptians are likely to be at home with the television on. Each year the "Riddles" features a female entertainer performing Westernized singing and dancing routines, complete with nightclub costumes and meaningless lyrics. Intricate camera work cleverly connects fast-paced entertainment sequences with the most sophisticated commercials on Egyptian television, for the most part advertising expensive Western products.[43]

Shakaa's measured legal challenge questioned the appropriateness of such programming during Ramadan. He used the court action to raise pointedly the issue of Islamic values and standards in public life, particularly during the Muslim holy month. To Shakaa, the "Riddles" represented "an affront to the righteous religion" and injected an inappropriate consumerism into an important religious moment.[44] Not only do these programs "violate religious and social values," warned Shakaa, but the provocative and invasive timing of the performances "antagonizes the religious youth and arouses extremist responses."[45]

Dr. Shakaa turned repeatedly and patiently to civil and legal means to press his case. Even when he sought a legal injunction against the Director of the Television and Broadcasting Corporation, which would require him to terminate this insensitive and provocative programming, Shakaa did so without charges against his personal status as a believer.[46] The High Administrative Court dismissed the case in the summer of 1988 and again in the spring of 1991, ruling simply that the Television and Broadcasting Corporation is charged to "present a variety of programs, some educational, some religious, and some for entertainment."[47] The ruling made no mention of the offense to Islamic values that so large a part of the population shares. The court also chose not to address the implications of broadcasting such a program during Ramadan.

Shakaa, nevertheless, persisted in making his challenges, insisting on the educational value of the cases.[48] The official press barely reported the Shakaa suit; detailed coverage appeared only in the Islamist newspapers and journals. The government press typically gave most attention to the attacks on the arts by violent groups. When the moderates were discussed, their views were most often distorted to present their positions as no different than the reactionary extremist attacks on all art forms.[49] The Shakaa story could not easily be made to fit this mold, however, since it lacks the stereotypical stock characters that abstractly frame the issue as religious obscurantism or terrorism versus freedom of artistic expression. A respected cultural figure who bears not the slightest resemblance to a terrorist turns to the courts to argue a point of public media policy. He seeks to condemn not the arts but rather the misuse of artistic expression in a publicly funded medium in ways that denigrate religious sensibilities. In doing so, he raises complex questions of meaning, quality, and boundaries that the regime prefers to gloss over. What role should the arts and the media play in the cultural life of an Islamic society? By what standards should the arts be judged? What limits to artistic expression can reasonably be set in an Islamic society?

By raising these difficult questions about Islam and the arts in the state-controlled mass media, Shakaa highlighted the absence of a coherent government position on all these key issues. His legal action points to confusions over fundamental values in Egyptian public life that create a vacuum into which the extremists can move. Shakaa's suit, in line with the New Islamist historical and cultural analysis, implicitly argues that the present-day heirs of the Free Officer regime have failed to project a vision of Egypt's future, as reflected in the media, the arts, and public education more generally, that harmonizes with Egypt's Islamic heritage.

Applied to the "Ramadan Riddles" issues, this general argument takes the specific form of exposure of the regime's responsibility for and interest in maintaining this entertainment policy. These implicit charges of government culpability find support in the writings of Sarwat Okasha, the most famous and accomplished of the Ministers of Culture from the early years of Free Officer rule. In his memoirs, Okasha documents his losing battle with the regime, which pitted quantity against quality and entertainment against culture. Rather than using the new media to educate the public in the broadest sense and in keeping with the values of the society, the regime pursued instead a policy that emphasized simple entertainment that would direct the people's interests away from serious cultural and social issues.[50]

This government cultural policy also came to have important financial implications. By making Ramadan the high season of television with premier entertainment programming, advertisers are sure of a captive audience and therefore state-owned television can generate huge revenues during the month. Impressive profits are also gained by selling these popular Ramadan programs to other television networks throughout the Arab world, where the Egyptian entertainment serials produced for Ramadan have a huge following.

The Shakaa suit pointed to the ways in which official programming had helped promote a very powerful consumerist approach to Ramadan that has gathered momentum with time. Ramadan once had a very different character. Naguib Mahfuz, for example, has eloquently explained the religious and communal meaning that Ramadan held for his generation. Mahfuz says that of all times in his life, "Ramadan is the best month for me, and my fondest lifetime memories are of that month."[51] The erosion of these simple traditions accelerated during the Open Door period under Anwar al Sadat, when Egypt opened itself to the forces of the world market.

As feared, a profound and disorienting deepening of Westernization occurred during the 1980s and 1990s. A weakened Egyptian regime could do little to contain the corrosive cultural influences carried by the world market. New and even more commercialized and consumerist trappings were added to Ramadan. Writing in 1999, Fahmy Huwaidy commented: "Ramadan is no longer the month of probity, fasting and reading the Quran all night. It has become related to other things in our minds, other worldly things like the 'Ramadan Riddles,' TV serials, the entertainment tents, and al-Nargilas or water pipes!" Huwaidy went on to catalogue the contradictions that now plague Ramadan. The month intended for prayer, reading the Quran and cultivating self-discipline, and reviewing one's responsibilities to self, family, and society has instead become a time of "pleasures and entertainment . . . that is used to justify doing whatever people want to do." In what is meant to be a time of fasting, people eat more than at any other time, and instead of self-control, people show their anger more and are less polite with each other. Instead of a time of hard work and discipline, Ramadan "has become the month of laziness and fall in productivity." Huwaidy singles out television broadcasting that "spreads the culture of entertainment in Ramadan." He laments the new invention of the "entertainment tents" set up to provide for a fee a steady stream of music and dance, culminating in the last meal before the fast resumes at daybreak. "None of these activities are carried out in the spirit of the religious importance of the month." Huwaidy reminds his readers of the *hadith* [a report of the words and deeds of the Prophet] that describes Ramadan as a month when "the doors of Heaven are opened and those of hell are closed and the devils are chained. Also the angels call good people to be happy and bad people to reform themselves." When viewing the contemporary spectacle of Ramadan celebrations, Huwaidy comments that it is hard to resist the notion of a conspiracy to subvert Ramadan and to make it a time when the "the doors of heaven will be closed and those of hell will be opened and the devils will be free to live their 'best' month!"

Huwaidy goes on to remark that this decline of spirituality in all the new Ramadan customs is turning this Islamic holy month into an occasion like the western Christmas, which has become a time of shopping and entertainment instead of a celebration of Christ's birth. More often than not, Huwaidy comments, the name of Christ himself is not even mentioned in the swirl of worldly festivities. "I do not exaggerate," remarks Huwaidy, "when I say that we are doing exactly the same thing to Ramadan." Huwaidy concludes his warning of the deterioration with a plea that "our demand is very modest and does not mean more than a call to preserve this holy month from all these miserable symbols that have been attached to it. Leave us this one month to pray to God and you can have the remaining eleven to do as you will!"[52]

Over the years, the government has defended itself against these charges of subverting the holy month by broadcasting during Ramadan a greater number of serials and programs with Islamic historical and religious themes. However, the New Islamists deride these official "Islamic" art forms for their mind-numbing dullness and hollow pedantry. In their view, the stiff and formal programming of what passed for Islamic art provided the perfect vehicle to drive people to the escape of the "Ramadan Puzzles" and other such diversions.[53] The Shakaa case had aimed early on to draw society's attention to these major contradictions. Public policy meant that talent and resources went into programming that contradicted rather than strengthened Islamic values. The New Islamists objected to this contradiction, insisting on the Islamic character of Egypt's cultural background. Their position, however, does not entail insensitivity to the large Coptic Christian population.[54] Nor is it a call to turn back the clock to an earlier age of Islamic splendor. Rather, they feel that Egypt is a part of the larger Islamic world, that all Egyptians of whatever religious faith share in the rich legacy of Islamic civilization, and that the fundamentals of Islam as a faith indelibly mark the contemporary character of Egyptian society. For the New Islamists, Islam provides "the cultural background," as Kamal Abul Magd puts it, for Egyptian society and culture, rather than detailed prescriptions of social or cultural forms. What Islam provides, he adds, are the basic and unchanging values that should inspire the arts as well as other social dimensions of Egyptian life.[55]

Shakaa's case aimed to expose the absence among the present-day heirs of the Free Officer regime of *any* coherent set of values, let alone one in harmony with its rich Islamic heritage, that could be reflected in the media and the publicly supported arts. Lacking vision, the regime could not set appropriate standards. The government, however, did have its own responses to the periodic controversies over the arts. In addition to sponsoring the sterile and useless official "Islamic" programming, the regime used the media to project extremists like Abdul Rahman as representing the position of the Islamic wave on the arts. No outlandish statement of even the most minor extremist shaikh, it seemed, went unreported. The magazine *Rose al Yusuf*, in particular, made fulsome commentary on these extremist and often lurid positions a staple. In this artificial context, the regime then cast itself as a defender of artistic and intellectual freedom. The louder the voices of the Islamist violent groups, the more left and even liberal secular opinion proved willing to turn to the government for protection against the threats of the Islamists. No longer armed as it had been in Nasser's years with a broad national and Pan-Arab vision, the Egyptian regime in the nineties was simply armed. Instead of such a vision, the regime relied on martial law, backed by control of the army and police. In place of the cultural policies that a strong sense of national purpose might inspire, the government turned again and again to security measures.

The New Islamists sharply contested this view. Their point was not that there were no threatening Islamist extremists who were violently attacking the arts. As targets themselves of these groups, they had no illusions on that score. Rather, they argued against the notion that all Islamists fit that description. In Egypt, as in the West, the identification of "threat" and "Islam" was all too often generalized to suit official purposes. The Egyptian government used the assault on the violent groups, ostensibly to protect the arts, as a cover to strike at all forms of political, social, or even charitable activity under independent Islamic auspices, including that of the Islamic mainstream. By casting what was essentially an assault on democracy as anti-extremist, the government won the support of elements of the left.

The arts become the site of a security clash, where the focus was on the force of arms the government controlled rather than the kind of national debate on cultural traditions, values, and national purpose that would only draw attention to their lack of a coherent national vision. The New Islamists struggled to shift the terms of the debate over the arts from a security to a civilizational grounding. Addressing a symposium on the causes of extremist violence, Shaikh Muhammad al Ghazzaly stated forcefully that Egypt's spiritual crisis could not be met simply with official repression to counteract the young extremists. The rules to guide an Islamic community, he argued, must be established through education, culture, and dialogue, not by force. Even in difficult circumstances, Islam should appeal to the logic of dialogue and not the gun.[56] The antidote to the distorted ideas of the extremists is Islam, correctly understood, and thus Ghazzaly emphasized the importance of taking the ideas of even the violent extremists seriously in order to show how they distorted Islam. He acknowledged that not all religious figures were qualified for that task, but he still believed that, in the end, "only the *ulama* [Islamic scholars] could amend and correct deviations in religious thinking. A Charlie Chaplin could evoke laughter among the British. However, no one imagined that a comedian could replace literature, philosophy, and especially religion in protecting the nation's values."[57]

At the same time, Ghazzaly and the other New Islamists had no illusions that the fight for Egypt's youth would be easy. Nor were they naive. Confronted by youthful armed militants, they supported the police and security efforts to disarm them, using force if necessary.[58] However, they understood the enormity of the problems confronting a whole generation and deplored the conditions that drove them to despair. Above all, the New Islamists argued, it was essential to listen to young people and respond to their concerns, even if the efforts sometimes failed.

As a "caller to the faith" or preacher, Muhammad al Ghazzaly repeatedly made his case as part of his numerous encounters with ordinary Egyptians. He often took stories from these everyday conversations and made them the subject of his regular newspaper columns. Ghazzaly had the unique gift of finding just the right story to address the complex issue of moderation as an end rather than simply a means, and to face the reality that even the firmest commitment was no guarantee for success.

In one column Ghazzaly reported his conversation with a university student, who told his story with the enthusiasm and energy of a young man sure of his course.[59] At a particularly inappropriate moment, some of his "corrupted" fellow students were planning a party. The young Islamist activist and his group opposed this ill-timed frivolity, and the young man had come to tell Shaikh Ghazzaly of their plans to disrupt the event by force. Ghazzaly responded by agreeing that the time was not right to hold a party. He urged the young man and his friends to "explain my own view that there is no place at this moment for happiness while we are passing through such a sad era on the local and international level." Ghazzaly advised the student to ask them: "How can we sing while there are thousands of injured and dead? The future of Palestine and Afghanistan is uncertain, while the number of victims of the Somalia civil war exceeds those of Afghanistan."

When the impatient young man brushed that advice aside, Ghazzaly urged that he not focus on the music or singing, which seemed to be the trigger for his anger. After all, explained Ghazzaly, Islam properly understood did not forbid either one. The issue was timing, and above all content. What kinds of songs did the students plan to sing, and what kind of celebration were they planning? Music and singing, Ghazzaly reminded his interlocutor, were just means, and they might be used in ways appropriate even to these difficult times.

The young activist responded that such arguments would have no effect: "I will not talk with them in the way you suggest. Instead, we will tell them that Islam forbids singing and we will break up the whole party by force." Ghazzaly responded, "You are a young caller, lacking experience. Why not listen to the voice of my experience, and not give your enemies the basis for misunderstanding you and your aims?" With characteristic honesty, a worried Ghazzaly ended his account with the simple comment that "he refused to listen to me."[60]

Ghazzaly's vignette illustrates the difficulties of defending a centrist position when extremists take to the field. Despite such setbacks, the New Islamists have given great emphasis in their theoretical and practical work to questions of education and cultural formation. However, there were limits. When the cultural wars of the 1980s were reduced to questions of personal belief rather than considerations of the fate of the nation, the New Islamists condemned them as a wasteful misdirection of energy and resources. "For a society that is backward and deeply in debt, facing thousands of challenges, public preoccupations with issues of individual belief and charges of apostasy lodged against artists and thinkers can only be considered a diversion from more essential priorities," pronounced Kamal Abul Magd. The great storm of attention that gathered around the issue of the *Satanic Verses* by Salman Rushdie represented just such a destructive diversion. The New Islamists did stand with others in the broad political mainstream in Egypt to judge that Rushdie's work was a "horror" and a "deliberate insult" to Islam that did exceed acceptable limits. Even discounting the latitude permitted in imaginative works, the novel, in their view, used language and images that were simply unacceptable in an Islamic society. It was instructive to note that the very title of the book revived the charge, a staple of anti-Islamic propaganda, that the devil delivered to the Prophet Muhammad verses that urged worship of idols rather than God, and these were the "satanic verses." This reference in the title, according to Fahmy Huwaidy, implies that the Quran, understood by Muslims to be the word of God, represents the work of the devil with Muhammad's connivance and nothing more. Huwaidy's reading goes on to catalogue the insults delivered to the Prophet's wives, who are represented as prostitutes working in a brothel, to the Angels, and to the Prophet himself. Such disgusting characterizations arouse, as he puts it, "a legitimate anger." Given the character of these derogations of the fundamentals of the faith—direct attacks on the Quran and the Prophet—Huwaidy rejects with "regret and disappointment" the view of some who see in Rushdie's work the rightful expression of his own opinion on Islam. Huwaidy concludes his assessment with a characteristic New Islamist expression of regret that the whole issue has taken "more attention than the book deserved."[61]

Typically, however, cases of possible infringement on the fundamentals lacked the directness and clarity of the *Satanic Verses.* At times—provided the extremists were not allowed to dominate the discussion—more ambiguous cases provided an opportunity for centrist thinkers to explore the complex issue of setting boundaries. A case several years after the Rushdie affair illustrates the latitude for artists toward which the New Islamists inclined. The incident involved a play staged in 1991 during an experimental theater festival in Cairo. A dancer ascended a platform for a representation of the Kaaba of Mecca, one of Islam's most sacred symbols, and performed rhythmic dances around the symbol. Sharply critical reactions ranged from articles in the press by Islamist critics such as Safinaz Qazim to expressions of outrage in the Friday prayers. The secular press immediately rose to the defense of the show and its director under the banner of freedom of expression.[62]

Reasserting the essential premise of the New Islamist aesthetic of belonging, Huwaidy rejected the abstract refusal of any limits on creative expression put forward by secular critics like Farida al Naqqash writing in *al Ahaly.* Naqqash argued for an absolute right of freedom of expression, which she felt the Islamists sought to infringe. Huwaidy proved very open, however, to the quite different substantive arguments made by the director of the play. Huwaidy noted that in his frequent interviews the director never once invoked any such absolute right of free expression. Rather, the director explained the actual intent behind the symbolism of the Kaaba in the play, stating that the play made the point that people today worshipped oil, and the wealth it generated, in place of God. To convey that message and warning, he needed a symbol of religion. In the world the play evoked, the transgressive dance represented distorted, materialist "worship." The message, in short, was a political one that had little to do with Islam and certainly intended no insult to the faith.

Fahmy Huwaidy responded to this argument with a general clarification of what the right to freedom of thought and expression meant in an Islamic society. He began with a clear affirmation. Human dignity and rights, Huwaidy noted, are sacred in Islam and belong to all, whatever their race or religion. Islam recognizes religious and other human differences as part of God's design for humankind and therefore not a legitimate basis for the denial of fundamental human rights. Finally, Huwaidy reminded readers that Islam encourages discussion and debate as a prelude to consideration of arguments like those put forward by the director of the play. "The Quran itself," Huwaidy said, "is a book of dialogue that engages all questions on the existence of God, and it does so on the basis of logical proofs." Huwaidy noted that an Islamic society extends to others "the right to abide by their own religion, to call for it, clarify its strengths, and discuss the reasons that explain why they cannot accept Islam. They can express their doubts about aspects of Islam, provided they do so without offense or insult."[63] Huwaidy then made it clear that he had been moved by the persuasiveness of the director's explanation and was convinced that his work, though provocative, had a rightful place in an Islamic society.

The government displayed a calculated deafness to all such moderate arguments. Secular intellectuals close to the regime hammered away at the theme that the "so-called moderates" were really just extremists with more cunning and patience. In the arts, as in all other fields, the Islamic moderates allegedly pursued the same ends, although with different, mollifying means. Set on the course of repression, the regime explored other ways to use the mass entertainment industry to mobilize the public against "terrorism," which more and more came to represent the Islamic wave across the board. In 1993, a number of television serials directly engaged the terrorist threat, initially with some popular success. However, the secular writers approved by the government to treat the issue of extremism at times proved inept in handling religious themes. The most controversial of all such efforts was the television serial "The Family," which initially captured a large audience before dissolving into a largely irrelevant theological debate that defined some limits to the regime's ability to manipulate the media.

The story line of "The Family" revolved around a moderate middle-class Muslim whose family life brings him into accidental contact with extremist elements. Written by Wahid Hamid, the leftist scenarist, the serial attacked terrorism with a broad brush. The language completely lacked subtlety, and the dramatic flow was frequently interrupted by political speeches that conveyed a general hostility to the Islamic wave. The notion of terrorism condemned in the serial applied not simply to those who throw bombs and arrange assassinations but was extended loosely and irresponsibly to indict the full range of Islamic phenomena, including by implication those who wear the *hegab* [head scarf], Islamic economic enterprises, shaikhs in their mosques, and various Islamic groupings. All manifestations of social Islam were indiscriminately implicated in the terrorist slander.

The series stumbled in its anti-Islamist propaganda effort, however, when a character in one episode questioned the clear Quranic notion that the suffering of sinners continues after death. The public reacted sharply. Both the Shaikh of Azhar and the Mufti of the Republic responded with public statements, following a flood of public inquiries about the episode that asked for correction of this heretical view.[64] The government was forced immediately to broker a conciliatory effort to quiet offended religious sensibilities. The attack on terrorism as the intended object of the serial was in the end overwhelmed by theological debate precipitated by an unintended misstatement on an abstract theological point.[65] Secular scenarists and government officials floundered badly, while their Islamist critics had a field day in indicating the limitations of their understanding of Islam. Taking advantage of official confusion, the Islamist press once again criticized the government's simple-minded belief that crude "artistic" propaganda could constructively engage the issue of violence by Islamist militants. The Islamists argued that the failure of the regime to project a compelling national vision to address the challenges of development and democracy had created the conditions in which radicalism of all kinds could flourish. Furthermore, by curtailing the work of moderate Islamists in all fields, the government was inadvertently aiding Islamist extremists by leaving the Islamic field to them. More pointedly, the Islamist writers suggested that a lessening of government repression and torture would be more effective than crude propaganda programming in the media.[66]

On the occasion of the prayers for the Feast in March 1994, Shaikh Muhammad al Ghazzaly brought this mainstream Islamist message to the crowd of thousands who had come to hear him speak. Citing the Quranic verses that deal with suffering after death, Ghazzaly pointedly criticized the writers and mobilized artists in Egypt who attempt to preach only to reveal their flawed knowledge of Islam, adding that art circles in Egypt are in fact compromised by a great many ills that antagonize believers. He concluded with the message for the regime that "the cure for extremism is Islam rightly understood and not ignorance."[67]

In a strongly worded response, the head of the Artists' Syndicate, Hamdy Gheith, expressed great surprise at Ghazzaly's censure, describing him as "one of the religious figures appreciated for their values and cherished for their enlightenment and comprehensive understanding of our era and our faith." Gheith nevertheless argued that the arts do have a role in religious and moral education, questioning as well the appropriateness of Ghazzaly's evaluation of artists' understanding of Islam.[68] The government, not for the first time, banned Ghazzaly from speaking publicly at the next prayers. Secularists conflated Ghazzaly's stance with extremist attacks on the arts, while Islamists retorted that Ghazzaly had, in fact, correctly raised the real issue of the accurate propagation of the faith through the mass media versus ignorant and misguided political propaganda that tarnishes not only the extremists, but all things Islamic.

Almost immediately, the Shaikh of al Azhar was drawn into the controversy. The scripts of the serial were sent to Azhar, where a committee of specialists confirmed Ghazzaly's judgment that the serial misrepresented the Quranic position. In response to this determination, the Minister of Information agreed to correct the errors in a subsequent episode. The furor over this incident triggered a court case to determine where authority over determining the accuracy of the treatment of religious issues in the public media should reside. Under the leadership of Tareq al Bishry, a leading legal authority and a part of the New Islamist circle, the State Council ruled that al Azhar has this expert knowledge and responsibility for assuring the accurate representation of Quran and *Sunnah* in the media.

Secular critics were infuriated by the ruling and denounced it as censorship of the arts. They also noted the central role of Tareq al Bishry in producing it. If a reputed moderate like Bishry could produce such a directive, the most extreme secularists asked once again, were there really any serious differences between moderates and extremists? However, Bishry, like Ghazzaly, was not so easily dismissed. Bishry matched Ghazzaly's stature as a religious scholar with his own reputation as a leading historian, respected in all quarters of intellectual and cultural life. The New Islamists had the collective advantage that it was not easy to misrepresent the views of such well-known public figures.

As participants in the public discussions, the New Islamists defended their centrist position, which recognized the value of the arts but insisted that, at the deepest level, the arts must preserve a positive connection to Egypt's Islamic cultural context. This meant respect for the fundamentals of the faith, the Quran and the *Sunnah*.[69] They had no illusions about the difficulties that surrounded efforts to draw such lines. Their own thinking and public interventions exhibited the same variation over time and responsiveness to a changing social context that marked parallel efforts to struggle with "free speech" issues in the advanced democratic societies.

In his dialogue with Naguib Mahfuz, Kamal Abul Magd had made the point that the spirit of Islam may well be most effective in the arts, as in other areas, when it is invoked naturally and "without strain." Moreover, that spirit may find expression in places overlooked or underestimated by those who should know better. In that quiet interview after the attempt on his life, Mahfuz reminded his readers that the Nobel Prize committee had recognized that his novel *Children of Gebelaawi* was about the search for spiritual values. Mahfuz expressed open admiration for Muhammad al

Ghazzaly as an Islamic thinker whose works he regularly read.[70] To the end of his days, Ghazzaly failed to appreciate the Islamic dimension of Mahfuz's celebrated novel. It is perhaps for that reason that Mahfuz so clearly valued Kamal Abul Magd's clear and eloquent recognition of the Islamic character of his most controversial work. Certainly, Mahfuz would not be the last such artist to find vindication another day.

Despite changes in their positions over time and differences of judgment among the major figures, the New Islamists never wavered from the principle that, however difficult in practice, the protection of the fundamentals did justify the setting of limits. However, they most often took the position that the maximum latitude, short of violation of the sanctities of Islam, should be tolerated. The New Islamists resisted efforts of extremist groups in particular to extend notions of what the fundamentals of Islam were in unwarranted ways "from the roots to the branches." They also consistently argued that the minimum of coercion possible should be used to enforce the essential limits. Above all, the New Islamists insisted that the Islamic wave maintain a balanced view that kept these cultural questions, and the debates they generated, in the larger perspective of all the great challenges that faced the community. It was essential that such cultural and intellectual questions be given attention, they argued, but not at the expense of the more pressing issues that Egypt faced. On more than one occasion, they suggested that other matters might be more deserving of attention. At other times, they showed themselves quite willing to defer the ultimate resolution of disputes over the arts and culture to some unspecified future for which the discussions seemed to be the enlightening though always incomplete preparation.

Idols, Statues, and the Aesthetic of Belonging

The arts, along with education, are critical elements of the Islamic civilizational project for which the New Islamists struggle. As defenders of the Islamic mainstream, they confidently face those secularists and others who fear Islam because they take the extremists at their word and accept their distortions as defining Islam. How could this be Islam, they ask, when the violent attacks on the arts and artists by the extremists contradict the clear evidence of the Quran and *Sunnah* and the rich artistic legacy of the heritage? The New Islamists confront just as forthrightly those who so fear for Islam that they seek to protect it by preserving frozen forms and rituals, while neglecting core values and higher purposes. How could this be Islam, when such rigidity contradicts the flexible and comprehensive character of "Islam of all ages"?[71]

The controversies over the role of the arts in society tried but did not break the confidence of the New Islamists as heirs and proponents of the Islamic mainstream. The aesthetic of belonging of the New Islamists occupies a middle ground between Islamist extremists, who denied the arts any place at all in an Islamic community, and their secular counterparts, who denied the right of the community to set any limits to the role of the arts. When a particular art form or opinion generated a controversy, the extremists of both camps entered the fray with simple and easy to understand banners. The secular extremists called for absolute freedom of expression. The Islamist extremists, like Ghazzaly's young interlocutor, called for banning and destruction of the arts. In sharp contrast, the New Islamists faced the far more demanding task of protecting a discriminating and nuanced middle ground that raised the complex but essential questions of community values and the ways in which the arts enhanced or undermined those higher Islamic purposes. It was a hard position to defend, in Egypt no less than in the larger Islamic world. However, the difficulty has only made the work of the New Islamists all the more important. Their vision and sense of responsibility in the arts, as in other fields, have extended beyond Egypt's borders. In those transnational arenas, as in Egypt itself, their moderate centrist position has faced daunting challenges. The New Islamists did not always prevail. Still, their articulate pronouncements and brave interventions have importance in preserving the possibilities of thinking and acting for Islamic moderation in the artistic sphere as in all others.

In the early spring of 2001, the assault on Afghanistan's historical and artistic legacy by the Islamic extremists in power directly challenged these New Islamist views. The irresponsible and at times destructive actions of the Taliban attracted attention around the globe to the issue of Islam's stance toward the arts. The ruling Taliban stunned the world by announcing that Islam mandated the destruction of "idols." The extremist regime denounced the presence in a country they ruled of such pre-Islamic religious artifacts and announced their intention of cleansing Afghanistan by smashing the "idols." The New Islamists refused to allow this retrograde position to define Islam in the eyes of the world.

Responding to the imminent threat to the historic statues and to the damage that such a criminal action would do to Islam's reputation, Yusuf al Qaradawy issued a *fatwa*. His ruling stated forcefully that "statues created by predecessors before Islam represent a historic legacy and a live historic presence for every nation and should not be destroyed." He added that such monuments should be seen "as an evidence of God's blessing on this nation as he liberated its people from worshipping idols through the revelation of Islam" and pointed out that "Muslims entered Afghanistan in Islam's first century and never considered destroying the idols they found." He reminded the Taliban that the first century was "the best in terms of how devout and militarily powerful Muslims were and still they never disturbed these monuments." The task of Muslims, Qaradawy wrote, was to liberate people and not to destroy history. He cited the example of Omar Ibn Khattab, who, when he entered Egypt, left fully intact its wealth of monuments to the gods of the ancient Egyptians. Qaradawy urged the Taliban to direct all their energy to the urgent tasks of providing food for every hungry person, shelter for the homeless, jobs for the unemployed, education for the illiterate, security for the insecure. Above all, he concluded, the Taliban should "work hard to stop the bloodshed that still plagues our beloved Afghanistan."[72]

The Taliban chose to ignore Qaradawy, as Fahmy Huwaidy learned later in the spring of 2001. Huwaidy was part of a delegation that went to Afghanistan to persuade the Taliban leadership and leading Afghan *ulama* to spare the statues. In a revealing account of his efforts, Huwaidy said that the *ulama* had approached the issue in the narrowest of textual terms. They memorized the texts, he explained, "and thought that such memorization was enough of a qualification to issue *fatwas* and soundly evaluate issues." What was missing was any sense of "the *fiqh* of reality, and this shortcoming made dialogue with them difficult." The meaning of the texts must be understood in the light of reality, with its balances and priorities, finding genuine interests and avoiding distortions or accepting a small distortion for the sake of avoiding a larger one. Huwaidy commented, "The grasp of such balances requires a mind that is capable of establishing priorities and, deplorably, we did not find such a mind in these *ulama*." Summarizing the long and frustrating experience of the New Islamists in dealing with the Taliban, Huwaidy concluded that the half-educated *alim* is worse than the ignorant. What they discovered in Afghanistan were *ulama* who knew from the texts that the Muslims had destroyed the idols in the Kaaba when Mecca was firmly in their control. The Afghans also knew from the texts and history that in all other subsequent instances the Muslim community had maintained the statues expressing earlier religious sentiments. However, these half-educated *ulama*, Huwaidy opined, had been "unable to grasp the idea that the demolishing was confined to the Arabian peninsula as the place where the message of God's oneness had been revealed"[73] because they had failed to place these particular verses and the events they described in the larger context of the Quran as a whole. The Quran made a clear distinction between statues as aesthetic creations and idols as objects of worship. Had the Afghan *ulama* read the Quran in this holistic way, rather than isolating particular verses, they would have discovered and considered as well those other verses where, for example, God is talking about Solimon and gifts from God to him, among which were "statues." These statues were valued for their beauty, but they were not worshipped. If the Taliban had understood the Quran and its message to Muslims in this way, it would have been inconceivable for them to describe all statues as idols and to incite Muslims against any artistic works, perceived as cultural products of beauty and not sanctified or worshipped. The half-educated *ulama* who ruled Afghanistan, Huwaidy stated, had a deeply flawed understanding of Islam and the ways in which it spoke to the needs of the modern world. They failed to grasp the meaning of the aesthetic of belonging to the Islamic world and the respected place it reserved for the arts in human life.[74]

In March of 2001, the world learned that the statues and monuments that had been Afghanistan's pride were no more. Ancient statues in the Kabul Museum, historical sites in Ghazny, and the spectacular Bamiyan Buddhas from the fifth century were all destroyed. The Taliban smashed the "idols" of their imagination, while the Islamic world suffered the loss of statues that had been part of the civilizational riches of its peoples. For the new Islamists, the destruction of the statues in Afghanistan reinforced their sense of the centrality of their interpretive project to understand Islam in the light of its core values and higher purposes. The unfolding of events in that ravaged land where distorted views of Islam had come to rule renewed the New Islamists' long-standing commitment to the *tarshid* of the Islamic Awakening as it struggled for a genuine Islamic community in Egypt and the larger world of Islam.

part II

Society

Writing from Egypt ostensibly in the year 2040, the economist and social critic Galal Amin reports on startling transformations of Egyptian society by the Islamic wave. The Islamist project, Amin's playful essay suggests, faces daunting challenges, none more damaging than the inclination of some Islamists to focus on minor issues. Wiser voices, like those of the New Islamists, point out that to do so might mean the neglect of the major questions of the shape of a just Islamic society and the demands of a productive economy to sustain it. By the year 2040, Amin projects, it is clear that distorted priorities have instead led to disaster.

The decline, as Amin reported in his December 2, 1987 article in *al Ahaly,* started innocently enough when a handful of women began in the 1970s to wear the *hegab* [headscarf]. They subtly pressured other women to do the same to avoid provoking the lustful male gaze. Intense theological discussions followed, and more and more women adopted the new style. Before long, the really virtuous women began wearing the *neqab* [face veil] with a long flowing dress and gloves. By the year 2010, Amin notes, "a foreign correspondent reported spending a month in Cairo without seeing a single female face or hands."

Amin then reports that a new debate suddenly opened in 2025. If women's bodies so easily provoked lust, clearly the male body represented a parallel danger. Male dress passed rapidly through the stage of the *hegab* and directly to the *neqab.* Cairo by the year 2040 has become a city of walking tents, with both male and female bodies safely covered. Meanwhile, Amin's account suggests, little else has changed.

chapter 3

Building Community

Bloody disturbances erupt in the winter of 1988 in Ain Shams, a poor neighborhood of Cairo, pitting security forces against Islamist militants.[1] Ain Shams attracts national attention because ordinary Egyptians from the quarter sympathize with the insurgents and resist their suppression by the government. The specter of violent Islamists coming to power with a coup supported from below hovers over the events at Ain Shams. In the name of centrist Islam, Shaikh Muhammad al Ghazzaly and the New Islamists intervene. Islam bases its injunction to build Islamic community, declares Ghazzaly unequivocally, "on faith, education, and national dialogue, while rejecting resolutely the resort to violence and the usurpation of the rights of others in the name of religion."[2] Ghazzaly speaks for the New Islamists, warning the radical *amirs* [leaders of Islamist groups] that by urging the path of violence they are misleading their youthful followers, distorting the message of Islam, and diminishing the prospects of genuine Islamic community. At Ain Shams, the New Islamists stand with the government, not so much to support the regime itself but rather to protect the prospects of peaceful reform.

The events at Ain Shams stand as an emblem of the confrontation between the regime and violent Islamist elements that dominated public life from the late 1980s until 1997. For the New Islamists, Ain Shams also represents one of the two major challenges of extremism that they face from within the Islamic wave: namely, those Islamist elements which, incited by government provocations, have too little patience in enduring adverse social conditions and the excesses of an unresponsive and authoritarian regime. From the late 1980s through 1997, these impatient extremists waged an unofficial war on the regime, resorting to violence in the hope of transforming society immediately. For the New Islamists, the danger of the use of force is compounded by the even greater threat of the distorted ideas of Islam that the violent groups advance to support their cause.

A second danger comes later, after the extremists have been suppressed. It takes clear shape at the end of the 1990s. Although it originates in the same deep disappointment with hopes for development and democracy, it finds expression in the opposite direction of passivity and too much patience. This brand of Islamist religiosity means abandoning all hope of reforming the public sphere. Energies are diverted into obsessive formalism of religious practice, more and more divorced from collective social life. At their worst, those who adopt these attitudes reduce notions of Islamic community to trivial rituals and empty incantations, devoid of social content and deeper values. While the last decade of the twentieth century opens with fears that dangerous and unproductive violence will engulf the Islamic wave and the nation, the century ends with the opposite but equally damaging threat of retreat into private worlds of empty religiosity.

From within the Islamic wave, the New Islamists stand against Islamist extremists of both kinds. They respond to extremist distortions of Islam with their centrist reform vision of a long-term project of peaceful yet profound social change to build a collective life based on the humane values of Islam. The reaction of the New Islamists to the events at Ain Shams spotlights in the most public way their principled assessment of the conditions and policies that prompt such destructive responses from the Islamic wave. Most important, the role of the New Islamists at Ain Shams throws into sharp relief the powerful centrist conception of the nature of Islamic community that would overcome the desperation and despair of ordinary Egyptians.

In the face of the violence of the militants at Ain Shams in 1988, Shaikh Ghazzaly acts decisively "to serve my religion and perform my obligation toward the authentic Islamic religion by condemning the ignorant preachers who are remote from the spirit of Islam and its true call." While condemning the actions of the violent groups and those who incite them, Ghazzaly also calls for serious reform by the government and a halt to indiscriminate official repression. He declares, "I am neither one of the government's religious callers nor one of the shaikhs of the police." Faced with the criminal violence of the young extremists in the service of a dangerous misreading of Islam, the New Islamists tilt decisively toward the established government. They do so, however, from the independent ground of their distinctive, centrist vision of an Islamic political community yet to be realized.

The New Islamist position rests on the firm judgment that, for all its limitations, the existing government shows no evidence of abandoning basic Islamic commitments. Moreover, the regime does maintain conditions of order and stability that enable the work of reform to go forward in both theory and practice. Given these conditions, the New Islamists are able to mount important interventions in the last decades of the century on such central issues of community as the role of women, non-Muslims, and secularists in an Islamic society.

In the spirit of the *Wassatteyya,* the New Islamists insist that resolution of differences should come through dialogue now and improved education for the future. The New Islamists define their own position as centrist interpretations of the faith and responses to the exigencies of Egypt's special situation. More often than not, they control neither the timing nor the framing of public interest in these questions. However, the underlying coherence of their interventions finds clear expression in the collective body of scholarship on Islamic community that they produce. Their writing on the fundamentals of Islam elaborates the guidelines and principles of interpretation on which they rely to develop their ideas and guide their actions on questions of the organization, purpose, and spirit of public life. Over time, an impressive shared vision of Islamic community emerges, both from the refinements of their scholarly commentaries and the living details of their engagements in controversial and important issues. By the end of the century, the New Islamists, through a rich fabric of intertextual commentary and an extensive record of collaborative social action, have significantly advanced the *Wassatteyya* conception of Islamic community they inherited.

At some points in the 1980s and 1990s, however, it seems as if violence is the only issue, overwhelming all else. While rejecting dangerous militants who assault the government as a regime of unbelievers, the New Islamists at the same time refuse to see all the young activists and the common people who respond to them simply as extremists and criminals, forever beyond the pale of redemption.

The story of Ain Shams begins with a prison breakout. Three inmates, sentenced to life for their role in the assassination of President Anwar Sadat, escape from Torah Prison on July 18, 1988. Central security forces, armed with bayonets and rapid-fire weapons, invade the poor quarters of Cairo in search of the fugitives. They are identified as members of the violent Jihad group, which later achieves worldwide notoriety for its links to Osama bin Laden's al Qaeda network. Pushing with undisciplined zeal into the crumbling neighborhood of Ain Shams, the security forces storm into mosques and make large-scale arrests. Mass anger at this heavy-handedness triggers a backlash of demonstrations and protests.

Hundreds of local residents pour into the narrow alleys of Ain Shams to block the invasive police searches. The security forces surround the five most important neighborhood mosques to prevent communal prayers and flood all the open squares where hostile crowds might gather in the densely populated neighborhood. By the time the first of the escapees is killed on July 26 and the second shot and a third arrested on August 8, hundreds of ordinary citizens have also suffered arrest, wounds, or death in the clashes.

On August 10, police investigators announce that the Jihad organization masterminded the Torah prison escape. The police charge Jihad militants with planning to use the fugitives in assassination plots against government officials. The Minister of Interior alleges that members of the underground group met at the Adnan mosque in Ain Shams to plot these acts of incitement. However, he offers no evidence to support the charges. Disturbances erupt again on August 12 and 13, when protesters try to march out of Adnan mosque to protest police brutality and the unsubstantiated charges that justify it. The demonstrators defy the security forces and block a police effort to arrest two young men accused of being Jihad members. The ensuing clashes leave over twenty people injured or dead (including a security captain who succumbed the next day to head injuries) and more than a hundred arrested. Security officials announce plans to bring some of those arrested before military courts on charges of aiding the prison escape as part of a plan to rebuild the banned Jihad.

Meanwhile, the local people of the Ain Shams quarter struggle to return to normalcy in the face of this forced entanglement in the clash of the regime and the radicals. Prayers resume in the mosques, with thousands in attendance, including entire families, in the hope that the presence of women and children will calm the security forces. Neighborhood efforts are launched to organize campaigns to collect funds for those wounded and arrested. Acknowledging that no weapons were found in the Adnan mosque, the police release about half those arrested. Meetings resume in the mosques of the neighborhood in the early fall of 1988. The government sponsors assemblies presided over by shaikhs attached to the Waqfs Ministry [Islamic endowments], who come "to preach true Islam and to urge the youth not to use violence." During one encounter at Adnan mosque, youthful members respond by urging the official shaikhs to place themselves above the "whims of the government." None of these officially sponsored meetings makes much headway.

Violence erupts once more on December 9, ending with further arrests. Leaflets appear in response, warning darkly of reprisals for the constant repressive measures. Clashes in the streets, originally between militants and the police, increasingly become little more than a battle between the regime's security forces and the common people from a poor quarter of Cairo. Ain Shams raises national fears of a general collapse into violence and repression.

Egypt's religious figures respond. Official Islam, closely tied to the government, speaks first. On December 26, 1988, the Shaikh of al Azhar issues a call for unqualified support for the state security forces. The al Azhar statement condemns "appropriations" by the extremist groups as theft, denies them the right to act to correct what they regard as society's ills, and sanctions police attacks on their mosques. Al Azhar urges the violent groups to "come to their senses," while encouraging "religious propagators, leadership elements, and the people to act in a decent way and to confront the rebellious groups by helping the state."[3]

The New Islamists, as much in response to the one-sidedness of this al Azhar pronouncement as to the events themselves, play a leading role in formulating a second statement of independent Islamic thinkers, signed by Shaikh Ghazzaly and drafted in part by Yusuf al Qaradawy. These centrists condemn the violence of the militants in terms as unequivocal as those of the spokesmen for al Azhar. However, the independent Islamic intellectuals also call for a long-term program of moderate reform. In this way, they stake out a distinctive third position between the government and the extremists. Unlike official religious spokespersons, the independent moderates clearly register the shortcomings of corruption, repression, and unmet mass needs in existing structures and policies. They do so while making it clear that the ignorance and destructiveness of the violent extremists constitute an even graver danger.

The centrist statement argues that reliance on the *Sharia* [the provisions from Quran and *Sunnah* to regulate human behavior] as the method for building Islamic community "stipulates clear ways for thwarting deviations from the correct path, that do not include irresponsible charges of unbelief nor undo haste in carrying out reforms." The scholars explain that Islam relies instead on the rationality, sound advice, and healthy argumentation enjoined by the Quran. They categorically reject the sweeping claims of the extremists that society and government in Egypt are un-Islamic: "We believe in the faith of the regime and we trust the regime's faith in Egypt." They declare that strategies to achieve the reforms necessitated by *Sharia* should be characterized by gradualism. While the moderates cite the verified *hadith* [saying of the Prophet] that provides that evil should be changed by hand, by tongue, and by heart, they explain that the communal responsibility to correct evil belongs to the legitimate authorities and not insurgent groups:

> It never happened in the era of the Prophet or his companions and their successors that a group appointed itself to execute the *hudud* [punishments provided for in *Sharia*] or rules without the permission of the legal ruler. It is proven in all ages that it is only the sovereign authorities that execute the *hudud* and change evil by hand.

Directly contradicting the pronouncements of the leaders of the violent groups and offering to "meet with any one of them to clarify the truth and guide him to the straight path," the New Islamist scholars state that unless these restrictions on the right to use legitimate force are honored, society will be threatened with chaos that "harms the interest of religion and the nation." Their statement also calls on the regime to be more careful to guard the truth and abolish falsehood by strengthening virtues and religious and moral values. It concludes by expressing the hope that, over the long term, and with appropriate encouragement from social and political centrist forces, the government will realize the aspirations of individuals and society.

The Muslim Brothers take yet a different stance. Their moderation is tinged with opportunism. While the Brothers during the Sadat and Mubarak years consciously opted to compete for power by abiding by the nonviolent rules of the game, their intervention nevertheless shows a much more overt political thrust than that of the New Islamists. In line with the Brothers' broad commitment to nonviolence, the General Guide of the Muslim Brothers firmly endorses the position of the scholars on the crucial issues separating all moderates from the extremists. Like the New Islamists, they deny the accusations that the Egyptian government is un-Islamic. They condemn as well the resort to violence by the militants.

In their statement, however, the Brothers also take advantage of the moment of crisis to press a series of political charges against the regime, thus distinguishing themselves from the New Islamist stance. The time frame of the Brothers is shorter, perhaps a decade. Their focus is on the immediate shortcomings of ruling power rather than prospects for its reform over time. They argue that the outbreaks of violence result from the continued enforcement of the state-of-emergency laws. Moreover, they seize on this moment to argue that the mass discontents rocking the country have their origin in the serious economic failures of the regime. They charge that the state-controlled media are fostering a climate of decadence and authoritarianism, while blocking Islamist channels of reform. They argue that an oppressive law governing the formation of parties prevents the Muslim Brothers from operating legally as a political party—a party that could answer the urgent "popular demand" of the Egyptian people for an

Islamic political orientation that would address these pressing national failures.[4]

The New Islamists show no such inclination to exploit a crisis situation in order to press immediate political demands on the regime. Characteristically, their calls for reform flow into cultural and educational channels rather than taking the form of political demands. They consistently search for inclusive common ground that can be consolidated over the long term. The shape of the community envisioned by the New Islamists is reflected in their refusal to see either the security police, or the misguided young militants and the common people who rallied to them, as forever beyond the possibility of community. Even in the heat of a national crisis, the New Islamists, along with other independent Islamic scholars, insist on a reading of events that focuses on the possibilities of peaceful cultural and educational transformation of Egyptian society.

Ijtihad and Envisioning Islamic Community

As their intervention at Ain Shams made clear, the New Islamists reject not only the violence of the militants but also the ends they pursue. These centrists emphatically do not share the vision of community advanced by the violent extremists. At Ain Shams the New Islamists condemned the goals of the impatient extremists as vigorously as their violence, judging the extremist vision of Islamic community to be deeply disfigured by grave misunderstandings of Islam. Unmoved even by the sympathetic popular response to the militants, evoked partly by the regime's excessive and indiscriminate use of force in their suppression, the New Islamists spoke decisively in favor of the maintenance of order and accommodation with the authorities. Without hesitation, they rejected any notion of violent resistance to the government that might open the way to a coup by Islamic extremists and imposition of their rule. They advanced instead a vision of community that called for gradual and peaceful social change.

The New Islamist School has used the opportunity created by the stable Egyptian regime to prepare the tools that would be needed to build the just and inclusive community they envision. Most important is their theoretical work on strategies for interpreting the fundamentals of the faith for guidance of that struggle. The New Islamist manifesto states simply and directly that there could be no renewal of Islam without a new *ijtihad* [an effort of interpretation of the sacred texts] of the fundamentals by qualified scholars. "Every movement of renewal," the manifesto states, "must fulfill this responsibility or risk slipping back into stagnation and imitation."[5] The New Islamists have asked in systematic and important ways how to deal with *Sunnah* [all the deeds and words of the Prophet; the second source of Islam, after the Quran], how to read Quran, and how to implement *Sharia,* as essential elements of the building of Islamic community. Their scholarship, engaging these core issues of interpretation, places them among the most important Islamic thinkers of the twentieth century.

While refining their interpretive approach to the fundamentals, the New Islamists have used reformed methods to produce a sophisticated, substantive body of commentary on the most important and contentious questions of community. The two strands of their collective efforts, the theoretical and the practical, are closely braided together. The main focus here will be on the centrist interpretive project of the New Islamists, and this chapter is organized around their contributions to the interpretation of *Sunnah,* the Quran, and *Sharia.* Interspersed with these discussions will be periodic summations of their most important work on the role of women, non-Muslims, and secularists, made possible by their new interpretative strategies.

How to Treat *Sunnah*

"In the night that prevails in the Islamic world," writes Muhammad al Ghazzaly in a striking passage of his most controversial work, "the danger comes from the half-educated and half-religious." Ghazzaly's classic study, *The Prophet's Sunnah between the People of Hadith and People of Fiqh,* gives special attention to the threat posed by extremist thinking to the youth of the Arab Islamic world. He emphasizes as well the ways in which "enemies of Islam in Europe and America exploit the superficiality of the ideas of the militants as a pretext to attack the new Awakening of our already deeply wounded religion."[6]

Ghazzaly aims to expose the mechanisms by which violent extremists and retrograde traditionalists generate their false and dogmatic ideas about Islam. While focusing on the pressing danger represented by the militants, he explains how both groups abuse the *Sunnah,* while ignoring the Quran. Ghazzaly's argument is blunt and uncompromising. "I am completely fed up," he writes, "with those who hardly have any knowledge at all of Quranic provisions and yet issue judgments based only on the *Sunnah.* They leave the nation in confusion." Paying scant attention to Quran, extremist thinkers either misread confirmed *hadiths* or rely on isolated and often questionable ones, without identifying them as such. In these ways, they are able to create the impression of support for dangerous views that have nothing to do with Islam. Ghazzaly advances his critique of such faulty extremist thinking with passion. "I'm overwhelmed with anger and distress," he writes, "when the people of *hadith* are poorly aware of Quran. They read a *hadith* on people without feeling how close or far it is from Quran." He argues further that *hadiths* must always be understood not only in reference to Quran but also in the light of reason as it illuminates the conditions of the contemporary world. On this count, too, the extremists fall terribly short. These ignorant interpreters of the texts all too often display the same lack of comprehension of the world around them.

Ghazzaly elaborates his thinking in ways that allow readers to feel the importance he attaches to the centrality of guidance from Quran when building an Islamic community. Only such an approach, he explains, is capable of revealing Islam's basic values and illuminating its central purposes. In contrast, Ghazzaly points out that most of the controversial *hadiths* invoked by the extremists involve secondary issues that do not pertain either to the Muslim's essential faith or to the well-being of the Islamic community. At times they focus on minor theological questions, such as whether the prophet Muhammad actually saw God or whether the prophet Moses attacked the Angel of Death. At other times, they take absolutist and retrograde positions on sensitive questions of community, more often than not restricting the rights of its most vulnerable members in some unacceptable way. They do so because they have either misunderstood a confirmed *hadith* or depended on an unreliable one. Yet they always misleadingly present their opinions as authoritative because they are backed by a text and therefore above questioning. They do not hesitate to denounce as unbelievers any who dare to disagree with them. Ghazzaly staunchly defends the centrist position that all such contentious issues of community should be within the realm of difference of opinion and interpretation, not a question of true or false faith. He adds that the energy exerted over misplaced accusations of disbelief or entanglements in secondary questions could be better deployed elsewhere.[7]

The contempt for the extremists that drives Ghazzaly's reaffirmation of the center is palpable and formidable. "Just like that," writes Ghazzaly, "Muslims fall into the hands of those who are looked upon by rational people with amazement and surprise."[8] The cloak of learning in which the extremist *amirs* wrap their simplistic provocations particularly angers Ghazzaly. "They are students on Saturday, teachers on Sunday, and professors on Monday," he comments. Little wonder, he concludes, "that on Tuesday they claim to be the peers of the great *ulama*, with the argument that they are men and we are men, too." With impressive erudition, Ghazzaly exposes not only their reliance on unconfirmed *hadiths*, but also the flaws in their reasoning and the inadequacies of their grasp of the larger textual contexts of *Sunnah* and Quran.[9]

Muhammad al Ghazzaly stood firmly against all such abuses of Quran and *Sunnah.* Speaking for the Islamic mainstream, Ghazzaly summarized four core propositions to correct these egregious and dangerous errors of extremist misinterpretation and to guide centrist thinking. First, all matters pertaining to Islam have their ultimate and most reliable source in the *Quran.* In some areas, the Quran provides explicit provisions; in others, guidelines for believing, thinking, and acting. In all cases, the Quran provides the rightful starting point. Second, since *Sunnah* came later, to elaborate and facilitate the understanding of Quran, *Sunnah* cannot contradict that which it explains. Quran and *Sunnah* must be taken together, but in the end, Quran has precedence. Third, since both Quran and *Sunnah* are texts that may have unspoken meanings that are not accessible to literal readings alone, both the necessity of interpretation and the acceptance of the differences that interpretation will unavoidably generate are an inherent element of Islam and one that is to be cherished. Fourth, the flexibility that *ijtihad* affords and the differences within *fiqh* that it yields explain the capacity of Islam to meet human needs in all times and places. What remains constant are the general purposes and higher values of Islam, expressed in Quran and *Sunnah.* Ghazzaly argued that the constancy of these broad principles and general aims, understood by the use of the mind, gives overall coherence to the Islamic civilization.[10]

The response to *The Prophet's Sunnah* came immediately. The book caused a fury of protest. Some critics charged that Ghazzaly had attacked the *Sunnah* itself. Others alleged that he disqualified certain *hadiths* without sufficient grounds, while still others disagreed strongly with some of his interpretations of particular traditions.[11] Supporters, in contrast, proclaimed that Ghazzaly had launched an intellectual revolution that undermined the claimed Islamic grounding for the thought of the violent extremists and immeasurably strengthened efforts to make centrist Islam speak effectively to the new age. The vehemence of the storm was heightened because Ghazzaly often highlighted his bold methodological positions by reference to the ways in which extremists, and in many cases traditionalist thinkers as well, distorted understanding of controversial questions of community.

Ghazzaly's work is an integral part of the broader effort of the New Islamist School to elaborate a centrist conception of community that embraces difference and draws the boundaries of community in the most just and inclusive ways possible. More concretely, this New Islamist conception argues for the advancement of women, the guarantee of a rightful and secure place for non-Muslims, and the inclusion of moderate secularists. The resulting inclusive conception of community stands in sharp contrast to the totalitarian and exclusivist impulses that drive extremist thought.

The Advancement of Women

Ghazzaly's pathbreaking work on the *Sunnah* aims to show how a sound method of interpretation strengthens the inclusive and tolerant *Wassat-teyya* vision of Islamic community. The frequency of references to issues pertaining to women, in particular, helped immeasurably to buttress the work of the New Islamist School for the advancement of women.

The New Islamist manifesto outlined the school's consensus position on women in the early 1980s, based on their interpretation of the male-led family provided for in the Quran.[12] This Quranic vision is juxtaposed to extreme views, ranging from "those that consider the relationship between men and women as one of struggle to those who regard woman as no more than the property of men, an inferior creation in value, capacity, and social status." In sharp contrast, the New Islamist manifesto proclaims that Islam "sees both men and women as the essence of humanity and an expression of the unity of creation." Islam unequivocally establishes "the principle of absolute equality between men and women in human dignity and responsibility. Woman is considered the sister of man." The rule in Quran is "absolute equality between men and women with only those explicit exceptions, few in number, that God set." Moreover, the manifesto notes, "the meaning [of these specified exceptions] is not that a woman's status is lower. Rather, they merely respect the truth of natural differences between man and woman and the consequent priorities of responsibilities delegated to each of them in the family and society." Family life, according to the manifesto, is "based on freedom of choice of spouses without compulsion or tutelage." The family depends on "sharing responsibilities, exchanging opinions, and love and compassion while asserting man's leadership. It is a leadership that doesn't decrease or denigrate the completeness of the woman's personality and its right to equality." Caring for the family is described as the first duty of the woman, since "no one else could substitute for her in this domain." Women, like men, also have responsibilities to society that depend on their own resources of time and energy as well as on the needs of their society. It is important to underscore that the acceptance of inherent differences and the delegation of family responsibilities in the light of those differences is grounded in the Quranic understanding of absolute equality rather than a conception of difference that implies inferiority.

The fact that this Quranic insistence on equality is more violated than honored in practice gives the New Islamist stance an inherently progressive thrust. The New Islamists acknowledge that the progress of women in recent times has actually been slowed in some areas and even reversed in others by misreading of these essential elements of the Quranic delineation of women's role in Islamic society. They aim self-consciously to reverse these negative trends and to achieve the full measure of advancement possible within the Quranic framework. To that end, the New Islamists stand firmly against the inclination to overemphasize and falsely generalize the differences specified between men and women or to understand them in ways that denigrate women. They also oppose the tendency to stress the rights of men, while paying insufficient attention to the fulfillment of responsibilities that justify them.

The New Islamist emphasis on essential human and spiritual equality stands against extremist Islamist notions of the inferior status of women and their generalized subordination to men. It opposes as well as a host of traditional and popular notions that constrain women, deny their rights, and even prompt disfigurement of their bodies.

Most impressive in the literature on women by the New Islamists is the sheer psychological strength and energy summoned to confront the weight of an entire culture of assumed male superiority and unchecked domination. To make their case for the advancement of women in the spirit of Islam properly understood, the New Islamists reassert the mainstream Islamic intellectual and spiritual universe. Feeling no need for foreign models, they write as the self-conscious heirs of the *Wassatteyya,* drawing on that tradition to address misunderstanding about women in their own time. However, their aim is independent and ambitious. They are never content merely to imitate the *ijtihad* of even their most trusted intellectual and spiritual mentors from the *Wassatteyya* or to simply react to their extremist adversaries without advancing clear and compelling alternative views. In short, the New Islamists have committed themselves to moving beyond restatement of inherited formulations and beyond the critique of prevailing customs and distorted practices. Their aim is to generate a new *fiqh* of community that will clarify thinking about women in both public and private realms on the firm Islamic ground of Quran and *Sunnah,* rightly understood. They develop their position against a backdrop of frank acknowledgment of the progress of women elsewhere in recent centuries, notably in the West. While they do not object to these foreign examples of progress serving as a reminder of shortcomings and an impetus to reform, they decline to take either the theory or the practice of others as models for rote imitation. They remind readers of the historical gains made by women under Islam in earlier centuries to discredit ideas that Islam cannot generate a social framework adequate to this challenge.[13]

The New Islamists' efforts to advance corrective ideas about the role of women have a strong personal dimension which they have openly discussed. Leading New Islamist figures have not hesitated to share with the public their support for the active social roles played by their own sisters, wives, and daughters. Kamal Abul Magd has on more than one occasion recognized the influence his wife exerts on his thinking and has drawn attention to her own active work in society. In a television interview discussing the new personal status laws, Kamal Abul Magd pointedly quoted his wife as urging that "this was something that Egyptians should support for the sake of their daughters." In the same spirit, Yusuf al Qaradawy has often registered his pride in the educational and career achievements of his daughters. When asked about his children in a 1998 interview, for example, Qaradawy prefaced his remarks with the observation that the education of both girls and boys is an Islamic duty. He vigorously condemned prevailing extremist thought that seeks to deny education to women, citing the Taliban regime in Afghanistan as only the most horrific example of what the extremists aim for. The treatment of women in Afghanistan, he said, reflects a false understanding of Islam "that must be rejected." The Taliban, Qaradawy continued, "prevented women from working and locked them in their homes, including thousands of widows who had lost their husbands in the war and who needed their work to support their children. Some of these women are intellectuals and others are university graduates." He then took considerable pride in noting that "I have four daughters, of which the first has a Ph.D. in nuclear physics and is now studying on a one-year scholarship in the United States, the second has her Ph.D. in chemistry, the third is doing a Ph.D. in engineering, and the fourth in genetics." Qaradawy then added that "I also have three sons, of which the first has a Ph.D. in engineering, the second is studying for a Master's in *Sharia,* while the youngest is working as an engineer in Qatar." To reinforce his support for the rights of his daughters and all Muslim women, Qaradawy concluded by saying that when one of his daughters was "still in college, a suitor asked me for her hand in marriage but indicated that he did not want her to work after graduation. I discussed the proposal with my daughter, who said she wanted to work, and so the marriage offer was rejected."[14]

Their public willingness to challenge extremist thinking on women has prompted some of the strongest threats by the violent extremists against the New Islamists. Unfailingly, Muhammad al Ghazzaly has been singled out for the bitterest criticism, including charges of apostasy for his ideas on the role of women. Although all of the major New Islamist figures have made important contributions to the struggle against extremist views, Shaikh Ghazzaly did indeed set an unflinching tone of defiant condemnation of the distortions of Islam with which the extremists sought to restrict women and diminish their rights. Refusing to back down despite the uproar his book on the *Sunnah* caused, Ghazzaly used the interpretive methods he outlined there as the basis for the elaboration of his ideas in his classic *Issues of Women between Rigid and Alien Traditions,* published three years later in 1994. Ghazzaly's pathbreaking studies created the nucleus of serious contemporary Islamic scholarship on women and family relations from a centrist Islamist perspective. This body of New Islamist writing goes beyond anything produced by the generation of either Abduh or al Banna.

Ghazzaly himself led the way in bringing these findings to the widest audience possible. Those who seek an Islamic rationale for the confinement of women to the private sphere have to contend with the scholarship of Muhammad al Ghazzaly and its capacity to erupt in condemnation, at once angry and authoritative. Ghazzaly consistently gave the new thinking about women its most humane and accessible face through his preaching and writings for the general public. In uncompromising terms, he insisted that Islam, rightly understood, sanctioned an active role for women in public life. In his discussion of the Prophet's wife Aisha in his landmark book on the *Sunnah,* Ghazzaly emphasized not only her love of literature and the arts but also how she addressed the community through them. At the same time, Ghazzaly drew attention to Aisha's status as an authority on the *Sunnah,* reporting that she issued important *fatwas* [religious rulings] for the community until her death. "Shouldn't Aisha," he asked, "be the proper model for women everywhere, or should we order them to stay at home, with no literature, no poetry, nothing at all?"[15] In his popular writings, in particular, Ghazzaly frequently reinforced his point with a sharp question: Could the backward societies of the Arab Islamic world really afford to ignore fully half of their precious human resources?[16]

Ghazzaly confronted directly the contrary arguments of extremists and traditionalists. Both trends frequently rely on *hadiths* to the effect that women are "second to men in mind and religion" and "not suitable as rulers." To strengthen their case, these flawed interpreters cite as well the example of the Queen of Persia, on whom the Prophet did in fact comment negatively. However, Ghazzaly points out that this criticism is unfairly generalized to all women as leaders by extremists and traditionalists alike. With scarcely disguised contempt, Ghazzaly insists that the words of the Prophet that "those who are governed by a woman are doomed to misery" must be read and understood in context.[17] It is an intolerable affront to tear the Prophet's words from the historical fabric of the lives of Muslims and the context of the sacred texts, he declares. The Persian Queen came to power at a time when the empire was about to fall to Islamic rule. It was governed by a repressive monarchy that completely neglected *shura* [consultation], relying instead on a dissolute and corrupt royal family. There was an opportunity after a disastrous defeat by the Romans for the Persians to reform themselves and restore their former power. However, an ignorant young woman ruled Persia, and her incompetence brought about the downfall of the empire. The Prophet's words, Ghazzaly notes, "came according to all this and as a description of the situation."[18] Ghazzaly concludes with this extraordinary comment on the meaning of the *hadith:* "Had there been *shura* in Persia or had the woman governed like the leader of the Jewish people, Golda Meir, there would have been a quite different comment." Ghazzaly drew the clear lesson that the individuals most qualified to meet the needs of their people, whether male or female, should be the leaders of their societies. To make this point, he reminded his readers that the Prophet also told the story of the Queen of Sheba, reported in the Quran, "who governed her nation and led them to faith with her intelligence and prudence." Thus, the *hadith* referring to the Queen of Persia could not possibly have the generalized meaning falsely given to it. "It is impossible," concluded Ghazzaly, "that a *hadith* would establish a rule that contradicts the Quran."[19]

If women might properly be called to serve as the political leaders of their communities, then clearly all manner of public roles should be open to them. In the name of the "true religion," Ghazzaly railed against inherited traditions "that lock women away and deprive them of rights and duties." If there are 100,000 doctors or 100,000 teachers, "there is absolutely no reason not to have half this number women doctors and women teachers." Ghazzaly periodically reminded readers of his weekly column in *al Shaab* of the strength and contributions to their own societies of a long list of contemporary women. He mentioned not only Golda Meir but Queen Victoria, Indira Ghandhi, and Margaret Thatcher as well.[20]

Ghazzaly's forthrightness was not confined to battles in Egypt. He did not hesitate to inject his views directly into the most controversial public debates about women's roles in the transnational Islamic sphere. In the 1950s Ghazzaly had taken refuge in Saudi Arabia to escape the heavy, repressive hand of the Nasser regime. His gratitude to the Saudis, however, did not extend to approval of the notorious restrictions that the Saudi regime, with the support of the official Saudi *ulama,* imposed on women. Ghazzaly directly attacked Saudi religious scholars, whom he charged with mistaking the backward, inherited customs of the Arabian Peninsula for Islam and its revelation and then arrogantly seeking to impose their limited understanding on others. By once again exposing the reliance on weak *hadiths* and failure to understand all *hadiths* in relationship to Quran, Ghazzaly established that practices such as the *neqab* [face veil] derive from the traditions of the Arabian Peninsula and have no basis in Islam. Reviewing the literature from the Gulf, and especially Saudi Arabia, supporting the *neqab,* he dismissed it as entirely unpersuasive. For example, one Gulf writer made the argument that Islam forbids adultery, and exposing the face opens the path to that sin. Ghazzaly objected that Islam explicitly requires the uncovering of the face during pilgrimage and prayer, so how can such logic be accepted? He commented to those who demanded that women's faces be covered that the Prophet saw uncovered women's faces in mosques and markets and never called for their covering. Are you, he asked the advocates of the *neqab,* greater protectors of the faith than the Prophet? Ghazzaly pointed to the Quranic verse that enjoins both men and women to "lower their gaze" as a sign of modesty in interactions with each other. Why, he asked, should men lower their gaze if there were any assumptions that women would be completely covered in the ways the traditionalists and extremists demanded?

Kamal Abul Magd vigorously seconded Ghazzaly's assessment that the *neqab* had no persuasive justification in text or *fiqh:* it was merely a retrograde social custom of the Gulf Arab states.[21] This battle of the face veil was the centerpiece of a wider New Islamist struggle against the traditionalist Islam that had made important inroads into Egypt as a result of the large numbers of Egyptians who worked in the Gulf states. On the related issue of the *hegab* [head scarf] that covered a woman's hair but left her face exposed, the New Islamists reached no equally strong consensus as a school. The *hegab* is, of course, far less restrictive and quite easily adapted to the most modern life-styles and careers. Some figures, including Muhammad al Ghazzaly, Yusuf al Qaradawy, Tareq al Bishry, and Fahmy Huwaidy, clearly favored the *hegab* and even regarded it as a religious duty, while others like Kamal Abul Magd and Selim al Awa appeared to assign far less importance to the issue one way or another. However, even those New Islamists like Fahmy Huwaidy who supported the *hegab* most strongly went out of their way to argue that it did not have a great priority. The question of the *hegab,* Huwaidy argued, was one of the "branches" and not a "fundamental root." It was not a religious duty with the same weight as prayer or fasting, for example. Thus, when girls in France were barred from schools if they wore the *hegab,* Huwaidy declared that they should take it off because their education was a higher priority than their dress.[22] In the same spirit, Ghazzaly had once decried all the attention to women's dress, declaring, "I am less concerned with the veil to cover the face than with the one placed over the mind!"[23]

When Saudi women staged a dramatic public protest in the fall of 1990 against the kingdom's ban on women driving, Ghazzaly immediately threw his support to the demonstrators. "I read with a heavy heart about the news of the demonstration of women in Riyadh demanding the right to drive cars," he wrote. Expressing utter amazement at the Saudi position, Ghazzaly stated that "cars are a new and modern means of transportation which replaced the horses, mules, donkeys, elephants, and camels that were used in previous times. As far as I know these old means of transportation were used by both sexes, in accord with the teachings of Islam." With scarcely concealed anger, he added that "I know that there are some muftis, warped in their thinking, who claim that women are forbidden to drive cars and airplanes, just as she is forbidden to play any leading role whatsoever whether in her home or in society." Ghazzaly pronounced such views intolerable. He also warned that they would have a demoralizing effect on Islamic societies in our modern age. The Muslim woman, Ghazzaly explained, reads in the newspapers and sees on television how women all over the world have risen to elevated positions in different areas of science, how they have displayed impeccable behavior as professionals in a wide variety of fields, how they have earned respect and honors in all of them, how they have explored space, led their people, and headed governments. What will be the effect of telling the Muslim woman that Islam forbids all these activities? Will not her faith be shaken if she is told that Islam denies her such a productive role in society? Such an outcome, concluded Ghazzaly, "would be our responsibility, for this is not Islam."[24]

Ghazzaly is not alone in shouldering this responsibility. In an influential weekly column, titled "On the Need for a New *Fiqh*," Selim al Awa has also very effectively brought New Islamist thinking on women to a wider audience. Given his own impressive qualifications as a legal scholar, it is not surprising that Awa's commentary not only makes the scholarship of the New Islamists accessible to a broad public but also deepens the thinking that underlies it. Patiently, Awa sifts through the *hadiths* used by extremists and traditionalists alike to denigrate the position of women. He identifies and dismisses unconfirmed *hadiths*. More important, he challenges the prevailing interpretations of confirmed *hadiths* that, he shows, are misconstrued to constrain women in ways never intended by the texts. Awa explains, for example, that the confirmed saying that women are "less perfect mentally and religiously than men" refers to very precise and circumscribed limitations, associated with legal testimony and prayer while menstruating, which were never meant to be essentialized and generalized into unalterable female subordination.[25] Awa states that in the effort to understand women's roles, "the foundation is provided by the Quranic verses that emphasize the essential equality of men and women as spiritual and social beings" rather than those that point to differences. Both men and women are created from the same spirit.[26] They are "protectors one of another," and they share the duty to "enjoin what is just and forbid what is

Muhammad Selim al Awa, Professor of Law at Zagazig University and a highly regarded public figure in Egypt and the Arab world. (photograph courtesy of Abul Ela Mady)

evil." Awa concludes that, given this clear thrust of numerous Quranic verses and confirmed *hadiths,* "anyone who might want to assert inequality must come up with very strong evidence to do so."[27]

These impressive efforts to counteract the distortions of *Sunnah* by extremist thinkers on core questions of community and especially the role of women signal the importance of the New Islamist interpretive project. The reassertion of centrist understandings of the *Sunnah* is matched in the corpus of the New Islamist scholarship by an equally sustained and rigorous attention to ways in which the Quran too is misread and misused.

How to Read the Quran

Edition after edition of Ghazzaly's controversial book on the *Sunnah* rolled off the presses, as just one sign that the corrective work of the New Islamist centrists had found a wide audience. The Quran too was subject to distortion by extremists and traditionalists alike, and the New Islamists responded to this with a reassertion of centrist interpretive strategies for the Quran itself. Once again Muhammad al Ghazzaly led the way, with the support and encouragement of the New Islamist School.

There were anticipations of the main lines of the work to come on the Quran in Ghazzaly's *The Prophet's Sunnah between the People of Hadith and People of Fiqh.* While Ghazzaly focused on rescuing the *Sunnah* from extremist misinterpretations, his examples inevitably brought into view the ways in which the Quran was misread as well. He noted that some of the most egregious misrepresentations of the meaning of the Quran by extremist shaikhs were advanced to support backward attitudes toward women.

These "half-educated" commentators, to borrow Ghazzaly's phrase, routinely misinterpreted the verse that describes men as the "maintainers and protectors of women." They argued that this verse means that women most probably could not and certainly should not play a role of strengthening and defending their societies as leaders, since God had reserved that function for men. With barely concealed impatience, Ghazzaly remarked that such scholars had neglected to read the entire verse and in that way produced a "totally unacceptable" interpretation. If you continue to read the verse, he explained, "you find that it deals with a man in his home." Ghazzaly made it clear that this definition should not be extended to the role of women in society, citing the example of the Prophet's successor as leader of the first Islamic community, who "appointed a woman as a judge in the market, and she had an unqualified right to her independent judgment."[28]

Ghazzaly's *Women's Issues between Rigid and Alien Traditions,* published in 1994, multiplied the examples of how the intolerable restrictions placed on women by both extremists and traditionalists rested on what can only be described as willed and biased ignorance of the Quran. In this study, he tackled directly the verse that allowed men to strike women, frequently used to clinch the argument that the Quran provided for generalized male dominance over women.[29] Ghazzaly insisted first that the verse be read carefully and completely. He pointed out that striking women was described as a last resort, and was only permitted under very precise and limited conditions. Those conditions were unfaithfulness and "the display of *nushuz,* an attitude that indicated a refusal to remain faithful" such as allowing strange men to enter the husband's house against his wishes, thereby "creating suspicion and shaking the foundations of married life." Ghazzaly noted, "I have found in *Sharia* only these two cases where striking a woman is permitted." He then reminded readers that this singular verse called on men to respond to these improprieties by first admonishing the woman and then refusing to share her bed, that is, suspending sexual relations. Only when men had exhausted these deterrents could they resort to striking. And even in this extreme case, Ghazzaly pointed out that the consensus of scholars specified that the resort to physical force should be very moderate in character and should not include either striking the face or uttering harsh words at the same time.[30]

Extremist as well as some traditionalist interpretations sought to evade all of these restrictions that surrounded the controversial verse. In doing so, they found support in a confirmed *hadith* attributing to the Prophet the words "a man should not be asked why he beat his wife." With stunning courage, Ghazzaly directly challenged the judgment that confirmed this *hadith,* stating bluntly that the *hadith* "contradicts the Quran and many other reliable *hadiths.* Aggression by men against women, just like that of women against men, is also rejected by logic and a sense of justice. I do not know how such words are attributed to the Prophet." Ghazzaly grounded his confident reading of the evidence by reminding his readers that one of the most important "general rules" of the Quran is that everyone will be held accountable for each and every little good or bad deed. "Is it conceivable," asked Ghazzaly, "that a wife would be the only exception and a man would not be asked why he beat her? How could it be that a man would have the right to beat her just for some deep reason inside himself?" How could such a view possibly be squared with the Quranic verse "either take them back on equitable terms or set them free on equitable terms," or the *hadith* that tells men to "take good care of women"?[31] With these uncompromising questions, Ghazzaly clearly signaled that such distortions of Quran, notably including those that had arrested the advancement of women, should not be tolerated.

Muhammad al Ghazzaly's full-fledged battle to reassert the *Wassatteyya* reading of the Quran in order to shield the interpretive process from distortions came with the publication in 1995 of *Toward a Substantive Interpretation of the Surahs of the Holy Quran.* "I have accompanied Quran since my childhood," wrote Ghazzaly in the introduction to his last book on Quranic exegesis. "I memorized it by the age of ten and I continue to read it in the eighth decade of my life." Yet, Ghazzaly commented, "it seemed to me that what I know of its meanings is little and does not rise above the direct meanings and repeated phrases."[32]

The modest spirit of these words captures an essential characteristic of the New Islamist School in general. Ghazzaly and the other major New Islamist figures made no effort to match the shouted certainties of the militants. They understood that the insights from Quran on how to organize life and give it an Islamic character would come only from, to borrow Kamal Abul Magd's phrase, a "huge effort of the mind."[33] They saw clearly the dangers of religious totalitarianism that lurked in absolutist religious claims, and their own explorations of how to read Quran offered no illusions of final answers. They provided their readings of Quran neither to displace all others nor to end the process of *ijtihad.* Instead, they managed to combine extraordinary commitment to the task of struggling for greater understanding with the modest realization that ultimately they were "deficient explorers." As Ghazzaly put it, he was simply using his "limited abilities" to make discoveries that would inspire "others to go further in serving Quran and uncovering its greatness and glories."[34]

Ghazzaly knew that his opinions on Quranic interpretation would generate storms of protest, precisely because he once again applied them to women's issues. However, Ghazzaly also knew that recent centuries had brought regression in the understanding of the rights and responsibilities of women that prevailed in much of the Islamic world. That debilitating trend must be reversed, he insisted. At the close of the twentieth century there were more than a billion Muslims in the world. As the first waves of accusations swirled around him, Ghazzaly calmly refused "to deny the dignity of 500 million women."[35]

In his book on Quran, Ghazzaly argued that a major cause of the contemporary misunderstandings of Islam's message was the wrenching of verses and even parts of verses from the surahs, or chapters, in which they occurred. Extremist thinkers, in particular, focused on such fragments to produce misleading and often damaging readings. To counter this abuse, Ghazzaly argued for holistic, substantive readings. It was essential to see each surah whole, he maintained, and then to understand its meaning in the context of all other surahs as well. Only then could meanings be grasped in terms of the higher purposes and core values that God's words brought to humanity.

Ghazzaly illustrated his method with the treatment of the lengthy and significant Surah on Women, offering an important new interpretation that would be impossible to ignore in any future consideration of women's role in the Islamic community. Ghazzaly stated his thesis simply and directly. The surah, taken as a whole rather than as a collection of discrete verses, treats the totality of human social relations and not simply issues of women. The most important misreadings of the surah's overall meaning result from separating particular passages on women out of this larger context. "I see the subject of the surah as general," wrote Ghazzaly. "It deals with all the community and its various components, and the discussion of women is simply one part of this whole."[36] Thus the surah understands the role of a woman in the broader context of the social world through which she moves as individual, family member, and part of the larger society. Ghazzaly brought the Quranic depiction of all those roles simultaneously into view as women shared them with men. Humankind was called to carry out great tasks on the Earth. Was it conceivable to accomplish them with only half of human talents and gifts?

Selim al Awa elaborated with great effectiveness the essential interpretive and substantive conclusions that flowed from Ghazzaly's authoritative statement on how the Quran should be read and interpreted. As part of his very accessible treatment of Quran, Awa provided a painstaking review of the three Quranic verses most frequently cited by both extremists and traditionalists to privilege males and deny women an equal right to a role in public life.

The first verse cited says that "women have rights similar to men but men are a degree above them."[37] Awa points out that this verse is inaccurately read as a broad statement of the overall superiority of men to women and flatly denies that the verse supports such an interpretation. He explains that the text, so often cited in isolation, comes in the Surah of the Cow as part of the treatment of divorce, where very detailed guidelines are provided for both men and women. The particular reference bears on the marriage contract. Awa argues that a verse that refers to a complex issue of the private sphere in very precise and limited ways simply cannot be generalized to public life without doing serious violence to its meaning. He concludes, therefore, that the verse cannot reasonably be construed to "forbid women to participate in public work through its clear meaning when read in context."[38] The second verse, even more often misread and misused, is from the Surah of Women, and contains the frequently cited phrase "men are the protectors and maintainers of women."[39] Here Awa follows the argument made by Ghazzaly that this sacred verse "cannot be taken as proof, and it does not mean that women should be forbidden from participating in public work or occupying high positions for which they are qualified by their abilities and education."[40] The third verse cited by those who seek Quranic justification for their efforts to exclude women from their rightful role in community affairs includes the injunction "stay quietly in your homes and make not a dazzling display as in pre-Islamic times."[41] Awa points out that the verse refers without the slightest ambiguity to the wives of the Prophet Muhammad and their quite distinctive responsibilities. The verse just before the one cited quite explicitly states: "Ye are not like other women." It is "simply not acceptable," Awa argues, to use a verse so clearly specified as relevant only to the wives of the Prophet as justification for applying restrictions on all women.

Having made the case that these frequently cited Quranic verses do not justify denying women a public role, Awa urges his readers to remember instead the many verses in the Quran that talk about "the origin of equality between man and woman in creation, rights and duties." Awa notes that the *Sunnah* taken as a whole confirms this Quranic insight. The clear injunction of essential equality finds expression in the *hadith* that he summarizes to say "woman is equal to man in participation in public work, and she is not to be taken away from it except for the same reasons which may take the man away and prevent him from doing this work."[42]

The engagement by the New Islamists with the ideas of the militants and traditionalists on these issues of women's roles in Islamic community represented a critical battle in a larger crisis of thought. The broader battle pitted the reasoned interpretive strategy of the New Islamist centrists against the rigid textualism of the extremist thinkers who inspired the violent groups and the most retrograde of the traditionalists. Kamal Abul Magd characterized those Islamists who adopt the textualist stance as "having but one principle, and that is to declare support for texts and willingness to apply them immediately and unconditionally. They see the issue as taking a clear-cut position on texts, either to accept them or to reject them." The New Islamists not only exposed the ways in which the texts or fragments of texts invoked were frequently misread or taken out of context; they also warned of the totalitarian impulse driving this rigid and absolutist stance. Abul Magd explained that the treatment of texts in this way by the extremists in particular most often translates simply into a demand to follow the *amir* [leader of Islamist group] and the particular understanding of the text that he holds.[43]

This is not Islam, the New Islamists state flatly. God's message to humanity relies on the use of the mind, as indicated by the very character of the texts. Yusuf al Qaradawy took the lead in explaining precisely why the linguistic character of the message required reasoned interpretation and not mechanical application. "God wanted some of his provisions to be clearly stated and others left unspoken," wrote Qaradawy. Clearly, implicit meanings could only be deduced by the mind. More to the point, "even among the specified texts, He wanted some to be clear-cut and others somewhat vague, so that minds would practice *ijtihad* to deduce their meaning." In a key passage in *The Islamic Awakening,* Qaradawy sums up the heart of the New Islamist case against the textualists. He explains that "had He so desired, God could have given all religion the same formulation, unquestionable and needing no *ijtihad,* so that those who disobey would immediately make themselves unbelievers." However, God did not do so "in order that the nature of religion would be consistent with the nature of language and of humanity in order to make things easier for those who believe."[44]

Addressing all elements of the Islamic wave, Qaradawy makes his broad argument for the necessity of reasoned *ijtihad* by beginning with the essentials of the faith that not even the most extreme elements question. The source of Islam, he notes, is Quran and *Sunnah.* Quran is a group of texts, and most of the *Sunnah* consists of texts as well. Then, moving to the distinctive position of the New Islamists, Qaradawy comments that "these texts of Quran and *Sunnah* are just like any other language text as far as understanding and interpretation are concerned." The texts use "the words and structure of the language." For Qaradawy and the New Islamists, the implications are clear: "Some words," he writes, "can have more than one meaning. Others can be understood either literally, figuratively, or metaphorically."[45]

The explicit recognition by the New Islamists that texts may have subtle and unspoken meanings places the interpretive project and the tolerance of difference that it demands at the very center of the effort to build Islamic community. "The unspoken always yields disagreements," writes Qaradawy. From a vantage point that rejects the kinds of misplaced certitude and absolutism shown by the extremists, he adds with unmistakable emphasis, "difference is a treasure because it triggers different *ijtihad* by different *ulama,* and with this *fiqh* is immeasurably enriched."[46]

The controversies over women's issues were not the only serious disagreements where these lines were drawn, setting the reasoned and tolerant flexibility of the New Islamists against the rigid and dogmatic arbitrariness of the textualists. Just as important were the controversies that arose over non-Muslims. Islam is innocent of any exclusionary impulse that would define the Islamic community as one that exists for Muslims only. However, questions do arise about precisely how the expected role of non-Muslims should be defined. Characteristically, the New Islamists have used their reasoned interpretive strategy to argue for the most expansive readings against the exclusionary impulses of the extremists.

The Secure and Rightful Place of Non-Muslims

Kamal Abul Magd has articulated with particular clarity the general principles that underlie the New Islamist approach to non-Muslims in the Islamic community. The starting point of all such discussion, Abul Magd insists, must once again be the unequivocal Quranic assertion of the essential equality of diverse humankind. Abul Magd acknowledges forthrightly the terrible gap between the promise of these Quranic ideals and historical realities. He takes note of prevailing conditions in Islamic societies where the balance tips too often toward the power of states rather than the protection of citizens, and where the rights of society's most vulnerable members, non-Muslims as well as women, are routinely violated.

These are the failings of Muslims, not Islam, Abul Magd argues. "Needless to say," he writes, "the situation in Islamic countries has never reached the level of equality expected by Islam. However, who would contend that such a human failing is found in the Islamic world alone? Regrettably, it is also the case in many other countries that have clear-cut constitutional statements on equality never attained by its people in real life as they continue to suffer from different forms of discrimination."[47]

The task facing the new generation of Egyptians, notes Abul Magd, is clear. Undaunted by the limited achievements of their predecessors, they must work to devise more effective institutions to realize the Quranic vision.[48] In facing that challenge, the New Islamists argue that Egyptians have a distinctive resource in the rich and complex religious tradition of their ancient land. Abul Magd points to the particularly tolerant and open spirit of religion as it has developed in a country with two major religious traditions, Islam and Christianity, whose historical interactions have contributed to the national identity. He notes that the most important values of the mainstream of both Islam and Christianity, such as truth, honesty, and justice, overlap and reinforce each other in an easy and natural relationship. Egyptians, suggests Abul Magd, must call on that unique experience to confront the divisive forces that aim to pit Muslims and Christians against each other, violating their common civilizational legacy and threatening national unity.[49]

All of the major New Islamist figures have contributed in important ways to this effort to create an inclusive national project that draws strength from Egypt's distinctive history, shared by Muslims and Copts.[50] The New Islamists argue that the dual religious tradition of Egyptians has created a context in which the open and inclusive thrust of Islam finds a particularly full expression. They advance this argument to address the secularizing impulse that would drive religion from the public arena. To do so would be counterproductive, they maintain, given Egypt's legacy of religious tolerance. The New Islamist manifesto stresses that the core values of Islam on which the Egyptian national community rests are deeply rooted in the hearts and souls of Muslims. They argue unequivocally that Christians hold these very same values as well. Thus, Islam and Christianity both contribute to the creation of a "civilizational religion" that provides a foundation for the national community.

On these grounds, the New Islamists reject the secularist inclination to explain sectarian difficulties by an excess of religious zeal, arguing instead that it is the dilution of *sound* religious education that has caused the sectarian conflicts of the last decades of the twentieth century. The New Islamist manifesto states that "secularizing society, in the absolute sense of isolating religion from life, cannot be the right solution for the sectarian problem in multi-religious societies. Secularism, in this sense, kills the patient in order to cure his illness." According to the manifesto, the proper Islamic solution to the sectarian conflict requires first of all "a guarantee of complete freedom of creed and worship," and second, adherence to the principle of "the right of the majority to rule" with "full rights for the minority." The New Islamists consistently maintain that when both religious traditions are correctly taught and encouraged, their civilizational commonalities will assert themselves and strengthen national unity.[51]

To address the periodic outbreaks of sectarian conflict that have blighted Egypt's recent history, the manifesto calls for "national unity and fraternity." The New Islamists state categorically that a strong national community requires complete equality between Muslims and non-Muslims in their civil and political rights as citizens. The constitutional guarantees of such equality, in their view, supersede any outmoded notions of the proper relationship between Muslims and non-Muslims, including those that extremists and traditionalists draw from the era of the Prophet. The manifesto calls on Egyptians to translate these principles of a civilizational national project into realities by means of a national dialogue that confronts problems and admits difficulties. In a series of important works published later in the 1980s, notably Yusuf al Qaradawy's *Non-Muslims in Islamic Society,* Fahmy Huwaidy's *Citizens, Not Zimmis,* and Selim al Awa's *Copts and Islam,* the New Islamists significantly advanced this project laid out in the manifesto.[52]

The distressing record of escalating violence between Muslims and Christians in the 1980s and 1990s underscored the importance of such a national dialogue between Muslims and Christians. The New Islamist insistence that the Islamic wave pay as much attention to the world around them as to their inherited sacred texts meant that they were unavoidably drawn into the national effort to make sense of sectarian conflict. In their *fiqh* of contemporary reality, the New Islamists registered their concern that current outbreaks of violence should not be allowed to obscure the deep, historical roots of fraternity that bound Egyptian Copts and Muslims, with their long and proud history of tolerance. Tareq al Bishry, in particular, has made a singular and widely acknowledged contribution to a rich historiography that documents the role of Egyptian Copts as full partners in Egypt's national struggles. The starting point of Bishry's thinking is cultural history. Islamic civilization, he explains, is the product not only of Muslims but of non-Muslims as well. Furthermore, Islamic civilizational boundaries are not drawn along racial, ethnic, or religious lines. It is precisely for this reason that the New Islamist School insists on the important distinction between an Islamic order and a religious one. The New Islamists emphasize that Islamic community is constituted on civiliza-

Yusuf al Qaradawy *(left)* represents Islamic scholars in one of the numerous public dialogues held in the 1990s with prominent figures of the Eastern Christian Churches. (photograph courtesy of *al Ahram* newspaper)

tional terms within which non-Muslims hold a secure and rightful place. Historical memory for the New Islamists includes recognition of the contributions of non-Muslims to the glories of Islamic civilization. More pointedly, they remind Egyptians that Copts played a critical role in the modern Egyptian national movement, giving the blood of their sons for the Egyptian national resistance. Thus they insist that Copts helped create the modern Egyptian identity and constitute an indispensable element within it. Bishry spoke for the New Islamists in declaring that, given the role of militant Islamist groups in bringing about violence, the Islamic trend as a whole, and its "moderate heart" in particular, had a special responsibility to declare clearly its condemnation of violence that targeted Copts.[53]

These balanced, though controversial, views on the issue of communal violence represented a crucial element in the New Islamist *fiqh* of reality. In addressing these pressing issues of contemporary Egyptian social realities, the New Islamists never abandoned their attention to the guidance provided by the texts as well. They combined their *fiqh* of reality, including its most distressing aspects, with an insistent *fiqh* of texts that would bring into view the higher purposes and values that should guide the struggle for resolution of all such dilemmas in a community of justice and inclusion. Nowhere is this balance between interpretation of text and reality more clearly in evidence than in the New Islamist approach to the implementation of *Sharia.* All Islamists agree that without *Sharia,* there can be no Islamic community. However, the centrists and the extremists disagree profoundly on what constitutes *Sharia* as well as how it should be implemented. From this vantage point, the New Islamists forcefully reject the notion that what most distinguishes the extremists is the violence of their means. In the New Islamist view, the struggle between the center and the violent groups at the margin is ultimately a contest about ends and not simply means. It is a struggle between two strikingly different substantive understandings of the nature of Islamic community and, more particularly, of the *Sharia* that regulates it. The community toward which the *Wassatteyya* is working is open, inclusive, and responsive to the world. The New Islamist conception of *Sharia* is consonant with such a community. In contrast, the community of the extremists is closed, exclusive, and hostile to the world, and their ideas about *Sharia* mirror these distortions and rigidities.

How to Implement *Sharia*

Sharia, as Yusuf al Qaradawy explains, moves Islam from the realm of ideas and values to the realm of the social realities of an Islamic community. As Qaradawy puts it, Islam is a belief, from which is derived *Sharia,* on which Islamic community is based.[54] The New Islamist School insists that successful implementation means discerning God's higher purposes expressed in the texts and using reason to realize those purposes in a particular community. Such is the aim of *fiqh.* This perspective distinguishes carefully between *Sharia,* which is divine, and *fiqh,* which is human. This distinction has great importance not only for the process of implementation but also for deciding substantive questions of how the community will be defined and its boundaries drawn. The issue of secularists, as will become clear, raises this important boundary question with particular clarity.

The basic premise of New Islamist thinking about *Sharia* is the proposition that wherever there is a community of believing Muslims, *Sharia* is already and necessarily a part of their lives. *Sharia* provisions come from the Quran and *Sunnah,* and in this precise way, *Sharia* has a divine dimension. For that reason, as Kamal Abul Magd explains, "a Muslim cannot be a Muslim unless he chooses to abide by *Sharia.*"[55] Fully elaborated and realized, *Sharia* would be a way of life, including all those provisions and general principles revealed by God to govern man's life in his relationship:

(1) to God, with prayers and fasting, for example, as provided for explicitly in the Quran and *Sunnah;* (2) with other Muslims, including requirements of moral behavior, like honesty and kindness, as well as material rules of relationships, such as inheritance; (3) with non-Muslims, requiring guarantees of their equal rights and value as members of the community; (4) with society, assuring that it is founded on principles of justice; and (5) with all other forms of life and the universe, assuring that they are treated with respect. These various dimensions of *Sharia* enable humankind to fulfill the responsibility "for acting as God's regent on Earth."[56]

Abul Magd cautions that Muslims should know, however, that "texts do not treat everything in detail in order to preserve the necessary flexibility to adjust to particular circumstances and needs. God elaborated on some things and not on others; it is a delegation to us to practice *ijtihad* and an invitation to use the mind."[57] Moreover, it is only logical that in those "vast areas" where there are no texts, the role of the mind must necessarily be even more expansive. The historical record of the implementation of *Sharia* indicates that it is fully able to meet this challenge. Islam as the religion of all times and places, Abul Magd adds, is in this sense neither a myth nor a miracle.[58] Yusuf al Qaradawy notes that "*Sharia* provided the basis for legislation and *fatwas* [religious opinions by religious scholars] in almost all the Islamic world for almost thirteen centuries; as such it was introduced into different environments, to different races and to a number of civilizations."[59]

How was this extraordinary achievement possible? For those areas of social life that needed clarification and elaboration of regulatory rules, a realistic grasp of social conditions and an understanding of the needs of people provided the appropriate reference points. The New Islamists argue that *fiqh* must have those conditions and needs, and not some unrealistic, general standard or ideal, as its "material base." The task of analyzing social conditions and meeting human needs is not a "philosophical or abstract action but is rather a practical way for those who rule to take care of people's affairs." New Islamist confidence that this challenge can be met flows from what Qaradawy calls the "comprehensiveness and flexibility" of *Sharia.*[60] In the New Islamist terminology, comprehensiveness emphatically does not refer to the prior existence within the body of *Sharia* of specific structures and concepts to deal with all the minute details of an evolving and changing world; instead, it refers to four clear and easily understandable mechanisms, two based on texts and two on social realities, by which the "higher purposes of *Sharia*" can be met by a variety of means responsive to particular circumstances. The *faqih* [an Islamic scholar, specially trained and recognized by peers as qualified to contribute to *fiqh*] can rely on analogy to other relevant texts, the exercise of choice among different interpretations of those texts to best meet prevailing conditions, an appeal to general human interests, and finally acceptance of existing and common practices, provided they do not conflict with the general aims of *Sharia*.[61] "All the various forms of judicial systems developed in the different Islamic eras," writes Qaradawy, "resulted from historical experimentation and development in accordance with these means. None of these forms were dictated by Quran or *Sunnah*."[62]

The New Islamists also developed pragmatic arguments consistent with the flexibility that *Sharia* afforded. *Sharia*, they insisted, could build on what already existed. They noted that often *Sharia* was already applied in the sense that existing laws, whatever their provenance, conformed to the purposes and values of *Sharia*. Such laws could be considered Islamic. It was ridiculous, in their view, to oppose this practical approach on the grounds that social laws and regulatory patterns had to be distinctive to be Islamic. Such a restrictive attitude would unnecessarily preclude creative borrowing from the experience of others. Islam, as Kamal Abul Magd explained, was the religion of all the prophets. Therefore, it should not be surprising that social regulations derived from other civilizations could meet the needs of those living in Islamic communities. Finally, the New Islamists pointed out that the *Sharia* itself rests on the Islamic conception that takes into consideration the necessity imposed by exceptional circumstances. "Hardship necessitates facilitation," both in fulfilling obligations and in giving license to that which ordinarily is not allowable. This practical attitude applies not only to individuals but to the community as a whole. As Yusuf al Qaradawy points out, the grounds for invoking these pragmatic forms of flexibility are "meeting the needs of the community and protecting it as an entity,"[63] and thus "we can say with an easy conscience that *Sharia* can accommodate any modern judicial system that is likely to realize justice and assure security."[64]

For just these reasons, Kamal Abul Magd has argued forcefully that the "practice of *ijtihad* is not an aggression on texts but rather a way to abide by them."[65] The scope for *ijtihad* is necessarily wide because "what is not addressed by texts exceeds that which is addressed."[66] The wide scope that God left to *ijtihad* and the *fiqh* it generates shows that we must assume that "God knows that life forms change and that people's problems take different forms because it is He who created this world and knows it best."[67]

The New Islamist principle that an Islamic community will be based on *Sharia* thus means that the divine dimension derived from Quran and *Sunnah* must necessarily be present, along with the contingent elaborations of *fiqh* that originate with *ijtihad* in response to the particular circumstances of the community. On this basis, the New Islamists highlight the critical distinction between *Sharia* and *fiqh*. "*Sharia*," Kamal Abul Magd summarizes, "is a group of fixed provisions by God and the Prophet, regulating people's actions and having their source in Quran and *Sunnah*." In sharp contrast, "*fiqh* is the variable work of people on behalf of *Sharia*, to explore the provisions, explain texts, and use analogy when there is no text in order to secure the welfare of people." Both are essential, but their weight and importance differ in striking ways. The rulings of *Sharia*, as Yusuf al Qaradawy points out, "do not change, regarding the duties, penalties, and forbidden actions stipulated basically by Quran and *Sunnah*." However, the interpretation "is linked to the 'intent' which a given ruling aims to achieve, and thus the rule may change in time and place." In his scholarly treatment of *fiqh*, Qaradawy illustrates that there is a basis in Quranic texts for the principle of changing religious rulings according to variable circumstances in order to respect their unchanging intent. He also cites parallel examples from *Sunnah*. All four schools of *Sharia* that developed later, notes Qaradawy, recognize this principle of variability.[68]

Extremists, Kamal Abul Magd explains, fail to make the critical distinction between *Sharia* and *fiqh* and thus fall into dangerous distortions in their ideas about community. All too often, they place *fiqh* and *Sharia* on the same level and describe the combination as "Islamic legislation or law," which they assert must be immediately applied. This misleading conflation heightens the dangers of their thinking, especially when they go even further in their dogmatism and make support for their faulty positions a test of religious faith. The New Islamists dissent sharply from such distortions. In a definitive formulation, Abul Magd states that while "*Sharia* is governing, Islamic *fiqh* is subject to anything applicable to all human endeavors." Driving home the distinction, he concludes that "the obedience of Muslims is to *Sharia*, not to *fiqh* and not to the *faqihs* who create it." Thus, Abul Magd explicitly addresses the false calls for the rule of clerics, that is, theocracy, so often advanced by Islamist extremists. Turning their accusations of disbelief back onto the extremists themselves, Abul Magd charges that by their "fatal mistake" of obscuring the difference between *Sharia* and *fiqh*, the extremists distort and undermine the faith by "adding to Islam things that are not Islam and committing people to things they should not be committed to."[69]

Against the impatient call of the extremists to implement *Sharia* now, the New Islamists respond that *Sharia* is not something external to Islamic communities to be imposed on them from without. Rather, *Sharia* is already partially implemented wherever there is an Islamic community, and the task is to use the mind to complete its elaboration. Kamal Abul Magd explains that, despite variations in the scope of its realization, *Sharia* and its interpretive extensions by *fiqh* have been an integral part of the culture and history of the Arab Islamic world for centuries. Moreover, in varying degrees it continues to be so today as "one of the expressions of its cultural autonomy and political independence."[70] The task for Islamists is not to start from scratch but rather to begin with these partial implementations of *Sharia* and complete their elaboration. "God gave us the mind," he wrote, "to cope with this continuous change and to respond to developments. It is only the mind that can protect *Sharia* and achieve its purposes."[71]

Only by mistakenly sanctifying and rigidifying *fiqh,* and thereby disfiguring its essential character, can the extremists advance their mindless slogan that calls for the immediate implementation of *Sharia.* The extremists misunderstand *Sharia* to be "a ready-made structure that can be invoked by society at the right historical moment, rectifying everything and driving all evils away."[72] In the most reductionist versions of this thinking, *Sharia* is further reduced to its legal dimensions, and those in turn conceived only as the *hudud* [punishments] provided for in the texts. The New Islamists categorically reject these views. Punishments cannot be the place to start, they explain, because every punishment specified by Islam requires first that people be given their rights. The application of *hudud* would require that a just society has been realized. To make this point, Abul Magd cited the example of Caliph Omar Ibn al Khattab, who refused to countenance the cutting off of the hand of a thief because the man stole because he was starving. Clearly, he had been denied basic rights. In the New Islamist view, Islam is not a message for disciplining people but a way of life that aims to meet their needs and assure their happiness. *Sharia* is the means to that broad end. How, then, could it possibly be reduced to punishments?

The New Islamists believe that such terrible distortions in the call to implement *Sharia* stem from the absence of thoughtful religious education. The void is filled by what Abul Magd calls "heard Islam." With this telling phrase, Abul Magd refers to those who know Islam only by "a word here and a speech there but have no knowledge of *fiqh* or *Sharia* or the sound rules of inference and deduction." Often, Abul Magd continues, even those who do learn something of the Quran and hundreds of Prophetic *hadiths* do so without understanding the rules of *fiqh* or grasping the meanings of the *Sharia.* Moreover, since they know nothing of the conditions of their society, how can they make sound religious judgments? Such figures, he concludes, "are in no position whatever to talk of religion, and those who do listen to them are even more ignorant and irrational for paying attention to those so unworthy of it."[73]

The New Islamists strive to rescue the issue of *Sharia* from the sloganeering of the extreme Islamists and all those who accept extremist views of the nature of *Sharia* and the means to implement it.[74] They seek to recenter the debate over *Sharia* in the Islamic mainstream and thereby bring it closer to Islam's real message. To do so means to affirm the mainstream's emphasis on core values and higher purposes, gradually implemented through a thoughtful *ijtihad*. They turn their own interpretive efforts to clarifying and strengthening that value-centered and gradualist position, and they begin by staking out an exceptionally muscular conception of *ijtihad*. Not even the existence of a text, Kamal Abul Magd argues forcefully, abrogates the use of the mind: "We should put the widely held view 'no *ijtihad* when there is a text' into its proper context." In the clearest terms, Abul Magd states that "the presence of a text (that is, verse or *hadith*) does not necessarily cancel the role of the mind and *ijtihad*. The understanding of the text and judgment about any possible contradictions among texts is itself an *ijtihad*."[75] Yusuf al Qaradawy explains the implications for interpretation of the fact that, as he puts it, "most holy texts laying down specific and detailed rulings are open to more than one interpretation." As a result, such texts yield different interpretations that have in turn been the bases for different schools and orientations in Islamic *fiqh*. For this reason, Qaradawy concludes that even the texts that treat specific matters should be regarded as "a guiding light and not a restricting bond" for the exercise of the mind. It often becomes clear that there are commonalities underlying apparent differences, anchored in "the intent" of the text and "the interest" of the Islamic community.[76]

The New Islamist School applies these fluid conceptions of intent and interest with particular force to the issue of human variety in the Islamic community. Islam, they declare, is innocent of a homogenizing impulse that would eliminate or diminish diversity. Kamal Abul Magd points out that there are numerous, clear-cut Quranic verses that recognize difference and emphasize its positive dimensions. "Man," he writes, "is a dignified creature, preferred by God over all other creatures. This preference has nothing to do with color, wealth, or even religion, but rather derives simply from his humanity. It is neither related to Muslims alone nor to Arabs alone." According to Abul Magd, this position that human rights inhere in a diverse humanity is expressed in a straightforward manner in several Quranic verses. The Quran makes it perfectly clear that the variety of humankind is an intended blessing from God. Surely, God could have made all men alike if He so desired.[77] Instead, the Quran tells us that human variety is one of God's signs: "And among his Signs is the creation of the heavens and the earth, and the variation in your languages and your colors; verily in that are Signs for those who know."[78] Just as God urges humankind to explore the wonders of the Earth, He informs all of humankind that they originate "from a single (pair) of a male and a female. God then made humankind into nations and tribes, that ye may know each other (not that ye may despise each other)."[79] *Sharia,* Abul Magd continues, takes this essential and shared human dignity as the starting point for efforts to assure that human liberties, rights, body, reputation, and property are untouched and respected. "These social duties," he observes, "regulate the relationship between individuals, and commit them to respect the rights of others, their lives, properties, and right to privacy. Islam, Abul Magd concludes, is exceptional in making the honoring of the rights of others a sacred responsibility. The only bases for making exceptions and recognizing differences are those advanced in the interest of protecting the rights of others or for the welfare of the entire community.

This nuanced understanding of *Sharia* has important practical implications. The New Islamist premise that all members of an Islamic community must accept in principle the notion that such a community is regulated by *Sharia* provides a general standard for drawing boundaries. Their distinction between *Sharia* and *fiqh* also plays a role in questions of inclusion and exclusion. Many restrictive ideas originate with *fiqh* rather than *Sharia,* and they are falsely judged to be authoritative. In the most general sense, the important debate over secularism within the Islamic Awakening centers around precisely this issue.

The Inclusion of Moderate Secularists

The underlying spirit of *Sharia,* as the New Islamists understand it, values difference. In their view, *Sharia* aims to facilitate the regulation of a necessarily diverse human community in ways that balance the rights of distinct groups with the collective interest. The treatment of secularists in the Islamic community illustrates how the New Islamists believe that such a just balance should be achieved. Secularists have a place in the Islamic community, they argue, provided they do not call into question or actively undermine its foundations, thereby endangering the community and depriving it of its Islamic identity.

In their manifesto, the New Islamists make a clear gesture of cooperation in the national interest to secularists and others outside the Islamic wave. They explain that revival depends on the "interaction among all the categories and elements of the nation" because "no one category can bear the burden on its own." They acknowledge difference, but signal a willingness to act in concert with others. Those others may share only "*part* of their vision." What is required of all is that they accept that Egypt is an Islamic nation, by the commitment of the majority of its citizens and the explicit provision of its constitution. Thus, the New Islamists call those in each creed who seek revival and those in each intellectual school who work for freedom and justice "to transcend the boundaries that separate such schools in order to strengthen each other in thought and action, taking as our slogan 'cooperation in areas of agreement and forgiveness for the differences we have.'"[80] Such broad cooperation must be based, they explain, on "rationality and freedom of minds as well as tolerant behavior toward others."[81]

While the New Islamists take for granted that the underlying framework of the nation is Islamic, they appreciate the strong presence and exceptional strength of secular intellectual and social trends in Egyptian society. Moreover, they regard this secular influence as less antithetical to Islamic principles than many assume. The very term "secularism," Kamal Abul Magd explains, is sometimes misunderstood even by scholars in ways that create a sense of opposition to an Islamic framework in areas where none exists. Many secularists in fact do accept the principle of applying *Sharia*. The New Islamists stress that acceptance of the principle of implementing *Sharia* does not preclude contestation of all of its *fiqh*. Moreover, the New Islamist understanding preserves a space for disagreement and active dissent on the important issues of how and when *Sharia* should be elaborated. All of these opportunities are open to secularists as the process of implementing *Sharia* unfolds. A secularism that can accommodate this understanding of the character of *Sharia* and of the appropriate process of implementing it is regarded as "moderate secularism." Such a secularism poses no problem for inclusion in an Islamic community.

Extreme secularists, in contrast, are defined as all those who reject the very *principle* that *Sharia* should regulate community life. This rejection would undermine an Islamic community, and therefore extreme secularists cannot be included. "What Islam rejects of secularism," Kamal Abul Magd explains, "is mainly the secularization of society or the isolation of religion from regulating social affairs." He adds that the notion of the separation of religion and society developed in the West, where it is consistent with the precept of Christianity to "render unto Caesar what is his and unto God what is His." In the Western cultural context, the principle is benign in its impact, explains Yusuf al Qaradawy, because Western societies have developed two separate and independent sources of power, one to sustain religion in essentially private spheres and a second to empower the state to defend society's common interests. Christianity, adds Qaradawy, never developed an official code regulating various affairs in life. Therefore, secular laws do not offend Christians because they do not replace a regulatory code derived from their religion. Moreover, Christianity "as a religion is not undermined by the separation of state and religion because there exists a religious authority, protecting and supporting this religion with no interference with the state. In the Islamic state, on the other hand, the result would be a religion with no authority to back it or support it." Thus, the New Islamists consider a secular state to be in harmony with Christianity. It does not destroy the authority of Christianity but merely defines its sphere in relationship to the temporal authority. In sharp contrast, a secularism that entails the separation of religion and society "completely contradicts the nature of Islam and constitutes a direct threat to its comprehensive code of life."[82] In rejecting the principle of applying *Sharia,* such a secularism would deny the comprehensiveness of Islam. If acted on in an Islamic cultural context, such a principle of separation would be a subversive and potentially destructive one.[83]

The New Islamists, however, approach such extreme secularist views with the argument that even a viewpoint rejecting the implementation of *Sharia* can simply be ignored, provided those who hold it undertake no actions to rally support for their conception. When questions of extreme secularism do come to public attention, the New Islamists most often downplay the threat that even these extreme secularists represent, arguing that the nation has far more important dangers to confront. In contrast to their tempered reservations about extreme secularists, the New Islamists regard the issue of the full inclusion of moderate secularists as one that is worthy of immediate community attention. In their view, this inclusion is important in order to strengthen the nation.

Kamal Abul Magd notes that the heart of the secular position is the conviction that in a secular order, political power originates in the civil sphere rather than springing from religious or theocratic sources. Contrary to the widespread misconception, Abul Magd points out that Islam has no trouble accepting such a principle. In fact, Islam explicitly rejects the idea of a religious state and can easily embrace the idea of the democratic state that many secularists champion, at least in theory, despite their support for various forms of authoritarianism. Abul Magd writes without ambiguity that the notion of a democratic state, with power deriving from the consent of the governed, is fully compatible with the call for an Islamic system: "Out of my analysis of political power in an Islamic state, I have no reservation about this element of a 'secular' state and I do not believe it clashes with the call for Islam or for establishing an Islamic political system."[84]

Confusion sometimes arises because the term "secularism" in Arabic is derived from the same set of letters as "science," and some incorrectly assume that the contrast between secularism and religion or Islam indicates a clash between religion and science. According to Kamal Abul Magd, Islam knows no such conflict. On the contrary, Islam exhorts human beings to use fully the gift of the mind in all scientific pursuits. There are no barriers to the full inclusion of moderate secularists who embrace reason and science in the Islamic community.

For still others, "secularism" is taken to mean a commitment to the equal civil, legal, and political rights of all citizens, regardless of race, religion, or other such distinctions. They regard this commitment as a key component of the secular orientation and one of the primary goals of secular movements. With these issues in mind, some claim that to stand against secularism is to deny the Universal Declaration of Human Rights. Again, in forthright language, Abul Magd states that "the Islamic character of a state does not violate this equality." Although particular Islamic regimes, like non-democratic regimes of all stripes, may in fact violate such human and civic rights in practice, these negative practices cannot be ascribed to Islam.[85]

The New Islamists believe that moderate secularists and centrist Islamists share an impressive set of commitments that provide an ample basis, in theory at least, for mutual understanding and collaboration as rightful members of an Islamic community. They explicitly credit various secularist trends with the pursuit of positive values such as justice, freedom, and rationality within their own Egyptian or borrowed Western secularist frameworks. Such secularists are singled out for inclusion in the "creation of a 'coalition' intellectual school . . . in which followers join in spreading charity, righteousness, good, and justice among the people."[86] The New Islamists see no barriers, in theory, to cooperation with moderate Egyptian secularists on all such national projects for the common good.

At the same time, the New Islamists do recognize that this great potential for collaboration has, in too many instances, gone unrealized. The New Islamists stand firmly against those Islamist extremists who indiscriminately attack secular trends, and they regard the "rationalization" of the Islamic body, with the precise meaning of correcting such angry and isolationist impulses, as a major priority of their own work.[87] At the same time, the New Islamists express surprise and disappointment at the position of some secularists who resolutely refuse dialogue and cooperation with even the enlightened Islamic trend.[88] In response to the call for dialogue by the reformist Islamists, these secularists respond that Islamists differ only in the ways they present themselves or the means they adopt to accomplish ends that are in fact the same as those of the Islamic extremists. Secularists with such views "seem determined," writes Kamal Abul Magd, "to refer to the trend without differentiation, assigning to it a long list of negative traits such as stagnation, irrationality, intellectual repression, and psychological suppression, as well as denying all forms of democracy and tolerating aggression and practicing violence and coups in public work."[89] Abul Magd reports that others among the secularists avoid such irresponsible sloganeering. They even credit the idealism and good intentions of the moderate Islamists. In the end, however, they too often dismiss all elements of the Islamic trend for a different set of reasons. They question whether the centrist Islamists, whom they recognize as potential partners, speak for anyone other than themselves as isolated individuals. These critics also express doubts that the centrists will be able to stand up to the more aggressive and extremist radicals. Won't such moderate voices, they ask, simply be swept away by those demagogic and violent Islamist "fanatics who have mastered the arts of political 'action'"? The practical result of both sets of responses is the same: there is no need for dialogue with the enlightened Islamists because when the real confrontation comes they will either betray their idealistic words or simply be pushed aside.[90]

Despite these discouraging responses from secularist quarters, all the New Islamists adhere to the common position that dialogue among all the major currents is in the national interest.[91] For the New Islamists, however, the issue of secularism does raise the critical question of how that national interest is to be defined. Fahmy Huwaidy explains that society is not just borders, land, and people, but includes the culture that links all of these elements—that is, the spiritual, intellectual, moral, and material values of any specific society. The New Islamists believe that the integrity of these essential elements is an objective condition for the exercise of all social rights and freedoms. Consequently, societies have the right to circumscribe those freedoms when that integrity is threatened. An Islamic society, they argue, cannot allow extreme secularists to take action that undermines the core Islamic commitment to the principle of implementing *Sharia* on which Islamic public order rests. It does welcome those moderate secularists who have their own contributions to make to build a community with a civic rather than religious character, a democratic political order, and a broad commitment to the enlargement of the sphere in intellectual and social life of reason and all the sciences that make human advancement possible.[92]

The issues of women and non-Muslims in the Islamic community enter into the debate over the implementation of *Sharia* in equally important but quite different ways. With these two groups, the issue is not one of boundary maintenance, as with the secularists, but rather the determination of just what their respective roles will be in Islamic community. Debates over implementation of *Sharia* sharpen the fundamental differences that separate the views of the New Islamists from those of both traditionalists and extremists on the rights and obligations of women and non-Muslims in a community regulated by *Sharia.*

Sharia and the Rights of Women and Non-Muslims

In the New Islamist view, the proper implementation of *Sharia* would affirm the essential equality of men and women in human rights and spiritual worth, set forth in the Quran and elaborated in the *Sunnah.* The leading members of the school, however, are fully aware that all sorts of un-Islamic abuses of women are falsely justified by appeal to distorted conceptions of *Sharia,* especially on women's individual and family rights. They therefore extend their own work on clarifying the message of the Quran and *Sunnah* on the role of women by discrediting misapplications of *Sharia.* They do so frequently and vigorously as specific issues arise, notably questions of inheritance and legal testimony, women's right to unforced marriage and divorce, and female circumcision. In all of these controversial areas, the work of the New Islamists centers on a corrective *ijtihad* that takes aim at a flawed *fiqh* that has contributed, in particular, to the erosion of the personal rights of women.

Faced with periodic public controversies over the meaning of *Sharia* for non-Muslims, the New Islamists have always invoked the Quranic spirit of embrace of human equality and diversity. The tolerant principles advanced in the Quran and elaborated in *Sunnah,* explains Kamal Abul Magd, provide the essential source, while "everything else is open to question so that *Sharia* can respond to changing conditions."[93] The Quran makes choice rather than force the crucial element in religion and assigns rights to humankind without reference to the religious choices made. With these principles as their guiding light, the New Islamists faced the shortcomings of both tradition and extremism when dealing with Christians in the Islamic community. This inclusive stance guided New Islamist involvement in frequent and often heated public debates centered on the legal and civic rights of Copts under *Sharia.* Questions of the rights of non-Muslims had a heightened importance against the background of sectarian tensions and outbreaks of violence that plagued Egypt in the last quarter of the twentieth century and threatened national unity. In all such interventions, the New Islamists insisted on the need for a continuous *ijtihad* to translate the spirit of the Quran into more tolerant social realities.

The New Islamists, as their work on Islamic community makes clear, are no strangers to controversies. Some are of their own making. A strong sense of intellectual and moral responsibility compels them to speak plainly to all who share the obligation to build the just Islamic community. In defining Islamic community, they lean decisively in the direction of openness, pressing for recognition of the rightful place of women, non-Muslims, and moderate secularists. They are unfazed by the opposition such positions generate. They believe that these issues of inclusion, viewed by others as marginal, in fact define the essential character of *Wassatteyya*, the largest and most important of the trends that make up the Islamic Awakening. At the same time, the New Islamists understand that the important national role of the Awakening itself is not an exclusive or solitary one. Neither the Muslim nor Islam is, or should be, alone in the national community and the world. Muslims, though not Muslims alone, are enjoined to build the just community. They are called to cooperate with moderates of all kinds to make Egypt whole. The women of Egypt and the nation's Coptic citizens are singled out as complete and indispensable partners in that effort. It will embrace as well moderate secularists, who are at times unfairly constrained or unnecessarily excluded. Even extreme secularists are welcome participants in those projects based on values they do share with the mainstream. This community building is seen by the New Islamists as only part of a still larger task to which Islam calls them. All of humankind—not just Muslims, Christians, or Egyptians—has the shared responsibility to build the world and work together to accomplish God's purposes on Earth. As public intellectuals and not policymakers, the New Islamists do not have a foreign policy. What they do have, as will be seen in the book's final chapter, is a clear sense of how Egyptians should engage the world and fulfill their responsibility to make a contribution to its betterment. These larger commitments are mentioned here because they serve to reinforce the logic of inclusion that animates their vision of a just community in Egypt.

This generous and ambitious spirit does have limits, however. Addressing the Islamic community, the nation, and the world, the New Islamists did not hesitate at Ain Shams to condemn armed and angry militants who cloaked themselves in Islamic justifications. There is no place for the violent extremist in the Islamic community they envision. Nor, as

Islamist intellectuals, can they condone the efforts of secular extremists to act on views that would undermine Islamic communal foundations. Just as decisively, as the last decade of the century drew to a close, Fahmy Huwaidy spoke for the school in denouncing the new threat emerging from within the Islamic wave. The New Islamists immediately saw the larger danger that lay behind the small instances of a self-absorbed religiosity that crowded out all sense of caring for the social whole. The egoist in pursuit of personal salvation also posed a threat to weaken the just Islamic community and the better world it promises. Huwaidy took the lead in launching a full-blown campaign against the new pietists before they overwhelmed centrist Islam.

In early 1999, Huwaidy deliberately provoked an uproar with his campaign in *al Ahram* to denounce the insidious threat of the "darawish."[94] A journalist as gifted as Huwaidy clearly understood the sarcastic connotations of a term used in the vernacular to describe those who have lost their minds through absorption in an imaginary world of their own making. Huwaidy had in fact found just the right term to pierce the unbearable sanctimoniousness of the hyper-religious, whose selfishness masquerades as Islam. "I have come to fear for the *umra*," announced Huwaidy, "at the hands of religious people." With these words, Huwaidy opened his blistering attack. Taking on a subject that a less confident figure would not dare touch, Huwaidy registered sharp disapproval of the growing practice of complementing the duty of *hajj* with the performance of innumerable *umra* [pilgrimages], often during the month of Ramadan. He expressed his "distress" at reports of planes chartered to carry hundreds of Egyptians to Mecca, noting that the number of pilgrims in Mecca especially during Ramadan was rapidly approaching those during *hajj*. With many planning to stay for as long as three months and coming from all parts of the Islamic world, Huwaidy wondered how any Islamic society would advance even one step forward if resources were diverted to such uses. Clearly, he acknowledged, expressions of religious attachment should be welcomed. But is this kind of personal excess really Islam? He reminded his readers that Islam emphasizes the social responsibilities of members of the community, and indicated that a just society would not countenance exaggerated attention to superogatory religious forms and practices when the basic needs of the people and the nation went unmet. The "darawish," he complained, had reduced the idea of worship and doing good to narrow rituals and traditional religious practices that they carried to an extreme in the hopes of winning greater rewards. "In doing so," wrote Huwaidy, "they are striving for their own salvation as individuals and ignoring the society around them. This causes a kind of unintended selfishness in their religiousness.

The main core becomes 'I' and there is no place for anyone else." Huwaidy decried this distortion of the priorities that Islam establishes: "This notion of employing worship and good deeds for one's own salvation contradicts Islam. *Istikhlaf* [Man's calling to act as God's regent on Earth] gives humankind the responsibility to build the Earth and to improve its societies. So the one who does service to others is considered the best."

The letters of protest poured in, as Huwaidy surely knew they would. He dubbed the angry reaction the "revolt of the darawish," who protested his attack on their kingdom. Isn't what you're criticizing better than terrorism? asked one reader. Another wondered why Huwaidy focused on the use of resources for multiple *umra* instead of attacking rampant corruption. Why have you joined those who seek to put out God's light with your pen? When we neglect our religion, you complain. When we express it, you attack us. What do you want from us?[95]

Huwaidy was ready with a compelling response that clarified the New Islamist view of the needs of community building. There are those, Huwaidy began, who seek to meet Egypt's challenge of developing and finding the community's place in the modern world by setting religion aside. There are others who drain Islam of its essential commitment to justice on earth, shared by all the world's great religions. Huwaidy argued strongly that either course for Egyptians would mean depriving themselves of their greatest resource, the culture and civilization inspired by their religious traditions that provide the bedrock of their identity and the source of their creativity. What is needed, wrote Huwaidy, was civilizational religion that was "committed to fundamental teachings and core values and always aware of larger purposes. It is that religion that links faith, sound behavior, and good deeds." "I would not be exaggerating," he continued, "to say that the renaissance of the nation depends on this kind of religiousness that I would hope the faithful of all religions, notably Muslims and Christians, would adopt." Huwaidy concluded that this challenge of restoring civilizational religion "should be at the top of the agenda of all patriotic intellectuals. I may take the risk and say that this task is in the foreseeable future the 'mother of all questions and issues.'"[96]

Huwaidy clarified the relationship of civilizational religion and the task of building community by contrasting it to the distorted religious ideas of violent militants, on the one hand, and self-absorbed pietists, on the other. Huwaidy recognized the militants' aim to change society but pronounced it wrongheaded and dangerous. "Their major mistake," he explained, "is to start by putting society on trial and convicting it in advance. Their relationship with the society is thus one of tension and clash, expressed in violence and *takfir*." Huwaidy warned that although the violence has been repressed, its causes have "not been fully studied nor treated at all." This limitation means that "the security achievement has been accompanied by a political and cultural failure. It is true we're talking here about an exceptional small sector, but it is also true that it is very active and has a loud voice. Being small should not lead us ignore it. All fire comes from small flames."[97]

In the first years of the new century, the more visible and perhaps even the greater threat has come from the distorted thinking and behavior of the darawish, Huwaidy added. They have no interest in society. They also separate ethics from practical dealings. Public duties have no room in their perception of religion. Huwaidy finds an example of the darawish in the public figure who will "pay hundreds of thousands to build a mosque bearing his name but not a school, clinic or factory." He sees them in the ordinary people who "give all attention to appearance, pray at the appointed times but do not go to work on time and do not perfect the work they are supposed to be doing. Some of them never stop mumbling verses aloud, although they don't mind insulting people or taking their money unfairly." Huwaidy says that, unfortunately, this form of religiousness has gained the widest number of adherents. It is characterized by an intellectual and social laziness; its followers neither think for themselves nor engage the world in creative ways. Huwaidy elaborates that "by the 'darawish' I mean the wide strata of people who perform what can be called the 'popular religiousness' in the sense of inheriting it, following what they have heard, never getting involved in a party or association. Most probably, they are not interested in politics. Their sole aim is to clear their personal accounts before God and live a quiet life." Huwaidy condemns such beliefs as "safe and easy faith or religion for free." Religion understood in this way, he concludes, "can be practiced without burdens. Most regrettably, it deprives society of the energy of its followers. I do not hesitate to say that this form of religiousness represents wasted energy."[98]

Not surprisingly, Huwaidy turned for support to the late Muhammad al Ghazzaly and Yusuf al Qaradawy to elaborate this centrist position that so harshly condemned not only the violence of the militants but the equally dangerous social passivity and misplaced emphases of the pietists. Ghazzaly had seen the darawish coming. Qaradawy, too, had early on warned against their misplaced priorities. Both recognized and stressed the distorted thinking at the root of these deviations from the Islam of the *Wassatteyya.* Ghazzaly was impatient with those who identified the impact of the powerful West as the only cause for the backwardness of the Islamic world. Decline had its internal causes as well, he insisted. Above all, Ghazzaly pointed to the intellectual failings that characterized the Islamic world. "Religion," he wrote, "had become dead traditions and practices full of myth and heresies." Muslims had withdrawn from the economic, political, and social fields. This overall decline "came foremost out of the death of the mind. Faith becomes an inheritance of traditions with no thought."[99]

Thus Huwaidy was supported by Ghazzaly's words and writing in his own efforts to face the darawish. "Shaikh Ghazzaly devoted the writings of the last ten years of his life," explained Huwaidy, "to the *tarshid* of the Muslim mind and the refreshing of the nation's consciousness." He did so, Huwaidy might have added, with those striking phrases and imagery that brought his thinking to life for the general public. "Religious thought," declared Ghazzaly, "is getting fat and has started to have a belly full of trivial, useless issues. This thought will never regain health until it gets rid of the 'fat' and the 'belly' and Muslims begin again to concern themselves with the critical sciences of life and rescue their religion from embarrassment." Ghazzaly could not bear "this miserable separation of religion from life, so contrary to Islam." He derided those who focused on such trivial yet dangerous issues as dress or the proper form of greetings, noting that these preoccupations all too often turned into attacks on the most vulnerable members of society. Ghazzaly would have none of an Islam that focused on the details of rituals and secondary issues of behavior while "ignoring its realistic and practical side."[100]

Huwaidy perfectly captured the thrust of this New Islamist message when he boldly reminded readers that "in the Quran, there are several verses that start with the expression 'they ask you about.'" He cites the examples "they ask you about doomsday, they ask you about gambling and wine, they ask you about the soul." Huwaidy decried the fact that those who speak in Islam's name and raise its banner have all too often failed to move beyond these inherited questions. They have failed, that is, to address the pressing social questions of their own time. "It is striking," writes Huwaidy, "that the majority of religious minds remain preoccupied with these same questions and never move on to contemporary issues." He comments that "if I were to adopt the Quranic style, I'd say: They ask you about democracy, accountability, human rights, and economic development . . ."[101]

In the chapters to come on economics, politics, and foreign policy, we will see in more detail how the New Islamists have provided guidance on how best to address precisely those pressing issues that the violent extremists approach only in dangerous ways and the quietists simply ignore.

chapter 4

Creating an Economic System

"The twenty-year experiment of Islamic banks," reports Fahmy Huwaidy in a celebratory article in *al Ahram* in the winter of 1995, "is a promising though unfairly treated one."[1] The sting of unfairness originates in the dismissive treatment of Islamic economics by influential Egyptian secular critics who regard the very idea as a "backward legend" unsuited to the modern world.[2] The sense of promise stems from the impressive record of this experiment in Islamic economics by more than fifty Islamic banks that made a mark in the world of international finance. Prompted by the Quranic prohibition of *riba* [usury], the Islamic bank is based on the concept of "an investing bank that shares in the profit and loss" of the commercial or productive activity it finances.[3] By rethinking accepted banking methods and inventing new forms of financial action in the light of the injunctions of the faith, the Islamic banks, in Huwaidy's view, take "bold steps that make them an influential reality that cannot be denied." This practical experience, according to Huwaidy, significantly enriches the *fiqh* [understanding derived from the Quran and *Sunnah*] of Islamic economics as it struggles to respond to the dominance of the global market economy in ways that answer the demands of a higher moral order.

New Islamist thinking in all economic matters is premised on the view that man in his worldly activities must act as God's regent to serve His purposes on Earth. One important implication of this concept of *istikhlaf* is that money is a sacred trust, rather than simply a commodity. Financial resources and institutions should serve Islam's purposes of creating a just human order, rather than simply accruing profit as an end in itself.[4] The idea that Islam speaks a moral language responsive to the needs of the age has elicited an appreciative response in world financial circles. Sophisticated financiers have noted that attentive groups are emerging around the world that, while recognizing the market as the driving force of any economy, seek to place it within a moral and ethical framework. Generally, the aim of all such reformers is to protect the weak and restrain the excesses of the strong on both international and national levels. In the post-Soviet and post-Marxist world, groups in the West identified with the left are attempting to formulate a socialist alternative to the politics of acquisitive individualism and unrestrained market forces. Others aim more modestly to build safety nets and retraining programs to assist the most vulnerable citizens in the effective adjustment to market forces. All such efforts seek to maintain some notion of human community with responsibilities to preserve human dignity. The possibilities for sharing these sentiments and the instructive social experiments they generate have grown. As Kamal Abul Magd puts it, "The world is now at our fingertips, especially with satellites, television, video, media networks, and research centers, and I can tell you there is a reaction against the materialism resulting from economic systems based on consumerism. It has taken the form of a trend of religiousness spreading around the globe."[5] New Islamist theorists such as Abul Magd and Yusuf al Qaradawy refer to the example of the Islamic banks when they confidently assert the heightened global relevance of the Islamic message at a time when, in their view, the world's dominant societies have lost their sense of moral purpose to unreflective consumerism.

Huwaidy takes particular pleasure in the fact that a survey of the global reach of Islam in the British *Economist,* the Western journal of preference for Egypt's secular economists, singles out international banking as an area where "Islam may have something distinctively useful to offer."[6] A conference on "Islamic Banking and the International Media," held in Dubai in December 1994, brought this novel notion of banking to the world's attention, though the first such bank had been established as early as 1975. Discussion at the two-day conference, attended by representatives of the major international banks, focused on the elaboration of economic principles inspired by Islam and also evaluated the actual performance of Islamic banks. The conference brought the positive record of bank achievements to the attention of the international media. By the mid-1990s, more than fifty Islamic banks were flourishing in Arab countries from North Africa to the Gulf, in Pakistan, Turkey, Iran, Malaysia, and Indonesia, and as far afield as South Africa. These banks, Huwaidy reports enthusiastically, enjoy substantial financial weight, which, in turn, is bringing them respectful international attention. Estimates of their holdings reach 60 billion dollars, while the total amount of deposits around the world is believed to be 120 billion dollars as of the mid-1990s. Moreover, these figures represent only about 15 percent of all bank deposits by Muslims worldwide. Islamic banks hope to attract at least 50 percent of that total sum in the first decades of the twenty-first century. The success of the banks thus far and their aggressive plans for expansion have prompted the international financial community, dominated by Western institutions, to move into the Islamic banking arena. Both CitiBank and J. P. Morgan have opened Islamic banks in the Gulf, indicating that the practice of Islamic banking has now found a secure place on the agenda of international financial institutions.

At the Dubai conference, some Islamic banks expressed misgivings about the competitive entry of Western banks into the Islamic field, fearing their larger capacities and longer international experience. Others, with the New Islamists supporting this stance, welcomed the challenge and the impetus it would give to improve performance and invent new services and tools. Despite the danger that the funds currently held in the Islamic banks might be drawn away from the Islamic world, Huwaidy explains that Islamic banks are not goals in themselves. Rather, they should be understood as means to use and develop new Islamic methods in finance and economic dealings. "If others accept such concepts (like ruling out *riba* and adopting notions of sharing both loss and profit), this would mean the success of these Islamic ideas and their globalization."[7]

Egyptian secular critics traditionally regard arguments of Islam's relevance in the economic realm as impractical at best and dangerous at worst.[8] They miss the fact that Islamic theorists and bankers have devised a number of inventive ways of coping with the problems that "interest" raises, their energies and creativity fueled by the very lack of a clear consensus on the issue among religious scholars. All Islamic thinkers agree that *riba* is prohibited; the disagreements center on whether or not modern-day bank interest constitutes *riba*.[9] Theorists who do extend the Quranic prohibition to bank interest are working with bankers to develop new interest-free practices. Their efforts take two general forms, either a trade or a production orientation. Both are understood to extend the concept of the bank from just a financial agent to an investment partner in either commercial or production activities with those to whom funds are advanced. This understanding of a bank as an agent in the commercial or production process rather than simply a provider of capital has caught the eye of foreigners for some of the distinctive advantages it brings. The idea of the "investing bank" gives the depositor a good incentive to guarantee that loans go to something useful. ("What a pity," the *Economist* notes sardonically in its report, "that the West's banks did not have that incentive in so many of their lending decisions in the 1970s and 1980s.")[10] In addition, the notion of partnership stresses the sharing of responsibility among all those who use the money, thus making the free market more open and possibly even more democratic. According to the *Economist,* these prospects explain why the economics of Islam does not deserve "the usually rather ignorant sneer" it gets from critics.[11] "Why," asks Fahmy Huwaidy, "do we only appreciate our successes when they begin to attract attention abroad?"[12]

Taking the measure of the Islamic economics involves, according to the New Islamists, a clear understanding that Islam requires that economic activity serve the higher purposes and reflect the core values of Islam, notably human dignity and justice. This view, however, should not be mistaken for the judgment of some Islamists that the dilemmas of Egyptian society stem essentially from a crisis of morality. In sharp contrast, the New Islamists view Egypt's crisis from a multifaceted perspective that searches for causes as much in the material sphere as in the realm of values. In blunt language, the New Islamists caution Islamist activists against narrow moralistic thinking. Such an approach leads to the mistaken view that the articulation of Islamic ideals could substitute for a realistic assessment of economic conditions and practical efforts to resolve problems. The New Islamist manifesto states that "it is unacceptable scientifically to describe the crisis of contemporary Muslim societies as simply a problem of morals and values, ignoring with this naive and one-dimensional view the multiple, complex, and interrelated problems of contemporary society." Clearly directing a warning to the impatient adherents of political Islam, they pronounce: "Those who rise to transform their society guided by such primitive thinking engage in a terrifying adventure." Instead, "Responsible reformers should exert more effort in understanding problems and recognizing their dimensions."[13]

In the late modern world, more than ever, those "dimensions" require analysis on a global rather than a national level. In broad strokes that draw on a cosmopolitan *fiqh* of reality, the New Islamists describe the global forces that have shaped problems at home and necessitated new thinking. They observe that the earlier scientific and industrial revolutions were followed by revolutionary developments in production, transportation, and communication, notably in the technology of storage, transfer, and use of information. All of these changes, in their view, have created new problems and given old ones new dimensions. More specifically, Islamist reformers must address not only the long-standing imperative of development but also social dilemmas such as the growing gap between rich and poor, as well as environmental damage that now appears to have global dimensions. Until Islamic reform movements address these and related contemporary economic issues, they will remain isolated from their societies, which will be hesitant to follow their lead and take their slogans seriously.[14] The New Islamists believe that Islamic societies can borrow from the knowledge and experience of others in meeting these challenges. However, they must do so in ways consistent with the values and purposes of Islam.

An Enabling Moral Framework for Economic Activity

The human economic activities of production, distribution, and consumption, according to the New Islamists, lie fully within the scope of Islam. Islam refuses any polarity between man as a moral being who responds to higher purposes and man as a physical creature with material wants and needs that must be met. God created man with both sets of characteristics, and they are an integrated part of the human nature that God intended for man. This essential character defines human beings everywhere, despite all their surface diversity. Transcendence of difference flows from the act of creation. God created all men and women from his spirit, making them brothers and sisters whatever their nationality, religion, or gender. Moreover, he created man as his regent on Earth, charged with building the Earth according to His will. This notion of *istikhlaf* means that all human beings, and not just Arabs or Muslims, have rights to dignity and justice. Human beings have an obligation to God that goes beyond simply living and enjoying the things of this world. They are to live in accord with the higher purpose that God intended for them, and they have the obligation to secure the conditions necessary to do so.

Istikhlaf thus means that the fundamental rights of all human beings, regardless of religion, nationality, or gender, are at the same time duties owed to God. Huwaidy writes that securing these rights, at once the rights of man and of God, are "the aim of *Sharia*." They range from the spiritual to the material. *Sharia* thus entails preserving "soul, mind, religion, honor, and money." Violating any of these human rights is also a violation of God's rights and a transgression against *Sharia*. In Islam, respect for human rights is thus a religious duty.[15]

God did not create man and subordinate all the other creatures of the Earth to him without a purpose. "The purpose," Huwaidy explains, "is to empower man to build and grow." He makes the critical point that "in Quran, the link between the creation and construction on Earth is very clear." Building the Earth is thus one of the purposes of *Sharia*. "Since progress is important for construction," argues Huwaidy, "the neglect of progress is an aggression against God's rights and constitutes a failure to fulfill one of the purposes of *Sharia*. All transgressions of man's rights to live in dignity and justice in accord with the nature God has given him are a violation of God's rights."[16]

In the light of this fuller understanding of *istikhlaf* as provided by the Quran, the importance of the banking experiment becomes clearer. Islamic economics should not be reduced to banking. However, the understanding that money belongs to God and that people act merely as its guardians lies behind the notion of the "investing bank." People do not "own" capital; they only have the right to invest it as they perform their role as God's regent on Earth. Because it is God's money, the nation has rights to it, as do the poor and the weak. Money, by these lights, must be used for productive and humane purposes. Islamic banking thus exemplifies how the abstract notion of God's rights can be translated into concrete practices. Economic activities seen in this light are an important dimension of a comprehensive civilizational project that aims to develop the nation based on the values of Islam. Justice is at the very core of these values, as revealed in the Quran. Moreover, the project is inclusive for, as Huwaidy stresses, the Quranic notion of *istikhlaf* is not addressed to Muslims alone but rather to all members of the human community.[17]

Among the New Islamists, Yusuf al Qaradawy has taken a leadership role in elaborating this Islamic civilizational framework for economics, although all of the major figures have made important contributions to this intellectual effort. Qaradawy's substantial body of work on the economy can be read as an elaboration of the meaning of Islam for economics. The framework is put forward to inspire and guide economic activity as well as to provide a standard to measure its achievements.

Taking the foundational concept of *istikhlaf* as his starting point, Qaradawy maps the divine dimension of the Islamic economy. He states that in an Islamic order "economic relations should be established and assessed according to their capacity to enhance the human relationship to divine purpose." At times, that connection to God's purpose is spelled out in specific injunctions or prohibitions that cannot be ignored or violated, such as *zakat* [obligatory alms] as part of worship and the prohibition of *riba* [usury] in financial exchanges. More frequently, man's link to the divine purpose flows in a less directive way from the status that God has uniquely conferred on him. While other systems of thought may "make bread their goal and give the economy the highest priority, an Islamic one will give importance to these things only as a means. The main goal remains the enhancement of man and his rescue from the injustice of materialism by lifting his moral and spiritual being."[18]

Given that economic activities should express the human relationship to God, Qaradawy explains that the Islamic economy should also be ethical, human, and balanced. Man, created by God to fulfill a certain role on Earth, cannot proceed in an unethical way in the material dimensions of life. This idea of divinely sanctioned limits and responsibilities is captured in the notion of God's rights, which refers to the claims God has on human beings that flow from their preferred status among His living creations. They are charged to play a higher role, and there can be no abridgment of the dignity implicit in this role, either by themselves or by others. Human desires, or even needs alone, cannot drive economic activity. For example, there are certain fundamental interests and rights of humankind, notably justice, that cannot be abrogated by either the market or politics because they are in fact derived from God's rights. Qaradawy explicitly rejects any notion of an "economic man" who is impelled by interest and profit alone to do whatever he likes: "No, he is restricted by belief and ethics."[19] In the same way, the economic system of "production, distribution, and consumption must respect these same core Islamic values and purposes."[20] For Qaradawy, there can be no conflict between these divine and ethical dimensions of an Islamic economic system and its human quality, since both rest on the premise of the inherent worth of man as the successor of God on Earth. Economic activities, conducted accorded to these ethical standards, should necessarily serve human needs. Basic needs to assure human survival in dignity come first. However, Islam does not seek to deny humankind the permissible pleasures that life on Earth can bring, provided they are pursued without excess. Qaradawy comments on the allowable enjoyment of good housing and clothing, as well as comfortable transportation. Arguing against the dour prohibitions of "angry" Islam, he explicitly mentions the need to cultivate a sense of beauty and appreciation for the arts.[21] Finally, Qaradawy explains that the Islamic economy could best achieve these ethical and human ends with economic arrangements that avoid extremes. Balance might mean avoidance of the exaggeration of the rights of the individual, as capitalism encourages, or those of society, as socialism does. Balance also cautions against excesses of personal piety when they come at the expense of meeting the social responsibilities that Islam enjoins.

This concept of the Islamic moral framework has more than abstract interest for the New Islamists. The framework, whether implicitly or explicitly invoked, gives overall coherence to their practical interventions on economic matters. It enables them to judge which issues merit activist attention, without the need for a rigid Islamic model of the economy. What is important to the New Islamists are the moral purposes realized in the divine, moral, ethical, human, and balanced dimensions of economic activity, rather than the specific institutions or processes through which they are realized. This comprehensive though flexible framework can be used effectively to evaluate behavior within *any* macroeconomic system, whether capitalist, socialist, or some combination of the two.

New Islamist understanding of the divine dimension of economic activity, for example, provides the point of entry into controversies that center on the obligations that possession of money or capital entails. The New Islamists view the debates on *zakat* from this perspective. Qaradawy explains that money comes suffused with moral obligations that it be spent "as God says, for the public good, assisting the poor and weak so that God's money is spent on God's creatures."[22] The New Islamists make *zakat* an issue in Egypt first because many Muslims regularly fail to pay the *zakat,* and second because those who do not pay often justify their lapse by arguing that the taxes they pay to the state fulfill this obligation. Others make the reverse case that, having paid *zakat,* they can justifiably evade state taxes. The New Islamists deplore such laxity in meeting the obligations of *zakat.*[23] They assume in their own work that all Muslims must honor their religious obligations that place *zakat* alongside the profession of faith, prayer, fasting during Ramadan, and pilgrimage as essentials of the faith.

The same attention to both personal and collective responsibility marks the New Islamist understanding of the ethical dimension of the economy in an Islamic order. They exhort Muslims to adhere to ethical standards not only in their own everyday dealings but also in those circumstances when society and the state have failed to protect the vulnerable. Qaradawy explains that "the Muslim when he buys and sells, borrows and lends, or deals in other ways with money is constrained by the provisions of God, i.e., not to profit from things God forbids, not to exploit through monopoly, not to lie or steal, and not to accept or give bribes."[24] However, in Islam religion regulates more than man's individual behavior and his personal relationship to God. Islam extends its set of values to all human interactions. This means that the salvation of individuals must be followed by the salvation of society. The injunction to "advance the good and stop the evil," according to Qaradawy, is a manifestation of Islam's rejection of "any isolation of the individual from the larger society."[25]

Fahmy Huwaidy makes this essential point of the overriding importance of social responsibility with a story of one of the great Imams of the first centuries of Islam. Huwaidy reports that the Imam customarily performed the *hajj* [pilgrimage to Mecca] each year, regularly entrusting his assistant with a sum of money for that purpose. About to leave the city with the convoy of pilgrims, he came across a little girl searching through the city garbage site. He stopped and asked her who she was and what she was doing. The child answered that she was an orphan, looking for something to eat. The Imam turned to his assistant and instructed him to give the girl all the money entrusted to him, saying simply, "this is our *hajj* for this year."[26]

This imperative to respond to human needs, as the story of the Imam makes clear, relies on human ingenuity, prompted by an Islamic sense of moral responsibility to right injustices. The creation of an economic system that achieves dignity and justice is a demanding human task for which God has not provided a direct or detailed blueprint. In particular, the New Islamists resist the simplistic idea that obedience to the very few explicit economic injunctions in the texts makes an economic system Islamic. Such a conception, in their view, is far too narrow. Of course, specific provisions of the Quran, such as the prohibition of *riba* and the obligatory payment of *zakat,* do have economic implications and must be honored. However, the prohibition of *riba* and the payment of the *zakat* constitute necessary but not sufficient causes to accept a given system as Islamic. It is easy enough to imagine a context where *riba* is banned and *zakat* is paid, yet basic human needs remain unmet. In the same spirit, the New Islamists reject the claims of some within the Islamic wave who seek to sanctify for all ages the economic practices and institutions of the formative early years of Islam under which these obligations were met. Neither text nor historical model alone, in their view, is sufficient to identify an economic order as Islamic. The full elaboration of an Islamic economic system is one of those areas left by God to the creativity of each generation, requiring that they seek inspiration for their efforts in the purposes and values of Islam, which set standards that go beyond any specific injunctions.

These higher-level Islamic values and purposes center on meeting basic human needs within the context of a community rather than expressing individual piety. Muhammad al Ghazzaly has most eloquently asserted this priority of creating a humane community before addressing individual spiritual preoccupations. Islam does not glorify poverty. Poverty and its sufferings in this world earn no reward for the hereafter. On the contrary, filling empty stomachs and allaying human fears for physical survival constitutes the first task in a just Islamic order. The God of the Quran fully understands basic human needs and the imperative to meet them. Ghazzaly derides the very idea of calling people to Islam or preaching ideas of religious reform without first addressing their physical needs. In his view, reform of material conditions stands as a precondition for the development of religious faith, not the other way around. Ghazzaly reminds his followers that the consensus of scholars finds that prayer arising out of hunger or fear is not prayer at all. Poverty and fear cannot be the gateway to Islam. Furthermore, he explains that all Muslims have an interest in overcoming these plagues of the human condition because, in order to be Muslims, they must have the company of their fellow human beings. Both Qaradawy and Ghazzaly stress in all their writings that an individual cannot be a Muslim alone, but only as part of the community of believers. Islam makes inclusion not simply a gesture of goodness but a requirement of the faith. Every Muslim has a responsibility for every other Muslim, especially for those who suffer deprivations. In Islam, the profession of faith, prayer, fasting, *hajj*, and alms giving, that is, each of the pillars of what it means to be a Muslim, has a collective dimension. *Zakat* and *hajj* are directly linked to society, since *zakat* expressly aims to help the weaker members of the community and *hajj* carries the obligation, however frequently ignored, that the assembled believers discuss the affairs of the Islamic community. Thus, two of the five pillars cannot be done alone. Fasting during Ramadan has its full significance as a communal experience of shared discipline and reflection on the meaning of the faith. There is also a clear preference that prayer, the fourth pillar, be performed in groups, a preference which becomes obligatory for the important Friday prayers. Finally, the profession of faith defines not only the individual's submission to God's message but also entrance into the community of Muslims. Thus, in its core devotional acts Islam places a distinctive stress on community.[27] For just this reason, Ghazzaly suggested, God kept the requirements of formal religious observance to a minimum so that there would be ample time for the myriad obligations to the community.[28]

Despite the sense of urgency prompted by the multiple failings of the economic system, when measured by the standard of its impact on Egypt's most vulnerable citizens, the New Islamists never lost their sense of balance and proportion when calling for reform, arguing consistently for gradualism. They were guided by more than personal moderation. As their manifesto explained, they believed that the radical shifts in orientation from Egyptian versions of capitalism to socialism and then back again did terrible harm to the economy. For much the same reason, they cautioned against those within the Islamic wave who looked to Islam to inspire a radical new turn in the economy. In economic matters, as in all key elements of the social change they envision, the New Islamists urged carefully paced change that avoided all extremes.

In their manifesto the New Islamists argued for a pragmatic and non-ideological stance to guide any economic reforms. They judged unacceptable any inclination to neglect promising ideas for reform, simply because they came from the non-Islamic world or from an orientation currently out of fashion in Egypt. They took the measure of socialist and capitalist ideologies and warned against extreme versions of either: they rejected the inclination of extreme capitalism to sacrifice the public good for the sake of exaggerated individual rights, and they took radical socialism to task for completely abandoning individual rights. Capitalism in its excessive forms, the New Islamists argued, can lead to an abandonment of standards of social justice, while socialism risks sacrificing freedom for the promise of material prosperity. Guided by moderate Islamic values, they maintained that both freedom and justice should be part of the goals for developing the economy.[29]

Later, when the effects of the worldwide religious revival registered their impact in Egypt, the New Islamists took the lead in warning against yet another form of excess. They stood firmly against excesses of Islamic personal piety at the expense of the social concerns that a strong economy should serve. While celebrating the new signs of religious engagement as a source of great hope in an otherwise bleak landscape, they also cautioned believers not to abandon the strong commitment to a productive and just community that lay at the heart of Islam.

Fahmy Huwaidy, as we saw in the previous chapter, took the lead in standing against the "darawish" whose excesses of pietistic zeal sharply diminished their capacity to fulfill their broader Islamic obligations to the welfare of their communities and their fellow citizens. Huwaidy made the case against the "darawish" with a personal story of his own small village in Manufeyya where villagers organized *umra* trips to Mecca during Ramadan. The *umra* [recommended but not prescribed pilgrimage to Mecca at times other than the *hajj*], while commendable as a sign of religious devotion, does not have an obligatory status in Islam. Huwaidy recounted how the villagers would rent a van for the first leg of their journey and would move slowly through village streets that were barely passable and overrun with sewerage. He commented that the villagers, although well-intentioned, never made any connection between resources spent on the *umra* and the neglect of basic sanitary conditions in the village. "No one thought," wrote Huwaidy, "that if the villagers joined forces and fixed the sewers in the village, they would come closer to God. Such an act would better serve God's rights than the *umra*."[30] In conclusion, Huwaidy went even further and argued that "the urgent duty of ameliorating the mud and dirt of the village" should take precedence over even the *hajj*, which after all was obligatory only if financial and other conditions allowed.

The New Islamists never confused the moral framework that allowed them to make such a distinction with the framework of a unitary and rigid Islamic economic theory or model. They never lost sight of the fact that these normative categories, even when fully elaborated, were not the same thing as the kind of "detailed system in this field" that a theory or model would provide.[31] Moreover, they believed that striving to create any fixed

Islamic system would be a misplaced effort, given Islam's worldwide commitment to address human needs in all times. No one set of institutions and processes could possibly suit the vast variety of conditions under which Muslims must tackle their responsibilities in the economic realm.

Not all Islamists agreed, of course. From within the Islamic wave came those impatient revolutionaries who made the simplistic assumption that Islam contained a full-blown economic theory that had only to be implemented once power was seized. More often than not, closer examination revealed no thought deeper than textualist ideas that the prohibition of *riba,* identified with modern bank interest, and provision for the payment of *zakat* rendered an economy "Islamic." At times, these slender textual sources were supplemented with historical references to such economic institutions as the *waqf* [Islamic endowment] to deepen the impression of a comprehensive Islamic economic theory. Such thinking in the camp of political Islam found reinforcement from the examples of so-called Islamic regimes that noisily defined their economies in just these ways. The New Islamists demurred. Although the Quran and *Sunnah* do provide provisions on *riba* and *zakat,* and the historical experience of Muslims has yielded institutions like the *waqf,* these two Quranic concepts in the New Islamists' view referred to sharply limited fields. Even the addition of economic fragments from the past, no matter how inventive for their times, produced at best an amalgam of circumscribed textual provisions and decontextualized historical remnants that fell far short of a general Islamic theory or model for the economy.

Experiments in the Economic Field

Given their conclusion that no fixed model for the Islamic economy existed or was even desirable, the New Islamists argued that building an economy in particular circumstances necessarily involved experimentation. It meant taking risks and getting one's hands dirty, grappling with real problems and searching for practical ways to resolve them. Egyptian Islamists rose to the challenge to innovate, as even their harshest critics acknowledged, often finding the most promising spaces for new initiatives in civil society. Their efforts did not go unnoticed. Perhaps not completely innocently, secular critics pointed to the extraordinary variety of initiatives, very often in the economic realm, that Islamist activists launched. Abdul Moneim Said, Director of the al Ahram Center for Political and Strategic Studies, commented that "while others talk about civil society, the Islamists go about creating one, including economic institutions. They establish their companies and banks, they play an influential role in professional syndicates, and they build such social institutions as schools, hospitals, and even hotels." Said concluded, "The Islamic trend is not satisfied with demanding a civil society as the leftists do nor just calling for it like the liberals. They go about building it in their distinctive ways."[32] Saad Eddine Ibrahim, head of the Ibn Khaldun Center, made the implicit warning embedded in this complimentary assessment explicit, stating that "the real political parties in Egypt" were the banks and companies that were creating an independent source of social power for the Islamists.[33]

The New Islamists themselves never indulged in such exaggerated claims for the social and potential political power of Islamic institutions. Nor did they accept the unstated assumption that the variety of initiatives had a coordinated and intentional character. In particular, they objected to the notion that the social experimentation of the Islamist activists aimed in some monolithic way to establish subversive Islamist cells as the nuclei of an alternative society. True, some extremist adherents of political Islam did indeed dream of building strength for a seizure of power. The New Islamists, however, actively opposed those aspirations of a minority. They spoke in the voice of the *Wassatteyya,* articulating quite different goals of open and democratic transformation.

The New Islamists understood that initiatives in the economic realm emerged spontaneously out of the Islamic wave and were beyond the control of any organized force or movement. Precisely for that reason, they directed their own attention to critiques of shortcomings and guidance for their correction. New Islamist support for reforms did not mean automatic approval of the results of all such efforts. What counted were positive results that advanced the interests of the community, in line with Islam's moral vision. In the case of corrupt financial investment companies, they recognized that, as the manifesto had warned, opportunists and undesirables of all kinds exploit Islamic symbols and damage the community. In contrast, they aggressively defended the Islamic banks for their constructive and innovative contributions.

It was the investment companies that dominated national attention in the late 1980s. The corruption story of the financial investment companies took on the dimensions of a national tragedy when investigations revealed that an estimated one-half million investors were involved, with capital losses estimated as high as 8 billion Egyptian pounds. No one told the tale in more affecting human terms than the highly respected columnist for *al Ahram,* the late Ahmed Bahaeddine. Concluding his series on the toll taken by this massive fraud, Bahaeddine described his own personal trauma as he became aware of the full extent of the destruction of lives that the fraudulent schemes had caused. "When writing this series," he reported of his running account of the tragedy in his *al Ahram* column at the end of the 1980s, "my day always ended with nerves racked by the unbearable stories heard over the phone, told through letters, or recounted personally to me in my office and even on the road." Like other responsible mainstream commentators, Bahaeddine recognized that the investment companies had used Islamic symbols to lure clients, and he understood as well that some elements from the Islamic wave had supported and benefited from the massive fraud. In the end, however, Bahaeddine concluded that the Islamic dimension played a decidedly secondary part. In fact, he came to believe that Islam and the very idea of Islamic economics had suffered manipulation and distortion. In his view, the whole concept of Islamic economics unfairly became one of the victims of the tragedy.[34]

The New Islamist assessment of the investment companies stressed underlying economic and political causes for the rise of the companies. Fahmy Huwaidy argued persuasively that the essential characteristics and strategies of the companies owed very little to Egypt's Islamic cultural background and even less to the basic ideas that drove Islamic economics. He noted that two key elements combined to explain the rise of the investment companies: first, the large volume of remittances or financial transfers from Egyptians working in the Gulf during the oil boom created a large new capital reserve; and second, the failure of the official banking system to create attractive investment opportunities for these surplus funds left a void that the investment companies filled.[35] The best of the studies of the companies by professional economists drew essentially the same conclusions.[36] Neither of these determining factors had any particularly Islamic dimension. The fundamental concept behind the companies mirrored that of "pyramid schemes" which have appeared, always with the same disastrous results, in the most varied cultural contexts around the world. The initially high interest rates that attracted investors resulted from the simple equation that underlies all pyramid frauds. Benefits distributed must always be less than new subscriptions received because gains are paid out of new deposits rather than from earnings on productive activities. The expansion of the number of recipients of benefits creates inexorable pressure to expand the volume of new investors. Pyramid schemes inevitably collapse when adequate numbers of additional subscribers can no longer be found. Following this pattern exactly, the investment companies in Egypt collapsed with the cooling of the oil boom and the drop in available capital from remittances. The logic of the financial investment companies had nothing to do with "Islamic blessings" in their initial expansion stage nor with the "evil eye" when they ultimately folded, although company representatives seeking to conceal their misdeeds invoked both.

Threaded through the assessments by such respected economists as Sayyid al Naggar and Mahmud Abdul Fadil, for example, is the common theme of the failure of the government to recognize soon enough that adjustments would have to be made in the money and investment markets to absorb the remittances. Moreover, these critics agreed that once it became clear that these questionable investment companies had managed to attract a huge proportion of the new capital reserves, the government did not move quickly enough to regulate their activities. The factors that made the companies so effective had far more to do with such government policy failures than with the beards and flowing robes the company owners donned to give their machinations an Islamic cover.

Fahmy Huwaidy adroitly picked up on this theme. Huwaidy's understanding of the extent of the damage wrought by these companies' exploitation of Islamic symbols went deeper than Ghazzaly's. He also understood just why the government appeared more interested in linking the companies to the Islamic trend than in curbing their misdeeds. Consistently, whether addressing the government or intellectual critics of the Islamic trend, Huwaidy rejected claims by the government and its secular allies that the investment companies represented the "economic arm" of the Islamic movement. He insisted, for example, that "al Rayan [one of the largest and most notorious of the companies] is not the Islamic trend."[37] In a review in 1988 of the annual report of al Ahram Strategic Center for Political and Strategic Studies, Huwaidy criticized the claim of connections between the companies and the Islamic movement. These unfounded accusations, he wrote persuasively, are simply assertions made without any proof.[38] At the same time, Huwaidy charged that a good part of the ineptness of the government in acting effectively to curb the abuses of the companies stemmed from the government's politically motivated obsession with searching for links between the companies and the Islamic movement. This misplaced effort, in his view, came at the expense of formulating effective regulatory policies.

Addressing the Islamic wave, though aware that his audience would be larger, Kamal Abul Magd drew the most important lessons from the experience of the companies. He explained that an economic process or institution did not become Islamic through reliance on external forms or unsubstantiated claims. Both were too easily manipulated for devious purposes. The investment companies had simply declared the benefits they paid to be *halal* [religiously permitted] in contrast to the *haram* [religiously forbidden] interest in regular banks. They made their case not with logical arguments but rather with assertions, reinforced by superficial symbols and images. Even the presence of religious scholars on the companies' advisory boards could not ensure that any given set of practices conformed to Islamic values because, while they might understand Islam, their grasp of economics might be too questionable to make them reliable guarantors of probity in financial dealings. Abul Magd made it clear that Islam provided no magic formula that abrogated the logic of the market. Rates of return that appeared too good to be true invariably proved to be fraudulent. Mystical evocations of "Islamic blessing" to explain windfall interest rates simply misused Islam to cover fraud. Abul Magd stated that an authentic Islamic approach to the economy would rely on strategies and tactics devised on an economic and scientific rather than a religious basis. An Islamic economy would honor the logic of economic science. It would do so, however, while placing economic science within the larger moral universe that Islam defines, so that the economy would serve the higher ends that Islam identifies.[39]

Abul Magd pointed out that some progress had been made in providing a *fiqh* of economics adequate to the age, notably in the elaboration of the general moral standards that an Islamic economy would have to meet. However, he also stated that serious work remained to be done on the level of providing clear guidance for practical economic work. The unresolved confusions about the meaning of *riba* and its relationship to the contemporary interest paid by banks, for example, had helped create the void that the investment companies exploited. The New Islamists themselves were divided on the issue of *riba.* Qaradawy believed that interest *was* in fact the *riba* that the Quran forbade. Ghazzaly, in contrast, sided with official Islam in judging that interest paid by modern banks differed from the exploitative *riba* denounced by Islam. Contemporary interest, he argued, served legitimate social ends. Abul Magd took a strong middle position. In his view, a textual resolution of the debate might not be possible.[40] The Quranic verses prohibiting *riba* were revealed late, he explained, and as a result reliable *hadiths* explaining their meaning were few in number and inconclusive. Therefore, the texts could not provide a clear basis for judging whether modern-day interest was *riba* or not.

Given this irresolution, Abul Magd argued that a plausible case could be made for both kinds of banks. In fact, he revealed that he placed his own personal savings in a national rather than an Islamic bank. However, he went out of his way to point out that the operations of the Islamic banks were on a par with all other banking institutions. Unlike the investment companies, the Islamic banks operated within a government regulatory framework and under the supervision of the Central Bank, and therefore they were constrained to follow sound economic logic. Moreover, in case of financial failure, they had the same kind of official protection for depositors as any other bank. For this reason, even those New Islamists like Abul Magd who dealt with the national banks objected strenuously when secular critics sought to lump the investment companies and the Islamic banks together as the economic wing of the Islamic movement. Some critics hostile to the Islamic wave even went further by characterizing the banks and the investment companies as representing the embryo of an alternative society, a new basis for political power, or the source of social chaos. The New Islamists contested the dangerous and misleading implication of these charges that all activities with an Islamic character represented essentially the same phenomenon. They understood full well that this misrepresentation provided support for the indiscriminate government policy of "drying the springs" that lumped moderate Islamists together with extremist and criminal elements who misused the Islamic banner.[41]

In the spring of 1997, the government newspaper *Akhbar al Yaum* launched a full-scale assault on the Islamic banks with apparent official support. The Shaikh of al Azhar, Muhammad Sayyid Tantawy, who earlier had held the position of Mufti, ruled that the interest charged by the banks should not be equated with *riba.* His opinion had important implications. If the interest in the national banks was allowable, there was no need for Islamic banking. The opinion was innocent enough had it not been for the climate of growing official hostility to all forms of Islamic economic activity. In such a politicized setting, the Shaikh's judgment set the stage for the assault on Islamic banks, which were rendered unnecessary by his logic and dangerous by the hostile climate. Almost immediately a flood of articles, quoting economic specialists and religious figures, made the tendentious case that the Islamic banks constituted the same kind of threat as the investment companies. A chorus of critics urged that they be shut down.

The New Islamists, many of whom disagreed with the Shaikh of al Azhar on the interest question, did not hesitate to challenge his views. Even those who sided with Tantawy's interpretation rejected the attempt by the government to give his view an authoritative status when the matter remained open to interpretation. Finally, with one voice the New Islamists defended the experiment of the Islamic banks and strenuously objected to the unfair press campaign that equated Islamic banks with the investment companies.

On the issue of whether or not bank interest is *riba,* Qaradawy and Tantawy, in particular, have a long history of public disagreement. In the early 1990s, then-Mufti Tantawy pronounced contemporary bank interest *halal* [religiously permitted] in an article in *al Ahram,* entitled "*Haram* and *Halal* in Banking and Finance." In one celebrated exchange, Qaradawy bluntly challenged Tantawy's credentials to make such contributions to

Islamic *fiqh,* despite his official position. At the same time, he criticized the substance of Tantawy's views, arguing that they sowed "misunderstandings and confusions among Muslims." Qaradawy concluded by expressing regret that Tantawy's official position gave visibility to his views. In response, Tantawy appeared to claim the status of *faqih,* that is, a scholar qualified to add to *fiqh.* He based this claim on his "studies and scholarly work" rather than his official position.

When faced with issues for which there were no texts or with principled disagreements on the meaning of texts, the New Islamists have insisted that such matters be left open. In debating these unresolved questions, they did give some weight to precedents and to viewpoints that enjoyed strong support among scholars. However, given their strong commitment to the necessity of the constant renewal of *ijtihad,* they most often preferred not to rely on the resolutions of the past. At such times, they would point to Islam's acceptance of four quite distinctive, yet authoritative, schools of *fiqh* as an indicator that, in some matters, diversity of viewpoints best serves Islam's higher purposes.

The New Islamists' acceptance of theoretical differences of opinion on interest and other important economic issues translated into a belief that contested issues could be resolved by reasoned deliberations of specialists. If such efforts failed, they counseled either resolution by democratic means, in cases where the impact on the public was substantial, or else tolerance of diverse institutional forms that reflected the unresolved differences. On the controversial interest question, Kamal Abul Magd cautioned, "the issue of Islamic banks is an important one that affects the lives of the people. It should not be discussed in a press campaign but rather in the context of serious, scientific research, appropriate to a scientific, rather than a political, issue." If the technical specialists could not resolve a conflict, the New Islamists proposed a democratic resolution. If the pressing character of the issue meant that a resort to politics was inevitable, they believed the best form of political resolution to be a democratic one. In such cases, they argued, scholars had the responsibility to formulate as clearly as possible the acceptable alternatives from an Islamic perspective. Then, if the choice among them could not be settled, they suggested that the practical policy question in which the issue was embedded be resolved by democratic vote of the elected representatives of the people.[42]

On the specific issue of the banks, Kamal Abul Magd offered a pragmatic and persuasive solution. In his view, there was no compelling reason to force a choice between Islamic and non-Islamic banks. Why not, he asked, simply continue to live with their current coexistence? Such an outcome had clear advantages over an arbitrary decision by the government, relying on what would be viewed as the coerced or opportunistic approval of official Islam. Even more emphatically, this solution would be preferable to having people turn to the radical *amirs* [leaders of Islamist groups] to seek resolution of the issue. "Since some people are suspicious of the national banks," wrote Abul Magd, "there is nothing wrong with their turning to the Islamic banks. Others who do not share these reservations should continue to deal with non-Islamic banks." He concluded with the tolerant equanimity characteristic of the Islamic *Wassatteyya:* "There is absolutely nothing wrong with having both kinds of banks at the same time."[43]

Development in a Global Age

The same quiet self-confidence that marked New Islamist interventions in the controversies over domestic economic issues, like the investment companies and Islamic banks, characterized their position on the large questions of national economic policy. Regarding national development policy and Egypt's relationship to the world market, the New Islamists took a strong centrist position, rejecting the extremes of de-linkage from the global economy, on the one hand, and complete integration on terms set by the dominant powers and international financial institutions, on the other. Instead, they argued that Egyptians must work for a development project defined as much as possible in its essential values and goals in ways consistent with the *Wassatteyya* conception of civilizational Islam. They understood the constraints that global forces would exert, and they emphasized that such a strategy would necessarily entail active engagement in an interconnected world. Their strategy was the pragmatic one of taking maximum advantage of whatever freedom of maneuver was open to the nation.

Isolation, or de-linkage from the world market, is simply not a realistic option in the New Islamist view. Kamal Abul Magd expressed his agreement with the "many writers" who have warned that "the technological revolution has made it difficult for peoples and cultures to remain isolated. All this means," he continued, "that the future will inevitably witness cultural interactions, whether friendly or hostile."[44] The real debate for the New Islamists centers on the choice between two competing concepts of development in the new conditions of globalism, the first of which calls for a development strategy to be as independent as possible and inspired by the civilizational project, while the second views unconditional imitation of the Western path as the only course open to Egypt. The New Islamists stand unambiguously with those who struggle for an independently conceived path to economic progress, though they are fully aware of the powerful international pressures for conformity to the Western model.

Given those external forces, the New Islamists believe that only with a strong national consensus on economic strategy can Egypt hope to maximize prospects to develop in conformity with its own vision of the country's future. From the outset, the New Islamists have committed themselves to drawing the Islamic mainstream into the center on national economic issues. To be sure, they have enthusiastically supported economic experiments inspired by Islam. However, just as important was their argument, apparent in Abul Magd's position on Islamic versus national banks, that existing economic institutions and arrangements need not be abandoned. On an impressive range of issues, the New Islamists have shown themselves quite willing to accept existing economic institutions and practices as adequate (if imperfect), provided they did not violate some clear and confirmed Islamic injunction. While open to change, they also displayed a seasoned understanding that radical shifts in the economy, especially on the macro level, had done great damage to the national community.[45] Thus the New Islamists emphasized gradual transformation that balanced the need for innovation with appreciation for past accomplishments.

An important part of this strong preference for gradualism stemmed from their centrist commitment to finding common ground that could define a national center on economic questions. In evaluating economic processes or institutions, they emphasized the contribution made to the common good rather than the derivation of any particular economic institution or idea from one or another of the competing twentieth-century orientations to the economy. The New Islamists showed themselves less interested in validating either Nasser's "Arab socialism" or Sadat's liberalizing "Open Door" than in retrieving the best for the future from each of those eras. This attitude finds clear expression in the New Islamist manifesto and the way the contrasting periods are discussed. Regarding the socialist impulses of the Nasser era, the New Islamists have sought to reassert the concern for the good of the community and the progress registered in education, health, and other forms of social development, while noting with regret the neglect of individual rights and freedoms. The subsequent era of the opening to the world market carried the promise of greater prosperity and an expansion of freedom that the New Islamists found attractive, despite the excessive manifestations of self-interest and the growing gap between the rich and the poor. The manifesto states candidly that it is time to drop ideological litmus testing; all that matters is whether or not any particular concept or practice contributes to the common good.[46]

This centrist and inclusive spirit manifested itself in the search for even small steps that could be taken together to register economic progress. The New Islamists worked to find underlying points of consensus on lesser, but still important, questions about which all major elements could agree. They cast these consensual elements in terms of the core values of justice and respect for human dignity that characterized their most essential Islamist commitments, but resonated as well with the thinking of other trends. They had no illusions that these areas of agreement could in themselves define an overall national strategy. However, they did consider such points of consensus as important movements in that direction. In this spirit, the New Islamist manifesto insisted that the basis for any development strategy must first be a concerted increase in productivity that flowed from the intensification of work and improvement of the management of public expenditures. Anything short of this effort, they argued, would mean "wasted efforts and false solutions that are just pain killers that only postpone the time of disaster." Second, they argued that the necessity to preserve social justice meant that "human labor in its different forms should be thought of as a principal source of revenue and value in society." Finally, they emphasized the critical importance of improving the work environment, in order to harness individual ambition and release the human creative spirit through work arrangements characterized by a minimum of bureaucratic hierarchy and maximum encouragement of individual and collective initiative.[47]

Anticipating the criticism that there was little explicitly "Islamic" or even new in such formulations, the New Islamists early and consistently sounded a fourth general theme that complemented their support for experimentation in the context of an overall gradualist strategy. They argued that it was neither necessary nor even desirable for Islamists to "have a distinctive position" on each and every economic issue. As the manifesto explained, Islamists "aren't required to prove their uniqueness and particularity by distinctive methods of economic reform."[48] An Islamic moral framework would allow them to accept ideas and structures that advanced the goal of justice, whatever their source, while integrating these borrowed elements into a drive for progress inspired by the civilizational project.

The New Islamist elaboration of the meaning of the civilizational orientation called for creative interaction with the world, eschewing any impulse to isolation. Who could doubt, they asked, that the West had surpassed the Islamic world in material productivity and technological innovation? Of course the Islamic world had a great deal to learn from the West about the new technologies and their applications to production. By these measures,

Egypt was certainly poor and vulnerable. Moreover, who could question that the revolution of Westernization had created a worldwide capitalist market that had a profound impact on development strategies around the globe? In an age of space-time compression, Egypt had no choice but to engage with a world linked together as never before.[49] Any realistic development strategy would have to take into account the broad context of a world transformed by American dominance, the technological revolution, and a unified world market. Since isolation from the world market was no longer feasible, serious questions now centered on the forms and character of linkages most consistent with self-defined goals. Such an approach would require a balanced understanding, one that appreciated the strengths of the West and its power to impose its economic will, while not abandoning the contributions in the economic realm that could come from Egypt's unique cultural heritage.

"Our contemporary world," commented Fahmy Huwaidy, "is experiencing a scientific and a technological revolution unknown before." The writings of the New Islamists convey a sophisticated appreciation that the world has indeed entered a global age, marked by an unprecedented acceleration of change. Writing in the late 1990s, Huwaidy captured the heart of the matter with his pronouncement that scientists judge the transformations of the last decades of the twentieth century to be "deeper and more important than all the changes that happened on our planet Earth since the appearance of humankind." More specifically, Huwaidy reported that scientific and technological revolutions have transformed economic life in the advanced states to the point where information now represents 80 percent of input, with capital, labor, and natural resources together constituting the remaining 20 percent. "We find the opposite in the developing states," notes Huwaidy.[50] The effect on economic standing for underdeveloped areas like the Arab Islamic world has been dramatic. For example, Huwaidy reports that the total national income of all twenty-one Arab states, with their combined population of 2.34 hundred million, represents only 21 percent of the German economy.[51]

On all these issues of the descriptive dimensions of the new world, New Islamist thinking could easily find common ground with the most advanced of Egypt's globalists. Where the break occurs with some influential globalists, however, is over the notion that any one set of economic prescriptions flows from an understanding of this new global condition. In particular, the New Islamists challenge the notion that given the global condition it is necessary to accept the specific set of policies urged by the United States and/or the international financial institutions. The New Islamists insist on the distinction between globalism understood as a description and globalism as ideology. The link between power, more specifically American power, and the new ideology of globalism does not elude them. The New Islamists understand that no society could really stand apart from the worldwide capitalist market and the scientific and technical revolutions that now undergird it. But they also realize, as their support for the Islamic banks suggests, that the forms and timing of the linkages to the global market represent critical issues open to negotiation and variation. Thus they adamantly refuse the notion that one pattern fits all.

The New Islamists also reject the well-known "end of history" arguments based on the global extension of capitalism and liberal democracy in its American form, regarding such arguments as a kind of ideological triumphalism that reveals more about American will and arrogance than historical inevitabilities. They do not accept the proposition that the great human questions have been resolved by the American formulas. They note first that the world simply does not have the resources to generalize the American pattern. America's prosperity rests on the consumption of a disproportionately large share of the world's resources, combined with the power to defend it. More important, they observe that the consequences for human beings and the planet from this American model have by no means been uniformly positive. Even if imitation were feasible, the New Islamists question its desirability.

The New Islamists understand "progress" for Egypt as having a distinctive and multifaceted meaning. While advancement of the economy does remain at the heart of their approach, the ways in which they address fundamental economic issues incorporate moral and civilizational imperatives as well as purely material needs. Addressing extremists within the Islamic wave, they caution that Islamist activists working in the economic field must not ignore economics as a social science, relying only on abstract moral injunctions. Knowledge of religion, they argue bluntly, cannot substitute for practical and theoretical knowledge of economics.[52] In particular, Western achievement in such fields as modern productive techniques and genetic and information technologies simply cannot be ignored. This admiration for Western advancements does not translate, however, into the uncritical embrace of any particular developmental model. The New Islamists believe that Western theories of development take changing forms that reflect shifting Western interests as much as objective distillations of economic experience. Caution is therefore warranted. This critique operates on two planes. On an abstract level, the New Islamists believe that development strategies inevitably reflect the values and standards of the societies that generated them, and these measures of progress may or may not reflect a stance that is suitable for other contexts. At the policy level, the New Islamists note the way that changes in policy recommendations from Western governments, through their aid programs or the international financial institutions they dominate, often reflect shifts in domestic configurations of power in Western societies at least as much as an altered international environment or new development needs. From this perspective, American notions of development provide a useful gauge of changing American definitions of national interest rather than a reliable record of either gains in knowledge or experience in development.

Egypt's "salvation" in the face of these challenges, to borrow Fahmy Huwaidy's phrase, comes with the knowledge that while Egyptians might be poor, neither their humanity nor their civilization is "underdeveloped."[53] The New Islamists believe that Egypt's history and cultural experience have enduring, positive dimensions that can make important contributions to defining progress and specifying strategies for its attainment. With the same lack of defensiveness that allows them to face calmly areas of "backwardness," the New Islamists draw attention to the strengths that flow from Egypt's history and culture.

The New Islamists believe that human communities have been charged by God to achieve progress according to standards that protect human dignity and serve justice. They view the Western record of economic advance through this prism and find it lacking in important ways. In sober terms similar to those of global humanist critics in the West, they note that even the most advanced of Western societies have not resolved problems of poverty. They also point to the growing political power of the wealthy minorities that dominate these societies and the threat to democracy that such concentrations of financial resources represent.[54]

The New Islamists approach the much-heralded "information revolution" in the same balanced way. They understand that the new global order has emerged from the marriage of the new information technologies to the world market, with profound consequences for all human societies. They stand firmly against those retrograde elements within the Islamic wave who see "the devil" in the computer and the Internet, arguing that Islam, as the faith of science and learning, must not reject such powerful new technologies. On the contrary, major New Islamist figures like Kamal Abul Magd and Yusuf al Qaradawy have taken the lead in warning that isolation from the information revolution is neither possible nor desirable.

In looking to the future, the New Islamists forcefully reject any rigid technological or market determinism. In their view, American dominance and the end of the Cold War did not in themselves define the precise characteristics and forms that a capitalist world order would take in the post-

Cold War era. In short, the New Islamists' realistic recognition of current Western dominance did not translate into acceptance of the permanence of that hegemony in any fixed form. Even for the present, they argue that there is still room for maneuver within the constraints set by the Western-dominated global market system; there are still important choices to be made.[55]

Taking this position means that the New Islamists stand as firmly against the misplaced certainties of the free-market "fundamentalist" advocates of structural adjustment as they do against the Islamic extremists. Both strategies of imitation, whether of historical patterns or by willing compliance with externally imposed models, have strong advocates in Egypt today. The New Islamists see the same rigidity and insensitivity to context in both kinds of thinking. Within the Islamic wave, the New Islamists argue persuasively against accepting models built to worship the false idols of a petrified past. In the larger public arena, they caution against the mindless acceptance of the misleading promises of a free-market future in forms designed to meet other people's needs. They recognize, of course, that U.S. backing means that structural adjustment prescriptions have to be taken seriously. However, these realities of power do not alter their belief that mindless compliance with ready-made foreign models holds little promise to meet Egypt's economic needs in ways that respond to the country's special circumstances, not to mention the moral imperatives of the faith.

Despite the shadows cast by Western power, the New Islamists nevertheless regard the Western experience with economic development as a particularly rich one from which the Islamic world must learn. In place of forced compliance or imitation, however, they argue for a strategy of selective borrowing—adopting what is best from Western and other societies while actively preserving those things of value that derive from Egypt's belonging to the Islamic world. At the same time, given the global power imbalances that weigh so heavily against Egyptians, the New Islamists urge vigilance and multifaceted resistance to economic impositions by external powers that further diminish Egypt's prospects.

The strong New Islamist position against acceptance of externally imposed economic strategies thus does not translate into isolationism or a movement toward de-linkage. Within the framework of a realistic understanding of the dominant international order, the New Islamists urge Egyptians to learn from others, even as they resist, when possible, external impositions that would have clearly negative consequences. Tareq al Bishry in fact argues that only by holding these two contrasting sentiments toward the outside world in tension can a self-directed strategy be actualized effectively. Only a level of consciousness that embraces both attitudes, Bishry argues, will allow positive development and change that can be made consistent with and expressive of a guiding Islamic moral framework.[56]

Because the New Islamists never mistake the organizational and technological advancements of the West and Japan as representing the progress that Islam enjoins, they never subject themselves to the invidious comparisons from which mere imitators have inevitably suffered. They are therefore able to suggest helpful guidelines both for drawing from the heritage and selectively borrowing from others as Egyptians struggle to attain a measure of self-defined progress. Their realism does not underestimate the external barriers to this effort. Understanding that Egypt must interact with the world and with the global capitalist market, they argue nevertheless that the character and timing of these linkages must be established on terms as congruent as possible with Egypt's rich and distinctive heritage and the enduring values that undergird it. They do not hesitate to suggest that at critical times it may be essential for civil society, including its important Islamic wing, to stand with the government to resist externally imposed conditions for global linkage that would be detrimental to Egypt's long-term prospects to realize progress in its own image. In the last resort, they recognize that the realities of the Western-dominated global system may defeat both the political system and civil society, leaving to the Islamic wave the task of preserving the possibility of alternatives to animate the struggles of tomorrow.

The New Islamists and the National Agenda

The New Islamists neither make nor implement domestic or foreign economic policy. Their sense of the importance of the Islamic *Wassatteyya* as a component of any possible political mainstream, however, impels them to address pressing economic questions of national importance. In the final years of the old century and the first of the new, the New Islamists insistently brought two such large economic issues to national attention. They related both to the new conditions of the global age that were everywhere exacerbating inequalities. In their view, globalization has meant a widening of the gap between rich and poor around the world, threatening social peace and diminishing hopes for social justice. The New Islamists reported in unsparing terms that Egypt had lost ground dramatically in the competitive international struggle for economic development. At the same time, growing social inequalities within Egypt were taking a particularly ugly form. The New Islamists did not hesitate to announce that Egypt increasingly was ruled by "tyrant wealth."[57]

Fahmy Huwaidy neither minced words nor spared sensibilities in driving home the point that, for all the official talk of a successful economy when measured by the rise in GNP, Egypt had nevertheless suffered a precipitous decline in its international economic standing. The New Islamists were not alone in pointing to such negative economic indicators as the declining rate of development in productive sectors, worsening unemployment, and the widening gap between rich and poor.[58] "If underdevelopment is a disaster," wrote Huwaidy, "it is even a greater disaster that we do not acknowledge the clear evidence that we are underdeveloped." We speak with such confidence of entering the twenty-first century, Huwaidy cautioned, apparently unaware that "we may not even belong to the twentieth century!"[59]

About a hundred and seventy years ago, Muhammad Aly, the founder of modern Egypt, spearheaded a modernization drive that attracted attention as far away as feudal Japan. To inspire their own revival, the Meiji reformers sent delegations to more advanced states around the world to learn from their experience. Egypt, Huwaidy noted, was one of those promising states. Today, continued Huwaidy with devastating effect, any comparison with Japan would be an absurdity. Egyptians must face the fact that their economy is now compared regularly with states "not yet standing on their own feet and who were not even mentioned on the map of success twenty years ago!"[60]

The New Islamists have argued that critical work needs to be done on both theoretical and practical levels to raise productivity and reverse the erosion of Egypt's economic standing in the world. Using his platform in *al Ahram,* Fahmy Huwaidy in the summer of 1998 wrote a series of articles explaining how the economic challenge of Israel gave these economic tasks even greater urgency. Citing dramatic figures, Huwaidy drew a daunting picture of the contrasts between Israel and the Arab world. Adjusting for the population ratio, Israel exceeds the Arab countries by more than ten times in the number of scientists, thirty times in spending on research and development, seventy times in scientific publications, and over a thousand times in inventions.[61] More to the point, Israel has successfully turned this scientific and technological lead to economic advantage. Lutfy Abdul Azim, the dean of economic journalists, responded to Huwaidy's series with the painful suggestion that Egypt's position had eroded even more dramatically than Huwaidy indicated. The rough parity between the Israeli and Egyptian share of total Middle East exports, preserved until 1995, had subsequently disappeared. By the late 1990s, the Israeli share reached 12 percent while the Egyptian share had declined to 2 percent, Abdul Azim reported. Similarly, whereas the Egyptian contribution to total Middle East imports in 1967 was 12.6 percent and that of Israel 4.2 percent, the two had reversed positions dramatically by 1996, with the Egyptian share standing at 8.5 percent while the Israelis claimed 20.6 percent.[62]

Aggregate figures on imports and exports may well understate the challenge. In the information age, the character of economic activity is more important than its quantity. Huwaidy drew the attention of his readers to the leadership role that Israeli information technology specialists were playing in cutting-edge electronics and Internet development, while Egypt was only just entering those fields. Citing Thomas Friedman of the *New York Times*, Huwaidy reported that Israel now held second position after the United States in the number of new computer and Internet-based companies in the 1990s.[63] He cited as well a *Newsweek* article that described Israel as having the only information technology industry capable of challenging Silicon Valley. By 1998, developed technology represented a full 34 percent of Israeli exports.[64]

To explain the relative decline in Egypt's world economic standing, the New Islamists resort to none of the standard scapegoats, rejecting out of hand the arguments of some secularists that Islam has caused Egypt's backwardness. The values of Islam in their view are fully compatible with economic advancement, though the violations by Muslims and the currently existing regimes systematically negate those possibilities. Similarly, the New Islamists acknowledge the historical setbacks to development caused by imperialism and recognize the challenges of unequal international exchanges set by the developed states. Still, they argue that a window of opportunity remains open that Egyptians must take advantage of by their own initiative and hard work.

Islam, in the New Islamist view, provides the broad precepts that can successfully guide such an effort of economic revival. New Islamist thinking on economic reform begins with the principle that all social change starts with the efforts of a people to reform themselves, thus rejecting any inclinations toward fatalism. Huwaidy speaks of this principle as a law of the universe, while Qaradawy regularly cites the inspirational Quranic verse that a people can change their circumstances only after they have reformed themselves.[65]

A second and closely related principle of New Islamic thought holds that development and culture are inextricably linked. Called upon to "build the Earth," humankind is enjoined to do so in keeping with the values and purposes of its diverse cultural communities. The striking absence of a homogenizing or unitary impulse in New Islamist thinking flows from their recognition that, if God had wanted a unified and homogenized humankind, he would have created but one nation. Human diversity is a reflection of God's will and so, therefore, are the diverse paths to the future. This inclusive notion guides the New Islamists' effort to rethink their own Islamic heritage from a developmental perspective, building on its strengths and seeking to overcome its weaknesses, not least by openness to the experiences of others. This line of thinking emerges most clearly in Huwaidy's discussions of the Korean example. Citing an academic study of development in South Korea, Huwaidy reported that the Koreans turned first to the inherited Confucian tradition.[66] They analyzed Confucianism from a developmental perspective, emphasizing those values and concepts that advanced economic growth while downplaying traditional beliefs and practices that would create barriers. The reformers focused the mobilization effort largely around such constructive Confucian values as hard work, discipline, achievement, lawfulness, respect for education, and responsibility for the family, while pushing into the background such accretions as formalism and rigidity that are also part of the tradition. Substitute Islam for Confucianism and Egypt for Korea, and you have a clear picture of the thrust of the New Islamist contribution to thinking about development and culture.

In the same spirit, Yusuf al Qaradawy has frequently sounded the theme that "productivity is a form of worship."[67] The New Islamists regularly decry the fading in Egypt since the 1970s of a public climate of respect for hard work, a commitment to excellence, and a sense of discipline, in favor of appearance, cleverness, fast earnings, and consumption.[68] As Muhammad al Ghazzaly has pointed out on more than one occasion, modern Egyptians have failed not only themselves but also Islam by not meeting the test of building productive economic systems. Ghazzaly understood full well the debilitating mechanisms of global dominance that secured the prosperity of Western societies and the relative deprivation of the developing world, to which the Islamic nations belong. Yet, with the same realism, he also generously acknowledged and celebrated the impressive creativity and, above all, hard work that ordinary citizens of the West bring to economic tasks. Ghazzaly would not lay all the blame for the backwardness of the Islamic world on Western depredations, pointing out that Westerners have earned an important part of their progress by diligence. There is no excuse for laziness of mind or body and for the prevailing laxity in a sense of public responsibility, according to Ghazzaly. All of the elements for an Islamic work ethic could be drawn from the Quran. Fahmy Huwaidy has discussed the numerous texts in the Quran that urge people to work hard and perfect what they do, calling on occasion for collecting these texts and organizing them as a *fiqh* of work ethics.[69] In a variety of ways, Ghazzaly, Qaradawy, the other New Islamists have repeated the message that Egypt and the Islamic world need to spend less time blaming others for their backwardness and more effort working to improve themselves.

Ghazzaly, in particular, drove home these unpopular arguments during interactions with the people who crowded around him whenever he appeared in public. On one occasion, a young pharmacist approached Ghazzaly with anxious questions about the proper form of "greeting the mosque." The reference is to a minor religious practice of saying a brief prayer of respect when first entering a mosque. The pharmacist wanted to know where Ghazzaly stood among the various schools of interpretation on the matter. Ghazzaly responded instead with a question of his own. "Why don't you serve Islam in your field," he asked with impatience, "and leave this issue to the specialists?" Ghazzaly went on to explain that the question raised was a minor one even for specialists and hardly worth the attention the young man gave it, whereas the community faced pressing needs in pharmacology. Ghazzaly reminded his questioner that the majority of medicines sold to Egyptians were manufactured abroad, indicating that "Islam is defeated and vulnerable in the area of drugs." He suggested that the pharmacist spend his time and energy on improving the capacity of Egyptian pharmacology to deliver the medicines and services that Egyptians so desperately needed.[70]

One particularly telling vignette spoke volumes to anyone familiar with the bureaucratic barriers to development in Egypt. Ghazzaly found himself waiting in a public office with the opportunity to observe the employee in charge. He noticed first how bored and unresponsive the employee appeared, even though people came to him for the services he was supposed to provide. Some he ignored completely, while others he simply delayed with endless excuses until the time for prayer came. The employee fastidiously began the preparations for prayer well before the appointed time. An exasperated Ghazzaly could no longer contain himself: "Do you not realize that the duties you have been neglecting are no less important than the ones for which you are now preparing? Serving the people in a timely and efficient way is just as much a part of our Islam as prayers and fasting."[71]

On another occasion, Ghazzaly was asked if the import of frozen chickens from non-Muslim countries was *halal.* Again, he responded with an instructive question. What should concern us, he explained, is why we are not producing our own chickens in sufficient quantity and why we are in need of imports at all! In one of his most frequently quoted statements, Ghazzaly dismissed out of hand the notion that the new availability of consumer products from abroad represented real progress. We have become so unproductive ourselves and so dependent on others, he said, that if the things we now import were taken from us, "we would stand naked before the world!"[72]

The New Islamists, in effect, were arguing that working for progress in the service of the people represented a religious obligation. The claim did not go unquestioned from within the Islamic wave. Fahmy Huwaidy reported one revealing challenge from a young man, holding a *meswak* (a tooth cleaning instrument from the time of the Prophet, used by those prone to exaggerated and often trivial imitation of the Prophet's behavior), who asked, "What evidence can you provide from the *Sharia* that progress is a religious duty and that we'll be accountable before God because of backwardness?" Huwaidy responded: "Backwardness is a sin because it means a neglect of the duty of *istikhlaf*."[73]

Convinced that a proper understanding of Islam emphasizes human responsibility to "build the world," the New Islamists have taken a particularly strong position against any escape from harsh material realities and challenges into the mindless activism of the radicals or the abstract spiritualism of the darawish. Neither version of Islamist extremism, in their view, would prove adequate to their economic vision for the new age. The New Islamists have worked consistently to make the Islamic wave a part of a centrist national effort to address core economic issues. Their own important contributions notwithstanding, they state categorically that Islamic thinking in the economic realm remains underdeveloped, and Islamist intellectuals must elaborate more fully a new *fiqh* of economics that aims to build Islamic economic systems in the new conditions of globalism. The major contribution of the New Islamist School in the economic realm resides precisely in their own first steps in this direction.

New Islamist interactions with the Islamic wave on economic matters center on the effort to direct attention to critical issues of national development, rather than on peripheral but controversial cultural and social issues. They regard with dismay the common inclination in the ranks of political Islam to raise diverting but secondary questions of Islamic dress or intellectual heresies. They despair of the manner in which secular critics of the Islamic wave compound the damage, by magnifying the false importance of these issues with their exaggerated responses. In the late 1980s and 1990s, the major challenge to the New Islamist approach came from the impatient hyperactivity and exaggerated claims for Islamic economics of political Islam. By the last years of the century, the increasingly widespread pietist reaction, including a focus on personal salvation and an intense preoccupation with secondary religious rites, threatened to further diminish constructive engagements in the social and economic arenas. The danger of such views was that Islam would be reduced to a refuge for battered identities, no longer able to cope with a world that appeared to be spinning out of control. The New Islamists took the lead from within the Islamic wave in opposing such personalistic readings of the faith. Islam, they argued, called on Muslims to live their faith through active involvement in social life, including its most material dimensions.

The New Islamists reject ideas suggesting that there is some secret formula for success that is somehow in the possession of the West and permanently out of reach of the Islamic world. Their most recent writings on economic development contain numerous references to the selective successes of others, in countries ranging from Korea and Malaysia to Ireland. In all cases, they argue, successful reforms begin with education and end with hard work in the context of a comprehensive national strategy. Writing of Ireland, Huwaidy invokes this formula as an antidote to depression and despair. During a short stay in England in the mid-1970s, he had noted parallels between the ways in which Londoners spoke of the naive Irish and the attitude of Cairenes to country folk from Upper Egypt, who could be conned into buying a share in the pyramids! In those days, Ireland's economy depended on growing potatoes and barley, raising cattle, and producing textiles. In Huwaidy's mind, Ireland seemed not so different from his own home province of Menufeyya, which evoked similar rural and nostalgic images.

By the end of the century, apologies to the Irish were in order. In two decades, reported Huwaidy, the Irish had transformed themselves from a poor agricultural country that, despite its location, belonged to the developing world into an industrial state that competed with the United States in the production of electronics and represented an important import market. "Although I am biased toward Menufeyya and hold it in deep respect and regard, I must confess that a comparison of my home province to the Irish would be a major insult!"[74] Startled by these Irish "surprises," Huwaidy asked the inevitable questions about the formula for Irish success. Everywhere he heard the same story: the reform effort flowed from a clear strategic vision that began with the educational system.[75] Huwaidy reaffirmed in Ireland the conviction "that there is no secret in the whole matter." The journey of success begins by passing through the gates of education, as Ireland, Malaysia, and Korea, along with Muhammad Aly, had done. As Huwaidy put it, you should "read" first in order to "know" and then "progress." Muslims should understand, he concluded, "that this is why the word 'read' was the first word God sent to the Prophet Muhammad."[76]

Egypt's slippage in the global arena is matched in seriousness by a second, and in some ways far more insidious, threat. "Tyrant wealth," in Huwaidy's telling phrase, gave a particularly dangerous Egyptian face to the ever-widening gap between the rich and the poor that was emerging everywhere as a central characteristic of the new global age.[77] Small incidents sometimes capture the essential meaning of major trends.[78] The death of a young swimmer, killed by a reckless speedboat at the luxurious North Sea community of Marina, proved emblematic of the insensitive attitudes of Egypt's new class of unprecedented wealth. The "Marina" people who populated such new resorts and gated communities, warned the New Islamists, placed themselves above ordinary Egyptians, the law, and morality.

The New Islamists were not the only voices that sounded this alarm. Acute critics from the left, right, and center have written of the dangers that unprecedented concentrations of wealth in a narrow stratum pose to social health and stability. Yet by casting their argument in the Islamic categories that structure all of their thinking, the New Islamists raised this issue in compelling terms, understandable not only to the political class but to the mass of Egyptians. This point was not lost on the government censors.[79]

Huwaidy had in fact alerted readers to the dangers of developments on the North Coast even before the fateful killing captured national attention, and he was not alone among the New Islamists in doing so. For years, Muhammad al Ghazzaly had questioned the wisdom and justice of government involvement in projects to establish tourist villages in Sinai, on the Red Sea, and more recently on the Mediterranean coast. Unlike the Islamic radicals, Ghazzaly defended tourism on Islamic grounds, citing the Quranic injunctions that humankind should travel the world and learn. However, he questioned whether these precious lands could not be given over to more productive enterprises. Ghazzaly feared that these tourist villages to which the elite flocked represented a frivolous tilt to the rich, unseemly in a poor country.

Voices from the left offered essentially the same assessment, though with a more pointed "class" message. Why, asked one prominent economist of the left, should public moneys be used to provide entertainment for wealthy Egyptians and foreigners? Implicit in the question is the charge that the complex infrastructure required for these tourist villages essentially came out of the state budget. National economic policies, beginning with Sadat's Open Door and continuing through current responsiveness to IMF-backed restructuring, made it possible "to steal the money of the hardworking poor." How many of these Marina people, the critic asked, were brought up in the era of the Open Door policy, grew to maturity in the period of IMF reforms, and then earned the title of "businessman"? The government was actively serving this new class by weakening the laws on fraud and the tracing of illegal profits, opening the way for even greater corruption and abuses of power. The economist concluded that "before the revolution, Egypt was a society of the half percent, where this percentage controlled and owned everything, while the rest owned only poverty. Now," he continued, "we have a more fierce separation than that of the past. Now, we are either Marina people or Non-Marina people."[80]

Huwaidy went to see for himself the "development" of the once pristine North Coast region. What he found instead were the dreaded "small signs of doomsday." The Prophet foretold, Huwaidy explained, that warnings of the coming of doomsday would first appear as small indictors that things were not right with the world, followed by unmistakable signs of impending disaster such as the sun rising in the west. Reporting from the North Coast resort region, Huwaidy related with pointed sarcasm how he had personally witnessed on the North Coast one of these small but telling reversals of the natural order of things, whereby divine displeasure is signaled.

In a crowded public square, Huwaidy had witnessed an unfortunate but common event in Egypt. A young driver in an expensive car had roared through a crowded square, barely sparing the lives of terrorized pedestrians. The ensuing commotion attracted the police, and an officer motioned the offending driver to the side. Huwaidy expected to see the ritual pleas and elaborate explanations by the driver to escape the inevitable fine. Instead, Huwaidy heard the boy scream insults and arrogantly tell the officer just whose son he was. The enraged teenager went on to tell the policeman what his father, one of the "big ones," would do to make his life miserable. The explicit threat was unnecessary; hearing the family name was enough. The police officer's manner totally changed. With an ingratiating smile, he started patting the boy on the shoulder, trying to calm and convince him that he had not meant to anger him.

A stunned Huwaidy spent the rest of the day telling this story of reversal to everyone he encountered. Their reactions taught him even more. "Those who heard my story," reported Huwaidy, "nodded and said it happens every day here in Marina. Some of them," he continued, "interrupted me to tell me the rest of the story as if they were present. It is true that the reaction of the officer in public was new, but the behavior of the sons of the big ones who are above the law has become commonplace." A small sampling of corroborating incidents did find their way into the press, each story imprinting the message with telling variations. Although the wealthy father remained offstage in the traffic scene Huwaidy had witnessed, other accounts brought these powerful figures to the fore. One centered on a small dog that disturbed a family enjoying the beach. When the dog got too close to one of his children, the father had pushed it away. The young owner of the dog reported the aggression to his father, who rushed to the site to insult the hapless bather, a doctor. Within minutes, the angry father returned with bullies in tow, who proceeded to beat the man in full view of the horrified public. When the doctor pressed charges, he got nowhere attempting to bring this "big one" to justice.

These patterns of behavior gave the subsequent tragedy of Marina an air of inevitability. The main outlines of the incident emerged clearly in the national coverage. A swimmer was struck and killed by a speedboat at Marina when the young and irresponsible driver ignored the ban on approaching the bathers close to the shore. The details, however, remained obscure. Was the culprit a young boy or an older man? Why had the victim's family declined to press charges and renounced any claims? These questions about the details of the accident lingered despite the glare of national press attention. In fact, the suspicion of a cover-up that these loose ends suggested helped sustain national attention.

Fahmy Huwaidy's article effectively brought out the larger implications of the incident. The innocent blood shed in the water at Marina lent powerful emotional force to an indictment of excessive and irresponsible wealth that threatened to undermine social peace. To introduce his assessment, Huwaidy relied on Dr. Ahmed Khalifa, a respected centrist figure, "neither a failure resentful of the rich, nor a Marxist moved by class antagonism, nor a fundamentalist seeking escape from contemporary life." Huwaidy presented Dr. Khalifa as a social science researcher who for years had headed the National Center for Criminological and Social Research before becoming Minister of Social Affairs. Khalifa addressed his warning against the dangers of "shameless wealth" which in its boasting style expresses the worst in people and threatens social peace.[81] "What kind of devil," asked Khalifa, "pushes the wealthy person to show his wealth through conspicuous consumption that causes pain to empty stomachs?" Such behavior, he continued, "requires abandoning anything related to heart and mind, religion and morals." Not only is it damaging to those who engage in it, but it is also a "terrible aggression against the rights of deprived people who are our brothers in citizenship."

In the past, there have been instances of quite different behavior by the rich in Egypt. In an important series on the *wafq* [Islamic endowments], Fahmy Huwaidy cited cases where Egypt's richest families had supported educational and social, as well as religious, work on an impressive scale. Where, asked Huwaidy, are such wealthy people today?[82] Instead of acts of humane generosity that would survive them, Egypt's richest citizens now regularly committed the kinds of aggression of which Khalifa warned. Weddings in the five-star hotels of Cairo and Alexandria set the standard for flagrant and irresponsible display. In the last decades of the twentieth century, the society pages of the papers were filled with ostentatious displays of wealth, and slick magazines appeared with photo spreads on the rich and powerful. Reporters relished the details of the embellishment of what were once simple marriage traditions in order to attract attention with ever more absurd extravagances. In Cairo's top hotels weddings typically cost from one to one and a half million Egyptian pounds, providing those hotels with up to 40 percent of their earnings. For some parties costs ran as high as 4 million pounds, with all of the food and beverages flown in from Europe, at times on private planes. In some prosperous societies, Huwaidy said, such expenditures might be defensible. But not in Egypt, where half of its people live in poverty, one-quarter of them live under the level of poverty, and some, numbering as many as 15 million, are barely able to survive.

Huwaidy drove home the social implications of such display by juxtaposing the unseemly extravagance of these wedding parties with the plight of poor Egyptians forced to sell their blood and even their body parts to survive. One Cairo newspaper carried a wedding story describing "flowers from Holland, incense from Saudi Arabia, meat from Switzerland, and singers from America." In the very same edition appeared a report of the exposure of a private laboratory that had sold 1,500 human kidneys.[83] Huwaidy pointed out that the report focused on the details of the crime, never asking, "Why were those Egyptians obliged to sell parts of their body and their blood in order to survive?" He concluded that the paper failed to note "the obvious connection between the two stories as both reflecting the same extreme and unbalanced social reality, too often ignored."[84]

The writings of the New Islamists are not animated by the class envy or hatred that at times colors the views of other critics. Yusuf al Qaradawy has stated, for example, that "we are not against richness and wealth, but we are asking God to bless whoever earned this money from legitimate work." With appropriate gravity, Qaradawy added that "in our Islamic culture when someone earns a lot of money in his work, this is considered a kind of reward and a call for him to spend from what God has given him in acts that benefit the poor. The Prophet (God bless him and grant him salvation) used to ask for God's protection from blasphemy *and* poverty."[85] To act for Islam in the world, the New Islamist School maintains, is to enlist in the struggle for justice and against extreme inequalities and poverty of individuals and nations.

part III

Politics

In the face of widespread despair over the prospect of cleaning up the corruption and ineffectiveness of Egypt's political life, the political scientist Manar al Shorbagy sees, with wounded amusement, a glimmer of hope in—the Party of Soap! Islamists are not alone in condemning rigid and authoritarian political structures that defend neither the domestic nor the foreign-policy interests of Egypt's people. There is also widespread discouragement about the corrosive impact of consumerism and market choice as a substitute for real democratic participation.

Shorbagy captures the essence of this critical thinking, advanced with particular force by the New Islamists, with a mock social-scientific report published in the March 1996 issue of *Nidaa al Jadid.* She announces the emergence of a "new political party" that works against these depressing trends. The new party, Shorbagy explains, originates in a hugely popular television show, "Gold Talk." Smiling representatives of the soap company that sponsors the program "campaign" by presenting themselves at the doorsteps of ordinary Egyptians. If the lucky citizens have empty boxes of the company's soap in their homes, they become party members on the spot and are rewarded with gold coins.

Shorbagy criticizes those Egyptian intellectuals who denounce the new party for trivializing political life and humiliating ordinary Egyptians by playing on their greed. Until such time, she argues, as Egypt's real political parties abandon "their empty songs of love for Egypt and service to the people" that only mask corruption and abuse of power, intellectuals are advised to suspend their contemptuous dismissal of the Party of Soap. The new party at least provides hope in the form of a few gold coins to the "lucky few."

chapter 5

Struggling for Islamic Renewal

"Let's Elect Copts!" exclaimed Fahmy Huwaidy in his article on the 2000 electoral campaign for the People's Assembly. This call from Egypt's most prominent Islamist journalist to support Christian candidates for parliament was striking in itself. For those who recalled seeing the headline and the article before, the effect was even stronger.[1] Huwaidy had issued the same call five years earlier during the 1995 elections. With his slogan, he drew attention to the fact that in all of Egypt only thirteen Copts had received nominations for the 1995 round of national elections. The ruling National Democratic Party failed to name even a single Coptic candidate for parliament. The Muslim Brothers matched the regime's shortsightedness. The opposition Labor Party, known for its strong Islamist sentiments, offered to nominate a Copt together with their candidate from the same district, Mamun al Hudaiby, a leading Brotherhood figure. Hudaiby declined. Huwaidy warned that a critical fault line along religious lines had opened up, and that neither the regime nor civil society, including its Islamist wing, had responded effectively to this threat to national unity. In a bold gesture, the newspaper *al Wafd* reprinted Huwaidy's article of 1995 to signal that the country's major political and civic institutions had made no progress on this critical national issue five years later.

The New Islamist School took the unambiguous position that Islam, rightly understood, provides for the full participation of non-Muslims as citizens of an Islamic community. Egyptians as a people, the New Islamists argued, are made up of both Muslims and Copts, who are the joint heirs of an incomparable shared history and culture. They must be fully equal as citizens. In advancing this position, the New Islamists regularly condemned the Islamic extremists who filled the air with poisonous attacks on the Copts. Huwaidy's argument in the context of the parliamentary elections went even further. He pointed out that not all the venom directed against Egypt's Christians came from militant Islamist quarters—that some Muslim electoral candidates having no affiliations with activist Islamist groups of any kind "themselves crossed the red lines." They used unjust and spurious arguments to claim that non-Muslims did not have the right to exercise leadership over Muslims. It was imperative, Huwaidy stated, to "mobilize the energies of reason and correct belief to counter such false assertions and restore the authentic image of Islam."[2]

To Huwaidy's consternation, the official National Democratic Party (NDP) itself was responsible for one of the most shameful incidents. It was like a "mined message," commented Huwaidy, "that exploded in my face as soon as I opened it." An unidentified reader sent him the offending pamphlet. It came with a brief note, asking "How do you like this?" The pamphlet baldly declared, "Those who elect atheists are atheists." This pernicious sentence echoed the extremist Islamist position that Copts and those Muslims who supported them for leadership roles were non-believers. By this argument, Muslims were dissuaded from voting for Coptic candidates.

Huwaidy admitted that at first glance he assumed an Islamist militant or perhaps even agents that sought to distort the Islamic Trend's image had issued the offending pamphlet. "But I did not believe my own eyes," he reported, "when I realized that the pamphlet came from one of the major figures in the ruling party." The candidate promoting himself in this deplorable way turned out to be an important NDP figure whose constituency was in the heart of Cairo. The phrase was not the thoughtless lapse of an ignorant supporter, nor a whispered private indiscretion, nor a gaffe in an electoral speech. Printed and widely distributed, the pamphlet played an important role in an official NDP campaign. Huwaidy noted that it would be difficult to convince people, especially Copts, that this influential figure nominated by the party represented only himself in using these divisive tactics. He concluded that Egyptians should not "be silent about electoral campaigns that violate the supreme interests of the nation in this way."[3]

Huwaidy's message in both 1995 and 2000 was that the government's mishandling of the parliamentary elections signaled a more general political breakdown, marked by political incompetence and ever more insistent reliance on repression. On the Coptic question specifically, Huwaidy made the explicit suggestion that "society" step in to make up for this failure. He called for direct, democratic action by Egypt's ordinary citizens over the heads of all political parties and bypassing the vulnerable institutions of civil society.

"If I were in charge," commented Huwaidy, "I would call for electing all Coptic candidates, whatever their political affiliations or even their policy positions." During this difficult period, major New Islamist figures, includ-

Fahmy Huwaidy, a weekly columnist for *al Ahram* newspaper and Egypt's most prominent Islamist journalist. (photograph courtesy of Abul Ela Mady)

ing Muhammad al Ghazzaly, Yusuf al Qaradawy, and Selim al Awa, along with other prominent Islamist intellectuals, published a clear and forceful statement in *al Shaab* affirming the sound basis in *Sharia* for Muslims to elect non-Muslims as their representatives.[4] In Huwaidy's view, electing Copts had become "an urgent national task" in order to affirm that Egypt's Christians are "an integral part of the fabric of our society."

Huwaidy, of course, understood full well that the government had, for the past fifteen years, shamelessly manipulated elections in Egypt. He also knew that mass attitudes among Muslims toward Copts had deteriorated. In the face of these dispiriting realities, Huwaidy appealed to the best in Egyptians, urging ordinary citizens to make their votes a symbolic gesture toward justice for the Copts and a politics of full equality between Muslims and Christians. Huwaidy understood that the attainment of this goal lay in a future beyond the current political practices and existing civil society.

Nevertheless, such a politics was worth acting for now. Huwaidy concluded by writing, "Although I'm not good at demonstrating and have not joined a demonstration for a quarter of a century, I'm tempted to call for a demonstration carrying the banner 'let's elect Copts.'"

The reprint of Huwaidy's courageous and insightful article generated more than an echo. In the year 2000 there was a response, and it came in a form remarkably close to the hopes that Huwaidy had expressed. It was almost as if a film director, disappointed with the first take, had revised the scenario and refilmed that scene of the prominent NDP Muslim candidate who sought to manipulate anti-Coptic sentiment to secure his election. The setting and the cast of characters remained the same. In the second take, however, the Coptic candidate, who had been opposed in such a dangerous and underhanded way, was resoundingly elected against the NDP incumbent. The energy for the reversal, it should be noted, came from below in the form of direct action by citizens rather than from government or civil society institutions, just as Huwaidy had imagined. The election results dramatically affirmed the democratic cooperation of the Muslim and Coptic citizens of one Cairo neighborhood in order to defend their rights. The sequence ended in 2000 with a real-life shot of "all the people of the district, children and adults, Muslims and Christians, pouring into the streets to express their happiness with the election of the Coptic candidate."[5]

Initially, it appeared that this positive experience of one Cairo district would not be the only indicator of progress registered during the 2000 parliamentary elections. Just as promising was the decision that the judiciary would monitor voting. To accommodate judicial oversight, the voting process was extended from one to three stages, with different districts voting on successive days, so that monitors could be present in all districts. Reports on the first stage indicated that the monitors' role significantly reduced abuses. As a result, the votes for the ruling NDP party declined. This signal was not lost on the regime.[6] The government found ways to go around the monitoring. Reports documented the manipulation of outcomes by busing government employees to the voting booths, as well as outright bullying of opposition supporters. The regime targeted the Muslim Brotherhood in particular, in this way revealing the official assessment of the balance of forces on the political street. In the months prior to the elections, there had been widespread arrests of Brotherhood figures. The worst instances of forceful intimidation during the elections took place in those areas where the Brothers ran candidates.[7] The regime succeeded in slowing the pace with which the NDP lost ground by reverting to its well-established repressive patterns.

In the end, however, the NDP still lost its majority. This erosion of NDP support sent the first of three clear signals on the meaning of the 2000 elections. There could be no doubt that the turn away from the ruling party validated the assessments of widespread political disaffection with the official political system. The victory of sixteen Brotherhood candidates carried the second message. It meant that the Muslim Brothers had become the largest opposition bloc, though still only a handful against an overwhelming NDP majority. The third sign from the electoral results, however, eclipsed the importance of both the NDP's decline and the Brotherhood's gains. The real winners in the elections were those candidates who carried no party affiliations at all and ran as independents. "The party of independents," claimed some analysts, "has become the largest party in Egypt." Others explained that this success of the independents indicated dissatisfaction with existing parties and a trend toward emphasizing the character and record of candidates, rather than their party affiliation.[8]

Post-2000 election developments only reinforced that sense of alienation from official politics. Real power lay with the executive, which, for all the talk of democratization, continued to rule by a system of emergency laws that relied on authoritarian control of the army and police. Understanding that no parliament could contradict these power fundamentals, a large number of independents announced a post-election shift of party affiliation to give the official NDP its usual overwhelming majority. Some were candidates who had lost the NDP endorsement, while others were genuine independents. They all recognized that only a People's Assembly with an NDP majority would be seated, and therefore they joined the NDP fold. Egypt thus had a dominant party incapable of mobilizing independent political support. At the same time, the country was also lacking opposition parties that could mount even a token challenge.[9] The only sign of independent political life came from the Islamic wave, represented politically by the Muslim Brothers.

Such a pallid political system held little attraction for those, like the New Islamists, with an interest in the kind of broad social and cultural transformation called for by their contemporary Islamic vision of gradual and democratic change. The New Islamists stood against those elements within the Islamic wave that sought to give political activity primary emphasis. In their view, there were few serious lessons in democracy to be learned in such an undemocratic political arena. In Egypt real power, they understood, flowed through other channels, inaccessible to democratic challenge. Therefore, an emphasis on political means would lead away from the fundamental democratization of social life in which the New Islamists were interested. It would inevitably rely on other, undemocratic means necessary to contest official power, notably violence and ultimately the idea of a coup to bring Islam to power. The New Islamists understood that in such a confrontation the center, and centrists like themselves, would be the first target. "If Islam were to come to power by force," wrote Selim al Awa, "it would be far worse than the current situation. Those who are in power today are in dialogue with us, which is far better than being slaughtered in the name of Islam."[10]

In place of a political orientation, the New Islamists have devoted their primary efforts to the *tarshid* [guidance] of the Islamic wave as a broad social force with far greater promise as both locus and agent of peaceful social change. The first task, by these lights, would be the transformation of the movement itself in line with the inspiration of the *Wassatteyya*. In this approach, the Islamic wave would be the primary object of attention and the place where anticipated changes would take place first. The second requirement would be to make the transformed *Wassatteyya* a core constituent element of a proposed centrist politics on Islamic ground. For today, the New Islamists encourage young Islamists especially to engage in constructive social action in whatever spheres open up to them, rather than placing any great hopes in the existing political order. For tomorrow, the New Islamists argue that the best hope for a better politics depends on the strengthening over the long term of a broad political mainstream drawn from the major social forces. That mainstream, in their view, must in turn articulate an inclusive, centrist national project that could galvanize real political action. Their long-term vision conveys a clear sense of the contributions that the Islamic *Wassatteyya* can make to the emergence of this mainstream, but never loses sight of the necessity of a broader coalition of moderates from all major social and political forces as the basis for a new politics.

The *Fiqh* of Texts: Justice and Democracy in an Islamic Framework

The New Islamists argue that a democratic politics, founded on commitments to independence and reform and set within an Islamic framework, holds the greatest promise of fulfilling the needs of the nation. They address their brief for democracy in the first instance to the Islamic wave, but intend it for a broader national audience as well. The essential New Islamist argument links democracy to the core Islamic value of justice. "Tell me where you are as far as justice is concerned," pronounced Fahmy Huwaidy, "and I'll tell you where you are as far as Islam is concerned."[11] Their bold *ijtihad* [effort of interpretation of the sacred texts] reaches the general conclusion that Islam establishes the realization of justice as the prime purpose of a political system. The degree to which justice is achieved in turn represents the appropriate standard for its evaluation. In the light of Islam, explains Huwaidy, justice is "an absolute and not a relative value. It must be adhered to in all cases and under all conditions, against enemies as well as with allies."[12] He underscores the centrality of justice as the highest value by declaring that "even if the banner of Islam is held on high and its religious teachings adhered to but justice is not achieved, the message is emptied of content and the means have failed to achieve the ends."[13]

In the New Islamist view, democracy in modern times affords the best means to achieve justice.[14] The New Islamists note that the idea of democratic political means has its own distinctive place in Islam, anchored by the concept of *shura* [consultation] with the ruler. However, their stance toward democracy is not an apologetic one. They recognize that the world beyond Islam's borders, most importantly the West, has developed the most promising modern democratic mechanisms and has the richest experience with democratic political institutions. They urge the Islamic world to look both to the heritage and especially to the experience of others to develop democratic political systems suitable for the global age.

The New Islamists propound this centrality of democracy while at the same time frankly acknowledging the historical record and contemporary reality of the despotism of most regimes, and the extreme vulnerability of civil society in Egypt and throughout the Arab Islamic world. They are painfully aware of the stark contrast between an imagined democratic politics of Islamic inspiration and the long authoritarian experience of Arab Islamic countries. Despite the democratic promise of the Islamic notion of *shura,* they acknowledge that political tyranny came early to the Islamic world and continues to diminish its prospects.

In the face of these daunting historical realities, the New Islamists assert that the inspiration of Islam speaks afresh to each generation. They refuse to be bound by what they see as the regrettable political mistakes of earlier generations or, for that matter, of their contemporaries who have relied on authoritarian political alternatives. "The abandonment of *shura,*" wrote Yusuf al Qaradawy unequivocally, "was the first thing that harmed the Islamic nation." The virus of dictatorship from the Roman and Persian Empires infected Islamic rule, based on the consent of the people, when the Muslims copied the worst features of these systems.[15] The infection of tyranny took hold early and persisted with devastating consequences. Fahmy Huwaidy has pronounced long stretches of the subsequent political history of the Islamic world "a series of disasters in which only the names and places changed."[16] The genius of Islam historically found its expression in fields other than politics. Thus, the New Islamists have not hesitated to challenge the usefulness of historical models from the Islamic world. For the most part, they remain equally unimpressed by the claims of contemporary regimes to represent Islamic models of democratic governance.[17] For positive guidance they turn instead to the histories of others, notably Westerners.

The New Islamist *ijtihad* of texts seeks to draw inspiration from the revelation rather than from the history of its abuse. Their reading of the texts develops the concept of *shura* as a means, provided for in the Quran and *Sunnah,* to achieve justice by rulership based on full participation and respect for the rights of people given to them by God. They identify these dimensions of the tradition as essential characteristics of any modern idea of democracy. Whether admonishing the regime, guiding the Islamic mainstream, or acting to contain the extremists, Huwaidy explained that the New Islamists aim to correct distorted ideas about Islam in order to bring this democratic reading of the legacy to the fore.

Islamic democracy in a form that responds to the needs of the age, they candidly acknowledge, is a project yet to be realized. The New Islamists, therefore, set their sights on the long-term task of laying the educational and cultural foundations for an Islamic politics that has justice as its core value and democracy as the vehicle for its realization. In particular, they argue that Islamic *fiqh* must appropriate the gains of Western political constitutional thought. Speaking with unembarrassed frankness, Muhammad al Ghazzaly pronounced Islamic constitutional *fiqh* to be "severely underdeveloped." He urged Islamic thinkers to borrow freely from Western democratic concepts and mechanisms. More precisely, the New Islamist School singled out the following notions as proven instruments of democratic rule that should be imitated: the separation of powers, multiple parties and competitive elections, constitutional guarantees of basic political freedoms such as speech and assembly protected by an independent judiciary, and limited terms for the highest offices. The New Islamists have worked to integrate these elements from the experience of others into a coherent theory and practice of Islamic democracy.

New Islamist theorizations have aimed for a democracy of just outcomes and not simply procedures. This position clearly precludes the uncritical imitation of the West. The New Islamists balance their appreciation for the nuts and bolts of Western democracies with a discriminating sense of their limitations, particularly in terms of the unjust outcomes that even the most advanced democracies tolerate. They draw particular attention to the destruction of values and culture by unbridled consumerism and the unacceptable disparities in material circumstances and life chances that characterize all of the Western democracies, especially the United States.

All of the key New Islamist figures have made substantial contributions to an impressive effort that has extended over the last three decades of the twentieth century to spell out the implications of these insights. With too few exceptions, observers outside the Islamic movement miss or underestimate the important innovations in political thinking that these efforts have produced. As Fahmy Huwaidy notes, most analysts of the Islamic wave, whether Egyptian or Western, direct their attention either to "the traditional face of the Islamic movement, represented by the Muslim Brothers, which dates from the twenties, or to the angry, subversive groups which emerged in the circumstances of the seventies, forming both al Jihad and the Islamic Group, as well as al Takfir wa al Higra, which then disappeared from the scene." Most of these researchers, Huwaidy points out, fail to survey the huge Islamic terrain beyond these narrow borders which saw "very important and very positive developments" in the post-Nasser era.[18]

At the heart of this new political thinking are the 1993 *fatwas* [religious opinions] of Yusuf al Qaradawy on pluralism and democracy. Qaradawy spoke for all the New Islamists when he unambiguously embraced political pluralism, including the competition of political parties. He explicitly rejected the contrary views of Hassan al Banna, founder of the Muslim Brothers. Reasoning by analogy, Qaradawy explained that Islam has no trouble tolerating diversity in *Sharia,* recognizing four major schools as authoritative, despite important differences among them. Clearly, Islam could, and should, value pluralism in the political sphere. With the same emphasis, Qaradawy took as a starting point the idea that the Islamic notion of *shura* with the ruler provided a secure conceptual anchor for contemporary efforts to build democracy. Again with the full support of the New Islamists as a school, Qaradawy unequivocally pronounced that *shura* was obligatory and not voluntary, as some within the Islamic wave contended. While the New Islamists do recognize the very general character of the concept of *shura,* noting, for example, that Islam allows the fulfillment of the obligation of *shura* in a variety of ways, their response is to regard this generality as enabling intellectual creativity in the elaboration of the meaning of such a concept today. In their own work, they put forward a strong argument for understanding *shura* in terms of the Western democratic mechanisms that are now part of the common heritage of humankind, inspiring democratic experiments around the world.[19]

Huwaidy comments that this critical *ijtihad* on pluralism and democracy has been willfully ignored. He notes that if even a minor figure from the contemporary *ulama* [Islamic scholars] denounces democracy and a multi-party system, his words become the subject of headlines and endless commentary by intellectuals in Egypt and abroad. However, when

"Dr. Yusuf al Qaradawy, a great Islamic scholar, issued his *fatwas*, his declarations fell on deaf ears." Wryly, Huwaidy adds that "those observers who rarely ignore anything related to Islam paid no attention to his declarations at all, leading one to believe that their intent must be to obscure the Islamic attitude toward freedom in general."[20]

Given his major platform in *al Ahram*, Fahmy Huwaidy has played a central role in efforts to bring elaborations of this new *fiqh* of politics to public attention. In two authoritative syntheses published at the beginning and the end of the 1990s, Huwaidy laid out the main lines of the democratic theory advanced by the New Islamists. In a concise and easily understood form, he specified the seven critical characteristics that New Islamist theorists agree a political system must have to meet the exacting Islamic standards of justice achieved through democracy.[21] The first specifies that legitimate authority rests with the people, who choose the ruler and have the right to remove him from power.[22] The second notes that society has responsibilities and duties that it exercises independently of any "call by the authorities or permission by the government."[23] The third, fourth, and fifth characteristics provide, respectively, for freedom as a right for all, equality of all citizens, and the explicit recognition of the rightful place of the "other," that is, the non-Muslim, as a full partner with Muslims in the just Islamic state. The sixth element of an Islamic political system understood in these terms makes any injustice *haram* [religiously forbidden] and its confrontation a duty of all citizens. Finally, the seventh characteristic recognizes *Sharia* as the source of legislation to which rulers as well as the people must yield. *Sharia* is understood by the New Islamists to derive from the divine injunctions of the Quran and the confirmed provisions of *Sunnah*. They also recognize the importance of *fiqh* in elaborating and explaining the applications of these injunctions, though they insist that *fiqh* is a fully human project, subject to criticism and refutation. This formulation that identifies *Sharia* as the source of legislation, the New Islamists explain, separates executive from legislative power and thereby creates the theoretical justification for constraints on the power of the executive.[24] Rulers, like all citizens, are themselves bound by the provisions of *Sharia*, and the legitimacy of their rule rests in part on fulfillment of their obligations to *Sharia*.

The New Islamists take these characteristics as a standard to assess whether and to what degree any particular political system, real or imagined, meets the Islamic standard of a democratic order that strives for justice. This measure is addressed, in the first instance, to the Islamic movement. For the activists of the Islamic wave, this normative theorizing makes the fundamental point that the simple acquisition of power cannot be the aim of the Islamic Awakening. The critical issue is the purpose for which power is used. The capacity to make and insist on this distinction sets the New Islamists apart. Others in the Islamic wave, especially those identified with "political Islam," too often succumb to the temptation to celebrate any wielding of political power by forces that identify themselves as Islamist, whatever the actual character of their rule. In important ways, the specter of "political Islam" drives the corrective work of the New Islamist School. To traditionalists and extremists alike who adopt this attitude, the New Islamists argue that injustice and tyranny, however they are cloaked in historical Islamic forms or legitimized by angry Islamic slogans, remain injustice and tyranny. They maintain that Islamic justice must define the purposes of power to be achieved through a patient process of cultural transformation that lays the basis for a democratic politics, rather than a sudden seizure of power.

Political Islam represents a direct threat to the attainment of this long-term goal. In some ways, it is even more damaging than the government's blockage of democratic advance. In insistent terms, advocates of political Islam call for *hakameyyet Allah* [God's rule], using this evocative phrase to justify rash bids for power. The extremists formulate the call in the strongest terms, but it also echoes in the words of traditionalists and some elements of the Muslim Brotherhood. Often these diverse advocates of political Islam give a falsely legitimizing, historical aura to such claims with loose references to the caliphate system or *wilaya* [a historical and therefore not binding concept of rule]. They capture headlines with noisy denunciations of "Western" democracy and its competitive political parties, focusing public attention on the alternative "Islamic" forms of rule they advocate.[25] As a result, political Islam has a strong presence both as the dream of salvation by those Islamists who seek the political kingdom, and as the nightmare of secular critics who fear Islam in power. Whether dream or nightmare, its essential features are those of the theocratic state, with power in the hands of religious figures who claim exclusive right to speak for Islam.

The New Islamists confront this specter boldly. They warn its advocates that their dream would be a terrible nightmare, violating Islam's opposition to the very idea of a religious state. To its critics, they explain that their nightmare reflects only the narrow political dream of a minority, far from the broad civilizational project of the mainstream Islamic *Wassatteyya* for which they speak.

With unrelenting precision, the New Islamists expose on Islamic ground the mistakes in interpretation that yield the distortions of political Islam. Political thought in an Islamic context, they explain, draws on three sources: texts, the interpretations of texts, and the historical experience of the Islamic community.[26] The specter of political Islam arises as an amalgam of these three elements, one that fails to distinguish among them and to understand their very different weight and authority. Political Islam relies, above all, on flawed or inappropriate historical models and questionable interpretations of texts.

The New Islamists state firmly that only texts, not particular interpretations or historical models, are authoritative. Moreover, they point out that those texts of Quran and *Sunnah* that relate to political rule are few in number and general in character, referring for the most part to values and purposes rather than means and structures. With this reasoning, they reach a strong conclusion: Islam, in their view, does not specify a particular system of governance, sanctified by text, to manage the use of power in human affairs. Political Islam asserts otherwise. It falsely advances particular models as "Islamic" in some universal sense. The New Islamists categorically reject these claims. In their view, all of the institutional specificities of the various concepts and models of political Islam derive essentially from interpretations, often seriously flawed, and particular histories, rather than texts. These include, in addition to political Islam's distorted understanding of *hakemeyya* [God's rule], its dangerous presumption of legitimate authoritarian rule by religious figures in a religious state, and its mistaken inclination to regard the caliphate or *wilaya* as models for such a system that are appropriate in modern times. To refute such ideas, the New Islamists argue first that Islam categorically rejects the sanctification of any such specific forms of political legitimation, leadership, or institutions. With intellectual authority few can match, the New Islamists go further to challenge all efforts to find an authoritative basis in Islam for absolutist and authoritarian political claims for any future project. Finally, they maintain that this age, like all others, must not be bound in political affairs either by earlier interpretations of texts or by the example of political arrangements adopted by previous generations. In their view, each age must have its own political *fiqh*. On this basis, they confidently assert their own new *fiqh* of politics, while challenging the faulty political claims of political Islam in clear and forceful terms.

"They are laughable illusions," wrote Shaikh Muhammad al Ghazzaly of the "strange religious figures" who dominate the dreams and nightmares of political Islam. Ghazzaly dismissed these images of "men in long beards and flowing robes, those inflated 'Imams' who would drive the country backwards by their preoccupation with issues irrelevant to life on earth, such as preaching on preparation for doomsday." He warned that "this is a terrible mistake," because in Islam there is no such thing as "men of religion" with a sanctified claim to rule. The extremist *amirs* [leaders of groups] do assert a claim to rule, and they base that claim on their allegedly superior understanding of Islam. Such a prospect, the New Islamists declare, should sound an alarm in all quarters. The New Islamists vigorously discredit the credentials of the extremist leaders to interpret Islam. However, their argument goes further: it challenges the very premise that scholars, even recognized scholars, should rule. Addressing this false claim from Islamic ground, Ghazzaly explains that there are indeed those specialized in the study of Quran and *Sunnah.* "These studies," however, "are just one part of the wider Islamic culture that includes endless arts and subjects." Moreover, the *ulama,* as Ghazzaly describes them, "are just a group of Muslims, neither above nor below any other group." He adds that those most trusted in understanding the texts never had key roles in building the Islamic state—that "in the golden ages of Islam the most highly regarded *faqihs* [an Islamic scholar, specially trained and recognized by peers as qualified to contribute to *fiqh*] were never candidates for ruling."[27]

Equally wrongheaded is political Islam's understanding of the call for *hakemeyya.* "It is unacceptable," declares the New Islamist manifesto, "to deprive Muslims of their political rights and responsibilities with the assertion that in an Islamic society 'rule is for God and not human beings.'" The New Islamists explain that the phrase actually means in both Quran and *Sunnah* that "the *values and principles* of Islam are God-given." As the New Islamist manifesto expresses it, "God's rule comes at the beginning and the end."[28] They interpret this phrase to mean that the Quran and *Sunnah* define the purposes for which power should be used "at the beginning" to inspire the effort to build a political system, and "at the end" to assess whether the system has in fact achieved justice as called for by Islam. Islam thus provides a larger moral framework on the basis of which a system of rule can be chosen and then assessed. It leaves to human beings the actual task of building a political system, selecting its leaders, and executing policies that meet people's particular needs and circumstances. It is up to each generation to accomplish these political tasks.

According to the New Islamists, the essential interpretive error of political Islam in its understanding of the concept of God's rule is the conflation of two issues that in Quran and *Sunnah* are kept separate. The first is the source of legislation, and the second is the basis for the obedience owed to the ruler. In Islam, they explain, legislation originates in revelation. *Sharia* has a divine character in those provisions that come directly from Quran and *Sunnah,* and both ruler and ruled are subject to these elements of *Sharia.* In contrast, the legitimacy of the ruler and of the political system itself in an Islamic society "depends on the consent of the people, meaning that Islamic government is a civil and not a religious government."[29] It is unacceptable to extend the rightful recognition of the divine character of *Sharia* as derived from Quran and *Sunnah* to the very different issues of the claims to rule by a particular political regime and leadership. The New Islamists believe that Islam, with no ambiguity at all, leaves these issues of rulership to the exercise of human discretion.

The New Islamists are not dissuaded by the fact that this confusion between the divine basis of legislative as opposed to executive authority has deep historical roots; they acknowledge that it can be traced back to the reign of the fourth caliph. Moreover, they are unmoved that the most important contemporary theorists of political Islam, including both Abul Ala al Maududi and Sayyid Qutb, have aggressively reasserted this confusion. "Rule is but for God" and "He is the Creator and the Ruler" are the two verses that have consistently been cited to blur the distinction between the divine basis for legislation, on the one hand, and the fully human claim to legitimate rule, on the other, in order to sanctify political authority generally. The New Islamists accept neither the authority of history nor that of interpreters from another time or place. They turn to the texts and offer their own readings. Kamal Abul Magd makes a strong argument that both of the texts usually cited to justify authoritarian rule refer only to the source of legislation or *Sharia* and not to the source of sovereignty. "Neither verse," states Abul Magd in unequivocal language, "has anything to do with the bases of political power."[30]

Adherents of political Islam often invoke historical references, notably to the caliphate, to buttress their misreading of the texts to legitimate authoritarian systems of rule. Models of politics from the first Islamic century (dated from the founding of the Islamic community in 622) are most often invoked, with such features as the lifelong mandate and unconstrained authority of the executive. The New Islamists readily acknowledge, as Selim al Awa expressed it, that "the era of the Prophet and the first four caliphs was the best time in which justice prevailed." However, in keeping with their core belief that each age has the right to its own *ijtihad,* Awa just as firmly rejected any implication that a caliph was therefore obligatory today. Instead, he pointed out that the caliphate of those first years was itself an *ijtihad* that changed and developed. "No detailed system is binding," wrote Awa, "unless it is chosen by the people who believe it achieves their aims and protects their interest; if not, they have the full right to change it." He noted that "prescriptions for the lifelong mandate of the caliph were written by *faqihs* according to their own times, but it is not a binding *Sharia* rule."

The New Islamists have likewise rejected the notion of rulership associated with the concept of *waliya.* This concept of rule is invoked by political

Islam almost as frequently as the caliphate to ground authoritarian political claims. Neither women nor non-Muslims, according to conventional interpretations of *waliya,* could assume rule. The concept is exploited today for exclusionist ends. The New Islamists reject all of these contemporary applications of the idea of *wilaya.* "I was asked by some young people," wrote Selim al Awa in the most thoughtful statement on the issue, "about the Islamic opinion on nominating and voting for Copts for the People's Assembly." The question arose, he explained, as a result of "the widely cited saying 'no command by non-Muslims over Muslims.'" They also asked him "about nominating and voting for women" because of their doubts arising from the *hadith* [a report, including the sources, of the words of the Prophet] that 'those who give authority to women fail.'" Awa's response to these inquiries, later published in *al Shaab,* was direct and unambiguous: "I said to them that both texts are used in the wrong context to prove something that has nothing to do with them." In an interpretation, endorsed explicitly by both Muhammad al Ghazzaly and Yusuf al Qaradawy, Awa bluntly declared that these restrictions on the political rights of women and non-Muslims derived from the obsolete concept of *waliya* and should be disregarded. Awa explained that the term refers to an absolute power to command and noted that the concept originally referred to the head of the Islamic state who had military and purely religious duties, notably leading prayers that were considered inappropriate for women or non-Muslims to perform. In Awa's view, none of these conditions can or should be met in contemporary political life. Therefore, in his judgment this historical concept is now irrelevant. "*Waliya* . . . no longer exists in any country," stated Awa. "The concept of government, its mechanisms and institutions have changed in such a way that today no one can be considered to have *waliya.*" In a memorable conclusion that underscored the link between the rejection of such antiquated authoritarian ideas and the New Islamist commitment to full political participation for all citizens, Awa advised the young people that "the proper criterion for accepting or rejecting candidates must be their qualifications to perform the consultative role, such as honesty, absence of corruption, and courage in facing evils." With strong emphasis, he added that "by these criteria Muslims and Copts are equal, as are men and women. The only permissible distinction is according to ethics, character, public record, and ability to support what is right and deter what is wrong."[31]

In line with this thinking, Awa put forward his own striking assessment of the meaning of the caliphate experience for the contemporary period. "If there is something to learn from this early age," he wrote, "it is that the caliphate was based on two pillars: first, the caliph was selected through *shura* among Muslims, with no particular group entitled to choose for the nation as a whole; and second, the nominee chosen never assumed power without clear-cut support of the people." Translating these lessons into contemporary language, Awa concluded that "democracy is the best way to choose among rulers since human beings have so far found nothing better than direct elections," and he stated further that the mandate of elections should not be lifelong. "Good for the Americans that they limited the terms of the President to only two!" wrote Awa with a dramatic and unexpected flourish.[32]

The New Islamists acknowledge that the capacity for such *ijtihad* requires knowledge and understanding "in knowing God's rule that are not present in the majority of people." However, they explicitly condemn "raising this slogan on the tips of swords and insisting on it." They use this historical image to criticize authoritarian preemptions of the right of *ijtihad* in the political sphere as in all others. Such usurpations, they warn, "were, in our recent and remote past, a prelude for evil and injustice." Neither reason nor text, the New Islamists conclude, provide any acceptable justification for the monopoly of the right of political *ijtihad* by either a single ruler or a small group.[33] This stance carries the implication that competent scholars will have the task of *ijtihad,* with the results of their efforts subjected to democratic mechanisms of arbitration and choice.[34]

In place of the rigid and misleading certainties of political Islam, the New Islamists offer the tentative and contingent findings of their own interpretive project. Their work explores an open-ended way the prospects for attaining justice by democratic means in modern conditions. In Islam there are no ready-made models, sanctioned by God for all times and places, to achieve the standard of justice. In challenging the positions of political Islam, the New Islamists argue that their alternative interpretations represent not only a more accurate understanding of texts, but also a further development of mainstream Islamic political thought, particularly well suited to the needs of the global age. From the work of earlier Islamic thinkers, beginning with Afghany and Abduh and extending through al Banna to contemporary figures, they offer a selective reading that emphasizes democratic strands such as the struggle for freedom from external oppression, insistence on civil rather than religious governance, commitment to peaceful and gradualist reform, work for broad participation in political life, and the setting of meaningful limits on ruling power. These promising elements from the New Islamists' predecessors have contributed to their own collective *ijtihad* for the sake of an Islamic vision of a democratic politics that aspires to realize social justice. While highly conscious of the place of their work in the stream of Islamist political thought about justice and democracy, the New Islamists have developed their thinking with close attention to the special political circumstances of their own time. Appreciative of the contributions of the founders of the *Wassatteyya* trend, the New Islamists nevertheless understood that theirs was wisdom for another time, that the last word on Islam and democracy in a global age could not be theirs. The new *fiqh* of texts developed in tandem with an equally important new *fiqh* of reality. The resulting realistic awareness by the New Islamists of their own situation and of the prospects of its democratic transcendence within an Islamic framework contributed greatly to the resilience of their political ideas in the changing and often adverse political circumstances of the last three decades of the twentieth century.

The *Fiqh* of Reality: Theorizing the Center

Historical context matters to the New Islamists. Political thinking, in their view, requires a *fiqh* of reality as much as a *fiqh* of texts, and they have developed a shared assessment of the most relevant dimensions of their historical situation. The New Islamist historical imagination directs attention first to the impact of the global wave of religious revival that reenergized the Islamic body in Egypt during the second half of the twentieth century. Second, they emphasize that Egypt's Islamic Awakening failed to generate an Islamist leadership fully able to respond to the opportunities that had been created. Finally, the New Islamists face squarely the authoritarian political context that constrains, but does not preclude, the intellectual and activist work of their school on behalf of the *Wassatteyya*. It is not simplifying the situation too much to say that the Islamic renewal sustains their hopes for a better future; the leadership void sets their essential task of educational and cultural reform; and the ebb and flow of authoritarian rule defines the terrain of their struggles. The New Islamists look initially for salvation to the "moderate heart" of the Islamic wave and then to other centrist social forces. Over the long term, they aim to translate their new *fiqh* of politics into reality by bringing the *Wassatteyya* into a broad national effort to create on Islamic ground a moderate politics of justice and democracy.

The New Islamists theorize and act within expansive boundaries of historical possibility. Over the last quarter of the twentieth century, these Islamist thinkers established themselves as important public figures who interact with all major social trends. In their commitments to social justice and democracy, they served as exemplary models for new generations of moderate activists. The extended time frame of their perspective allows them to avoid entrapment in a conception of political life limited by the unhappy prospects of both official politics and civil society in current conditions of undemocratic rule. Their inclusive thinking starts from the premise that the centrist elements of all national major trends aim to realize the good of the nation, discoverable in recognizable, though varied, embodiments. They also believe that the moderate centers of all these social forces share a history of constructive interactions more important than their current divisions. From this perspective, the New Islamists see a history of past collaboration and a future of possible cooperation for a wide spectrum of moderates.

The gradualist political thinking of the New Islamists lays the groundwork for a future where the Islamic wave would be an integral part of the mainstream of Egyptian political life. They regard such a future as distant but reachable, and they work patiently for its realization as their first priority. The New Islamists stand firmly against the contrary and impatient strategy of political Islam that aims to capture targeted institutions of civil and political society. In this vision, these Islamist "islands" or "beachheads" would form the nuclei of an Islamic society to displace dominant arrangements, by force if necessary. The New Islamists explicitly reject these "infiltration" and "counter-society" models in favor of gradual, peaceful social and cultural change of the whole society.

To meet this challenge, the New Islamists cultivated a strong sense of "civilizational belonging" that saw Egypt as part of the Arab Islamic world. They defined that world in terms of its own intrinsic worth rather than in critical contrast to the West. Emerging from its own rich and distinctive Islamic roots, the civilization to which Egypt belonged had always interacted freely with the wider world and must continue to do so. In the New Islamist view, the remaking of Egypt would require the confidence to learn from all quarters, without, however, forgetting the distinctive Egyptian purposes of that learning. It would require the discriminating ability to return to Egypt's past without drowning in it. It would be essential to find in that past materials that would help to build new pathways to an evolving and very different future.

The New Islamists thus built their centrist position on solid Islamic ground without isolating Egyptians from the main currents of contemporary thought. This new thinking expressed the insights of the Islamic wave in theoretical ways that captured the essence of successful experiences, while responding with openness to the new conditions of the global age. In this way, the New Islamists' theoretical work on civilizational identity helped to provide an anchor for Egyptian efforts to create an autonomous path into the future in the face of potentially overwhelming hegemonic influences from the West. Its bedrock was the civilizational confidence that the Islamic wing of the national movement had preserved and the New

Islamists had refined. Its instrument was the rationalized Islamic wave as a component of the political mainstream. Its orienting strategy for the long term was the evolving national project to which the *Wassatteyya* aimed to contribute.

The importance of the New Islamist conception of civilizational identity was not restricted to the Islamic wave. The ability to cultivate a distinctive and confident identity, particularly among the young, was important to all trends. The balanced and sophisticated forms that the New Islamist thinkers gave these insights helped bring them to the mainstream of political life where they would be within reach of all groups. Such inclusive thinking about the civilizational identity of all Egyptians helped to overcome divisions, enabling moderates of all kinds to build coalitions and other forms of cooperation for their often courageous and always daunting efforts to act politically in an authoritarian political context.

Acting Politically

The New Islamists understand that young activists in particular need ways, however circumscribed, in which to develop political and civic skills. For that reason, these theorists of the center have kept themselves alert and open to all practical opportunities to act today for the new politics they imagine for tomorrow.

This emphasis on the cultivation of the young has elicited a surprisingly positive response for a "school" that controls neither a party apparatus nor, for that matter, any institutional structures at all. Young Egyptians have responded to the major New Islamist figures, especially Muhammad al Ghazzaly and Yusuf al Qaradawy, as they did to few others in public life. While it is possible to identify other important intellectuals who have identified with opposition political trends and played leadership roles in civil society, none have attracted as wide a following among the youth over so long a period.

Finding constructive outlets for the energies of activists has been a continuing challenge for the New Islamists. They never forget that the whole edifice of political and civic activity rests on the acquiescence of a government yet to be democratized. They see how deep the absence of values and mindless deference to authority goes in all the institutions of public life. They understand, moreover, that not all of these weaknesses can be attributed to authoritarianism. Opposition political parties that might provide an alternative for the new generation instead mirror many of the worst characteristics of the NDP. Year after year, the opposition parties grind out the same tired ideologies and platitudes, lacking in imagination and any capacity for self-criticism. The same aging figures monopolize all key positions, blocking access by younger activists to leadership roles. Internal divisions and splits, most often based on personality issues, further weaken all the opposition parties. Many of these same failings mark the major organizations of civil society: their internal practices are often just as undemocratic as those of the parties, though there are some notable exceptions. However, the same petty internal squabbles, as well as preoccupation with minor issues, plague both sets of institutions. The Muslim Brotherhood enjoys more success than other groups in drawing young people to its ranks. Yet these same internal failings mar the Brotherhood organization, notably the disinclination to give meaningful organizational roles to young people.[35]

In the face of these obstacles, the New Islamists seek to guide youthful activist energies into whatever productive channels become available, provided they are consonant with the ends of political life they imagine. They aim to encourage even partial realizations of the larger dreams that the *Wassatteyya* embodies. Precisely because the New Islamists do not look to the government or even civil society with great expectations, they are able to take their measure accurately. They are adept at adapting to successive waves of repression, responding adroitly to periodic openings.

The decade of the 1980s offered many such positive opportunities. In retrospect, it is clear that during those years some of the most enduring roots of moderation took hold, especially important for the "lost generation." Practical experience was gained that bore fruit later. True, in the wake of the dismal elections of 1995 and 2000, it takes more and more imagination even to recall the optimism felt when Sadat's rule ended. Yet at that point Egypt did seem poised for a deepening of democratization that would include the Islamists. At just this historic juncture, the New Islamists drafted their manifesto and first advanced their claim for a leadership role as the "mind" of the *Wassatteyya.*[36] The New Islamists worked to provide *tarshid* for the efforts of the Islamic "body" in the civic and political spheres that were expanding in those promising years. They did so, moreover, in a balanced way that set them apart. They never pushed criticism of the regime so far as to question its authority. At the same time, they avoided too close an identification with a system of rule that in the end remained undemocratic.

The deepening of democracy never took place. By the late 1980s, any illusions about the character of the regime and the possibilities that it would reform began to fade. Selim al Awa in his unsparing *The Political and Constitutional Crisis in Egypt,* published in 1991, laid bare the absolute unwillingness of the regime to respond to legal, judicial, and popular demands for any effective constraints on its power.[37] The New Islamists understood that although repression might periodically be lightened, the underlying government monopoly of real power would most likely continue for the immediate future. However, they did not find this political reality as debilitating as other social forces did. For them, this harsh political situation meant that the Islamic center must look beyond politics and even civil society. Their own most promising role, as the New Islamists saw it, was to rationalize the Islamic wave and make it an essential element of moderate social forces, drawn together from across the political spectrum and bridging the gap between Muslims and Copts. In the long run, they looked to these forces of moderation to create new political horizons of opportunity.

During the last years of Sadat's rule and the first of the new regime, Islamists established themselves in the faculty clubs of the universities, forged alliances with political parties, successfully published the important *Dawa* journal, and made themselves a dominant element in the professional associations. The most visible victories in the 1980s came in parliamentary elections. The Muslim Brothers cooperated first with the Wafd party in 1984 to win eight seats, and then in 1987 with the opposition Labor and Ahrar parties to win an unprecedented thirty-five seats in the Egyptian parliament. Supporters as well as critics came to respect the improved skills of the Islamist activists in playing the game of democratic politics, however they might differ in assessing their ultimate goals.

The New Islamists welcomed and carefully assessed this peaceful expansion of the activities of the Islamic body through democratic channels. In no sense did they control or direct these diverse and often spontaneous activities. Their role was rather to provide *tarshid* wherever and whenever possible. In the end, their experience in the middle-class professional associations with democratic elections and administrative responsibilities proved most valuable of all in enhancing the political skills of a new generation of moderates. Islamist activists in the numerous associations (for doctors, lawyers, teachers, veterinarians, and so forth) competed for leadership roles in compliance with democratic rules, accepting defeat and the circulation of power. They were instrumental in expanding the narrower professional functions of the associations to take positions on issues of public policy. The Islamists succeeded in enlarging the associational role in civil society, notably through forums and discussions sponsored by the professional associations that enliven Cairo's civic life. The Doctors' Association went furthest, expanding its social service efforts on behalf not just of doctors but of less privileged elements of the population in the interest of social justice. On occasion, the Doctors' Association succeeded in doing so on a national scale, especially when the country was struck by some national disaster to which the association responded.

The New Islamists made their stabilizing and enlightening presence felt in these new forums, giving lectures and participating in public debates and discussions that gave Islamists the collective opportunity to assess their experience critically and reflect on its importance for the long term.[38] At the same time, the New Islamists demonstrated a willingness to criticize any lapses of behavior, particularly in those professional associations where the Islamists had a strong or even dominant presence and could therefore reasonably be held accountable for outcomes. The New Islamists did all they could to call attention to these lessons in applied democracy. They responded, for example, to an electoral failure of Islamists in the Veterinary Association with a blunt call to welcome the results of the ballot box. Islamic activists who complained of the outcome did not expect to be told that defeat in the elections most likely meant that they had failed their constituency and should work for self-improvement and reform. Selim al Awa delivered precisely this message. The Islamists in the Veterinary Association had initially won a landslide victory. However, after two years in office not a single candidate was reelected. Disgruntled, they approached Selim al Awa in his capacity as a lawyer with clear Islamist sympathies and asked him to handle a case charging fraud in the elections. Awa asked for all their records of their time in office. Reviewing the materials, he concluded that "during their term, they did absolutely nothing for their constituents aside from holding a number of religious symposiums on prayers, fasting, and so on." Awa told these Islamists that, given their record, their leaving office was a "good thing," and he refused to take their case.[39] This capacity to accept the discipline of democracy and to respond with positive self-criticism proved to be a distinctive characteristic of the activist Islamic wave, in no small part due to such guidance by the New Islamists.

The New Islamist School welcomed this work in the professional associations as an important "postgraduate" course in civic involvement for a whole generation of Islamists who were able to channel the activism of their university student days into these new democratic channels of civic engagement. However, they consistently registered the cautionary note that the associational realm, like other areas of civil society in Egypt, remained weak and vulnerable to government manipulation. Thus, the New Islamists resisted any exaggeration of the role the associations could play. Though they strongly supported Islamist activism in the associations, when the government crackdown and ultimate dismantling of the Islamist presence came, the New Islamists were neither caught unawares nor provoked into making the issue one of confrontation with the regime.

The regime in the end reacted very negatively not only to these associational activities but also to all developments that suggested the Islamic body would thrive in a democratic environment. Beginning in the early 1990s, the government launched a systematic crackdown on civil society, with particular attention to curtailing the professional associations where the Islamists had registered such important gains. The decade of promise was over. Civic action in Egypt was besieged and faced with hurdles at every turn. Ironically, the promise from the first years of the new regime of a deepening of democracy and the rule of law found its only lasting expression in the use of the law as the major tool of repression. The government relied on its compliant parliamentary majority not only to renew endlessly the state-of-emergency laws but also to pass a whole series of laws that provided a highly articulated "legal" framework for repression.[40]

At the same time, the regime mobilized and encouraged a segment of the intellectual elite, notably those from the left who were visibly alarmed by exaggerated fears of the Islamist extremists, to support these measures against political democracy and a strong civil society. They did so in the name of protecting Egypt's "nascent democracy" from the Islamists. Systematically, the regime and its supporters dramatized the actions of the Islamic militants and exaggerated their impact. At the same time, they downplayed the positive contributions in theory and practice of the moderates. Most dramatically, the government sought to incapacitate the professional associations by legal measures that effectively undermined their governing boards.

Secular critics of the Islamists paved the way for the government repression by evoking hostile images to characterize the alleged intent of the Islamists in the associations. The liberals linked the important role of the Islamists in the associations to their work in other areas such as health care, social services, and the economy, giving the whole project of the Islamists in the associations a vaguely subversive coloration. Other elements of the left attacked even more aggressively. Images of Algeria and the Islamist violence there were regularly evoked in connection with Egypt's Islamists, with scant attention given either to the Algerian military's preemption of the democratic process or to the very different historical and social context. The left most often judged that the cultural, social, and humanitarian work of the Islamists in Egypt merely provided a cover for their underground political organizing, and a screen for their links to the violent radicals who they believed would be the storm troops of an Islamist fascist coup. The evidence of democratic behavior in the associations, the left argued, was not really reassuring. In their eyes, democracy for the Islamists simply provided an alternative means to achieve their goal of the seizure of power. Evoking the rationale that the Algerian military had used to abort the democratic election of Islamists, extreme secularists in Egypt argued that if Islamists were to achieve power democratically in the national political arena, the first free election would be the last.

Two new laws, the first in 1993 and the second in 1995, turned these sentiments into new repressive realities by reformulating the rules for electing the governing boards of the associations. These antidemocratic laws had the clear intent of crippling the Islamists. As the government intended, none of the associations in which the Islamists had registered their gains proved able to hold elections in accordance with the new restrictive terms. The governing boards where Islamists dominated were dissolved and the associations were placed under legal custody, effectively losing their legal autonomy and their somewhat insulated status as institutions of civil society. The full force of this "legal" repression was felt in 1995 when leading Islamist syndicate figures, most notably Essam Eryan of the Doctors' Association, suffered arrest, trial, and sentencing by military courts to long and unjust prison terms.

Steeled by their larger sense of purpose that centered on the Islamic wave and their tough realism about the regime's limitations, the New Islamists displayed a self-assured resiliency in the face of these government assaults on political and civic freedoms, as well as lapses of good sense by elements of the Islamic wave. Their affirmative conviction of the intrinsic importance of their own work in the Islamic sphere, difficult though still possible, carried them through. They recognized that official repression had, by the late 1990s, reduced political and civic discourse to a desert. Yet they also saw that the sole exception was the Islamic trend, which, despite its lapses, had distinctive sources of energy and vitality that were beyond the reach of government repression. They knew that the Islamic trend could draw on the deep springs of faith of the majority of ordinary Egyptians, as part of the worldwide resurgence of religious commitment that had characterized the late modern world. Despite the regime's efforts to dry and despoil these springs, the New Islamists remained convinced that these attempts would fail. Historically, the sources of faith in Egypt run too deep. That did not mean, of course, that there was no corrective and nurturing work to be done. Lapses by Islamists could be serious and could have unfortunate consequences. Though the Islamic Awakening appeared to have the strength of a force of nature, the New Islamists clearly understood that it nevertheless required active attention and cultivation, a task they judged far more important than the incessant parrying of government repression.[41]

This cautious optimism of the New Islamists periodically found vindication. Despite the apparent success of the regime's repressive moves, the impression that the Islamist experiment in the associations and other spheres of civil society was completely over by the mid-1990s proved deceptive. The Islamists once again displayed their resiliency. By the first years of the new century, Islamist activists showed signs of regaining some of their earlier momentum in the associations. The success of Muslim Brotherhood candidates in the 2000 elections to the People's Assembly was matched by their comeback in the associations, notably the Bar Association. In the 2001 elections to the Bar Association, the Islamists regained control in a major reversal.[42] The New Islamists responded with measured enthusiasm to these signs that once again Islamist activists could bring new energy to public life. They were encouraged by the fact that, among all the important trends, only the Islamists consistently succeeded in attracting youth and providing them with a sense of larger purpose, as well as various sites within which those purposes could be realized.

The New Islamist focus on the rationalization of the Islamic sphere alerted them to dangers to Islamic moderation other than government repression. At times, extremists from both Islamic and secular quarters proved even more dangerous to the moderate center occupied by the New Islamists than the authoritarian regime. The New Islamists regarded extremism of all kinds as a dangerous diversion for the Islamic movement and for the nation. At a time when there was serious work to be done, extremists often focused attention on minor personal and cultural issues and diverted energies into unproductive channels. The *fiqh* of priorities dictated that the "mind" of the Islamic movement should ignore or downplay these diversions, and keep attention on the long-term tasks of rationalizing the Islamic "body" and making it a part of the national center. However, the strategy of gradual social transformation required at a minimum a framework of public order. When radicalism of any kind threatened to undermine that precondition, the New Islamists overcame their reluctance to engage with what they regarded as peripheral issues. They responded to the destabilizing threat the extremists posed, most vigorously when radical actions jeopardized the emergence of a strengthened center.

From their centrist Islamist perspective, the New Islamists faced down extremists of all kinds. As Islamist intellectuals, they had a particularly important role in confronting Islamist extremism, as the events in Ain Shams in 1988 indicated.[43] However, the moderation of their own Islamist positions also enabled them to deal with the very different problem of secular extremists. In some ways, the character of their commitments as Islamist centrists who spoke for the *Wassatteyya* stood out even more clearly when seen against the background of interactions with the secularists.

Unlike the Islamist radicals, the secular extremists did not resort to violence. The New Islamists never lost sight of this critical distinction. When Islamist radicals took up arms to advance their cause, the New Islamists did not hesitate to stand against them and with the regime, as the only force that could contain armed militants. In contrast, they understood that the secularist extremists mounted their attacks in the intellectual and ideological realms, to which they urged appropriate and proportional responses. Ideas, even the most distasteful and destructive ideas, were to be countered by better ideas, not by guns, and not even by the authority of the courts if that could be avoided.

In all of their interventions to counter extremism, the New Islamists acted to preserve a space for dialogue where the center could assert itself. For this reason, they opposed the cultural wars that raged in the final decade of the twentieth century, pitting extremist Islamists against militant secularists. Whenever possible, they distanced themselves from entanglement in these unproductive exchanges that focused on marginal issues. When they did take part in these cultural conflicts, they aimed to place the issues in the larger context of national needs and to reduce the vehemence of the exchanges. Clear patterns emerged in their actions. If Islamist extremists resorted to terror, they showed themselves willing to stand against them and with the forces of order. The New Islamists responded, for example, to the assassination of the secularist Farag Foda in 1992 with an unambiguous condemnation. Still, it was not always possible to avoid being drawn into the controversies around such deplorable incidents.[44] Shaikh Muhammad al Ghazzaly, for example, was called to testify as an expert on *Sharia* for the defense in the trial of Foda's murderers. He did so in a strict and unimpeachable way, but nevertheless he was vilified when his testimony was distorted in tendentious ways as a justification of the assassins.

Ghazzaly does bear some responsibility, however, for the uproar his testimony generated. Though technically correct, his final response on punishment for those who take it upon themselves to punish an apostate was too brief and too insensitive to the context within which this narrow legal question was posed. Earlier in the court session, Ghazzaly did elaborate on the *fiqh* surrounding the issue of apostasy, and he did indicate clearly his own opinion. He could and should have done so as well on the issue of those who usurp authority. After all, what was at stake in the trial was precisely the fate of those accused of the murder of an alleged apostate, and such an elaboration would have been even more germane than the one he offered on apostasy. Because he failed to take this opportunity, Ghazzaly made himself vulnerable to attack.

Just as the New Islamists deplored the violence that took the life of Farag Foda, so too they condemned the excessive and destructive zeal that disrupted the private life and destroyed the professional career of Nasr Abu Zeid, a young academic at Cairo University, who in 1993 was accused of apostasy for his interpretive work on Islamic discourse. Fahmy Huwaidy emphasized the dangerous consequences for an Islamic society of such ill-considered treatment of a scholar. He did not hesitate to say that the Islamists who brought the case against the researcher were just as bad as the government, which was threatening to imprison reporters whom they saw as expressing "contempt" for the ruling political system. "Both of these elements," Huwaidy wrote, "refuse to cope with difference of opinion; they deny the value of dialogue and work to decrease the space of tolerance."[45]

The threats to the tolerant center, however, arose not only from misguided young militants who sought to define a revolutionary political path for the Islamic wave. Exaggerated and intemperate responses by the Islamic wave to secular critics, especially the pointed attacks on the extreme secularists, threatened to undermine moderate purposes just as thoroughly. The New Islamists argued persuasively against viewing secularists as one undifferentiated group: they made important distinctions between moderate and extreme secularists. They defined the areas of potential cooperation with both groups, expansive in the first case and constrained in the second. The New Islamists never lost sight of the fact that even the most extreme secularists advanced their positions essentially on intellectual grounds, even though they were forced to acknowledge that those positions did provide the justification for government repression of the Islamic wave as a whole. Still, they held fast to the conviction that intellectual challenges could be safely met on intellectual grounds alone.

The New Islamists accepted with equanimity the reality that some of these disputes might not be resolved. They urged that these matters be put aside and attention focused instead on those areas where agreement made cooperation possible. After all, the New Islamists argued, the theorists and activists of the Islamic wave had a demanding agenda, and many of its elements had a more pressing importance. Resolution of the most intractable issues could be delayed, even repeatedly delayed, in order achieve progress in areas that held greater promise. It was critical to draw back from these engagements with extremists whenever possible in order to theorize and act for the center, both of the *Wassatteyya* and of the nation. The New Islamists believed that the best prospects for the nation rested with a moderate Islamic wave that would be part of the political mainstream. Quite unexpectedly, a group of young activists, spearheaded by younger elements within the Muslim Brotherhood, appeared on the political scene in 1996 to give tangible if not fully realized expression to these hopes. This group countered even the most extreme secularist ideas with the calm and confident presentation of the viewpoints of the Islamic center, if possible in appropriate academic and intellectual forums.

In helping to neutralize extremists of all kinds, the New Islamists made substantial contributions to the strengthening of the hope for the emergence of a broad political mainstream. Whether dealing with the fringes of Islamist or of secular opinion, their aim was always to reassert the center, not only of the Islamic wave but also of the nation as a whole, in order to refocus attention on the task of building as inclusive a national community as possible.

Guiding the Next Generation: The Wassat Party Experience

The news came early in 1996, in the midst of an aggressive regime policy of "breaking arms" directed against the new forms of Islamist activism in the professional associations and other sites in civil society. Several members of the younger generation of the Muslim Brothers officially applied to found a political party, which they called the Wassat Party. They did so in cooperation with a small number of women and Copts, including Rafiq Habib, the son of a prominent priest.[46] Although the membership drew most heavily from the Brothers, the party differentiated itself as a civil party that included Muslims and Copts and sought to address the concerns of all Egyptians.[47] These young activists, of whom the engineer Abul Ela Mady was the most prominent, adhered to the path of peaceful change. Their guiding ideas bore the clear imprint of the political thinking that the New Islamists developed in the last quarter of the twentieth century.[48] The moderate message of justice and democracy had penetrated deeper than conventional views suggested.[49]

It is impossible to read the Wassat Party program without hearing, between the lines, the voices of the major New Islamist figures.[50] Theirs is not the only influence, of course, and in some important ways the document falls short from a New Islamist perspective. The new party aims to speak to both the older and the newer elements within the Brotherhood. The traditional thought of such past and current Brotherhood leaders as Omar Tilmisany and Muhammad Mashur left its expected traces in the document. At the same time, the young activists have responded to nationalist thinking coming from sources outside the Islamic wave, such as Muhammad Hassanein Haikal's Arab Nationalism and Nemat Fuad's sense of

Egypt's unique identity. Within this amalgam, however, the single most powerful source of intellectual inspiration, and the source that gives the platform its most original and distinctive features, comes from the New Islamists. Thus, commentators familiar with the work of the New Islamists could not have been surprised when the Wassat Party's founder, Abul Ela Mady, explicitly cited Kamal Abul Magd, Muhammad Selim al Awa, Fahmy Huwaidy, Yusuf al Qaradawy, and Tareq al Bishry, among other independent intellectuals, as major sources of guidance for the young activists who made the decision to form the party and took the lead in formulating its program.[51]

The Wassat Party's platform clearly shows how effectively these centrist Islamist intellectuals have conveyed to a new generation their insights on how civilizational Islam could respond to the contemporary needs of Egyptians.[52] Complex New Islamist concepts find expression in the party platform, not least in the core substantive notions of civilizational Islam and appreciation for the historical roots of the broad *Wassatteyya* trend that expresses it. In the clearest terms, the party platform states that the civilizational project "goes beyond religion and all artificial divisions." Islam is understood in terms broader than those of religion, and the platform makes the explicit point that the Islamic civilizational project embraces both constituent elements of the Egyptian national community, Copts and Muslims. "Everybody is called upon to join this project, which unifies groups without eliminating their differences," announces the document.[53] The young activists have absorbed both Qaradawy's view that Islam is broader than religion and Abul Magd's arguments that civilizational Islam provides the generous foundations for a pluralistic and inclusive national project. They explain that their "use of the term 'civilizational Islam' does not reject Islam as a religion; on the contrary, religion is part of it and adds to it." The slogan emerged from the effort to identify a referential context that represents everyone. The document adds that "Islam as a religion remains as such for those who believe in it; religion gives strength to Islam as a civilization. Islam as a religion represents the majority which preserves 'Islam as a civilization' that represents the unity of all."[54]

The party platform notes that this inclusive stance represents a break with the past, when Egyptians too often retreated into narrow and exclusivist "sub-affiliations marked by religious slogans and defense through devout acts." While understanding the defensive logic of this response that aims to protect the nation's religious sanctities, the Wassat group argues that their generation must pursue a different course that emphasizes "the pan-affiliations of Islam as civilization rather than the sub-affiliations of Islam as religion." Thus the distinctive thrust of New Islamist thinking about civilizational Islam as a project for the future of the entire nation permeates the Wassat Party program. With Kamal Abul Magd, the Wassat youth argue that Islam as a civilization encourages an identity able to transcend fearful and reactive defensiveness and to inspire "work for progress and development" of the entire nation.

The confidence of the party program comes in part from the understanding that the Islamic civilizational project is an integrative one, as Qaradawy emphasized, that draws together the diverse strands of the Islamic wave. Above all, these young activists have understood the necessity, in the first instance, of reuniting the intellectual and activist wings of the Islamic wave. "In recent years," the party platform notes, "these elements were scattered and torn apart." Theory developed in its own separate sphere, while activism remained isolated from it. Selim al Awa in particular had frequently warned that one consequence of this split was that although "some people were convinced by the civilizational project, they doubted that it could ever be implemented."[55] Indicating that this lesson of the New Islamist *tarshid* had registered, the party program states that the task of the Wassat is to unite these two strands of thinking and activism. Such a combination of theory and practice, of mind and body, would "legitimate theory by connecting it to the masses and legitimate political action by making it the implementation of theory that aims for progress." Renaissance needs "a vision, renewal, and *ijtihad* as well as political action."[56]

The party platform also elaborates the rich connotations of the term *Wassatteyya,* as the Wassat circle has come to understand them. They recognize first that the concept finds its ultimate grounding, as Qaradawy has often explained, in the Quranic verse where God says "I made you a Wassat nation." This phrase is taken to mean that the Islamic civilization is a unique and independent one with an impressive will to survive. Neither minor nor marginal in world history, Islamic civilization has proved to be durable, with contributions still to be made.[57] In accents reminiscent of Kamal Abul Magd, the platform goes on to celebrate the "sophistication and balance" of Islamic civilization when compared to Western and Asian paradigms. With a pointed reference to the Native Americans decimated by colonization, the young activists state categorically that "as the children of this civilization, we will not allow its destruction."[58]

The name "Wassat," the platform also makes clear, is intended to invoke the venerable tradition of the *Wassatteyya* and its distinctively moderate understanding of the imperatives of Islamic reform. In explicit terms that again echo the arguments of the New Islamist manifesto, the platform affirms the understanding that moderation is "a direct expression of the nature of this nation." In this sense the *Wassatteyya* cannot be pushed aside, for it speaks for what is most central in national life. Moderation, rather than being simply the opposite of extremism as a choice of means, is understood in the party platform "as a way of life." This means that moderation is "a commitment to legitimate means and a real desire to achieve progress through peaceful methods" that respect the integrity and unity of the country. The Wassat group thus explicitly commits itself to "struggling for a better future, but without dismantling society or doing harm to the nation's soul."[59]

Drawing on the work of Tareq al Bishry, the platform explains that the *Wassatteyya* strategy is to approach its tasks by first distinguishing between what is constant and what is changeable in the national heritage. The capacity to recognize and act on this distinction gives reformers the flexibility to make concessions in many secondary areas while preserving things that relate to the core of the nation. In the language of Fahmy Huwaidy, the Wassat circle affirms that this nation, like all others, has certain "sanctities" that cannot be compromised. At the same time, the party platform strenuously curbs the retrograde inclination to sanctify everything. In this way, it is possible to avoid a vision so tied to the past that neither progress nor development is possible. The past cannot be repeated, though the values that brought glory to past ages can be made to illuminate the pathways to the future. "For all nations there are some constant things or sanctities," the platform states, and these provide "the principles and values that frame behavior." At the same time, "there are also changeable things." In a call to creative intellectual and practical engagement that echoes the best work of Selim al Awa, the platform notes that the vast area of the changeable defines the arena of the "*ijtihad* of different generations" that "neither sacrifices the nation's identity nor falls into the trap of repeating past experiences."[60]

The Wassat platform notes finally that the *Wassatteyya* orientation does illuminate a distinctive civilizational path to the future, defining the relationship to both the heritage and the Western experience, while charging each generation to bear its responsibilities accordingly. "When we know the constant and the changeable, we know the road." This confident assertion means that "to alter the constant would be Westernization and self-destruction." Following Bishry's logic, the Western achievement should be considered "not with fascination" in its own terms but rather in the interest of preserving the values and principles of the heritage. "We have to sort it out," the Wassat group explains pragmatically, "in order to determine what we can and cannot use."[61]

These activists also offer a generational understanding of "Wassat" as signaling the special responsibilities of the middle generation. They gratefully acknowledge the work of the pioneers and willingly accept responsibility for those, notably university students, younger than themselves. At this stage, however, they believe that their own generation, the middle generation, has its own distinctive potential, having "absorbed the experience of previous generations while remaining sensitive to the challenges we face." The Wassat generation "is nearer to the future without being disconnected from the past." Therefore, the middle generation is positioned "to achieve the goals of the *Wassatteyya*" and has to "carry the torch and undertake its duties."[62]

Along with these elaborations of the central concepts of civilizational Islam and the *Wassatteyya,* the Wassat Party platform addresses specific social problems. It does so in ways that suggest how the experiments mounted by civilizational Islam, informed by the theoretical work of Islamist scholars, can place policy questions in the context of both the latest Islamist thinking and the most recent developments in the national and global community. Not surprisingly, education is given special emphasis and treatment in ways that show the influence of the sophisticated commentary on education developed by the New Islamists.[63]

In the platform, education is seen as the heart of a broad, forward-looking commitment to gradual and peaceful change. The platform calls for comprehensive reform, including the curriculum, teacher training, running of the schools, and the overall administration. More important, it sees these individual areas as elements of an inclusive Islamic civilizational vision that derives from a consensual national project that can provide the basis of what the young are taught and to what ends. In explicit terms, the generation of the Wassat Party see their efforts as directed to bringing together the thinking of Islamist intellectuals and the social work of the Islamic movement, with education at the center of that synthesis. Echoing all the major New Islamist themes, they call for attention in educational programs to the determination of the specific needs of Egyptian society and the ways in which educational programs can meet them. They are strong advocates both of updating the curriculum to meet the needs of a new age and of making the educational system the vehicle for fostering among the young religious values and commitment to a consensual national project within an Islamic framework.

Given this ambitious goal, the Wassat Party platform extends the notion of education in ways consistent with New Islamist thinking to the "meaning-producing" media. An entire section is devoted to a series of demands to make the national media a more effective educational instrument. In particular, the platform calls for the banning of advertisements that contradict society's values and promote foreign interests, as well as the prohibition of media acceptance of foreign funding. It also advocates the removal of restrictions on the media, enabling it to confront the cultural hegemony of the foreign media and to represent all major social forces within the country. Finally, the platform calls for greater emphasis on Arabic as the language of the media and on the cultivation of creativity, especially among the young.

Although these sections on education of the Wassat Party platform show unmistakable imprints of New Islamist thinking, they also reveal just as clearly the ways in which the document, and indeed the party itself, should not be thought of too simplistically as either the work of the New Islamists or the culmination of their efforts. Very little of the profound New Islamist rethinking of the heritage finds its way into the discussion of the substance of the curriculum, apart from the emphasis on Arabic. The platform invokes the idea of the civilizational project but gives too little indication of its content. The rich body of scholarly work on inherited culture and its relevance to our age that the New Islamists have produced is scarcely tapped. The Wassat platform recognizes the imperative of national consensus for a comprehensive vision for the future, but conveys little of the sophisticated New Islamist understanding of the complex participatory social and political process that alone could produce such an outcome in a democratic way.

Instead, when it comes to implementation, the spirit of the Wassat Party platform draws more from the outmoded Muslim Brotherhood model of administrative and bureaucratic instruments that ultimately would have to be sanctioned by ruling power in order to achieve their ends. The platform's comments on the media and public education reflect very clearly the defensive, reactive, and "banning" approach of the Muslim Brothers, rather than the more open, liberal, and confident views of the New Islamists. The education section reads as though the only real problems in education stem from government censorship, corruption, and Western intrusions. Little real thought is given to the intellectual and moral challenges of educating young people in a world where the most powerful threat to the sense of community and to values more generally comes from the consumerist ideology and the impact of global market pressures which, unless confronted by powerful countervailing social and cultural pressures, adhere to no standards other than profit. Similarly, the sections on the role of women in society take the conservative stance that women's place is in the home, failing to build on the more progressive strands in New Islamist thinking. Yet for all these limitations, when contrasted with the exacting standard of the best of New Islamist thinking, the initiative of the young Wassat activists remained a bold and courageous step.

Consistent with the regime's strategy of repression and "drying the springs," the official committee with the power to license new parties lost no time in refusing to recognize the new party. To an Islamist party that explicitly refused violence, pledged its adherence to democratic participation, and included among its founding members important Coptic figures, the committee blandly responded that the Wassat Party was unnecessary because its platform contained "nothing new or distinctive."[64] The sensationalist magazine *Rose al Yusuf* almost immediately began to mobilize opinion hostile to the Islamic wave, with unsubstantiated charges that the initiative was a Brotherhood "conspiracy," with only a cosmetic Coptic "cover."[65] In the spring of 1996, security forces arrested three of the party leaders, along with thirteen members of the Muslim Brothers, as part of a repressive sweep against Islamist moderates.[66]

In sharp contrast to the government's reaction, some of the more independent critics writing about the Islamists recognized the important new features of the Wassat initiative. One particularly astute assessment signaled clearly that the "unfair" judgment by the government committee on parties overlooked the fact that the platform usefully "defined moderation not simply in opposition to extremism but rather substantively as the belief that concessions on the fundamentals would mean the destruction of the nation, while overreaction would mean drowning in the past." Just as important for this analyst was the fact that the Wassat Party distinguished itself by having a separate and prominent platform plank that reasserted the overriding importance of national unity between Muslims and Copts.[67]

The Islamist reaction proved the most interesting and least predictable. Although the press initially described the party initiative as the work of the Muslim Brothers, the leadership of the Brothers strongly attacked the new party and worked actively to undermine it. The aging leadership of the Brotherhood regarded the work of the young activists as a breach of discipline that threatened the bureaucratic and hierarchical organizational structure of the Brotherhood. They expelled the party founders for arrogance and disobedience that threatened to undermine the movement. They also instructed those members of the Brotherhood who had responded positively to the initiative to withdraw their support, whatever their personal relations with the founders, warning that this challenge to the regular authority structures would produce anarchy within the Brothers organization.[68] Even though the Wassat Party platform showed clear deference to the historical role and current importance of the Brotherhood, the Muslim Brothers still chose to disown their assertive offspring.

In sharp contrast, the New Islamists welcomed this bold initiative of the young as a sign of vitality and hope. In their public responses, they chose to pay attention to the most progressive and forward-looking aspects of the party platform, taking them as hopeful signs that the Islamist body could act in moderate ways that fully engaged the energies and talents of the younger generation. Yusuf al Qaradawy lent the full weight of his prestige to support of the Wassat Party, sharply criticizing the Brotherhood leadership for its disavowal.[69] Kamal Abul Magd saw in the new party a contemporary affirmation of the powerful centrist current of moderation that had asserted itself from within the Islamic Awakening. Reading the initiative of the Wassat Party founders as a dissent from the rigidities of the Brotherhood organization, Abul Magd unequivocally identified with it. "The idea of moderation adopted by the Wassat youth," he wrote, "is precisely the same idea about which we were enthusiastic in the fifties." Referring to the hostile government response, he added that "regretfully, what is happening currently with the centrists is exactly what happened with the group of moderates in the fifties." Abul Magd explained that the moderates of that period had questioned whether the "thought" of the Muslim Brothers was adequate to the need for a comprehensive framework to present Islam to the world; the moderates' answer then, as now, was that it was not, and that other sources, beyond the framework of the Brotherhood experience and thought, would be needed.[70]

Muhammad Selim al Awa vigorously protested the unwarranted attack on the moderate activists in 1996 by the "storm of rejection and denunciation from the Islamic movement and other sides as well." He called on the Islamic movement, and civil society in general, to recognize and celebrate the "real intellectual development behind this action that pushed this Islamist group to go beyond the familiar frame of action for the Islamic movement in Egypt." As Awa described it, these young people, under the most difficult circumstances, "tried to found a party that would operate under a highly complicated and restrictive set of laws and regulations that govern all parties in Egypt except the ruling party."

Awa pronounced the initiative by the Wassat founders an "*ijtihad* of the youth" that deserved backing from Islamist activists and intellectuals. The experiment, if supported and allowed to go forward, would have given these young people "a chance to interact with the state institutions and laws to show the real truth about the scope of political freedom allowed to those who want to form a distinctive party that introduces a new project for the nation, built upon its fundamentals, but also taking into account changes in contemporary life." What happened, concluded Awa, was just the opposite in both activist Islamist and official circles. Egypt's youth suffered "yet another series of assaults."[71] In subsequent legal wrangles aimed at challenging the party committee ruling, Awa acted as lead attorney for the Wassat Party, enlisting at one point the aid of the prominent Brotherhood thinker Taufiq al Shawy in an open conflict with the Brotherhood leadership over its treatment of the young activists.[72] Awa strongly criticized the Brotherhood leadership for cooperating with the government in the repression of political freedom.[73]

The Wassat circle responded to the setback with restraint, yet perseverance. They mounted two further applications for the party, using slightly different names. With each new application, they made amendments to the platform designed to show how their effort would broaden the existing range of political parties by introducing a moderate party that had civilizational Islam as its inspiration. Both applications were summarily denied, though the documents generated as part of this effort are important for the reaffirmation of the open and inclusive position that they take. The second application, for example, stated even more explicitly that it was an expression of the *Wassatteyya* trend.[74] The slightly larger group that endorsed this application contained both women and Copts.[75] The revised platform sounds the major themes of New Islamist thinking even more clearly and eloquently.[76] The core commitment to rethinking the heritage as the basis for political action is expressed as "a continuous *ijtihad*" that establishes "an effective relationship between the intellectual project of renewing Islamic civilization and political action." The party founders explicitly recognize their debt to "those generations of intellectuals who were working, away from distractions and political battles, on presenting the fundamentals of the heritage in a contemporary manner, leaving aside those elements that were not essential." Defining the role they hope to assume, the group announces that "these serious and continuous theoretical efforts were only in need of a movement to apply it." The mind-and-body notion of the New Islamists has clearly captured their imagination. They write optimistically that their movement "with God's help brings the embryo of the Islamic civilizational intellectual work into the world of action." Yet, as part of the genuine confidence that energizes their movement, the Wassat circle explicitly repudiates any totalitarian claims for their intellectual orientation or for the program they derive from it. In open and tolerant language that recalls such New Islamist figures as Selim al Awa or Kamal Abul Magd, they pronounce that "the supporters of this platform do not claim that they own the truth." Continuing in the same vein, the revised platform states that "what we introduce is just a human interpretation completely open for disagreement, amendment, and development because there is always a need for *ijtihad,* and our hearts and minds are ready to learn from anyone." This openness finds its most important political expression in the clearly stated intention to make the Wassat group part of a broader, inclusive national consensus. The revised platform announces a hope "to reach a national consensus that answers the legitimate questions raised by the national forces which once doubted the motives of the Islamic renaissance movement." The aim is "to reach out to everyone to create a political environment where consensus increases and differences are reduced."[77]

Finally, the activists of the Wassat Party do not hesitate to claim that they speak for a renewed legacy that aims to make a serious contribution to the world. The Wassat generation understands that the global age has brought the most diverse peoples into intimate and continuous contact in ways that often threaten breakdowns and conflicts. They seek to transcend these destructive cultural clashes with the message of civilizational Islam, with its "religious, human, and civilizational values that sanctify the dignity of human beings and respect religious and cultural plurality." In their view, "the contemporary interdependent and closely connected world needs centrism to achieve integration while preserving plurality." They recognize without defensiveness that "we need the advanced world and reach out for it in a spirit of amity and cooperation to obtain material progress and new methods." At the same time, they confidently assert that "the advanced world needs us, too, to give it a value-based and pluralistic model of cooperation built on respecting cultural specificity and human dignity, which have been eroded by materialism and torn apart by conflicts."[78]

The official party committee turned down the revised applications. Faced with these denials, the young activists sought other outlets for their energies and their hopes, as the example of the New Islamists suggested they should. Abul Ela Mady and others from the Wassat circle applied for a newspaper license, but that request, too, was denied. A new Islamist journal called *al Manar al Gadid* was licensed, however, and Wassat writers appeared regularly in its pages, along with others from the Islamic wave.

In April 2000, Abul Ela Mady, representing the Wassat group, announced the formation of an Association for Dialogue and Culture. The association was approved and registered by the Ministry of Social Affairs. In the words of its founders, the association would not be a substitute for the party, for which they intended to continue applying. The mission of the new association, instead, would be the related one of enhancing the national culture of dialogue with all social forces. The founders announced that the association was neither a party nor a professional organization but rather a meeting place in civil society for all trends. They indicated that they would enter these discussions on the premise that solutions to national issues should emerge from dialogue and be drawn from Egyptian culture, but without relying on "ready-made slogans and mottoes."[79] The young activists then turned to Selim al Awa to act as chairman of the Association.

Tareq al Bishry addresses the celebration in 2000 of the founding of the Association for Dialogue and Culture. (photograph courtesy of Abul Ela Mady)

Explaining the aims of the Association to the nation, Awa elaborated on the importance of both culture and dialogue to Egypt's future. "Culture" referred to the culture of the nation, as inherited from the past and developed for the future. It drew on "all the components of the national civilization, including religion, history, language, and the rich heritage of the people." To face the future, Awa commented, the nation must add to the riches inherited from earlier generations, making use of imported elements in ways that enriched the heritage and did not block access to its sources.

The Association would understand "dialogue" as interaction "with all and for the good of all." It would be a dialogue among those who differ, no matter how great those differences or the character of their origins and the forces that perpetuate them. No participant in the dialogue would be asked to abandon his or her creed, basic beliefs, or cherished ideas. The purpose of dialogue would be to clarify distinctions and differences in these areas, giving everyone a chance to make their contributions and to appreciate those of others. The only thing excluded from the dialogue would be the acceptance of humiliation and aggression, and the condoning of the abandonment of basic rights of the nation, its territories, and its beliefs.

Though open to all generations, the Association aimed to work for the fullest inclusion of the young, who must have priority because they are the hope of the nation. A special effort would also be made to include women in the dialogue and to address issues of importance to them.[80] Awa emphasized the importance of civility and of the extension of the dialogue into all aspects of society, including the personal spheres of family and friendships.

The broad aim of the Association would be to deepen the understanding of Egyptians for what such a pluralistic dialogue could bring to their personal and collective lives. In the widest terms, this multifaceted dialogue would center on the challenge of "reaching a balance between reviving the cultural heritage and its renewal in ways that will give the nation's origins and fundamentals an understanding appropriate to the present and future, and open to others, in order to learn from their experience and achievements." In elaborating this mission, Awa mentioned such specific foci as the right of freedom of expression, diversity within the framework of unity, movements of change and reform, the changing and the constant in Egyptian culture, and Egypt's cultural role in the Arab Islamic world. He concluded that success in this purpose would help "revive the national memory in order to eliminate the widely held illusion that Egyptian struggles for renaissance for over a century have failed, or are declared dead without an heir to revive, or even preserve, their legacy."[81]

Acting on this ambitious agenda, the Association hosted its first important event in the spring of 2001, a two-day conference on "The Right of Freedom of Expression and the Nation's Fundamentals." Held at the Journalists' Association, the conference attracted a diverse audience numbering several hundred. Islamist activists from a wide variety of trends were present along with other intellectuals, eager to hear such speakers as Tareq al Bishry for the Islamists and Salah Eissa for secular intellectuals discuss the issue of free speech and the fundamentals. Selim al Awa acted as host and moderator.

With this gesture by Selim al Awa, who played a leadership role in creating a new opening for the younger generation, the New Islamists signaled that they would continue their support for youth in high-profile ways. Clearly, the New Islamists had accrued a reservoir of intellectual and moral capital that they were already passing on to the next generation of Islamist moderates. At the same time, they had attained an impressive national profile as intellectuals with a respected place in the moderate mainstream.

The State, the World, and the Islamic Awakening at the Start of the Millennium

Three of the major New Islamists, Selim al Awa, Tareq al Bishry, and Kamal Abul Magd, received invitations to participate as speakers in the annual Political Science Conference of Cairo University in early December of

1999.[82] Each year the faculty of Economics and Political Science organizes a conference designed to report to the nation the best thinking on a critical issue. At the dawn of a new millennium, whatever the official title, the theme could be none other than "Egypt in the Global Age." The prominent representation of the New Islamist School signaled the important place their work had won in Egyptian public life.

Unlike such conferences in other countries, the Cairo Conference is never purely an academic affair, and press coverage enables participants to speak to the informed public. Leading scholars and intellectuals from all fields whose work has made a contribution to the subject under discussion are invited. Each formal presentation has a designated commentator who is most often a prominent public figure or an important intellectual engaged with the issue. The audience, too, is not confined to academia. The two- to three-day conference always attracts academics and students but also journalists, figures influential in civil society, and decision-makers as well as the attentive general public.

Bishry, Awa, and Abul Magd moved comfortably into this setting. Their prominent inclusion signaled general recognition of the importance of their scholarly work on political affairs and their stature as public intellectuals who reach a wide audience. Though they are neither shaikhs nor directly linked to official Islam, their Islamist orientation is known to all. At the same time, they are fully at ease in a gathering of cosmopolitan intellectuals with a predominantly secular orientation. The invitation extended to them signaled that the Islamic current had once again produced major figures who had won a place of intellectual leadership in academic and public life. By the close of the conference, it was clear that these three came not only as distinguished individuals but also as leading participants in a school of Islamist thinkers who had produced a cohesive body of collective scholarship and built an impressive record of coordinated public interventions.

The Islamic current, usually spoken *for* in such gatherings, this time had its own powerful voice. While each of the three speakers made an individual contribution, their commentaries had an overall coherence that reflected the shared Islamic vision of their school. Bishry analyzed continuities in patterns of state dominance in Egypt, while Abul Magd described the changing global context and its implications for the relationship between the state and society. Awa in turn reviewed the record and the promise of the broad Islamic wave of reform and renewal in the face of the authoritarianism of the state. Their combined reflections on the new global environment, the state, and the Islamic wave provided an enlightening tour of the horizon at century's end from a centrist Islamist perspective. Their words, reinforced by their very presence in this setting, signaled the imperative of including the Islamic center in the political mainstream. The three New Islamists made the case that only a mainstream strengthened by the inclusion of the *Wassatteyya* could hope to crystallize a compelling national project to meet the heightened challenges of the new century.

With the assurance of a leading historian, Tareq al Bishry laid out the central dilemma of Egyptian politics. The strong state dating back to Muhammad Aly completely dominated social and civil affairs. It did so quite independently of the character of constitutional arrangements or ideological orientations. Under feudalism, capitalism, and socialism alike, the power of the state consistently overwhelmed civic and social action, and weakened what Bishry called "communal society." Although Bishry used the term in ways similar to the more usual Western term of "civil society," his phrase avoided the idea of any opposition between the "civil" and the "religious" and thereby eliminated the tacit implication that Islamic institutions were to be excluded. The dominance of the state, Bishry argued, either preempted or censored independent efforts by relatively autonomous and often contending social forces to articulate the mainstream national interest. At the same time, successive regimes proved unable to articulate a comprehensive and compelling sense of national direction and identity. Bishry was here invoking his well-known critique of the imitative projects of both monarchical and revolutionary regimes that could not shake the hold of Western models and that, in the end, did not respond to Egyptian needs.

Bishry then linked this fatal disconnect between state power and national purpose to the unconstrained and arbitrary character of state power. The Egyptian state had refused the inherited Islamic framework for legitimating state power, turning instead to Western secular models. It did so, however, without subjecting state power to limitations established by a public consensus on democratic principles, as was the case in the Western democracies. The result, Bishry explained, was not simply authoritarianism. What emerged was a system of arbitrary rule with no organic and meaningful links to larger social purposes. There were no recognized and effective disciplinary mechanisms to guide state practices and policies in order to bring them into line with genuine national interest. In an Islamic system, the power to legislate is constrained by the higher purposes of Islam. In Western democracies, legislative power must function in ways responsive to the democratic principles that lie behind the mechanism of democratic rule. Neither set of defining constraints operated in the Egyptian context. In this sense, the power of the Egyptian state, Bishry explained, was set adrift from any larger framework of higher purpose shared with or generated by the people.

Bishry concluded his analysis with an assessment of changed external conditions which, he believed, created new dangers. In the age of globalism, new and exceedingly powerful forms of external pressures were acting on small nations. By the end of the twentieth century, the capacity of the Egyptian state to contend with these foreign forces had declined precipitously. Thus, while the state remained overwhelmingly strong in the domestic arena, it had become weak and vulnerable in the most important external environments. Only a concerted effort by a strong communal society in support of the state's effort to resist foreign intrusions, Bishry warned, could hope to preserve a distinctive Egyptian cultural identity and advance the possibility of autonomous development. By overwhelming and dominating society and its strong Islamic wing, the state had denied itself that support. From this distinctive angle of vision, Bishry argued that state repression of the Islamic wave as a key element in communal society undermined the national interest.

Kamal Abul Magd extended Bishry's analysis by characterizing the new global context. The space-time compression of the late modern world, Abul Magd explained, had made isolation impossible and participation in the global order a necessity. At the same time, he made it clear that recognition of the new realities should not be confused with any naive celebration of globalization. The new, penetrating global forces had a differential impact that was as dangerous for the weak to ignore as it was difficult to counteract. Old thinking about the dangers of colonial powers, however, no longer captured the essence of the threat. The weaker nodes in the global system of connections, like Egypt, faced not a unified material civilization intent on occupation, but rather the autonomous and alluring fragments of that civilization, from McDonald's to the icons of popular culture, which had a penetrative power unlike anything seen before. The state was ill-equipped to counter such new forms of intrusion, with their potential for securing market access and cultural hegemony for the West. Abul Magd stressed that globalization was not simply a description of new elements of the late modern world brought about by technological advance, but rather "an interested prescription, pushed by powerful American-dominated global financial institutions and by the United States itself as the single superpower." He suggested that the changed character of the external environment enhanced the protective role of communal society. This understanding of the decentered character of the assault reinforced Bishry's sense that the best hope of resistance lay in cooperation between the state and a revitalized communal society. Unstated, though clearly understood, was the necessity to lift the state's siege of the Islamic wave so that it could play its role as an indispensable element of that strengthened communal society.

Selim al Awa completed the analysis by providing a centrist characterization of the Islamic wave and a candid delineation of the pattern of regime repression to which it has been subjected. The regime, with the help of secular intellectuals, tells the story of Islamic activism as one of degeneration, as the title of an influential but misleading study put it, from "reform to violence."[83] It does so in order to justify the repressive strategy of "drying the springs" that targets not just radicals but the Islamic wave as a whole. By identifying the violent radicals as the telos toward which the Islamic wave inevitably moves, the entire tradition can be homogenized and discredited. Moderates are seen to differ from radicals only on tactical issues of timing and means. The Islamic order they envision is alleged to be the same.

In this presentation at Cairo University, Selim al Awa asserted the right of the Islamic *Wassatteyya* to define and shape the legacy of Islamic political thought and its distinctive interpretations. In an impressive tour de force, he restored the complexity of the Islamic legacy that had been obscured by the distorting simplifications of hostile commentators. Awa showed how the *Wassatteyya* selectively drew from a tradition with both radical and moderate strands to create an Islamic mainstream that carried a distinctive Islamic vision of reform explicitly repudiating violence. There were no apologies, for example, in his recognition of the revolutionary al Afghany as the fountainhead of Islamic political thought in the late nineteenth century. From Afghany came the broad goals of reform and autonomy. For the mainstream, Afghany's most enduring contribution was his championing of the principle of the open-ended right of each generation to *ijtihad*, rather than any specific lessons on how those goals might be defined or achieved. Afghany had sanctioned a method that might well be used to define a strategy quite different from his own. On crucial issues, the *ijtihad* of the confident moderate center did depart from the formulations of the founder. The reformist Muhammad Abduh (Afghany's most celebrated follower), Awa indicated, had provided the substantive core of alternative mainstream commitments, with his call to build a public opinion for constitutional and representative political action instead of revolution. From Abduh, the *Wassatteyya* also took the related principles of the civil rather than religious character of government and the priority of education and intellectual work over politics.

However, the New Islamists made it clear that Abduh's was not the last word on these issues. The revolutionary activist Hassan al Banna, founder of the Muslim Brothers organization in the late 1920s, defined the next significant moment in Islamic political theory at mid-twentieth century, from which the New Islamists drew important inspiration. In the centrist view, it is possible to recognize al Banna's pivotal role, while again borrowing only selectively from his legacy. Mainstream figures, including the New Islamists, have developed a pointed critique of al Banna that emphasizes his rigidity in organization and ideology, the general neglect of theoretical work, and an overemphasis on the political sphere. They explicitly reject the shadowy and violent underground activities of some elements from the Brotherhood. The New Islamists have added to this assessment a rejection of al Banna's negative views on pluralism and a refusal to accept his implicit judgment that the current regime had abrogated its Islamic responsibilities. They have also elaborated a much more inclusive view of the role of women and minorities in the Islamic community.

Nevertheless, Awa's characterization of al Banna at Cairo University clearly signaled that the centrists also insisted on the constructive and innovative dimensions of al Banna's thought and practice. At the heart of al Banna's project, Awa pointed out, was a reassertion of the comprehensiveness of Islam. The breadth of his engagements opened an extensive range of social fields, from education to the economy, within which the organization he founded could operate. Al Banna had shown how the Islamic wave could expand from elitist confines to a mass participatory movement. On that basis, the Muslim Brothers forged an unprecedented range of popular connections that showed how to turn an intellectual awakening into a movement of broad social transformation.

Awa did not shy away from treating the controversial figure Sayyid Qutb, who pushed these political views of al Banna to extreme conclusions in the 1950s and 1960s. Qutb's later work provided the theoretical underpinnings of political Islam in its most radical form. Awa acknowledged that Qutb had pronounced the Egyptian regime un-Islamic, and had provided the theoretical rationale for a minority vanguard to replace the regime, by force if necessary, with an extremist version of *hakemeyya.* The New Islamists forcefully rejected these arguments.

At this point, however, Awa's presentation took an unexpected turn. He used the acknowledgment that Qutb had turned al Banna's legacy in a radical direction to insist, with an impressive lack of defensiveness, that Qutb's extremist progeny did not own al Banna's legacy. In a significant departure from the usual interpretations of the al Banna story, Awa pointed out that there were mainstream thinkers within the Muslim Brothers who had made important theoretical contributions to a moderate interpretation of al Banna's place in Islamic thought. There was no imperative to move from al Banna to Qutb to the extremist, violent minorities. Awa singled out two Brotherhood intellectuals, Hassan al Ashmawy and Taufiq al Shawy, for their contributions to a contrasting moderate line of development. Ashmawy, according to Awa, strengthened the foundations of gradualist thinking by sharpening the distinction in Islamic political thought between what is unchanging because it is from God, and what is variable because it is human. Ashmawy also clearly rejected the notion of religious government as un-Islamic and placed a strong emphasis on individual freedom. Awa reported that al Shawy added to this contribution with his work on the concept of *shura* and its centrality in Islamic political theory, as well as his insistence that religious leadership be separated from the rightful political leadership of elected officials.[84] Both Ashmawy and al Shawy found justifications for these positions in al Banna's complex legacy, and to that degree reclaimed him for the moderates.

Awa then discussed the most recent period, from the mid-1970s to the present, which offered new opportunities and challenges for the development of centrist Islamic thought. On the one hand, the worldwide religious revival had a positive impact in the Islamic world, bringing large numbers of new activists into the Islamic wave. The modest regime liberalizations that held out promise in the 1970s allowed the emergence of Islamic journals and newspapers where Islamic intellectuals could exchange ideas. On the whole, however, Awa felt that the activist Islamic movements were not up to the task of rationalizing the Islamic wave, remarking that they "never presented an intellectual vision capable of turning this spontaneous wave into continuously renewed Islamic Awakening." The thought of this period was for the most part a "thought of crisis," defensive in tone, that responded to an agenda set by adversaries. Nevertheless, outside the confines of organized activist movements there were individual intellectuals who did make progress with "building rather than defense and mobilization," and Awa alluded to the work of figures in all Arab and Islamic countries who strengthened the intellectual foundations of moderate thought. Although Awa did not elaborate on these figures in his paper circulated at the conference, commentators during the discussion period made it clear that the New Islamists, including Awa himself, had been among the most productive in these efforts.

In discussing the new generation of moderates, Awa singled out the Wassat Party project, with their "thought distinct from the Islamic organizations that adopt violence and, at the same time, from the Muslim Brothers to which many of the members of these organizations went after the failure of their own organizations." Awa left no doubt that in his view, centrist Islamic thought had found its most compelling activist expression in the work of these youthful moderates.

Awa did not end on an optimistic note, however. In an unflinching conclusion, he spelled out the record of repression of the intellectuals and activists of the Islamic trend, which began with the fate of the founders and continued to the present day. Awa reminded his listeners that Afghany was opposed, exiled, and imprisoned in India, Persia, and the Hijaz. Abduh, too, was imprisoned, exiled, and denied the right of return to Egypt until he had categorically abandoned political activity. Al Banna, Awa commented wryly, was "accused of everything until he was finally assassinated and then buried without recognition or ceremony." The distinguished jurist Sanhury, though never a member of any organized movement, was beaten, insulted, and confined to his home in a Cairo suburb for what were understood to be Islamist sympathies. The radical but brilliant Qutb was imprisoned twice and finally hanged, while the moderates Ashmawy and Shawy were both imprisoned and exiled. Ashmawy lived as a fugitive for three years in Upper Egypt, before escaping to live in exile for fifteen years. Shawy's release from prison and exile came only after mediation by the King of Morocco. Sadat's decision to allow exiles to come home made it possible for him to return to Egypt.

The New Islamist "new *fiqh* of politics," dealing with such core questions as democracy, citizenship, and human rights, enriched and extended the political thought of the resilient mainstream tradition out of which their school emerged. Acting within an authoritarian context, they struggled against the daunting obstacles that Selim al Awa catalogued to exemplify the ways in which their innovative thinking might inform responsible political action. In doing so, the New Islamists inspired Islam's next generation of centrists.

The political arena, however, was never the primary focus of the New Islamists' attention, though they did not fail to encourage the Islamic mainstream to make the most of the opportunities it occasionally offered. They themselves exemplified the ways in which moderate Islamic public figures could play a constructive role in political and civic life. Still, the New Islamists focused their primary efforts on the guidance of the Islamic mainstream, rather than on politics or civil society as ends in themselves. They did believe that the government, for all its limitations, maintained a system of order within which their long-term efforts to rethink the heritage could go forward. However, they had no grand illusions about what could or even should be accomplished in either the political sphere or civil society under such authoritarian conditions. They believed that opportunities for political and civic action would be modest, though worth pursuing. They considered other priorities, notably educational and cultural changes, more significant. In general, the New Islamists reserved their larger aspirations for the strengthening of the *Wassatteyya* and the refinement of its collective thinking and action. Reaching beyond politics and civil society, they aimed to make the *Wassatteyya* a force for the gradual social and cultural remaking of Egypt. In their new political *fiqh* and in the record of their public interventions motivated by this political thinking, they spelled out the political implications of this long-term transformation.

chapter 6

Engaging the World

"It is as though we are not part of this age," laments Yusuf al Qaradawy. "The West invents the computer, and then we argue about the appropriate name for it in Arabic. Israel manufactures satellites capable of monitoring the most minute details of our lives, and we endlessly debate whether [its] pictures are *halal* [religiously permitted] or *haram* [religiously forbidden] in Islam." Qaradawy will not tolerate from Islamic activists such ignorance of the modern world, masked by empty "theological" discussions.[1] His words carry no hint of the simplistic moralism that mars the thinking of so many Islamist intellectuals who fail to engage the late modern world in all its complexities. The New Islamists condemn all signs of irresponsible thinking that misleads young people. In their view, empty Islamist slogans and random acts of violence distort the message of Islam and do nothing to advance the genuine values of the Islamic revival nor to alter the reality of Western hegemony. A different approach is needed.

Qaradawy is fully aware of American strength. He nevertheless rejects the conclusion that current Western dominance demonstrates a civilizational superiority that is forever beyond challenge. He questions the pessimism of leading secularists who have abandoned the belief that the Islamic world has anything valuable to contribute to world civilization. He grounds his optimism in the encouraging signs of a transnational Islamic Awakening, on the one hand, and a critique of the underlying weaknesses of the structures of Western dominance, maintained today by the United States, on the other. The West celebrates the collapse of the Soviet Union and world communism as a triumph of its own values. Qaradawy and others in the New Islamist School see it rather as the failure of one version of Western civilization. To them the grand illusion of Soviet socialism reveals the basic flaws of all Western-inspired global projects built on materialist foundations. All such undertakings, they believe, will not withstand the test of time. They see in the United States the same arrogance of power and amoral, bullying behavior that weakened an overextended Soviet Union. While they appreciate the scientific and technological advances of the Americans, they are not impressed by the consumerism and unbridled power of wealth that undermines democracy, trivializes values, and vulgarizes culture. They see the worldwide resurgence of religion, with Islam in the forefront, as a powerful harbinger of changes to come. The New Islamists are confident that their forward-looking, centrist Islamic project offers to Egyptians, to Muslims, and indeed to all of humanity an attractive alternative model of how to live in the global age.

The austere main hall of the Doctors' Association in central Cairo provides the setting for this call to think and act with realism and confidence on behalf of the Islamic civilizational project. Established as a major bastion of Islamist influence in Egyptian civil society and a preeminent national forum during the 1980s and into the 1990s, the association hosted a series of colloquia and dialogues in the mid-1990s on the prospects of the world's Islamic societies in the twenty-first century. Qaradawy's reputation, secured by a prodigious scholarly output with a transnational appeal, draws young people to fill the hall to overflowing on this warm evening in August 1995. Additional chairs are brought in to accommodate an audience predominantly of young men in their twenties, including a substantial number of non-Egyptians whose dress and accents identify them as students at the national universities from places as nearby as the Sudan and as distant as Malaysia.

How does Qaradawy so effectively reach the youth of the Islamic world with his characterization of the role they should play in an uncertain future? The subdued but authoritative manner of Qaradawy's entrance and the measured, respectful introduction he is accorded reinforce the sense of a distinguished academic addressing young people who, under the influence of his writings, already think of themselves as his students. Qaradawy speaks candidly of the terrible weaknesses of Islamic societies. He drops the euphemisms of "underdeveloped" or "developing" in favor of blunt recognition of backwardness in the face of the overwhelming technological and scientific strength of the West. Qaradawy's assessment of the state of the world makes clear as well the enormous costs of Western dominance, demonstrated so clearly in the Gulf War and the continuing tragedy of Palestine. However, his realism does not require the abandonment of hope by his young listeners, only its deferral.

Unlike the great Egyptian modernists, such as Muhammad Abduh who wrote at the end of the nineteenth century, Qaradawy and the New Islamists are no longer caught in the thrall of the West. The history of the twen-

Yusuf al Qaradawy *(right)*, Professor and Dean of the Faculty of Islamic Studies at the University of Qatar, participating in a 1997 transnational forum on the Islamic heritage. (photograph courtesy of *al Ahram* newspaper)

tieth century has taken its toll. On the one hand, the West's power of worldwide transformation is fully acknowledged. The New Islamists urge Islamist thinkers and activists to come to grips with a world revolutionized in the nineteenth century by Western technology and industrial management, with its spectacular productive capacities, and, in our own time, by the postindustrial revolutions in transportation and information technologies, with their capacity to collapse the barriers of space and time. Yet, even as the worldwide revolution of Westernization reached completion at the end of the twentieth century, the terrible failings of the Western project stood out just as clearly for these Islamist moderates as its triumphs. Their image of the West includes the human costs of colonialism and repeated neocolonial interventions, the brutalities of European civil wars misleadingly described as "world" wars, the horrors of Nazism and Stalinism, and the irresponsible consumerism and moral emptiness of contemporary Western societies, plagued by drugs, unimaginable violence, and, amidst abundance, the terrible neglect of the poor. Not even the social amnesia encouraged by the "glittering media" and the "wonderful computer," to borrow Qaradawy's phrases, can wipe out these haunting images of what the twentieth century has brought to those marginalized by Western civilization.

Is Islam a "threat"? asks Qaradawy. Yes, it is a threat to the reigning global patterns of oppression and injustice created by the dominant West, but never to "human beings and their chances for happiness." The New Islamists join critical thinkers around the world and the social movements they sometimes inspire in developing a sustained critique of the limitations of Western versions of universalism. The Prophet Muhammad laid the basis for another kind of civilization, Qaradawy assures his listeners, one that is balanced and integrative, a civilization of science and faith, of energetic production and just distribution, of material progress and spirituality. According to Qaradawy, Western civilization has not fulfilled universal human needs. It is a civilization that has reached the moon but fails to live on earth in a humane way; it is a civilization of means, not of ends; it is a civilization that does not give humankind social justice and spiritual happiness. To the young of the Islamic world, Qaradawy and the New Islamists do not offer the theatrical despair or ironic indifference that characterizes so much of the postmodern intellectual response to these failings in the West. They advance, instead, a vision of a social world rebuilt on the balanced foundations of Islamic civilization, rethought and translated into terms appropriate for a global age and promising a way out of the dilemmas of a troubled world.

Qaradawy's hopeful message comes at a time of deterioration at home, when the first signs are emerging that the government's campaign against Islamic extremists will be extended to moderates as well. In 1995, the space for dialogue is already contracting. A harsh, reactive shrillness creeps into the responses of even mainstream Islamists, who sense their vulnerability. These coming shadows are anticipated in the failure of Qaradawy's secular interlocutor to appear for what was originally planned as a dialogue. At the same time, the arrangement of the hall reflects the heavy-handedness of the Muslim Brothers' dominant role in the Doctors' Syndicate. Women are separated from men, with the women directed to the balconies. The proceedings are interrupted by the call to prayer in what purports to be a civic forum in accordance with behavior once reserved for mosques and churches.[2]

Still, even in these contracting circumstances of the mid-1990s, Qaradawy shows that a message of moderation can appeal effectively to the youth of the Islamic world. His youthful audience listens with rapt attention. Many take notes. Written questions circulate continuously to the front in anticipation of the question period. Throughout the proceedings, the packed hall remains uncharacteristically quiet and attentive as Qaradawy issues his call to young people in Islamic countries to undertake constructive engagements in public life, undeterred by the barriers erected by authoritarian regimes at home and the shadows cast by the ascendant West in the larger world.

Qaradawy understands that, in order to respond, young people will need a spirit shaped by realism but infused nevertheless with confidence that they can build a better future. What is most distinctive about Qaradawy and the New Islamists is precisely the capacity to project just such an energizing spirit. This assurance comes from a powerful blend of appreciation for the cultural attainments and possibilities of Islamic civilization and fearless openness to the world beyond Islam. It is made visible to the young in outspoken interventions by these centrist Islamist intellectuals in Arab, Islamic, and world forums. The New Islamists step forward with independent positions on critical Arab issues like the Gulf War and Palestine. However, these interventions, which attract the most attention by the international press, by no means exhaust their contributions. At the same time, they focus on developments in the broader Islamic arena for which they feel a special responsibility, ranging from the use of new information technologies in the service of Islam to criticism of the retrograde policies of the Taliban when they ruled in Afghanistan. In addition, the New Islamists have put forward an impressive model for an engaged Islamist role on the world stage in this global age when all the world's peoples and cultures are interacting as never before. With one eye on the higher purposes and basic values of Islam and the other on rapidly changing realities, the New Islamists take advantage of opportunities in all these forums to speak and act for the better world their contemporary Islamic vision promises.

Principled Realism and Deferral: From the Gulf War to the Struggle for Palestine

The New Islamists take strong centrist positions on the pressing issues of war and peace that face Egypt and the Arab Islamic world. During the Gulf War in 1991, they participated actively in the debates over the causes and conduct of the war, registering the distinctive voice of the Islamic *Wassatteyya* in the arena of foreign policy. The New Islamists mounted a strong centrist challenge to the views of the more radical Islamists, who gave uncritical support to the Iraqis. At the same time, they dissented vigorously from the official government policy in its unconditional cooperation with the American-dominated international coalition that liberated Kuwait and then assaulted and isolated Iraq. The centrists recognized the immediate cause of the crisis to be the criminal act of a dictatorial Arab regime that the Arab Islamic system proved unable to contain. But they also pointed out on a more fundamental level that the Arab weakness and disunity revealed by the crisis was particularly dangerous because of the larger threat of unconstrained Western power in the so-called New International Order.

The New Islamists feared that the preponderance of American power displayed during the Gulf crisis would have a profound and disturbing impact on the question of Palestine. In their view, the sequence of events that led from the Gulf War to the Madrid Conference in 1991 through the Oslo Accord of 1994 and into the Palestinian-Israeli negotiations that continued without meaningful results into the new century confirmed those fears. This series of agreements represented the backbone of what came to be known to the rest of the world as "the peace process." The New Islamists consistently refused this terminology, viewing it as seriously misleading: "It is absolutely not true that the Palestinian-Israeli negotiations in its various stages can be described as a peace process."[3] Peace, they insisted, could only come with justice. Speaking for the New Islamists, Yusuf al Qaradawy explained that "we do not oppose comprehensive and just peace, but oppose 'peace' if it is in the form of surrender that compels us to give but not take, 'peace' that concedes rights and sanctities."[4] The New Islamists argued that the framework created by these agreements reflected the current balance of power that overwhelmingly favored Israel and offered only a "peace of submission" to the Palestinians, signaled above all by the unrelenting Israeli colonization of the occupied territories.[5] The outcome of any such "peace process" would only ratify the final defeat of the occupied Palestinian people and legitimate the loss of Palestinian lands.

The weakness and disunity of the Arab states meant that they did not have the capacity to shield the Palestinians from this fate. Only resistance from within Palestine itself could keep the promise of justice alive, if only for future generations. The Palestinians suffered their humiliations alone, and out of their sufferings came a spirit of desperate defiance. The Palestinians rose up alone in the fall of 2000, just as they had done in the first Intifada [uprising] of 1987. The New Islamists hailed this second Intifada, named the al Aqsa Intifada after Jerusalem's famed mosque, just as they had the first. They did so not for its prospects of success but simply as a sign that resistance would continue. They took hope from the fact that strong Islamic sentiments were much more clearly in evidence in this second round of Palestinian national resistance. The violence of Israeli occupation had taken the quietly brutal form of expropriations of land and water and the erasure of the rights of the indigenous Palestinian people by "settlers." It would be met by the counter-violence of Palestinian resistance, once again beginning with stones thrown by Palestinian children and youth but this time ending with the suicide bombing of martyrs of resistance. Israel had one of the world's most powerful armies. It was a nuclear state. It enjoyed the backing of the sole superpower. The New Islamists openly admired the fortitude of the Palestinians, who knew from the outset that the blood to be shed would be overwhelming theirs.

Like most observers, the New Islamists noted that it was then Defense Minister Ariel Sharon who provided the immediate provocation that drove Palestinians beyond despair and into the streets to confront the tanks and helicopters of the occupiers. Sharon, accompanied by an army of guards, ostentatiously intruded on al Aqsa while the Barak government was ostensibly giving serious consideration to the latest American proposals. However, in the New Islamist view, it was U.S. President Bill Clinton who provided the strongest justification for a resistance so costly to the lives of young Palestinians, so unlikely to win any tangible Arab support, and so distant in its promise of advancing the Palestinian cause.

In the last months of his presidency, Clinton had arranged a second Camp David meeting with Israeli Prime Minister Barak and Palestinian President Yasser Arafat. The proposal that Clinton put on the table for "a final settlement" to the Israeli-Palestinian conflict claimed to give Palestinians 95 percent of the West Bank. The Western media hailed this as the "last best chance for the Palestinians" and the "most generous offer" the Palestinians were ever likely to get. The al Aqsa Intifada aborted the effort, toppling Barak and bringing Sharon to power. The Western media opined that once again the Palestinians and their Arab supporters had demonstrated their irrationality in what might well prove to be a final act of historic irresponsibility.

Fahmy Huwaidy responded with anger to the calculated distortions of this global media campaign and with outrage to the actual content of the American proposal. Huwaidy apologized to his readers for the uncharacteristic passion of the article in which he assessed the U.S. proposal, saying that he was still reeling "from this spit in the face and kick in the stomach." He deeply resented the contempt for the Palestinians and the Arabs that the disdainful and hypocritical terms of the Clinton proposal signaled. Offered as a final gesture from the departing president, the proposal in Huwaidy's view displayed more flagrantly than usual the American view of Palestinians as "an inferior people who did not deserve to live [as human beings] and therefore have the obligation to accept what Israel dictates."[6]

"The percentage sounds reasonable and encouraging," wrote Huwaidy, "because, if you are defeated and occupied, 95 percent is a good deal."

Huwaidy then provided a detailed and sober analysis of the Clinton proposal, exposing the myth of this American "gift" that, on the surface, made such eminent good sense. On closer reading, he explained, the reasonableness dissolves under the impact of the policy of building Jewish settlements on occupied Palestinian territory—a policy that every Israeli government, whether Labor or Likud, had assiduously pursued. The West Bank referred to in the Clinton proposal is not the West Bank of 1967. Rather, the proposal involved acceptance of the additional expropriations that the occupying Israeli power made in violation of international law over the long period of occupation after 1967. According to Huwaidy, Israeli annexations to Jerusalem during that period had claimed 18 percent of the best West Bank lands, which were taken off the table. But that was not all, he explained. The proposal also supported the Israeli demands to annex an additional 5 percent of the West Bank lands and the long-term lease of another 3 percent, in addition to annexing yet another 1 percent on which Jewish settlements are built, thus subtracting an additional 9 percent. When all such prior subtractions were made from the West Bank to be returned, Huwaidy calculated that the mythical 95 percent that made such a dramatic headline would be reduced to something at best on the order of 69 percent of the West Bank as constituted before the Israeli occupation in 1967.

Further provisions of the proposal provided for an exchange of land to compensate Palestinians for the loss of territory to the Jewish settlements; arrangements for the refugees; the resolution of the issue of sovereignty over the Muslim holy places in Jerusalem; and the final form of the Palestinian state. Each of these elements, in Huwaidy's view, has a poisonous dimension. Most innocent-sounding is the exchange of lands to accommodate the settlers. Israel would annex 80 percent of the land on which settlements are built in exchange for giving the Palestinians 3 percent of the land under Israeli control. The just solution would have been to give these settlements to the Palestinians so that the refugees could live in them, especially in view of the demolition by Israel of 420 Palestinian villages. This is not what happened. Instead, what is proposed is the annexation of the settlements in exchange for some other land. The proposal fails to mention that the Jewish settlements had taken the best agricultural land, with control of water resources and having strategic importance. In contrast, Huwaidy describes the lands the Palestinians would receive as "an area of desert with no life and no water and that had been used by Israel as a toxic waste dump."

The treatment of the refugee issue, writes Huwaidy, is even more heavyhanded. Estimates of the total number of Palestinian refugees range from

4.5 to 5 million. For the overwhelming majority of refugees, the Clinton offer proposes a plan of monetary compensation that "will not reach 2 percent of their losses, with the cost of even that trivial compensation covered by the Gulf States. Israel will not pay a penny." Huwaidy describes the other element of the refugee solution as "symbolic or, to speak more truthfully, comic." Israel would allow the return of only 150,000 of the refugees who left in 1948, at the rate of one to two thousand a year to reunite families. In this way, the proposal would dispose of the internationally recognized right to return of the Palestinian refugees.

"Jerusalem is no exception in this series of deceptions," continues Huwaidy. East Jerusalem is understood in the proposal to comprise two parts. The first part inside the wall contains the Muslim and Christian holy sites, including the most important Christian church in Jerusalem as well as Armenian, Christian, and Muslim districts, while the second consists of several additional quarters, some of which are described as Jewish.[7] The principle advanced in the proposal is that the Jewish areas would be under the Israelis, while the Palestinians would control the Arab sections. The proposal, in short, provides that Israel would retain West Jerusalem and would add to it these newly partitioned parts of East Jerusalem. The sovereignty of the 35-acre sacred site called by Muslims the Haram al Sharif, and known to Israelis and world Jewry as the Temple Mount, would go to the Palestinians. However, Palestinian sovereignty would apply only for its "above ground" part, while any excavation below ground would require agreement by both parties. This convoluted formula, Huwaidy fears, dilutes the sovereignty of a weak Palestinian state adjacent to a powerful Israel to such a degree that the Palestinians might well be unable to protect al Aqsa mosque on the southern-most end of that site from subterranean excavations. Huwaidy draws attention to the disturbing fact that this unprecedented notion of dividing sovereignty above and below ground succeeded for the first time in winning explicit American support for an Israeli claim to sovereignty over the land on which al Aqsa mosque stands. Finally, sovereignty over the Wailing Wall, which serves as one of the walls of the mosque, would go to Israel, even though, as Huwaidy notes, during the British Mandate international bodies called to study the question ruled "it should go to the Palestinians as it is part of the holy mosque." Huwaidy makes it clear that these provisions fail to meet minimum requirements for sovereignty over East Jerusalem.

Finally, Huwaidy notes that the American formula proposed for the character of the Palestinian state was even more biased to Israel and unhelpful to the Palestinians. He reminds his readers that the debate over the Palestinian state had crystallized in two positions. The Israelis demanded a demilitarized state, while the Palestinians insisted on a state with limited military capacity. The Clinton language describes the new state as "unmilitarized" without explaining what the difference between a "demilitarized" and an "unmilitarized" state would be. Huwaidy can find little of use to the Palestinians in such a vague formulation.

The United States claimed that this proposal, if implemented, would end the Palestinian-Israeli conflict and would reflect the full implementation of UN resolutions 242 and 338. The basic formula underlying these resolutions was the return to the Palestinians of the land seized in 1967 in return for peace. Only by accepting the glittering but misleading figure of 95 percent and overlooking all of the actual restrictions and qualifications imposed by Israel and endorsed by the United States could the proposal be read in this way. Only by ignoring the unacceptable dilutions of their right of return, their claims to Jerusalem and the al Aqsa mosque, and their aspirations for a viable state could the Palestinians regard the proposal as more than "a spit in the face," as Huwaidy put it. Placing the Clinton proposal in historical perspective, Huwaidy notes that this "final settlement" would mean that as the price for living in peace with the Jewish state, the Palestinians would have legitimated the surrender of all but a small remnant of their homeland occupied in 1948, far less than the 22 percent represented by the pre-1967 Gaza and West Bank. They would have done so, moreover, without receiving even a modicum of justice on the issues of the refugees, Jerusalem, and the form of the Palestinian state. "I do not hesitate to say," he concludes, "that the only good thing about the actual text of the proposal is that it clarifies that the hope for an honorable political settlement with Israel is still remote until further notice. The only hope, if there is any, is therefore the Intifada, the first, the second, and maybe the tenth as well."

The New Islamists had consistently asserted the interest of the entire Islamic world in the outcome of the Palestinian-Israeli negotiations, particularly on the issues of Jerusalem and the refugees. Yusuf al Qaradawy celebrated the final Palestinian refusal of this second Camp David meeting and hailed the Palestinian leadership's ultimate decision not to agree to the unacceptable terms proposed for the future of Jerusalem. "Palestine without Jerusalem," commented Qaradawy, "would be like a body without a head." Given a proposal that effectively denied Palestinians real sovereignty over the holy places, Qaradawy welcomed the collapse of these negotiations. He reminded the Palestinians, however, that they were not free to dispose of Jerusalem as they saw fit: "Jerusalem does not belong to the Palestinians alone, but rather to all Arabs, Christians as well as Muslims." In a message to the Palestinian authorities, Qaradawy added that the whole nation and not just one particular leadership has the permanent responsibility for

Jerusalem. "If any leadership of any generation," he said, "is unable to carry this responsibility, it should not impose this incapability on all subsequent generations."[8]

The New Islamists reacted just as strongly to the inadequacy of the provisions in the Clinton proposal for the Palestinian refugees. During the negotiations Huwaidy wrote an article with the striking title "Right of return is more important than Jerusalem." In the body of the article Huwaidy went on to clarify his position, saying that "giving up Jerusalem was a dangerous thing, and giving up the right to return is even more dangerous." The article produced a storm of protest in Islamist circles, many having incorrectly read Huwaidy's position as underestimating the importance of Jerusalem to Muslims around the world.[9] Huwaidy's clarification reminded Arabs and Muslims that while Jerusalem had received great attention, if not action on its behalf, the cause of the roughly five million refugees was relatively neglected, and his article was meant to redress this imbalance. Huwaidy added that to the degree they discussed the issue of the refugees as one of compensation rather than the internationally recognized right of return, the Arab regimes were "selling out the cause."

The American backing for the "peace process" initially had divided the Egyptian political class. Support for the "peace process" had begun to make important inroads based on the conclusion that realism dictated accommodation with the world's sole superpower. Sadat had advanced just this argument first. A much smaller group of Egyptian intellectuals went still further and argued not simply for support of the "peace process" but for active normalization of relations with Israel even before final settlement of outstanding issues in Palestine. The most important cluster coalesced as the so-called Copenhagen group. The group looked beyond governments to the creation of "peace camps" of civil institutions in Israel and Arab countries in order to break what they called the cycle of violence and war in which governments were locked. The Copenhagen circle remained small and never showed any signs of attracting a large following. However, the prominence in public life of some of its adherents, notably Lutfy al Kholy, a leftist luminary, and Abdul Moneim Said, head of the Al Ahram Political and Strategic Studies Center, gave them a weight beyond their numbers. The Intifada and the disproportionate force of the Sharon regime's efforts to repress it cast shadows over all of these accommodationist positions. For all practical purposes, they had collapsed by the summer of 2001.

The New Islamists believed that the Clinton proposal had the sole advantage of demonstrating that America could not broker an honest peace in Palestine. With the same logic, they anticipated correctly that Sharon's rule would be even more violent than Barak's in terms of the character of the war he waged against the Intifada. However, they also believed that Sharon in power would also bring into the full light of day the real character of Israeli rule of the West Bank and the plans for its future. The New Islamists understood that this would mean that the quiet but devastating suffering and humiliations of the Palestinians would be replaced by overt and violent repression. About this, like the Palestinians themselves, they had no illusions. It was harder to predict what the final impact on Israel, the United States, and the world at large would be of the devastating violence that Sharon's rule brought. One thing, however, was clear. The pre-Sharon configuration already spelled disaster for Palestinian aspirations. When the Hizbullah resistance forced the Israeli public to confront the costs of occupation, the withdrawal became possible.[10]

The New Islamists hailed the Israeli withdrawal from southern Lebanon. They also acknowledged that the Israeli peace movement played an important role in mobilizing sentiment against the continued occupation and the toll it took. They were unwilling, however, to exaggerate the power of the peace sentiment within Israel, especially when it came to the West Bank and Gaza. The New Islamists noted with regret that most elements of the peace movement identified with the Barak initiative and the Clinton proposal, thus revealing just how inadequate their conception of the just rights of the Palestinians was. Huwaidy also pointed out that the policy of aggressive military action against the Intifada, condemned by voices around the world, had the support of a strong majority of the Israeli people. Someday, there might well be effective partners for a just peace with Israel. That day, the New Islamists concluded, had not yet arrived.[11]

In response, the New Islamists urged something more thoughtful than either return to the empty rhetoric of the past, when the Arab regimes simply mouthed slogans, or the unacceptable silences of the present, when they quietly acquiesce in Israeli depredations under the cover of the "peace process." Their alternative relies on an Islamic habit of mind, given classic expression in the Quranic injunction that evil must be resisted by hand, by tongue, or by heart, depending on circumstances and responsibilities. God enjoined man to act according to the values he had set, notably the realization of justice. However, He did so in ways that allowed humans to preserve themselves and their families. Although there were moments when martyrdom was called for, they were unusual. For the most part, man was to respond to moral imperatives in the light of a reasoned attention to the realities within which injustice occurred and according to the appropriate means at hand.

In the Lebanese Hizbullah the New Islamists read the testimony of the martyrdom that resistance sometimes demands. They did not doubt for a moment that it was the tireless struggle and sacrifices of those fighters under an Islamic banner that defeated the Israeli occupation.[12] Fahmy Huwaidy hailed the victory not only for ending the occupation but also for shattering the myth that the Israeli forces were invincible. While celebrating the martyrs of Hizbullah who lost their lives fighting the Israeli occupation, Huwaidy also praised numerous instances of nonviolent resistance, including a celebrated action by unarmed Lebanese university students who succeeded in "liberating" a village that the Israelis sought to incorporate into their security zone.[13]

Thus, the New Islamists celebrated the Israeli withdrawal from the Lebanese territories as a galvanizing victory that should inspire actions of resistance, both violent and nonviolent, elsewhere. However, they characteristically drew that lesson with care and a sense of responsibility. While the Palestinians could draw inspiration from the victory of Hizbullah, they had to acknowledge as well that the tenacity of Israel in the West Bank and Gaza would be incomparably greater than in southern Lebanon. Their battle would be harder and longer, and their prospects for success in this generation less likely. The Palestinians, Huwaidy pointed out, appear to have understood these differences, even as they looked to the example of Hizbullah. They waged the second Intifada without illusions about what its costs would be. In effect, given the stark imbalance of power, any resistance to the Israelis was suicidal. "The scene," wrote Huwaidy, "has the dimensions of a tragedy . . . it is as if the Palestinian is fated to lift his own dead body and the bodies of his children every day and carry them to the top of the mountain without any hope of reaching his goal, like Sisyphus of Greek legend." The Israelis had eliminated all options for a defeated and occupied people except revolt and the sacrifices it would demand. Huwaidy was struck by the attitude toward death that characterized the Palestinians. If you want to be accurate, he observed, "they regard death not as a choice but rather as a duty." They understand that death will become the companion of those who seek to "live with dignity in their homeland and who struggle to retrieve it from brutal Israeli control." In the land of the Intifada, death has taken a unique form. It is something for which people "congratulate rather than console themselves." The Palestinians and especially the youth, wrote Huwaidy, now leave their homes with stones in their hands, welcoming martyrdom as they raise the banner of resistance. The scene was repeated again and again of Palestinian children and young people courageously facing one of the world's most powerful military machines, backed by the United States. Those images in themselves, whatever the outcome of particular confrontations, provided a "confirmation of the failure of the efforts of erasure and the conspiracy of destruction. It is an open refutation of the claims of Palestinian surrender. It expresses an uprising that many had considered over. It means that the invaders will not enjoy in peace what they took from their victims by terrible crimes that will neither be forgotten nor forgiven."[14]

Egyptians, too, could learn from Hizbullah. Again, however, the New Islamists cautioned that the lessons should be drawn in ways that suited their circumstances and purposes. They rejected out of hand the calls for terrorist strikes put forward by the most extremist voices of political Islam. Moreover, they judged that the realities of global and regional power precluded, under current conditions, a military option for Egypt. However, facing that limitation squarely did not, in their view, dictate abject submission. Even though a military option to confront the Israeli war against the Palestinians was impossible, they also felt that full normalization of Egyptian-Israeli relations before the basic rights of the Arabs and Palestinians had been secured was equally unacceptable. The New Islamists therefore rejected any "warming" of the relationship with Israel. The Egyptian-Israeli peace should be a "cold" peace so long as the oppression of the Palestinians continued. Egyptians might not now be able to act for justice and resist the Israelis by hand, but they could and should resist their continued violation of Palestinian rights by their tongues and in their hearts.

Alongside their refusals to "warm" the peace with Israel, the New Islamists urged alternative nonviolent expressions of support for the besieged Palestinians. "There are other ways of assisting Palestinians," wrote Huwaidy, "such as sending food and medicine." Even better, added Selim al Awa, would be "support for small productive projects."[15] The search for a middle ground of possibilities for action between the extremes of terrorism or war and submission characterized New Islamist thinking about Palestine. They started from an expanded conception of what resistance might mean, envisioning the broadest possible participation of citizens, rather than simply governments, in a wide variety of arenas with as much attention given to economic and cultural initiatives as political ones.

Ultimately, the New Islamist position was one of deferral of the conflict until such time as the balance of forces held out some greater hope for the Arab cause. Selim al Awa argued that realism about the current limited capacities of the Egyptian state did not have to mean the abandonment of all principle and hope; there still existed possibilities of resistance on the mass level. The New Islamists felt that every opportunity, no matter how small or apparently inconsequential, should be seized upon to give people a sense that their actions could make a difference.

To suggest these possibilities of resistance within existing constraints, Awa took to calling those intellectuals and public figures who actively opposed normalization with Israel "the Egyptian Hizbullah." Along these assertive lines, the New Islamists actively supported the call to boycott not only Israel but the United States as well. Again, they did so without illusions. Awa, for example, celebrated "the 'annoyance' the boycott would cause Israel and those who supported the Zionist state." The word was chosen carefully to avoid exaggeration. Awa understood that the economic effort had little chance to drive Israeli products, let alone American ones, completely from Arab markets. However, he did believe that it would not go unnoticed. As evidence, Awa cited the signs of worry from American companies in Egypt over the call to boycott American goods and services. He noted that some American companies and affiliates have prepared lists of the nationalities of those who work for them; others have begun broadcasting religious songs on their internal radio systems; and still others have taken to establishing Ramadan tables to feed the poor during Ramadan.[16] Awa also made it clear that even the unlikely success of going further and driving these companies from the Egyptian market would not seriously hurt either Israeli or American economic power. The call for the boycott was a gesture to assert a principle, and the New Islamists acknowledged this honestly. However, they still urged that these symbolic actions be taken. How, asked Awa, could the Egyptians and others from the Islamic world do any less to show their support for the Palestinian youth who were daily confronting the Zionist enemy? A boycott would create for Egyptians a means to participate in the resistance. If they could not return Israeli blows to Palestinian and Arab rights directly, at least they could do so indirectly by using their own financial resources. "It was simply unacceptable," Awa wrote, "at a time when Palestinian youth were being killed, for Arabs to enjoy the food, clothing, and other goods from this Zionist enemy or his primary supporter, the United States." Moreover, Egyptians should support the boycott for the sake of their own self-respect. Just because one is unable to resist the enemy by force, "that is no reason to help him with money to become stronger, and allow him to feel that his active animosity toward us will have no repercussions." Awa warned that "if the enemy feels this way, it will be more humiliating to us than a thousand military defeats!"[17]

The New Islamists thus supported the boycott against Israel and the United States as a popular action, one that did not involve the state. Fahmy Huwaidy's assessment of the Palestinian al Aqsa Intifada stressed that it had inspired ordinary citizens of the Arab world to reenter the field of political action on behalf of Palestine. Strong indicators had been mounting that the Arab political street had deserted the Palestinian cause. However, the courageous renewal of resistance by the new generation of Palestinians against such terrible odds once again prompted ordinary citizens of the

Arab states to ask what they could do to support the youthful Palestinian fighters. The New Islamists never called for a state-level boycott, a withdrawal of ambassadors, or a halt to diplomatic relations. "For years we have been saying," commented Huwaidy, "that the governments have necessities, while people have choices and thus more freedom."[18] Because citizens do not have the same constraints as states do, there are actions the people can take that go around state power. Awa explicitly called on "ordinary, simple, honest people to adopt the boycott as a way to express their anger toward the enemy." "The very least help that any one of us can give to the heroic Palestinian youth," he wrote, "is that every one of us should boycott the Zionist and U.S. goods to the degree that he can." Awa noted that this kind of citizens' boycott "is really harmful to our enemies because governments will not be able to combat it and the agreements made between states will not stop it; not even the meetings of the official Palestinians secretly with the Israelis can dampen its effects."[19]

It was their civilizational perspective, culturally confident and anchored in a strong sense of history, that energized the New Islamists, steeled them to the costs that principled actions would exact in an unjust world, and shielded them from lapses into despair or desperation. They opposed the extremes of support for either the accommodationist strategies forced on the Egyptian regime or the irresponsible calls for terrorist strikes of the extremist Islamists. Their sense of belonging to the Islamic world provided a distinctive and longer-term vantage point from which to assess the current power imbalance, to absorb realistically its immediate devastating consequences, and to focus on long-term strategies to overcome it. The New Islamists refused to accept American global and related Israeli regional dominance as permanent and unchanging facts of international political life, however powerful they might be at this moment. History, they argued, had no permanent resting places, and the Islamic world, including Jerusalem, had known even more trying times of conquest and occupation.

Theorizing and Acting for Islamic "Belonging"

The interpretive effort of the New Islamists to develop Islamic guidelines for acting in international affairs depends on the idea of a historical and cultural Islamic world to which Egyptians, other Arabs, and non-Arabs as well belong. This view requires attention to the fate of Muslim communities around the globe and not just those within the Arab circle. All of the New Islamist positions on the question of Palestine rest on a powerful commitment to the Islamic world. That broader commitment means that Palestine cannot be the only focus for the New Islamists, even though it is the most important. The New Islamists never acknowledge any tension between their support for resistance of the Soviet invading force in non-Arab Afghanistan, for example, and attention to the West Bank and Gaza where an Arab people suffer military occupation. Rather, they view all such attachments and commitments, including the commitment to Palestine, through an Islamic prism. To understand the struggle for Palestine in Islamic terms does not, however, mean to see it as one of Islam versus Judaism. "How could it be," asks Yusuf al Qaradawy, when the Jews are "a people of the Book with whom it is permissible to marry, just like Christians? How could it be when Jews always lived in the lands of Islam with all dignity and attained the highest positions as professionals and ministers?" No, he concludes, the struggle is not about the religion of the Jews. "We must fight them because they seized the land, caused bloodshed, and made people homeless. And what land did they seize? The land of the Prophets."[20] The New Islamists believe that the erosion of the Arab position in Jerusalem stands as the most horrific price paid for the weakness and decline of the Islamic world. Thus the shift in primary focus from the Arab to the Islamic sphere does not diminish or dilute for them the centrality of Jerusalem and the struggle for Palestine.

Muhammad al Ghazzaly explained the Islamic wellspring of this commitment when he reacted to the Madrid Agreement that inaugurated the direct Palestinian and Israeli negotiations. Students at Cairo University responded with anger and dismay to the terms of the agreement when they were announced in fall of 1991, fearing that a weak Palestinian authority would never be able to defend Jerusalem. In response to government urgings, the Minister of Awqaf organized a symposium at the university that included prominent Islamic figures, Ghazzaly among them. In his remarks, Ghazzaly first restated the unique importance of Jerusalem to the Islamic world and reaffirmed that its liberation was a sacred duty for all Muslims. He commented acidly that the issues of Palestine, the receptacle of Jerusalem, could never be reduced simply to questions of land and security, given the spiritual significance of the city. Finally, Ghazzaly argued that only the long-term rebuilding of the strength of the Islamic world would create the conditions for the return of Jerusalem. The gradualism of the New Islamist position was expressed in this final argument. Ghazzaly urged Egypt's young people to work hard to create the conditions necessary for the return of Jerusalem and warned them to avoid being drawn into the diversions of minor demonstrations and disturbances on the local level. In the core confrontation with the expansionist Zionist adversary, the Islamic world had to exploit every opportunity for legitimate resistance. In the end, however, given the forces arrayed against them, the peoples of the

Islamic lands might have no choice but to accept deferral of full confrontation, though they had no right before God to accept defeat.[21]

This commitment to legitimate resistance in all its forms against the occupation of Jerusalem characterizes not only New Islamist thinking but also that of the Islamic mainstream more generally. Although the New Islamists became critical of the rigidities of the Muslim Brothers organization, they never lost sight of the historical importance of that group to Palestine in defense of the rights of the Islamic world. No page in that history was more stirring than the role of the Brothers as resistance fighters in Palestine. At the time of his own affiliation to the Brothers, for example, Muhammad al Ghazzaly led a group of volunteers to Palestine, an experience that shaped a lifelong commitment to the liberation of Jerusalem. Similarly, in one of his most influential works, *The Fiqh of Priorities,* Yusuf al Qaradawy described his admiration for the Brotherhood leader Hassan al Banna for his role as a pioneer in the struggle to liberate Palestine, organizing conferences, lectures, and generally mobilizing people at a time when most Arab and Muslim leaders were unaware of the gravity of Zionist designs on Palestine. "It is indisputable," wrote Qaradawy, "that since its foundation the Islamic movement has ranked the liberation of all Islamic lands as a highest priority. . . . In 1948, the Brotherhood fought in Palestine. This is the rightful role of the Islamic movement against occupation of all kinds."[22]

The New Islamists are neither alone nor incapable of coalition with others in their call for resistance to Israeli power in Palestine. All the major opposition currents in Egypt, for example, stand with them on this position. The point is rather that they have come to this common position out of their own unique history. In the New Islamist view, the issues raised by struggles in Palestine are too important to be left either to the regime or to the Islamic extremists. The *Wassatteyya* has its own stance on the issue of Jerusalem, and the New Islamist School has given that position a particularly sophisticated expression, notably in the work of Tareq al Bishry.

Bishry's historical studies have heightened awareness among centrists of the distinctive history of opposition under the banner of Islam to the colonization of Palestine, and of the responsibilities it imposes on the *Wassatteyya* to participate in the struggle for justice in Palestine today. In the late nineteenth and early twentieth centuries, Bishry relates, Islamic sensibilities helped rally the Arab population to face the pressure of the Zionist colonizing forces. From the outset, Islamist thinkers have understood the fight for Palestine as part of a civilizational resistance to the worldwide imperial expansion of the West. In their view, the resistance against the Jews of Palestine and Europe was of one piece with the struggles, for example, of the Algerians against the French or the Libyans against the Italians—and, indeed, of peoples all over the Third World who stood against the aggressive power of the West. Yet at the same time, the importance of Jerusalem give this particular battle a greater resonance than any other. The disasters of 1948 and 1967 were blows to the entire Islamic world because they placed not only the land of Palestine but also the city of Jerusalem and its holy places in jeopardy.

Throughout the 1950s, 1960s, and into the 1970s the traumas of defeat translated into the travails of a grinding occupation that sought to destroy systematically the identity of the Palestinians as a people and to appropriate as much of the best land and water of Palestine as possible, all the while targeting Jerusalem. In this extended process, Bishry reports, "Israel was backed by the West, especially the United States, which has its own 'pioneering and settlement' experience of displacing the Native Americans while depicting them as barbarians standing in the way of history."[23] The world stood by as Jerusalem was declared the eternal capital of Israel. In ways too depressing to catalogue but familiar enough in the histories of Western colonization and displacement elsewhere, the Palestinians in Israel, Gaza, and the West Bank were crushed. They were "legally" terrorized into permanent submission, or so it seemed for these long decades of "deadly silence" from within the occupied territories.

Meanwhile, the Palestinians in forced exile outside their historical homeland created an organization of national resistance on the pattern of such resistance movements around the world. These were Westernized anti-Western forces in the sense that in order to combat the West most effectively, they adopted many Western organizational and ideological forms of struggle, including the banner of secularism that was the hallmark of the PLO with its call for a "secular, democratic state." Bishry's assessment centered on this paradox of the Westernizing role played by the PLO. From their Islamic civilizational perspective, the New Islamists opposed this imitative strategy, even as they supported the PLO's struggle for national liberation. Bishry understood the PLO as the product of the needs and conditions of dispersal, explaining that the PLO "went beyond the concept of a political organization into becoming the representative of the Palestinian nation. It fulfilled a role needed by the dispersed Palestinians and provided a symbol of unity for a people scattered in different places." At the time, the emergence of the PLO seemed natural enough, paralleling the emergence of "movements of the same colors in the 1950s; it aimed at liberating the land and building a Western-style social and political system." The PLO ranged itself among the secular liberation movements and the state systems that some succeeded in founding. The PLO naturally looked to the

Arab states for support in the struggle against Israel, and in many ways, PLO structures mirrored those of the Arab governments, including some of their worst anti-democratic features.[24]

The New Islamists viewed the politics of these secular Arab nationalists with ambivalence. As Bishry put it, "Secular liberation movements tended to compromise with colonization and to accept half-solutions on issues of national independence." Tied to the compromised Arab state system, the PLO shared in its precipitous decline in the wake of the 1967 defeat. The crushing defeat by Israel made it impossible to conceal the weakness of the regimes on which the PLO liberation strategy depended. Deterioration struck the PLO itself. Years marked by internal struggles, punctuated by assassinations and clashes with Arab authorities, notably Jordan, followed.[25]

Then in 1987 the Arabs within the occupied territories surprised the world with their first Intifada. This was a decisive moment in the Palestinian struggle, as the New Islamists assessed it. The PLO, operating from the outside, had sought to replace the nation with its own structures. Suddenly, in 1987 revolt erupted within historic Palestine. The Intifada and the new leadership cadres it generated emerged from the very heart of the nation. Not surprisingly, these new political actors reflected more accurately than the exiled PLO leaders the civilizational characteristics of the Palestinian people, notably the strong religious affiliations of both Palestinian Christians and the Muslim majority. Bishry noted that by this act of self-assertion on Palestinian land, the Intifada underscored the weaknesses of the dispersed PLO. Suddenly, the PLO faced an alternative liberation movement with a strong Islamic coloration.

At its high point during 1988, the first Intifada held great promise. Bishry's evaluation stressed the new forms of struggle that emerged from the battles. Children and teenagers took a leading part. Initially, the bodies of Palestinian youth and the stones of the earth were the only real weapons in what came to be known as the "Uprising of Stones." The New Islamists generally drew attention to the fact that the young appeared to act out of religious rather than secular inspiration. Bishry noted that the Muslim majority in the occupied territories adopted a *jihad* perspective that called for resistance. Christian young people found the same inspiration in their faith to fight occupation. Somehow, the mosques and churches had nourished the impulse to resist in a generation that knew nothing other than the humiliations of foreign military occupation.

As the struggle continued, the New Islamists called attention to the spontaneously generated forms of resistance that multiplied. In an early, detailed report based on Israeli sources, Fahmy Huwaidy sketched the inventive ways in which the Palestinians integrated the struggle into their daily lives and thereby sustained it against overwhelming odds.[26] While they appreciated the depth of the support from all elements of Palestinian society, the New Islamists' view of the Intifada put particular emphasis on the return of Islamic inspiration. However, they always situated that particularistic interest in a larger strategic assessment. Bishry stressed that the Intifada shifted the struggle to a direct confrontation between Palestinians and Israelis, unmediated by Arab regimes. In such a context, Palestinian unity became absolutely critical. Huwaidy characterized the preferred approach as one that "rejects clashes with any Palestinian force, whether Islamic or secular; it gives scope to all forces and does not monopolize the right of resistance. Instead, the door must be opened wide to all kinds and forms of resistance."

The PLO responded defensively to the successes of the Intifada. Understanding the potentially serious challenge to its leadership, the PLO became preoccupied with organizational loyalty, which, as Bishry pointed out, "was not equivalent to nationalist loyalty." The PLO's main goal, he continued, "became the international recognition to empower itself not in the face of other countries but of the competing Palestinian movement in the occupied territory." The PLO "sought recognition even from adversaries, and even if it meant concessions in goals."

The decline of the first Intifada meant that the PLO strategy of concessions would prevail. The Intifada began essentially as a spontaneous rebellion. To sustain the challenge to the occupier, it was necessary to turn the sporadic and unorganized confrontations in the streets into a comprehensive civil disobedience movement. Success of such an internal revolt depended ultimately on the ability of the Palestinians to decouple themselves to some degree from the Israeli economy.[27] The will to do so was clearly in evidence, especially in the first year of the struggle, and some progress was registered. For this move toward greater economic autonomy to succeed, Palestinians would require the support of the Arab states, particularly those of the Gulf with the resources to make it happen. Unfortunately, sufficient support was not forthcoming, and the New Islamists regularly criticized the Arab regimes of the Gulf for the inadequacy of their support.

The Iraqi invasion of Kuwait then sealed the fate of the first Intifada. The Palestinians in the streets of the occupied territories responded to events with support for the Iraqis. The logic of that support was straightforward. Whatever their assessment of the regime of Saddam Hussein, Palestinians saw Iraq as the only Arab power willing to challenge the Americans, who, in the final analysis, made the continued Israeli occupation of the West Bank and Gaza possible. The Gulf regimes, led by Kuwait, responded by halting their financial support for the Intifada. It was, as Fahmy Huwaidy put it, "a kind of collective punishment of Palestinians for their stand during the crisis." The consequence, Huwaidy argued, was to undermine the Palestinian resistance and strengthen "the terrible Israeli dreams of a greater Israel."[28] The world's attention shifted to the Gulf, and coverage of the Intifada slipped from the front pages. The PLO reconsolidated its leadership over the national movement. The way was open to Madrid.

By the time the "peace process" that began with Madrid was launched, the New Islamists had concluded that the PLO had in effect exhausted its earlier emancipatory role. They searched for a formula, as Fahmy Huwaidy described it, "for relations with the PLO, while rejecting its approach and without escalating inter-Palestinian conflicts."[29] The adverse terms of the Madrid Agreement that Arafat accepted heightened the dilemma. The agreement, as Huwaidy had put it earlier, was the "legitimate son of the Gulf War which shattered the Arab nation."[30] With the subsequent Oslo Accords, the New Islamists felt there could be no doubt that, as Bishry said, the PLO had "established itself as the Palestinian internal authority" at the cost of unacceptable concessions to Israel.[31]

The New Islamists were thus from the outset extremely wary of PLO participation in the American-backed negotiations with Israel. With an eye to the compromised PLO leadership, they declared openly that the fate of these Islamic lands did not rest in Palestinian hands alone and should not be decided in the current circumstances of extreme Arab weakness. The special importance of Jerusalem to the Islamic world provided the linchpin of this argument.

"We are all responsible for Jerusalem before God," explains Tareq al Bishry in an important new publication by Islamist intellectuals called *My Nation and the World.* In the 1999 inaugural issue of this new strategic annual, Bishry provides an extensive treatment of the role of Jerusalem as a key element of the history and memory that undergird the Islamic sense of belonging. "For us," he writes, "Jerusalem is not just an issue of religion, but rather of religions, community, history, and culture. It has an importance that is historical, contemporary, and part of our future." From an Islamist perspective, the role of Jerusalem defines the centrality of Palestine to the Arab Islamic world, or, as Bishry puts it:

> Palestine is the container of Jerusalem. Jerusalem is the identity of Palestine. Jerusalem is not simply a city in a nation called Palestine. Palestine is rather a nation in a city called Jerusalem. Palestine without Jerusalem has no more importance than the Sinai or the Golan Heights, that is, it becomes simply an issue of pure political liberation.

The implications of these judgments are not merely rhetorical. Bishry observes pointedly that it is not for the Palestinians alone to decide the fate of Jerusalem. "Palestine is not the responsibility of the Palestinians only," he writes. "We are all responsible for Palestine, whether we are Christians or Muslims, according to all these historical, cultural, religious, and political ties." Acknowledging the extreme political weakness of the Palestinians, Bishry concludes that "since Palestine is not owned by the Palestinians alone, any concessions by a political entity representing the Palestinian people is not binding on us, provided that we are up to our responsibility."[32]

Bishry urges that the current struggle be placed in a long-term framework. In looking at Jerusalem, the past as well as the present must be in front of our eyes. "What we understand of the past must be present with us," he writes. The present time of troubles for Palestine is not the first, nor even the worst. For about two hundred years, Bishry reminds his readers, from the eleventh to the thirteenth century, Palestine was a land of conflict. In the modern period the conflict has resumed for another century thus far, with no end in sight. While acknowledging all the political and strategic dimensions of the struggle for Palestine, he nevertheless concludes that its historical and religious meaning for the Islamic world takes precedence. Attachment to the city of Jerusalem, writes Bishry, "is an amazing common thread" that binds Muslim to Christian, those most attached to religion with those more drawn to the worldly life.[33] "Jerusalem cannot be transformed simply into a capital," Bishry continues. "It is not 'Berlin' which can be replaced by 'Bonn' in the German consciousness, or 'Istanbul' to be replaced by 'Ankara' for the Turks. It is Jerusalem, with no replacement. It is not a land whose people alone can determine its fate."[34]

The shared responsibility for Jerusalem means that all who feel that pull should contribute to its redemption in ways appropriate to their own circumstances. New Islamist intellectuals felt a particular sense of obligation to respond to what they regarded as the manipulation of Islam to support the unjust negotiations. From this perspective, the *fatwa* [religious opinion] published in January 1995 by Shaikh Ben Baz, the Mufti of Saudi Arabia, could not be ignored. Ben Baz provided an unequivocal Islamic justification for the peace process with Israel if the ruler finds it in the interest of Muslims. In support of his ruling, he cited both a clear Quranic verse and a verified *hadith* [a report, including the sources, of the words of the Prophet]. Yusuf al Qaradawy spoke for all the New Islamists when he directly challenged the *fatwa.* Islamic law rejects "peace" as the Israelis and Americans understand it, he wrote in an *al Shaab* article of January 17, 1995.[35] He then laid out the logic of his dissent. His reasoning provides a model of the essential structure of the New Islamist interpretive project as applied to foreign policy.

Qaradawy first made it clear that no religious figure is above questioning. He reminded his readers that for all his eminence, Ben Baz is a human being who could be either right or wrong in his thinking. "Apart from the Prophet Muhammad," Qaradawy wrote, "we learned from our predecessors that the words of any man must be sorted out to discern whether they are true or false." He cited a quotation attributed to Ibn Taimeyyeh that "the Shaikh of Islam is beloved by us, but the truthful word is even more beloved than he." No reader could miss the point that the same admonition applied to Ben Baz and, for that matter, to Qaradawy himself.

Qaradawy then showed that knowledge of the Quran and the *hadith* was not in itself sufficient to guide the Islamic community. He did so by recognizing, without any reservation, the authenticity of both the Quranic verse and the *hadith* that Ben Baz had cited. To reinforce the point, he acknowledged that the Mufti is rightfully regarded as "one of the most distinguished scholars of our time, trustworthy in his knowledge and religion." The basis for Qaradawy's challenge was the Mufti's flawed understanding of the contemporary reality to which he applied these authentic texts. According to Qaradawy, it was in his *fiqh* [understanding] of reality that the Mufti Ben Baz fell short. Qaradawy argued strongly that the conditions for the application of the sacred texts were not met in current historical circumstances.[36]

The Mufti had correctly cited the Quranic verse that reads, "If they want peace, you should opt for peace and trust in God." Ben Baz had also pointed out, again accurately, that the traditions of the Prophet contain examples where he accepted both permanent settlements and interim truces in war. From these examples, the Mufti concluded that peace with Israel should be accepted.

Qaradawy agreed that the message of the sacred texts was to respond to a peace offer. However, he vigorously challenged the claim that Israel had in fact ever made such a genuine initiative for peace. In Qaradawy's view, Palestinian weakness had forced acceptance of an imposed truce in the Madrid and Oslo Accords under extremely adverse conditions. For precisely the same reasons, they were being pressured to negotiate under terms that could not possibly yield a just outcome. To clarify the implications of these conditions, Qaradawy argued that the terms of the American-backed negotiations meant that even under the most favorable outcome, the land to be returned to the Palestinians could not exceed 15 percent of historic Palestine. With that underlying fact clearly in mind, Qaradawy offered this analogy:

> What the Jews did with the Palestinians is just like a man who took your home, and occupied it with his sons and followers by force. He forced you out, making you homeless. With your sons, you continued to fight him to regain your rights. After a while, he says to you: "Let's make peace. I'll give you

> one room of your big house provided that you renounce the struggle against me. I'll exchange this room for peace." Can such a person be considered a person who opts for peace?

Given the unfavorable international and regional imbalance of forces, talk of "peace" was simply a screen for Israel's exploitation of the power imbalance in order to legitimize its seizure of the bulk of Palestinian lands. In such a historical context, Qaradawy argued that the Quranic verse that should be applied advises: "never become weak and opt for peace while you should be the victor." Consistent with the interpretive approach of the New Islamist School, Qaradawy pointed out that it was never enough to understand the Quranic verses and *hadith* alone. It was always essential to understand the reality to which they applied.

Qaradawy rejected the notion that the Prophet's example of accepting truces with the enemy provided a framework for understanding the PLO accommodation with Israel at Madrid and Oslo. He concluded his response to the *fatwa* of Ben Baz by respectfully advising that, just as experts on the economy or medicine should be consulted before *fatwas* on economic or medical matters are issued, so authorities on Islam and its understanding of war and peace should be consulted before making a judgment on an issue as critical to the Islamic world as the fate of Jerusalem. Therefore, the texts cited by Shaikh Ben Baz are not applicable and the *fatwa* does not have force. Qaradawy added that "the land of Palestine is not owned by Palestinians alone but rather by the whole nation and all of its generations." He ended by saying: "If Palestinians abandon the land, it is the duty of the whole nation to defend its rights. If it can't do so by fighting, then it must at least do so by words."

Qaradawy's final recommendation signals the New Islamists' awareness of the overall weakness of the Arab states in the face of overwhelming Israeli power. Yet they refuse to accept the argument that there is no alternative other than compliance with the imposed negotiations. They point out that Israel repeatedly drains the idea of "peace" of any real meaning by its arrogant displays of expansionary power, most painfully in the unrelenting settlement of occupied lands and the suppression of the occupied Palestinian people through employment, tax, and residency laws. The New Islamists say frankly to the youth of Egypt and the Muslim world that, in our weakness, we have failed to protect the Palestinian lands. However, they refuse to abandon the principle that the occupied lands must be recovered. Instead, they urge a long-term strategy of deferral. The New Islamists maintain that the Arab and Islamic worlds must hold on to the possibility of a just resolution of the conflict with Israel. At the same time, it must be understood that this will be realized only when political and economic development creates a more favorable balance of power, allowing democratic Arab regimes to act within an Islamic framework to secure Palestinian rights.

The New Islamists realize that the Egyptian regime is subject to powerful pressures to adhere to an imposed process of negotiations. In these circumstances of regime compliance, they look to the people to resist. In this context, Muhammad Selim al Awa quotes approvingly the distinguished Lebanese cleric Muhammad Mahdi Shams al Din, who is head of the Islamic Shiite Council in Lebanon. "His opinions on the Arab-Israeli struggle," wrote Awa, "are worth remembering because he said that it is not important to settle it now." During this period of postponement, Shams al Din urged Arab peoples to remain steadfast and to ignore the Israelis at every opportunity. In elaborating this strategy, Shams al Din made a distinction between the governments and the people. As he put it, governments have dilemmas they must address, but the people have choices. He noted that while "governments may continue the peace process that is forced on them by international pressures," the people can exercise the choices open to them. In practice, Shams al Din explained that this does not place an unbearable burden on the people, requiring "no more than refusing economic and cultural cooperation, fighting only when the Israelis attack Arab lands."[37]

The New Islamists have adopted this general position of pacific resistance in the short term and postponement for the long term. Bishry explains that Egyptians should understand the Camp David agreement as turning the conflict with Israel from a military one to "peaceful forms of resistance, like that of Gandhi's liberation movement in India."[38] Speaking to a group of young people at the American University in Cairo, Awa elaborated on this general strategy of deferral in the idiom of Egyptian experience. When asked his opinion of the accords periodically generated by the American-backed negotiations, Awa responded that he opposed them, asking, "Why should we concede our land?" When one of the students asked what the young people of Egypt could do, Awa responded that "in rural areas if someone seizes someone else's land and the victim is too weak to take it back, what does the peasant do? He keeps on telling the story to his sons and grandsons, generation after generation. Don't forget your land. I think that this is what we should do. If the current rulership is too weak, we should tell the generations that follow. Perhaps one of them will return the land."[39]

This logic of deferral is the heart of the New Islamist position on Palestine as a core Islamic issue. It finds its justification in a vision of a renewed

Islamic world, able to redeem at some future time rights that are currently out of reach. In the worst case, the deferral might well be indefinite. Even in that case, however, the people of the Islamic world would at least live with the knowledge of their rights and with hope to redeem them preserved for future generations.

To preserve any optimism at all, therefore, it was essential to take a very long view, and not just on Palestine. Signs of the rise of extremist forms of Islam were deeply troubling to the New Islamists as the century came to an end. Even the shared distress over this negative development, however, reinforced a sense of connection and responsibility. The Taliban rule in Afghanistan provided a case in point. "It is a great gift for those who hate Islam," pronounced Fahmy Huwaidy in 1996.[40] Initially, Islamists of all shades, including the New Islamists, had vigorously supported the Afghan resistance to the Soviet invasion of Afghanistan. They encouraged the young men from various parts of the Arab and Islamic world who went to fight with the Afghans under Islamic banners. When the Soviets began their withdrawal, the response throughout the Islamic world was electric. Islamic fighters, or so it seemed to many, might be stymied in Palestine, but they were victorious over a superpower in Afghanistan. In fact, enthusiasm for the Afghan cause became so great that some seemed to place Afghanistan ahead of even Palestine as an issue, an inclination the New Islamists resisted. Yusuf al Qaradawy wrote, for example, that "Palestine remains the first Islamic issue, and it is not true that the movement has forgotten Palestine for the sake of Afghanistan."[41]

The long-suffering Afghan population had little chance to celebrate the Soviet withdrawal in 1989 before the internecine struggles of the resistance factions degenerated into violent civil war. At its worst, some seventeen Islamic parties vied with one another for control of the country. Major New Islamist figures, notably Yusuf al Qaradawy, Muhammad al Ghazzaly, and Fahmy Huwaidy, attempted mediation between the rival factions, but to no avail.[42] The civil war dragged on from 1989 to the mid-1990s, with devastating results. Writing in 1994, Ghazzaly claimed bitterly that the resistance fighters in the name of Islam had become simply marauders and bandits seeking power and the spoils of war, thus besmirching Islam's reputation.[43]

The New Islamist assessment of the Taliban placed their origins in this murky climate of internal violence and foreign intervention. They rose to power against a background of shifting strategic interests that had global importance. With the collapse of the Soviet Union, undoubtedly hastened by the debacle in Afghanistan, the mineral and oil resources of Central Asia were suddenly opened to an international scramble for influence. Afghanistan, in ruins and vulnerable to all kinds of interventions, stood as a gateway to that strategic area. Among the regional powers, Pakistan made the most aggressive move to influence developments in its favor through support for the Taliban. At the same time the United States moved heavily into Central Asia, with the Chevron oil company alone investing an estimated $10 billion in oil explorations.

New Islamist opposition to the Taliban was grounded firmly in their condemnation of the violence of their rise to power and of the terrible distortions of Islam they perpetrated once in power. The Taliban, wrote Huwaidy, "destroyed the capital and the whole government system in Kabul." He denounced the troubling ways in which they used the power they usurped "that began by forbidding women from working and closing schools for girls, asking men to grow their beards and cover their heads, and other stupid injunctions which humiliate Islam and its *Sharia*." The Taliban, Huwaidy said, failed to understand that "justice is the core of *Sharia*." They grasped neither "the *fiqh* of balance nor the *fiqh* of priorities." For the New Islamists, the actions of the Taliban confirmed that "they are ignorant Muslims who confuse religion with traditions and, even when they know the texts, understand nothing of their purposes. In their state of ignorance, they damaged Islam for which they falsely claimed to speak."[44]

Qaradawy spoke of Afghanistan from a perspective of responsibility for that Islamic land, abused by its Taliban rulers. "Beloved Afghanistan," as Qaradawy described it in the summer of 1988, did not belong to the Taliban alone. As rulers in the name of Islam, the Taliban had responsibilities to the world of Islam. Qaradawy did not hesitate to say that they were failing to meet them in egregious ways. A regime was Islamic by the measure of the progress it enabled toward justice, Islam's core value. In failing so completely to meet that standard, the Taliban had "broken our hearts," Qaradawy said, with their backward and violent ways that caused terrible damage to the name of Islam everywhere.[45]

The New Islamists struggled to create new possibilities to strengthen the ties that bind the Muslim world, and celebrated those that existed by finding innovative ways to revitalize them. They worked to counter the damage to those connections brought about by extremists of all kinds, including those in distant Afghanistan. For all this emphasis on the world of Islam, however, the New Islamists always saw the Islamic lands as part of a larger human community to which respectful attention must also be shown. They insisted that the varied peoples of the Islamic world were part of the broader human community with which they shared the planet. They had responsibilities to that global community too, and they were called to play an important role in it.

God's Will and Mercy: The Worldwide Human Community

New Islamist hopes for the success of the Islamic revival anticipate an enlightened and confident Islamic world. Yet in none of these dreams does Islam stand alone, as an island unto itself. The presence of others, both within and beyond the boundaries of Islam, is taken for granted as part of divine intention. Islam, as the New Islamists understand it, is innocent of a totalizing impulse to remake the entire world in its image. Human diversity provides an expression of "God's will and mercy." The history of the Islamic world is unimaginable without complex interactions of all kinds with non-Muslims. What worries the New Islamists is not the generalized anxiety about the "other" that characterizes Western thought. They are concerned rather that the peoples of Islamic lands, traumatized physically and psychologically by the superior power of the West, risk losing the confidence to act in the larger world in the ways that Islam enjoins.

Kamal Abul Magd has thought deeply about the implications of this contemporary erosion of confidence and the incapacity it threatens. He believes that the impact of the West has taken two distinct, but related, forms. There are those so dazzled by the West, especially by the engine of science and technology that drives its civilization, that they lose themselves in imitative admiration for all things Western. They are worshippers of a future that is conceivable only in homogenizing Western terms. Their actions reflect not the values and purposes of Islam, but faint versions of Western ends. Others are so paralyzed by fear of the power that the same Western science and technology have generated that they withdraw into a distorted reconstruction of the past to shield themselves from what they see as a hostile contemporary world. They are prisoners of history, imagining it as a defensive shield rather than a resource for creative action with others unlike themselves. Abul Magd concludes that both groups risk losing forever the ability to carry out the constructive roles that God has ordained for them in the world, which would enrich the experience of all humankind.

Abul Magd therefore makes the argument for a middle way in defining Islam's place in the world, aware of its distinctive history and contributions but open to the experience of others. In the body of his work on world affairs, he returns again and again to the conclusion that Islam precludes all unitary views of the human future, whatever their source, and he notes the radical pluralism built into Islam. The New Islamist School has absorbed into its thinking the Quranic celebration of human variety. The Quran is clear that if God had wanted humankind to be of one nature, He would have created them all of one piece. This Quranic message, as understood by the New Islamists, includes but goes beyond tolerance. It sees divine purpose in human difference. Thus, as Islamic thinkers, the New Islamists reject all influential homogenizing Western theories, whether they speak of the melting pot, a chosen people, a master race, or new socialist man. New Islamist thought sees positive good in precisely the durable distinctions of ethnicity, race, and class that have been consistently marked for subordination or elimination by such Western concepts. While this Islamic version of pluralism offers a shield to protect the vulnerable, it does not have its genesis in unfavorable power differentials. The appeal to the value of difference is not simply a defensive weapon of the weak. Rather, this attitude of mind and spirit springs from a confident faith and civilization that see positive value for the strong as well as the weak in the active embrace of human variety.

This positive preference for a plural humanity reinforces a second Islamic notion that there are rights and responsibilities shared by all human beings, whatever their place in the diverse human community. As Abul Magd explains, "Man is a dignified creature, preferred by God over all other creatures. This preference has nothing to do with man's color, wealth, or even religion as it is based simply on his being human." He adds that "no ambiguities surround this message . . . it is a simple and clear-cut position in the Quran expressed in a straightforward manner in the verses. The dignity is linked only to being a human being. It is neither related to Muslims alone nor to Arabs alone."[46] Thus, New Islamist thought points to the conclusion that human differences, however deep they may appear, neither enhance nor diminish fundamental human rights and responsibilities. Human beings are in this sense both the same and different. The New Islamists believe that this tension between sameness and difference defines the human condition as preordained by God.

It is possible to imagine a wide range of theories of world affairs generated by these broad Islamic principles. This, too, is no cause for disquiet. The New Islamists explicitly recognize that there is no singular Islamic theory of international relations. However, there is a Quranic standard that any such theory, whatever its other characteristics, must embrace the conception of a plural humanity endowed with intrinsic rights and responsibilities in order to be considered Islamic.

This New Islamist rejection of all totalitarian and homogenizing views of the human condition applies with special force to those advanced by political Islam. The New Islamists are fully aware that the meaning they ascribe to these Islamic principles is contested by many in the Islamic world. They thus understand that insistence on the positive worth of a plural humanity by Islamist intellectuals constitutes an act of self-criticism to which they attach great importance, especially as it applies to the actual practices of Muslims toward differences in religion, race, and gender in Islamic communities around the world.[47] They acknowledge freely that Muslims have all too often fallen short of what Islam demands of them, not only in tolerance but in embrace of differences. At the same time, the New Islamists recognize that, from different cultural starting points, non-Muslims have at times reached these same moral and intellectual understandings about the plurality and intrinsic worth of human beings. These insights do not belong to Muslims alone. For this reason, the New Islamists believe that ours is a time when these powerful insights arising from the world's great religious and cultural traditions, neglected and violated throughout the ages, can come alive in the tentative efforts now under way to build a world community. They contest the claims of those in the Islamic world who question the value of plurality and seek to repress difference, and they offer themselves as partners to those from other cultural worlds, including important minorities in the West, who embrace difference and struggle for justice for all human beings.

Armed with this spirit, the New Islamists move with remarkable ease across a daunting world landscape. They assume that a common meeting place for all of humanity can be discovered, knowing that this remains a task for humanity's future. To the task of building a new world community, they bring a vivid sense of the relevance of their Islamic heritage. The New Islamists do not expect to find the distinctive features of their own civilization mirrored in the faces of the others they find there. Quite the contrary, they anticipate explorations of human variety. Nor do they carry with them an Islamic blueprint for humankind's collective future. They understand that no one people or culture can write the future for a diverse humanity. Their self-assurance comes instead from the warm acceptance of human difference and appreciation of the common rights and duties of all human beings. From their Islamic perspective, they have reached the understanding that only a world built out of differences while respectful of common human rights and responsibilities could possibly be shared.

The New Islamists do take note of the special animus toward the world of Islam that emanates regularly from some quarters in the West. They respond calmly to such attacks, engaging only their more sophisticated forms and then always with restraint. One such conservative theorist has suggested that the fault lines of future global conflict will be civilizational and has identified an Islamic-Confucian axis as the major threat to the West. Kamal Abul Magd responds to this notion of a "clash of civilizations" with the competing concept that the coming pattern should instead be one of enhanced "communication of civilizations." He then explains the ways in which the revolutions in transportation and communication enable positive interactions. Abul Magd cautions that the Islamic world should not allow hostile critics in the West to monopolize its attention; there are alternative currents representing the "other West" that actively attempt to counter these hostile and unhelpful characterizations of the world of Islam. With such intellectuals and movements, the New Islamists believe, active cooperation in the human interest should surely be possible.[48]

This strong sense of a positive global role to play with like-minded others takes on a sense of urgency because the New Islamists understand the great needs of humankind. Like other enlightened minorities around the globe, they have allowed themselves to feel directly and personally the common dangers facing vulnerable humans and their abused planet—the worldwide plagues, the environmental destruction, and the unending ravages of poverty and war. Their collective statements and individual writings bear witness to active concern with these pressing human needs. They stand with those ready to renounce the old ways of self-centered greed and senseless violence and, as their manifesto expresses it, to compete instead in good works for the sake of humanity and the building of the Earth.[49]

Critics of the Islamic wave have found it easy to obscure this readiness of centrist Islamists like the New Islamists to engage the world community. They simply put all Islamists in one basket and then call attention to the most outrageous statement or action of the most closed-minded among them. However, when meaningful distinctions are made among the voices of the Islamic wave, a dramatically different picture emerges. At home, the New Islamists have stood consistently against the defensive narrow-mindedness of those Islamists who are so afraid for a vulnerable Islam that they shun involvement in efforts at global cooperation. One critical way in which this attitude of openness expresses itself is the New Islamists' embrace of the global struggle for human rights. They have taken an active role in the first tentative efforts to give this abstract idea a tangible expression that can resonate worldwide.

The idea of fundamental human rights, shared across boundaries of all kinds, underlies all efforts to create a worldwide human community. It is impossible to hear the New Islamists in a sustained conversation about the situation of humankind or to witness their active role in national, Islamic, and world forums without grasping their unshakable commitment to the idea that human beings everywhere have intrinsic rights that must be protected. To be sure, they come to this idea out of their own history, and it takes on particular Islamic shadings. These distinguishing traces of the Islamic origins of the idea, however, in no way preclude finding common ground with others.

All of the major New Islamists support the idea of universally shared human rights. As on other key issues, however, they do so with quite different emphases. The variety of their ways of understanding and supporting human rights serves to enhance their capacity to bring this critical conception to the widest possible audience. Whatever their other differences, a sharp critical edge characterizes the treatment of the concept of human rights by all of the New Islamists. They take pointed exception to those in the West who take for granted a purely Western genealogy for the idea. At the same time, they criticize the dismal record of abuses in Egypt and the larger world of Islam, where human rights are routinely violated. It is sometimes overlooked that both sets of criticisms affirm a strong commitment to the principle itself.

Muhammad al Ghazzaly regularly raised his voice against the arrogance of the West in casting the human rights concept in purely Western terms and ignoring the contributions of others to its elaboration. In addition, he was persuasive in pointing out the hypocrisy that too often inheres in the selective application of the human rights principle when it becomes an instrument of foreign policy, notably in the American case. Ghazzaly displayed just as much passion and considerably more courage when he condemned human rights abuses in Islamic lands, including the record of the regime under whose power he lived.[50]

Fahmy Huwaidy, too, bemoans the fact that the people of the Islamic world are painfully ignorant of the contributions their own history has made to the notion that all human beings have certain basic rights. He notes that the world's attention has gone to the celebration of the International Declaration of Human Rights, while the Islamic world has failed to pay attention to crucial historical events that have given the idea secure roots in Islamic cultural life. Huwaidy's intent, however, is to separate the notion of human rights from a genealogy that is purely Western in order that ownership of the concept might be more broadly shared. At no point does he call into question the concept itself. For example, despite his annoyance, he comments that the celebration of the International Declaration is fully deserved, calling only for recognition, not least in the Islamic world, of the contributions to that shared human good that have sprung from the history of the Islamic world.[51]

Selim al Awa has elaborated exactly how the concept of human rights might be shared as a collective achievement and goal of human beings everywhere. Awa is an active participant in the human rights movement and serves on the governing board of the Egyptian Human Rights Organization. He is fully at ease in working with a range of other actors who come to human rights work from very different starting points. In an open exchange with the liberal economist Sayyid al Naggar, Awa made this essential point by remarking that he saw no need to dwell too long on the difference in pathways taken to reach the common conclusion that human beings have intrinsic rights. Rather, Awa emphasized the necessity for these different actors to explore together the common ground that would make effective action on human rights violations possible.[52]

The New Islamist rejection of the fixed ends of Western ideologies, and the rigidities of the proposed means to attain them, does not translate into closed-mindedness to the dominant West in general. They understand that such an approach would be unworkable, given the penetrative power of the West. They also feel that not all the developments that originate in the West have the same rigid and self-absorbed character. In this spirit, the New Islamists have responded with positive interest to the rise of global social movements, most notably those working for human rights and social justice. They do so in strong opposition to those exclusionary voices of political Islam that attack all such conceptions and movements as alien Western intrusions. At the same time, the New Islamists are aware that these movements carry no natural immunity to the distortions of Western political, economic, and cultural power. When their offshoots appear in the Islamic world, they register concern about how and why their particular agendas are set. Moreover, they do not always agree with the formulations put forward by these aggressive non-governmental actors on the world scene. They also recognize that many within these movements view all Islamists with suspicion and criticize what they take to be Islamic positions on human rights, women, and minorities. In this regard, the New Islamists often find these groups no better informed about the diversity of Islamic opinion, and particularly of the Islamic *Wassatteyya,* then others in the West. Yet despite all these important reservations, the New Islamists give careful attention to the considerable promise of these new social movements, seeing them as potential partners of Islamists in their struggles for human rights and social justice.[53]

The public responses of the New Islamists to the world conferences on global issues, where the role of the new social movements has been most striking, provide a tangible and revealing measure of their interest. More than any other development, this series of world conferences has provided hope that at least the scaffolding for a worldwide human community can be erected in our late modern world. Out of the interactions, tentative and guarded, at these world meetings has come a loose yet enabling framework of cooperation. Within its uncoordinated and proliferating networks, potential co-workers in the project of building human community can recognize each other. They do so while preserving their differences that allow them to remain effective local as well as global actors. The New Islamists have taken note that the existence of this tenuous human community, built at once of sameness and difference, gives hope for collaborative interactions in the human interest.

Many in Egypt, and not just the radicals of political Islam on the fringe of the Islamic wave, greeted all such efforts, notably the UN global conferences, with the old rhetoric and hostilities of a vulnerable people faced with outside intrusions. Others rushed in with equal thoughtlessness to embrace the latest formulations of the leading Western institutions, as though Egyptians and others from the Islamic world could bring nothing distinctive to these international forums. Against this background of refusal or self-abnegation, the reactions and initiatives of the New Islamists stood out in sharp relief. Their collective responses modeled a balanced alternative of positive yet critical engagement, demonstrating that the Islamic world is more than the wounds it has suffered or the dilemmas it faces. The New Islamist interventions extended an invitation to cooperate in the search for solutions, explicitly to like-minded people, Muslims and non-Muslims, around the globe.[54]

The most evocative sketch of the great promise for humankind of the new efforts at global cooperation came from Fahmy Huwaidy. He consistently used his platform in *al Ahram* to draw attention to the series of world conferences, urging that the Islamic world give them full attention.[55] On the eve of the Conference on Social Justice held in Copenhagen in the winter of 1995, for example, Huwaidy portrayed the work of this social summit as part of the effort to write nothing less than a "global constitution." Huwaidy explained that the Copenhagen Conference would be the fifth in the series of seven international meetings that included the Conference on Children in New York, Conference on the Environment in Rio de Janeiro, Conference on Human Rights in Geneva, Conference on Population and Development in Cairo, and Conference on Women in Beijing, with a final Conference on Crime. Each conference would issue a charter that expressed the international consensus reached on the particular issue. The seven charters, taken together, would comprise the new constitution, intended "to settle the major issues and regulate the affairs of the world on this basis."[56]

While eager to publicize and support these efforts, Huwaidy expressed a realistic understanding of their limitations, explaining that "these announcements and covenants are not binding, from the legal and practical points of view." Huwaidy understood that the vision to build human community exceeded both enforcement capabilities and, even more fundamentally, the capacity to achieve consensus that went beyond general principles to matters of practical application. Nevertheless, he emphasized the moral impact that even nonbinding international standards could have. "These international covenants," he wrote, "are ethically important, and they become more and more so as each day passes. They have this effectiveness because they do show, from an international perspective, what should be the nature of the world."[57]

Thus, the New Islamists welcomed the work of the conferences as real though modest progress toward building world community. They immediately saw that international standards agreed on in such global settings would act to stimulate and support local reform efforts, provided of course that they represented a genuine international consensus. To that end, they urged the Islamic world to participate fully in the democratic forums that brought the whole world together to formulate these principles. The New Islamists showed themselves as ready to learn from the experience of others as they were eager to share the insights of their own Islamic heritage and history. As the work of the conferences unfolded in full public view, they developed a deep appreciation of the complex processes of international consensus building and publicized in their writing these lessons of a democratic global politics. In evaluating the substantive work of the conferences, the sophistication of their thinking enabled them to identify broad areas of general agreement with the international consensus, even as they clarified the particularities of their own Islamic understandings. More often than not, they were able to formulate agreement on critical general principles, while preserving cultural differences in the ways in which those principles were realized.

The self-assured New Islamist reaction to the world conferences came from their conviction that Islam enables layered identities and multiple human attachments. Not all elements of the Islamic wave agreed, however. When it was announced that the Conference on Population and Development would be held in Cairo, for example, Islamist voices denounced the very idea, fearing that the discussion would inevitably turn to controversial issues of sexuality and broader questions of the role of women that so frequently led to Western attacks on the Arab Islamic world. The New Islamists refused such a defensive view and looked forward to participation on the world stage on matters of such obvious global importance. They believed that Islamist intellectuals would learn much from such exchanges. They were equally confident that they would bring a great deal to this discussion, inspired as they were by confidence in the values and higher purposes that Islam held out to all humanity. The New Islamists believed that even the acknowledged failures of Muslims to realize these higher purposes might provide lessons for themselves and others. After all, where in the world today could a troubled humanity find that community of justice to which Islam called humankind? By that exacting standard, there were neither ready-made models nor historical records free of terrible failings.

Abul Magd did not exaggerate when he wrote that the Cairo Conference on Population "brought the world to Egypt." The uproar surrounding discussion in the Egyptian press of such issues as abortion and sexual behavior, as much as the work of the conference itself, illuminated for a brief time the new landscape of global political action. In Cairo in the fall of 1994, one could see representatives of all parts of the world struggling in the frankest of terms with the divisive yet critical issues of population and development. The new forms of human interaction made possible by the Information Revolution were everywhere in evidence. The unrelenting flow of images and information brought all kinds of disturbing realities into full view. At the same time, new connections, particularly those among the nongovernmental organizations, suggested how global networks of political action could be developed around the need for action on problems worldwide in scope.

For Egypt in the short term, however, the conference brought out the worst features of a frayed public life. The most retrograde Islamist elements even urged the stoning of the conference. The most polemical of the critics of the Islamic wave seized on such irresponsible statements to misrepresent the position of Islamists in general. Statements to the press told more about the damaging scars of civilizational insecurity and the defensive scramble for partisan advantage, than about how an endangered human species might do less damage to itself and the earth.

Viewing this spectacle, Kamal Abul Magd was silent at first, until the deterioration of the debate made continued silence impossible. When he did speak, two things were clear.[58] First, Abul Magd had no angry words to add to Egypt's cultural wars between Islamists and secularists. Second, in the events surrounding the conference, where others paid attention only to opportunities for partisan advantage, he saw something more.

In the pattern of words and actions that swirled around the Conference on Population, Abul Magd read the rough outlines of an answer to a larger question: What did the task of building a worldwide community demand of humanity? And, in a more pointed version of the same question, what did it demand of Egyptians as part of the Islamic world? Nothing less, Abul Magd believed, than "a leap into time and space." There, he continued, a new dimension of worldwide political action would eclipse differences and emphasize the common rights and duties of men and women working as architects of a worldwide community. Belonging to this new world would require the confidence to undertake the collaborative design and building of these new forms of global interaction, the courage to face daunting new realities that could no longer be kept at bay, and the creativity to develop new ways of belonging to the world so that common dangers would be faced and shared values expressed.

Abul Magd understood full well just how fearful many Egyptians would be of his call to take up these challenges of the new age. The long years of resistance to cultural dependence had taken their toll. Egyptians, like others in small and vulnerable countries, had acquired "an emotional and intellectual state of mind in which the fear of others prevails." In his view, this trauma has distorted Arab and Islamic thought by a self-imposed isolation, marked by a defense of anything local and a reluctance to interact with others. As a result the illusion persists that key problems can be remedied as local issues without the cooperation of the rest of the world. In addition, he notes that in searching for solutions thinkers too often look only to the past, "with an intense devotion to the pages of history as if culture only flourished then." While understanding their origins, Abul Magd rejects such concepts as "authenticity" and "cultural specificity" when they are misused in support of these paralyzing attitudes. Many people erroneously believe, he writes, that "to preserve 'authenticity,' we should necessarily tighten the relation with history and the past." They have become so fearful that "they regard delinkage from any of the elements of the past as a denial of cultural specificity and the first step toward the destruction of the inherited culture." The result of such thinking would be the ossification of Islamic culture, warned Abul Magd. It would stop developing and rely instead on contrived glorifications of an imagined past.

Abul Magd then pointed out that the Cairo Conference had "brought other cultures to us after we had refused to go to them." The revolution in information technologies had made it impossible for peoples and cultures to remain isolated from one another. Whatever dubious merit the strategy of isolation may once have had, such an approach was no longer feasible. Abul Magd charged intellectuals of all kinds to "continue the march out of isolation, building on the 'shock' that the Conference held in Cairo created."

Abul Magd did not take the idea of a shock lightly. His own comments on the most controversial issues addressed at the Cairo Conference stand as a bold example of the kind of courage required of Egyptians to be actors in a global society. He noted simply that the debate focused on abortion and human sexuality. Egyptians, he argued, were part of the world and had no choice but to confront and deal with all the realities of contemporary life:

> When it was announced that the population conference would take place in Egypt, the uproar started on the issues that had been placed on the agenda. The debate focused on abortion and sexual freedom. I haven't taken part in this debate because in my view and with all respect to the opinions about it, it was just another manifestation of the absence of awareness of what goes on around us in this world. It was also a manifestation of the continuing self-imposed isolation from space and time. Also, it was an insistence on treating our urgent vital issues with a purely local approach, believing that isolation is possible.

Abul Magd was not a man to tolerate the throwing of stones to confront ideas. He noted that the controversial views and practices involving abortion and sexual behavior did not emerge from the conference; on the contrary, they have been part of the social agenda in other societies for decades. That the echoes of the discussion of such matters would reach Egypt should be both expected and accepted as inevitable. Egypt's isolation, he concluded, only "delayed this and in turn delayed our expression of our opinion on such matters."

Abul Magd's formulation made it clear that the New Islamist position involved a willingness to listen to the position of others so that ideas could be evaluated in terms of their own civilizational values. The responses of other New Islamists to the conference demonstrated concretely just what this might mean. At times, the exchanges brought out unexpected similarities. Despite noisy attention to differences, Selim al Awa pronounced that "the statements of the Cairo Conference on the empowerment and equality of women are just a repetition of basic Islamic values."[59] Furthermore, Awa dismissed as groundless the fears expressed by some that the conference provisions on female rights of inheritance might undermine specific provisions of Islam in that area. In a carefully reasoned statement, he explained first that inheritance rights between men and women did not always differ in Islam. Moreover, when they did differ, a case could be made that the differences were proportional to the unequal social responsibilities between the sexes and were for that reason just. Awa acknowledged that clarification of these matters required a "new *fiqh*," and he cited his own work and that of other New Islamists as contributing to precisely this effort within Islamic societies.[60] At the same time, he noted that the conference properly shielded such matters from external interference with its clear provision that "the application of the final document provisions" would take place "according to the respective values of each society."[61] The absence of defensiveness in Awa's assessment enabled him to acknowledge openly issues concerning women that require internal attention. Awa showed himself completely open to reminders of obligations to women that Islam has clearly recognized in principle, though too often neglected in practice. He commented approvingly, for example, on the provision in the final document that men should share in household and child-rearing duties. Given his worldly experience, Awa must surely be aware that large numbers of Western men fail to act in any meaningful way on this obligation, no less than men in Egypt, whatever their class position or ideological orientation. With classic restraint, he remarked that "the participation of men in household burdens concerning the upbringing of children is a *Sharia* duty on husbands that the document did not invent," and that "if the conference reminds us of our duties toward women, it should be thanked for that."[62]

To know "the positions of our Islamic and Arab civilization on major issues," added Kamal Abul Magd, one needed to understand the meaning of any particular text within the larger context of the higher purposes of Islamic *Sharia.* Making sense of the world in Islamic terms would require more than the citation of partial texts and a focus on isolated events. When dealing with complex issues like the role of women, population, and development, it was essential to see both the texts and the world as a whole and to understand the larger implications of specific verses and isolated events. Just being a Muslim did not mean that one automatically understood Islam; just living in Islamic lands did not guarantee access to the Islamic heritage. Such awareness would require precisely the *fiqh* of sacred texts combined with the *fiqh* of reality on which all New Islamists insisted.[63] As Abul Magd put it, what is required "is an awareness that goes beyond the opinions of the predecessors, puts texts in their correct relationship to a changing world, and completes the inherited interpretation of the texts by contemporary ones that respond to new realities."

These lessons went beyond the specific concerns raised at the Cairo Conference on Population and Development. An Islam that was locked in its past and closed to the world could not hope to register its intellectual and moral voice in contemporary struggles. Those who would speak for Islam's message could not do so in reactive and defensive tones. Islamic culture was neither so fragile nor so limited as these excessive fears suggested. It was essential, Abul Magd wrote, to "encourage self-assured behavior among Arabs and Muslims, who must realize that they are the bearers of a message for human beings everywhere who cannot be reached if the messengers retreat into abnegation, withdrawal, and isolation."[64] While understanding the moral courage that such openness to the world and willingness to engage the opinions of others would require, Abul Magd maintained that Egyptians could shoulder that responsibility and more. This task would require self-assured awareness of oneself, of others, and of the common human condition. In regard to the culture of others, Abul Magd wrote that Egyptians would need a "brave critical spirit," which, in the best tradition of the Islamic *Wassatteyya,* would "evaluate other cultures objectively, without under- or over-estimation." He urged Egyptians not only to face the realities of a complex and dangerous world, but also to be creative actors in responding to these realities and shaping their consequences.

How prescient for the Islamic wave and for Egyptians generally those words would sound in the wake of September 11, 2001.

Interpreting September 11

"Our hearts bleed because of the attacks that have targeted the World Trade Center, as well as other institutions in the United States," declared Yusuf al Qaradawy.[65] Qaradawy based his condemnation of the murderous assault on the Quranic verse that says: "If anyone slew a person—unless for murder or for spreading mischief in the land—it would be as if he slew the whole people; and if anyone saved a life, it would be as if he saved the life of the whole people."[66]

Even in times of war, Muslims are justified in killing only those with whom they are fighting, sparing women, children, and the aged.[67] The moral clarity of Qaradawy's judgment did not come at the expense of inattention to historical circumstances. His reaction took account of the historical rights and interests of the Arab Islamic peoples as well as the new conditions of the global age. In his statement, Qaradawy explicitly noted that this condemnation of the murder of American civilians was made "despite our strong opposition to the American biased policy toward Israel on the military, political, and economic fronts." Qaradawy stated further that the vulnerable Arab Islamic world had its own special stake in the assertion of religious principles that aimed to protect the sanctity of human life. "We Arab Muslims are the most affected by the grave consequences of hostile attack on Man and life," he said. Qaradawy pointed to the suffering of the Palestinians under occupation, lacking a state or an army that could protect them, enduring death and the destruction of their homes and property, leaving "innocent orphans wailing behind." Still, he insisted that not even active American complicity in this record of Israeli oppression could justify the murders in New York City.

The nuanced character of the New Islamist response to September 11 was even more apparent in the lengthy *fatwa* issued by a group of Islamic scholars on September 27, 2001, in response to an inquiry from the most senior Muslim chaplain in the United States Armed Forces.[68] The chaplain asked whether it was permissible for Muslim Americans to participate in the military campaign prompted by the attacks on New York. The ruling declared unequivocally that American Muslims were obligated to serve in the armed forces of their country, even when the United States was at war with a Muslim country. The influential *fatwa* stunned and angered many in the Arab Islamic world, familiar with Qaradawy's record of outspoken criticism of the misuses of American power.[69] In his controversial and courageous ruling, Qaradawy was joined by Fahmy Huwaidy, Tareq al Bishry, and Muhammad Selim al Awa, along with two other Islamic scholars.

In their *fatwa* the scholars acknowledged that the inquiry reflected "a very complicated issue and a highly sensitive situation for our Muslim brothers and sisters serving in the American army as well as other armies that face similar situations." However, before responding to those contextual complexities, they addressed directly the core issue of the appropriate response to the crimes committed. "All Muslims," the *fatwa* stated unequivocally, "ought to be united against all those who terrorize the innocent, and those who permit the killing of non-combatants without a justifiable reason." The ruling invoked the same Quranic verses that Qaradawy had cited earlier, declaring "the spilling of blood and the destruction of property [to be] absolute prohibitions until the Day of Judgment."[70] The scholars declared that "whoever violates these pointed Islamic texts is an offender deserving of the appropriate punishment according to their offense and according to its consequences for destruction and mischief."

The *fatwa* then informed those Muslims serving in the American armed forces and affected by the ruling of their responsibility "to make this stand and its religious reasoning well known to all their superiors, as well as to their peers." It was important that they do so in order to convey "the true nature of the Islamic teachings, which have often been distorted or smeared by the media." From the perspective of *Sharia* and *fiqh,* the scholars indicated that the assault on New York would be judged a "crime of 'Hirabah'" (waging war on society). The perpetrators would be punished like those who "wage war on God and His Messenger and do mischief on earth."[71]

Given this judgment in the light of *Sharia* and *fiqh,* the scholars concluded that it was imperative to "apprehend the true perpetrators of these crimes, as well as those who aid and abet them through incitement, financing, or other support." The *fatwa* called for the criminals to be brought to justice "in an impartial court of law and to punish them in order to deter them and others like them who easily slay the lives of innocents, destroy properties, and terrorize people." Muslims were called "to participate in this effort with all possible means, in accord with God's (Most High) saying: 'Help ye one another in righteousness and piety, but help ye not one another in sin and rancor.'"[72] By this reasoning, Muslim Americans were enjoined to serve in the armed forces of their country, even if that should mean fighting against their fellow Muslims.

The scholars did not gloss over the anguish that their ruling might cause to American Muslims serving in the military, especially given the ambiguities of a war where it would very likely be all but impossible to differentiate between "the real perpetrators who are being pursued and the innocents who have committed no crime at all." They acknowledged as well that *hadith* that had traditionally illuminated this dilemma in the abstract were not relevant to the novel situation of American Muslims who found themselves the citizens of a state and members of a regular army. In these new conditions, they reasoned, the American Muslim has no choice but to follow orders; otherwise his allegiance and loyalty to his country could be in doubt. The American Muslim, the *fatwa* stated simply, "could not enjoy the privileges of citizenship, without performing its obligations." The scholars argued further that "the Muslim soldier must perform his duty in this fight despite his feeling of uneasiness of 'fighting without discriminating.'" To assuage the sense of guilt, the scholars counseled the soldier to preserve the pure intent of his own role as one that aims for the highest goals, such as preventing further aggression and bringing the perpetrators to justice. Even though the conflict might in fact produce other negative effects, the Muslim soldiers should not hold themselves responsible for actions they cannot control. The scholars explained that "all deeds are accounted (by God) according to the intentions." They added: "God does not burden man with more than he can bear. Muslim jurists have ruled that what a Muslim cannot control he cannot be held accountable for, as God (the Most High) says: 'And keep your duty to God as much as you can.'"[73]

The scholars also reminded the Muslim American service personnel that, if they should shirk their duty, the impact of such actions on millions of fellow Muslims would be highly injurious. For that reason, "even if fighting causes discomfort spiritually or psychologically, this personal hardship must be endured for the greater public good." To be sure, if there are opportunities to substitute service or support functions for a direct fighting role, Muslims may avail themselves of them, provided such action does not "raise doubts about their allegiance or loyalty, cast suspicions, expose them to false accusations, harm their future careers, shed misgivings on their patriotism, or similar sentiments."

Summing up, the *fatwa* states that "it is permissible, God willing, for the Muslim American military personnel to participate in the fighting in the upcoming battles against whoever their country decides has perpetrated terrorism against them." The combatants are reminded that they should as individuals preserve the "proper intention" in all of their actions, while at the same time taking care to avoid any course of action that would cast doubts on their loyalty or cause them other harm. This ruling, the *fatwa* concludes, is "in accordance with the *Sharia* rules that state that necessities dictate exceptions, as well as the rule that says one may endure a small harm to avoid a much greater harm."

These New Islamist responses to the human tragedy of September 11 provided a high watermark of sympathy for America and anger at the criminals responsible for the terror. However, in the months that followed from the fall of 2001 to the early spring of 2003, that sympathy eroded as the meaning for the Islamic world of the American war on terrorism, mounted in response to September 11, became clear. Despite their hostility to the Taliban regime, the New Islamists registered dismay at what they saw as a full-scale American war against an already ravaged Afghanistan as the centerpiece of the first stage of the American campaign against global terrorism. At the same time, they judged that the American tilt toward Israel had expressed itself with unprecedented clarity, as the Sharon government waged its own "war against terrorism" in the occupied territories with explicit American approval. And they viewed with even greater alarm the developing U.S. campaign against Iraq as a "terrorist state," allegedly linked to al Qaeda.

Tareq al Bishry's book, *The Arabs in the Face of Aggression,* published in the summer of 2002, summarized the New Islamist assessment of the implications of these developments for the Arab Islamic world. The United States, Bishry argued, had defined itself unambiguously as the enemy of the Arab and Islamic world by its assault on Afghanistan, its preparations to strike Iraq, and most tellingly its support for Israel in the occupied territories. "When we were young," wrote Bishry, "we used to jokingly repeat a phrase by an actress in a 1940s movie: 'The victim has forgiven the perpetrators but the perpetrator hasn't.'" He went on to say, "Today after fifty years I find no expression more serious and accurate to characterize the U.S. relationship to the Arab Islamic world. What happened in Palestine after World War II was a crime and it remains a crime today. The perpetrator was and is the U.S. The issue is not just Palestine. As we all know, it concerns all Arabs." Bishry expressed the hardening of hostility to the United States that post–September 11 U.S. policies had precipitated. He drew a direct line from Palestine to Afghanistan and Iraq: "The U.S. that expressed animosity for us in Palestine for the last fifty years is the one we face today in Afghanistan. It is the same hostile power which built military bases in the Gulf, laid siege to countries, and imposed boycotts."[74]

By the spring of 2003 Egyptian analysts across the political spectrum agreed that the Arab Islamic world faced new and unprecedented "necessities." A new era in world politics had emerged, and it was marked by sharply rising levels of hostility toward the United States—not just in the Arab Islamic world but around the globe.[75] In March 2003, the United States led American, British, and Australian troops in the anticipated attack on Iraq, with the diplomatic and political support of a "coalition of the willing" that did not include the French, Germans, Russians, and Chinese. The attack was launched without an explicit U.N. resolution authorizing force at this juncture. While the short-term military victory was never in doubt, the long-term political implications would take years to become clear.

Responding to War against Iraq

During the months from September 11, 2001, to March 2003 when the war against Iraq began, the New Islamists had struggled to hold the middle ground between those in the Islamic world who sympathized with the violent strikes against the United States and its allies, on the one hand, and those prepared to accommodate or even assist a second U.S.-led strike against Saddam Hussein's Iraq, targeted by the United States as a terrorist state. Despite their strong disapproval of American policies pursued during this period, particularly the seemingly unconditional support for Israel, the New Islamists condemned the continuing acts of violence against civilians by the Islamist extremists, whether they targeted a synagogue on the Tunisian island of Djerba in April 2002 or a tourist hotel in Bali, Indonesia, in October 2002. The synagogue attack killed nineteen, including fourteen German tourists. An al Qaeda spokesman broadcast a claim of responsibility for the attack on the Qatar-based al Jazirah television channel, claiming that "the young man who carried out the operation could not stand seeing his brothers in Palestine being killed and yet he sees the Jews in his city roaming around, having fun and carrying out their rituals. He was angered and the spirit of *jihad* rose in him and he carried out this successful operation."[76]

Yusuf al Qaradawy challenged this logic and the immoral attacks it condoned. "In Islam," Qaradawy explained, "it is not permissible to attack places of worship such as churches and synagogues or attack men of religion, even in the state of war." Qaradawy condemned the murder of all civilians, arguing that this act by al Qaeda and its extremist allies was a heinous crime "which is no more than a total barbarism that is devoid of morality and human feeling as well."[77]

Responding to the attack in Bali, Qaradawy said, "Strikes of this kind are proscribed by Islamic *Sharia* as 'an act of spreading mischief in the land or *hirabah*,' . . . a crime in Islam for which a severe punishment is specified, without discrimination as to race, color, nationality, or religion of the culprit." Muslims should never aid nor celebrate such sinful acts of criminality, no matter how provocative their alleged causes. Qaradawy directly questioned the reasoning that justified such violence as arising from the suffering and killing of Palestinians at the hands of the Israeli occupying forces on the West Bank and Gaza. "All Muslims," Qaradawy explained, "are thus required to stand hand in hand to wage war on oppression and transgression low and high, regardless . . . of the nationality of victims, be they innocent Australian tourists or wronged Palestinian citizens or any other person in the world."[78]

The New Islamists' opposition to extremist violence did not, however, translate into support for American policies, most notably on Palestine and Iraq. In Cairo on February 5, 2003, "Islam on Line" hosted a symposium to discuss the impending war in the Gulf with leading intellectuals, including Tareq al Bishry, Fahmy Huwaidy, and Selim al Awa, who all played major roles in the discussions. In their contributions, these New Islamist figures supported the Islamic right of defensive *jihad* in the face of aggression, for which Qaradawy had called, and they did so in terms that they argued were consistent with both democracy and international law. They addressed their assessment to the transnational Islamic community as a whole and not just to Palestinians and Iraqis. They recognized as well that the character of resistance and the roles of Muslims situated in different parts of the Islamic world would of course vary with circumstances.

Bishry opened the Cairo discussion of defensive *jihad* by placing strict limits on the use of force that defensive *jihad* justified. He asserted that the only legitimate use of force was that used to repel invaders and occupying forces. In particular, he cautioned against violence directed against Arab regimes that supported the coalition strike. "It is impermissible," said Bishry, "to employ violent means between Arab Islamic peoples and their rulers." Awa explained that this cautionary stricture aimed to restrain attacks on regimes that cooperated with the United States in the campaign against Iraq, even if their legitimacy is in question. Despite the fact that "we believe that some Arab and Muslim governments have 'usurped' the helm of power in their countries," Awa noted, "we should only confront them via democratic and legal frameworks enforced within the country." For his part, Huwaidy made the point that the U.S.-led invasion should not be understood as religiously motivated but rather as driven by political and economic objectives. He emphasized that it was important not to "jump to the conclusion that there is a battle against Islam," asserting, "several indicators confirm the opposite." Huwaidy warned that although some people want to depict the issue in this way, they must not be given the chance "because this is not in our interest." Bishry added a further qualification to the understanding of a legitimate *jihad* by sharply restricting its target, stating that only the invading military forces and not civilian diplomats, tourists, or other Westerners could be legitimate targets of *jihad*. Bishry explained that "they include our friends, and a large number of them are staunchly against war and the policy currently adopted against us by the American administration."[79]

Selim al Awa argued that a defensive *jihad* in response to war against Iraq was legitimate according to international law. He noted that the U.S. government had not made a convincing case that Iraq posed an imminent threat to the United States, as required for exercise of the right to resort to war in self-defense. The most credible delivery system for the weapons of mass destruction that Saddam allegedly possessed was by passing them to the terrorist network of al Qaeda. Awa dismissed the U.S. allegations of links between the Iraqi regime and al Qaeda as "unfounded." He also questioned the plausibility of the coalition's other justifications for the war, notably Saddam's undeniable human-rights violations and the repressive character of his regime. Awa noted that Iraq had been ruled by dictators ever since its independence from British colonialism: "Why do they speak now about democracy?"[80] He concluded that the motivations for war had little to do with Saddam's crimes.

When the coalition launched the war in March 2003, the Islamic Research Academy of al Azhar issued a strong condemnation, calling for a *jihad* by Muslims everywhere to resist this "Crusader war." The distinctive character of the New Islamists' response to the second Gulf War emerged most clearly in their reaction to the al Azhar statement. Although they strongly supported the call for a defensive *jihad*, they objected to the characterization of the attack as a "Crusader war"—that is, as a religiously motivated conflict of Christians and Jews against Muslims. New Islamist condemnations of Israeli policies had consistently maintained a distinction between Judaism and the policies of a particular Israeli government. On the eve of the second Gulf War, they also rejected the idea, implicit in the outmoded al Azhar language, that Christianity was behind the attack on Iraq. Tareq al Bishry pointed out that Christian Arabs, including Egypt's Coptic community, stood in solidarity with Muslims against the aggression. They also drew attention to the millions of citizens from Europe and American, most of whom were Christian, who took to the streets in condemnation of the invasion. In particular, the New Islamists drew a sharp distinction between Americans and a particular American government and the hostile policies it pursued. The New Islamists recognized friends and allies in the West across all of these barriers and reached out to them.

For all these reasons, the New Islamists publicly objected to the al Azhar characterization, subsequently modified, that the conflict represented a generalized war between Islam and Christianity.[81]

None of these refinements of their position, however, diluted the New Islamist opposition to the invasion of Iraq. In late March 2003, Tareq al Bishry, Selim al Awa, and Fahmy Huwaidy joined other leading Egyptian intellectuals in publishing a sharp and direct critique of an Egyptian government declaration that Saddam Hussein bore responsibility for the war as a result of his record of aggressive actions, notably by his invasion of Kuwait in 1991. These prominent public figures from civil society argued instead that this was an American preemptive strike, in the absence of a legitimate threat, to assure unchallenged American political and economic control over the oil-rich Gulf area and indeed the entire the Middle East area.[82] In the end, the New Islamists concluded that the United States, by its one-sided support for Israel and its attack on Iraq, had made itself the unavoidable and legitimate object of a defensive *jihad* in the eyes not just of extremists, but of New Islamist centrists and some of the most moderate forces in the Arab Islamic world. The forms and depth of this enmity would, of course, be shaped by the policies the United States pursued in the post-Saddam Middle East.

In the spare and elegant language of their manifesto, reinforced by their interventions as public figures in the decades that followed, the New Islamists had made clear their understanding of the complexities of the global age. "No movement for the reform of Islam," they pronounced, "will be able to isolate itself from the larger world. Our age no longer allows for such isolation. The interconnectedness of interests does not give anyone the opportunity to live in isolation."[83] How much sense did it make to talk of a "clash of civilizations" between Islam and the West, when Muslims by the thousands served in the American military yet sought moral guidance from the leading scholars of the global Islamic community? By what logic did the violent extremists condemn all Americans and other Westerners when literally millions of them took to the streets to protest the American-led war against Iraq? The New Islamists declared that neither the prevailing world ideologies nor the dominant understandings of Islam were adequate to respond to these new conditions and provide direction for pathways to a better future. As the representatives of an intellectual school, they call for a new vision of international relations that will address positively the core global issues of uneven distribution of wealth, persistent patterns of exploitation, the misuse of the world's resources, and questions of war and peace. They pronounce the old understandings as not only morally bankrupt from an Islamic perspective, but also irrational and inadequate for a global age of rapid, destabilizing change and inevitable interconnectedness. To respond to these conditions, it is necessary to develop relations characterized not by reluctant recognition and resentful tolerance, but by "positive cooperation for the common good, the cultivation of mutual interests and joint action to find new formulas by which nations can relate to each other."[84] Even in the wake of the U.S.-led war against Iraq, the New Islamists insist that there are groups and movements in the West with whom cooperation is possible.

The New Islamist School thus draws its inspiration from an inclusive understanding of Islam as a message that speaks to all of humanity, while recognizing and celebrating human variety, including differences in culture and religion. Like centrists everywhere in the Islamic world, the New Islamists find that message in the Quran. They cite in their manifesto the evocative verse where God speaks to all mankind and not just to Muslims: "O mankind! We created you from a single (pair) of a male and a female, and made you into nations and tribes, that ye may know each other (not that ye may despise each other.)"[85]

All too familiar with the disappointing history of Muslims and human beings everywhere in responding to that message, the New Islamists recognize that ours remains a violent and unjust world, marked by terrible conflicts and an unacceptable gap between the rich and the poor, the powerful and the weak, where we can scarcely hope to "know each other." In the face of these realities, and as Islamist intellectuals, they boldly call for a "new *ijtihad*, liberated from the remnants of history and from the imprints of these remnants on our heritage of *fiqh*."[86] The New Islamist response to the events of September 11 and to the subsequent American-led war against Iraq displayed just how bold that *ijtihad* would have to be in order to honor the inclusive spirit of the Quran as they read it and the realities of the global age as they understand them.

Conclusion

At the start of the twenty-first century, the New Islamists have struggled to keep their interpretive intellectual and social project open to the world and to the future. With more optimism than conditions warranted, they pressed for a bold leap into the turbulence of the new global age. They faced formidable obstacles, though not those usually imagined.

The real danger of the continuing cultural wars at home was not so much the challenge of secularism per se. It was rather the fearfulness of a great many Islamists, whether traditionalists or extremists, that a world dominated by the West and changing at terrifying speed somehow favored a secularist direction. Afraid *for* Islam in this emerging new world, these reactive elements sought refuge in closed and simplistic inherited formulas. They did so in order to escape from the uncertainties and undecidabilities of *ijtihad* [effort of interpretation of the sacred texts]. Against such impulses, the New Islamists insisted that only an *ijtihad* without fear, which understood reason and science as integral to the unfolding of Islam's compelling moral message, could provide the new *fiqh* [understanding of Quran and *Sunnah*] through which Islam would speak to the global age.

For precisely this reason, the real menace of an assertive West was not its invasive culture and staggering military power alone. More deadly still was the West's capacity to use the power and prestige of its technological and military prowess to undermine the self-assurance of the Islamic world, by invidious comparisons within a debilitating framework of externally imposed definitions and standards. In the brave new world of "good and evil" over which the American leadership saw itself presiding, you were either with the West under U.S. leadership, or you were part of the problem to be rooted out.

Elements on the margins of the Islamic wave responded with a violent and retrograde refusal that matched the shallowness of this American official vision. These Islamist extremists had only the power to disrupt and destroy, and they did so under the banner of their distorted understanding of Islam. In the end, their reactions only amplified the message that Islam had nothing to contribute to the emerging global civilization. These violent extremists who understood neither Islam nor the new forces shaping the global age reinforced the official American view that there were no credible alternative understandings and policies worthy of consideration and support. In this way, the West and those Islamists who feared the West in such exaggerated ways threatened to join forces to deprive the Arab Islamic world of the confidence to shape its own future. Should such a vision prevail, Islamic communities would be denied the opportunity to respond to the invigorating challenge of *istikhlaf*, that is, God's call to all of humanity to build a better world. The New Islamists responded vigorously to these attacks on their right of *ijtihad* to understand the world, focusing especially on those that originated in the fearful Islamic wave. At the same time, they displayed in their own *ijtihad* just how their *Wassatteyya* understandings of the changes defining a new world could be expressed in theory and practice.

In the final years of the twentieth century, the New Islamists refrained from an active role in the increasingly mindless public conflicts between secularists and Islamists over what seemed to be an endless series of minor and diversionary incidents. However, when Islamists embroiled in the cultural wars threatened the critical right of *ijtihad* itself, they responded vigorously. The precipitating incident was the public controversy over the book *The Story of Creation between Myth and Reality* by Abdul Sabbur Chahine. "For some time," explained Kamal Abul Magd, "I have been reluctant to respond to the urging of my friends to write this article on Abdul Sabbur Chahine's book." Abul Magd had grown weary of the loud uproars incited "by some angry people in protest of this article or that book, under the banner of defending God's religion and the fundamentals of *Sharia* and creed." By the end of the century, this deterioration in public dialogue had produced a debased climate in which elements of the Islamic body responded to perceived attacks on Islam "by hasty accusations without evidence, misrepresentations of intentions, which are known only to God, and a stunning expansion in the definitions of what the fundamentals [of Islam] really are." Abul Magd feared that "participation in public exchanges that had acquired such a character might be misconstrued as approval of this inaccurate and misguided approach to issues of creed and *Sharia*."[1]

In the end, however, the New Islamists were compelled to intervene when the voices of immoderation from the Islamic wave launched a frontal assault on the very foundations of their own interpretive project. A charge of apostasy was lodged against Abdul Sabbur Chahine for his discussion of Adam's role in *The Story of Creation between Myth and Reality.* Ostensibly criticizing Chahine, misguided Islamists threatened the right of each generation to exercise *ijtihad.*

This was not the first time, Kamal Abul Magd pointed out, that a scholar was facing an avalanche of accusations for interrogating secondary issues where a tolerant Islam in fact welcomes a multitude of opinions. Abul Magd noted as well the particular ironies of the storm aroused by Abdul Sabbur Chahine's work. The accused, he reminded the public, had earlier played the role of accuser. It was this very same Abdul Sabbur Chahine whose loose charges against the scholarly work of Nasr Abu Zeid had launched the campaign that dragged that young Cairo University scholar into the divorce courts as an apostate whose marriage should be dissolved.[2] "History thus repeats itself," wrote Abul Magd, "with this deplorable practice of bringing intellectuals to court to deprive them of their opinions, bury their writings, and even divorce them from their wives." It was imperative to break this destructive cycle, and not just because energies were wasted, careers derailed, and lives permanently disrupted. These periodic attacks, in Abul Magd's view, undermined a promise and carried a deadly threat. The promise was no less than the capacity of Islam, rightly understood, to respond to a need felt not only in Egypt but around the world for the higher purposes and values, moderation, and rationality that Islam could offer. The threat was to deprive thinkers and scholars of the essential process of *ijtihad* without which Islam could not hope to speak in this way to the global age. Abul Magd expressed his "increasing feeling, felt by other scholars as well, that the world is in a dire need for the true Islam with its clear, pure creed and its tolerant view of human nature." In his judgment, "the fate of the current wave of religiousness growing in the Egyptian society and throughout the Arab and Islamic world depends on the degree of moderation and soundness that defines its intellectual and practical approach." In such a form, he concluded, the expansion of the Islamic wave will be "a gift to people and a mercy."

Over several decades, the New Islamists have given a palpable and compelling expression of their shared sense of just what form this "gift" and "mercy" should take for Egypt and the Islamic world beyond. Under authoritarian conditions, they have constituted themselves as a flexible and resilient "intellectual school," neither attached to one particular movement nor an extension of official authority, yet nevertheless able to give coherence to their collective interpretive and practical work in a multitude of fields. Their scholarship has strengthened the intellectual foundations of a bold interpretive project, infused with the spirit of the *Wassatteyya,* to guide the renewal in ways responsive to contemporary realities. In addition, they have devised imaginative mechanisms to overcome the division between intellectuals and ordinary Egyptians, to make their project as accessible as possible and thus an active force in the world. They have enjoyed a success especially among the young unmatched by any other trend in Egypt. On a wide range of issues—education and the arts, community and economics, politics and Islam's place in the world—the New Islamists have realized an impressive *ijtihad* of thought and social action. The resulting substantial new *fiqh* represented an important but as yet unfinished legacy for the new generation. It was imperative that their work and the work of the next generation of centrists should continue.

Given these accomplishments and promises, the New Islamists refused to watch passively as the right of *ijtihad* was subjected to "arbitrary confiscation" during the controversies over Chahine's book. Such an unwarranted attack on a scholar and thinker threatened all these advances and could not be tolerated. In a striking passage, Abul Magd wrote: "Islam calls for thinking and moving on earth in search of knowledge and learning." He added, "God protects the expression of opinion from any aggression," citing the Quranic concept of "no harm to an author or witness."

Chahine's study deals with the creation of Adam, attempting to reconcile scientific understanding with the account in the Quran. His argument rests on the contention that Adam was not the first human-like creature but rather was preceded by others who, through thousands of years of evolution, eventually took Adam's shape. Kamal Abul Magd explained that the issues raised by Chahine had nothing to do with the fundamentals of the faith and were therefore the appropriate subject of contending views. The correct response to such an interpretation was to confront it with another interpretation and not to drag its author into court.

In that spirit, Abul Magd offered his own dissent from Chahine's method and conclusions, while at the same time defending his right of *ijtihad.* In Abul Magd's view, the very subject matter of Chahine's study made it impossible to reach the kind of firm and generalized conclusions for which the author aimed. Neither science nor the Quran offered the bases for the kind of reconciliation that Chahine sought. For all the advances of science, Abul Magd pointed out, the story of human creation remains conjectural and contested, without definitive documentation. Moreover, the verses in the Quran on creation do not deal with the details of means or timing; such matters are "neither part of the Prophet's functions nor the purposes of the Quran." Abul Magd explained that "the Quran simply tells the stories of predecessors so that people discover the rules of God and learn something helpful in their present and future."

These limitations, in Abul Magd's view, made it impossible for Chahine to realize his aim of "understanding the categorically confirmed verses of the Quran on the story of creation and in light of the scientific perspective." Such a goal could not be realized because the position of science is not clear-cut and the Quran and *Sunnah* do not present detailed and precise positions on the beginning of creation and the truth about Adam. Thus, Chahine's work "is not really an attempt to reconcile science and religion." Rather, Abul Magd concluded, it is "an attempt by a specialist in linguistics to fathom the Quranic verses in order to reach conclusions that can never be reached only through the study of language."

Abul Magd made it clear, however, that his most important point was a defense of Chahine's right to his views as an *ijtihad* in an acceptable area. His own willingness to engage precisely the same set of issues was a bold and effective reassertion of that right. The appropriate Islamic response to a controversial *ijtihad* like Chahine's is a contending scholarly interpretation. Abul Magd also pointed out that forums for learned exchange existed in abundance in Egypt, and they were the appropriate venue for free and unfettered discussions in those wide areas where differences of opinion were allowable. The use of the courts to decide such questions was an abuse. Allowing the court cases in turn to spill over into the media only made things worse by poisoning the atmosphere of public debate and diverting the nation from more essential tasks.

While Abul Magd believed that Chahine's book did not deserve all the public furor it had raised in the media, he decided that the discussion did provide an opportunity to make a more fundamental point. Although the fate of the nation did not rest on the understanding that scholars developed of Adam's role, it did depend on the prior right of intellectuals to *ijtihad*. Thus, Abul Magd in the end decided to intervene in the Chahine case "to stand up against the raids launched every now and then against the right of the *ulama* and intellectuals to practice *ijtihad*." For a thousand years, such silencing had been tolerated. This the New Islamists would no longer sanction. The collusion of those who feared excessively for Islam with those who feared Islam would not, this time, succeed in closing the right of *ijtihad*. That right was both Islamically legitimate and imperative for each generation. Without the guidance of an *ijtihad* that enabled the texts to speak to each age, Abul Magd warned, the promise of the Islamic wave would be lost. Instead, "if moderation and reason are absent, the expansion of the Islamic wave would only be a gateway to terrible conflicts dominated by narrow-minded thoughts, intolerant hearts, and fanatical souls."

As part of the broad Islamic *Wassatteyya,* the New Islamists were determined to face down intimidation and preserve the opportunity represented by *ijtihad* "to get out of backwardness and the closing down of any hope that Arabs and Muslims would contribute in directing the contemporary global civilization." In this spirit, Kamal Abul Magd reminded readers that in an earlier apostasy case when the right of *ijtihad* was also questioned, the judge commented in his verdict that "foreigners are preoccupied with what is useful and you are preoccupied with what is not useful." This wise sentence, said Abul Magd, should be repeated "to those who raise such uproars, break into courts calling for blaspheming those who offer interpretations and divorcing them from their wives because of an opinion or a suspicion." Such actions, he warned, "would close the door of *ijtihad* by intimidation and terrorism." Intellectuals and scholars would be silenced by "fears of the arrows of these hunters." In dealing with such angry and loud people, our time of confrontation must instead be a time when God's verse "so fear them not, but fear Me" rings clearer.[3]

The events that unfolded in the wake of September 11 heightened the grave meaning and relevance of Kamal Abul Magd's counsel. Egyptians had witnessed at Luqsor in 1997 the cruel actions of al Jihad extremists, who slaughtered innocent tourists in an orgy of mass murder that shocked the nation. On September 11, 2001, the al Qaeda network, with which al Jihad had merged, wrought havoc on an even more devastating scale with a crime against humanity in the very heart of America. However, the American reaction to the attack of September 11 aimed to impose a sweeping new global agenda under the banner of an unconstrained "war on terrorism." It was to be, of course, an emphatically American agenda, defined by American interests, projected by the Western media, and enforced by American power. With the support of its traumatized people, the American leadership expressed its own version of that metaphysical longing for simplicity that has been the most dangerous reaction of some to the numbing and often terrifying complexities of the global era. President George W. Bush spoke in terms shorn of the usual diplomacy. Osama bin Ladin and the al Qaeda network were pronounced guilty, without hesitation, by the same American security apparatus that had not had sufficient evidence to prevent the assault. The perpetrators of September 11 and those, like the Taliban, who shielded them were "wanted dead or alive." If you are not with us, you are against us, warned the American President, while vowing to "smoke out" the terrorists wherever they sought refuge and to punish those who harbored them. Osama bin Ladin became the evil outlaw, with a price on his head and the forces of good in hot pursuit. However, this self-anointed expansion of authority would represent the only change in American policies. The United States had been attacked for its goodness, its freedoms, and its prosperity, the President explained. No changes in its fundamental foreign policies, including those in the Middle East, were warranted. A wounded yet righteous America declared itself the leader of a global war to "rid the world" of terrorism, defined by its own lights.

Not even overwhelming American power, the New Islamists argued, could make the world that simple. The New Islamists spoke for the future in emphasizing the necessity of understanding the complex issues that had given rise to the criminality of Osama bin Ladin and his network of supporters. They had immediately condemned the murderous acts against civilians in New York. They had also signaled the necessity for careful and reasoned resistance to the global agenda of counter-violence that the United States was enacting. The New Islamists offered their assessment from their home places in Egypt and the Arab world and also through the new media of the Information Age. They did not hesitate to take their *Wassatteyya* message directly to the West. There is no better way to conclude this book than with a composite picture of the interventions of the New Islamists in assessing the world-changing events of September 11.

The intervention of Yusuf al Qaradawy from Qatar was marked by both candor and incisive analysis. Of the New Islamists, Qaradawy has established the strongest voice and most forceful presence in the new electronic media. He provided the major intellectual force for the influential Islam Online Internet site, and he was also one of the first Islamic intellectuals to establish his own Web site, which attracted an impressive global response. At the same time, Qaradawy's regular program on the al Jazirah channel secured him a prominent place in the new Arab satellite media.

In the wake of September 11 Qaradawy used these multiple platforms to speak plainly as an independent critic of the passive and unimaginative policies of Arab and Islamic regimes, cowed by the new American assertiveness. At home in Qatar, he used the occasion of the meeting of the foreign ministers of Islamic countries in Doha in early October 2001 to challenge the American war against Afghanistan. In a sermon during the Friday prayers, Qaradawy criticized the passive position taken by the foreign ministers on the U.S. war as "far from the feelings expressed on the Islamic street, as a result of their fears of the United States." The overflowing crowd at the mosque responded with "amens" when Qaradawy denounced the British and American military attacks on Afghanistan. In a subsequent press conference, Qaradawy argued that it made little sense to attempt to deal with terrorism without addressing the conditions that gave rise to it. Moreover, he criticized the United States for using violence in ways little different from those of the terrorists. He explicitly defended the "independence" of the al Jazirah channel, which had "so shaken the U.S." Finally, Qaradawy advised that "the United States review its foreign policy to understand why millions of people feel hatred and resentment toward it."[4]

While Qaradawy spoke to the world through the new media, Fahmy Huwaidy and Kamal Abul Magd brought their message directly to Britain and the United States. Huwaidy hesitated when the invitation first arrived in late October of 2001, but in the end he agreed to participate in a closed seminar, sponsored by the University of Exeter and held at the British Foreign Ministry.[5] Huwaidy had long understood that America and the West did not constitute a monolith. On more than one occasion, he had written insightfully and appreciatively of the diversity and range of Western opinions on issues of concern to the Arab Islamic world, including Palestine and the quarantine of Iraq. At the same time, because Huwaidy was himself a skilled polemicist, he was wary of giving the West any opportunity to manipulate Islamist intellectuals into compromising situations by appearing to endorse Western views to the detriment of the Arab Islamic world. In explaining his decision to go to Britain despite these reservations, Huwaidy cited his desire to present the Arab Islamic view without any mediation and the need to hear British positions directly from those responsible for them. Finally, he indicated his respect for Professor Tim Niblock of the Center for Islamic and Arab Studies at the University of Exeter, whom he recognized as "an honest and devoted scholar in his understanding of issues of the Arab and Islamic world."

There were twenty-eight participants in the seminar on "Radical Islam and the Current International Situation" that Huwaidy attended. Eight came from five British universities, while the remainder came from the Islamic world, including an Indian scholar and representatives from Egypt, Iran, Pakistan, Algeria, Palestine, and Kuwait. Huwaidy was gratified by the ease with which participants clarified the seminar topic, agreeing at once that the title of the sessions might be misleading, since Islam is of course but one, and all terms such as "Radical Islam" carry the possibility of abuse. The issue disappeared, however, when the participants agreed without dissent that "what is meant is the radical understanding of Islam, and this means that it concerns the behavior of some Muslims rather than Islam itself." Many of those presenting papers at the seminar explained further that "radical Islam means the Islamic trends or movements that use violence to achieve their goals."

Huwaidy noted first that there was no disagreement on the most general point "that people are not born terrorists but they become so as a result of certain political and social conditions. This relationship explains the otherwise mysterious facts of why terrorists appear in some states and not others and why they emerge during different periods in the life of the same nation." This conclusion also provided a partial response to a second general question concerning whether radical Islam was rising or declining. The participants were divided in their responses. However, it became clear that the varying responses reflected different conditions prevailing in different places and times within the Islamic world. "Anyone who reviews the map of the Arab world," commented Huwaidy, "can trace the environments in which there are reasons for extremism and terrorism and those in which these reasons have withdrawn."

Huwaidy reported that "there was near agreement that the current campaign against terrorism will have doubtful results because terrorism cannot be effectively fought by military means. It must be fought by eliminating the underlying reasons for it, and this can only be accomplished by other than military means." The participants in the seminar elaborated that the "main sources of anger and resentment in the Arab Islamic world are the Israeli occupation in Palestine and the sanctions on Iraq." One of the British participants commented that "if these two problems are not dealt with in a fair way, Western peoples should not expect the anger directed against the West by some of the Arabs and Muslims to subside. This anger was one of the main reasons for the attack on the United States."

Huwaidy also summarized the assessment made of the effects of the September events on the Arab and Islamic world. During the discussion, it became obvious that there was a general pessimism about consequences stemming from the fact that "recent events have provided an excuse for some systems to strengthen their security control. . . . This finds expression in the increase of arrests in some states and bringing a number of active Islamists to trials and the increase of violations of human rights." Moreover, the participants shared the fear that the military actions "would only increase the tensions in the area, resulting in the creation of new generations of extremists and terrorists."

Huwaidy remarked that the Foreign Ministry seminar constituted "one of the paradoxes of our time, in that a Western government seeks the advice of Islamic intellectuals in dealing with terrorism and its relationship to the Islamic world. It is a paradox because these intellectuals come from states that do not even think to consult them in such things. The officials in our states," he said, "know everything and do not need the advice of anyone." He added that "the irony here is obvious because this invitation was extended at a time when the Islamic street is mobilizing hostile feelings toward the West and calling what is happening now a crusade launched by blasphemers against Muslims." Huwaidy also commented appreciatively about the role of universities and society more generally in these dialogues with those responsible for making policy, noting that "we lack this kind of cooperation." He concluded by saying that "I don't know whether they benefited from us or not, but on the personal level I learned a lot from them and I respected their civilized behavior."[6]

Kamal Abul Magd's efforts took him to America. The United Nations declared the year 2001 the year of the dialogue of civilizations. Abul Magd is no stranger to this concept; in his writings over the years, he has often commented on the most important Western theories of cultural interactions in the global age. Therefore, it came as no surprise that this articulate and cosmopolitan Islamist intellectual would be the choice of Arab League head Amr Musa to represent the Arab League in the dialogues and symposia to be held around the world in response to the U.N. call.

Abul Magd's appointment as the Arab League spokesperson on the dialogue of civilizations assured him increased access to the media. In a lengthy interview on the television program "Underscored in Red" on March 12, 2002, Abul Magd provided a detailed account of a recent trip to the United States where he had represented the Arab League.[7] In his discussions in America, Abul Magd emphasized the point that the decentered character of the networks of terrorists meant that they did not need a "formal authorization nor incitement from anyone to act." Their actions flowed rather from their own direct reactions to the American policies that enraged them and hundreds of thousands of others. Of those policies, none produced greater anger in the Islamic world, Abul Magd told his American audiences, than the one-sided U.S. support for Israel. In particular, as an international lawyer Abul Magd questioned the legal force of any treaty with Yasser Arafat while he was held as an actual or virtual prisoner by the Sharon government. Abul Magd stressed to his Egyptian and Arab television audience that the Zionists worked tirelessly and with great skill to shape the global media in ways to advance Israeli interests and to the detriment of the Islamic world. He also cited the frequent misinformation and misrepresentation of Islam to American audiences by prominent commentators, such as Thomas Friedman of the *New York Times,* that too often went unchallenged. Noting that the Americans did not have the kind of colonial history in the Arab and Islamic world that both the British and the French did, he argued that the Arab Islamic world had failed to take advantage of this historical reality as the United States increasingly moved to take up the mantle of an imperial and colonial power. What, he asked, could be done to reverse or at least moderate this damaging development? Finally, Abul Magd reported to his Egyptian audience that his experiences in America had reminded him in very concrete ways that there were moderate voices and forces in America. It was imperative that the moderates of the Arab Islamic world make connections with these American moderates that could be the basis for common projects to advance their shared values and interests.

Selim al Awa played his role at home, where he displayed little patience with simplistic and fundamentalist thinking, whether Islamist or American. Awa presided over the symposium on "The Events of September 11th and Their Impact on the Global Media," organized by the Association for Culture and Dialogue in March 2002. Awa's moderating presence permeated the event. When introducing the speakers, Awa took pains to explain that CNN correspondents had been invited to participate but had declined. Undoubtedly, he remarked, they are "somewhere in a far corner of this earth but unfortunately cannot be with us here in Cairo today to present directly an assessment of CNN's coverage of events in Afghanistan." In their place, the association had turned to an Egyptian academic specialist on American politics, Dr. Manar al Shorbagy of the American University in Cairo. Though CNN chose not to attend, the al Jazirah channel had sent an important representative, prepared to explain that channel's extraordinary role in Afghanistan.

There were no empty chairs in the large conference hall at Shepherd's Hotel, with the media strongly represented. The Islamist presence, particularly from the generation of the Wassat Party, could be strongly felt. Few failed to notice, as well, the presence of American diplomats. In his brief opening remarks, Selim al Awa noted that there should not be empty talk of an "objective" media. Interests always played a part in shaping the news, he said, and it was the responsibility of the audience to identify these interests as precisely as possible and to determine just how they affected the news reported. Moreover, there was no need to overstate the difficulty of the task. The Arab media, for example, typically opened with a report on the relevant President or King, then moved to pronouncements by his key deputies, wrapping things up with reports of lesser official figures. Did it really take more than a few moments, al Awa asked, to assess what kind of media this was? By the same token, the Western media carried the influences of the society that produced them, notably the dominant corporations that owned the major outlets. Was there any reason to assume that al Jazirah was somehow shielded from societal influence? Openness to the various global media, while at the same time understanding the influences that shaped them, provided the best hope for developing one's own positions and also for using the media to project them, Awa explained. There was, of course, no guarantee of just how much of one's message would come through the different filters, nor any assurance of what effects it might eventually have. Still, he argued, it was imperative that the Arab Islamic world strive to make its voice heard through all available platforms.

The formal presentations at the symposium, also brief and pointed, provided characterizations of CNN and al Jazirah, in both cases shorn of illusions. Dr. Shorbagy of the American University in Cairo emphasized the self-censorship of the CNN coverage, and linked it to the unusually secretive character of policy-making by the Bush administration. The representative from al Jazirah concentrated on explaining that the exclusive access of that channel resulted from CNN's decision not to take advantage of an earlier opening that the Taliban government had extended to the international media. Al Jazirah found itself essentially alone in Afghanistan and, for the first time, succeeded in making an Arab media channel the leading global news source for developments of worldwide importance.

The real importance of the symposium, however, came with the discussion. Selim al Awa intervened selectively but effectively to express the centrist perspective of the *Wassatteyya* on the events of September 11. At one point, Awa objected strongly to another questioner's drawing a comparison between Osama bin Ladin and Omar Ibn Khattab, the revered successor to Muhammad as Caliph of the Islamic community. In his flawless and authoritative Arabic, Awa pronounced that such a comparison was simply unacceptable. The most revealing intervention, however, was Awa's comment on a statement by an ex-military figure with extremist views. The retired officer remarked that national and world events had brought him extreme pleasure on only two occasions. The first was when he heard the news of Anwar al Sadat's assassination, and the second when he received word of the attack on the World Trade Center in New York. Awa did not let that comment pass. He interrupted and bluntly remarked that he wished the man had not shared his subjective reactions. He insisted that the attack on the Twin Towers was a crime against humanity, as was the subsequent American assault on Afghanistan. Awa did not hesitate to assert the centrist New Islamist vision against the extremist positions from within the Islamic wave.

The larger story of the New Islamists of Egypt ends here, as it began, with sketches such as these of the ongoing struggles of the New Islamists to create the moral and intellectual foundations of a more fully realized Islamic community. All of the representations in this book, including those in this final chapter, begin as self-portraits of the New Islamists. These images are crafted in the first instance from the words, actions, and self-understandings of the New Islamists themselves. Throughout the book, I have taken care to listen to New Islamist voices and faithfully record their actual gestures. The literature of those who "know" the Islamists and their aims, without bothering either to read their works, listen to their statements, engage them in conversation, or participate with them in joint projects for human betterment, is already far too abundant. Nevertheless, empathic reconstructions have their own dangers of losing critical distance. For this reason, I have made every effort to draw these sketches from an external angle of vision broad enough to embrace the interlocutors of New Islamist dialogues and the subjects of their criticisms. The thinkers of the New Islamist School willingly engage the world, and attempts to understand them must contextualize self-understandings with the critical assessments of those who challenge their efforts to remake Egypt and bring the message of centrist Islam to the world.

The sketches of the New Islamists presented in this chapter, as they continue to speak out in the media and other public forums, provide a good basis for a concluding assessment of the weight and meaning of the New Islamist record. Interventions like Kamal Abul Magd's on the right of *ijtihad,* and comments of all the major New Islamist figures on the responsibility to respond to the unconstrained assertions of American power, can be read in the light of the accumulated evidence reviewed in earlier chapters, showing how in multiple ways the New Islamist social project speaks to the real needs and hopes of Egyptians in the face of events that demand definition and dilemmas that cry out for response. Words and gestures concerning these critical developments in the first years of the new century echo and reinforce positions developed over several decades of scholarship and active public engagement. They point to the continuing New Islamist effort, under the most trying circumstances, to develop a centrist model of Islamic political community in Egypt and to define a place for Egypt in the global arena.

The energizing faith of the New Islamists is anchored in the foundational belief that the Quran and the *Sunnah* of the Prophet provide the spiritual inspiration for a distinctive Islamic vision of human community. However, these Islamist architects of community differ sharply from the militants in their refusal to build complex social arrangements on emblematic fragments wrenched from the story of Islam, such as the *neqab* [face veil] or a random *hadith.* Nor do they accept a notion of guidance that reduces itself to repetitions of numbing and empty slogans like "Islam is the solution," or arrogant assumptions by any individual or group that they alone have the right of *ijtihad* or that their interpretations have a sanctified character placed beyond challenge. Above all, the New Islamists resist unreflective imitation of past models of the human effort to actualize the divine guidance of the Quran and the *Sunnah.* Just as decisively, they reject the mindless imitation of the experience of others.

The New Islamists embrace instead the difficult tasks of interpreting the meaning of the revelation for their own time and place, inventing new forms, adopting elements of the heritage or borrowing from others depending on current needs and circumstances. They demand that any particular *ijtihad,* including their own, be left open to the challenge of another interpretation. They insist that all such understandings of Islam must be evaluated in the light of not only the texts but also an informed and pragmatic grasp of the realities of the actual world in which the faith must be lived.

The New Islamists thus struggle for structures that are at once moral, intellectual, and social. Their efforts demand a profound rethinking of the core components of the Islamic heritage and a gradual remaking of the social world. As intellectuals and social actors, they are acutely sensitive to the constraints of social context, without succumbing either to a quietism that marks cultural defeatism or to an impatient and unreflective hyperactivism that turns inevitably into disfiguring violence. The New Islamists remain centrists in the precise but fluid sense that they stand between the dispirited souls who regard a distinctive Islamic civilizational project as impossible to attain and the ignorant, often manic enthusiasts who trivialize and distort the difficult path to its realization. As Fahmy Huwaidy explains:

> The subject of Islamic practice is not as simple as some might imagine. The belief of some that the establishment of the Islamic community awaits a decision, a law, or even the implementation of a body of legislation is a shameful simplification. This honorable goal requires honest and persistent work that needs a positive atmosphere that would permit seeds to grow, the cultivation to continue, and the harvest to occur in its appointed time. Furthermore, the reader of these words would be wrong if he concludes from it that the "Islamic solution" is ready and waiting for formulation and approval. What I wanted to say is that this solution is "possible" if we work hard at it. This solution is not "deficient" as has been rumored by some, nor is it "impossible" as others would like us to believe.[8]

Radical in their ultimate commitments, the New Islamists do not waver in the pacific gradualism of their means. Their hardworking and self-conscious gradualism aims for retrieval, restructuring, and creativity in facing new conditions. In all their collective efforts, they seek to embody their vision in existing or reworked social arrangements, building when possible on what has been achieved rather than indulging destructive extremist visions of totally new beginnings. Whenever possible, they lend their support to reconciliation and peaceful dialogue to move their project forward. The human character of their effort appears in the unusual capacity for self-reflection and self-criticism that marks the New Islamist social practice. The New Islamists understand and acknowledge that their work, while inspired by the Prophet's perfect vision of the kind of community best suited to humankind, remains unavoidably flawed by their own human failings of understanding and shortfalls of wisdom, as well as by the particular constraints under which they must work. An Islamic community for this world, they understand, will always reflect the particularities of the opportunities available and the inevitable limitations of those who seek to realize them.

Despite the strong imprint of these shared beliefs and the long-range strategic commitments that flow from them, the public faces of the New Islamists are far from identical. As earlier chapters have shown, the central figures of the New Islamist School by no means reach full agreement on all substantive issues of domestic and foreign affairs, nor do they aim to do so. Nevertheless, their common commitments and joint projects make them recognizable as a group, while their differences continue to mark them as individual and distinctive personalities, rather like individual members of the same family. Fahmy Huwaidy, with his unprepossessing public demeanor and fervent interest in foreign affairs, is very different from the late Shaikh Muhammad al Ghazzaly, whose personal warmth and charismatic public presence effortlessly dominated all public gatherings, even while his own attention was most often focused on the personal needs and private concerns of Egyptians. Dr. Yusuf al Qaradawy projects himself as a scholar and thinker in a rather traditional Islamic mode. In contrast, Kamal Abul Magd, Muhammad Selim al Awa, and Tareq al Bishry appear as urbane and worldly figures, the first a practicing international lawyer and professor of constitutional law, adviser to governments, and former government minister; the second also a distinguished professor of law who has written with authority on the most difficult legal and moral issues of a modern community; and the third a man of the law who had a remarkable career as one of Egypt's most highly respected judges and also established a distinguished record as a leading historian. Qaradawy speaks with particular effect to the transnational Islamic movement. Huwaidy writes with skill and verve for the attentive Arab and Islamic publics, while Abul Magd, Awa, and Bishry command more varied vocabularies that articulate the thinking of the New Islamists in ways more accessible to the broader secular world.

Despite all these personal differences of style, emphasis, and audience, these Islamist intellectuals nevertheless cohere as a "school" of Islamist centrists. They talk to each other in a language rich in shared understandings; they regularly read and cite each other's works; they develop common positions on complex issues; and they act together frequently, though in shifting combinations, to establish a collective public presence. The New Islamist identity thus emerges from a fluid and creative play of similarities and differences which they resolve, when resolution is required, by the agreement to embrace those elements that draw them together and to respect the distances yet to be bridged. Through their collective efforts in difficult authoritarian conditions, they succeed in making real public choices that leave a discernible record of the kind of community they envision and the means by which they hope to realize it. These concluding portraits capture the New Islamists' firm reassertion of the right of reasoned and realistic *ijtihad* and their brave efforts to project their centrist, contemporary Islamic vision to the world beyond Egypt at a particularly dangerous time. They show yet again how the New Islamists' actions embody the promise of the Islamic *Wassatteyya,* the generous heart of moderate Islam that reaches out to centrists in Egypt and around the globe, to cooperate in building a better Egypt and a more just human future.

Notes

Introduction

1. In his account of the incident that precipitated his article, Yassine remarks that he read the manifesto of the New Islamists earlier but welcomes the opportunity to reread it and publish his assessment. Whatever their opinions of the New Islamist Trend, by the mid-1990s it was clearly impossible for secular critics to ignore them. *Al Ahram,* May 30, 1994. The response by Kamal Abul Magd appeared in *al Ahram,* June 8, 1994, and the second article by Yassine appeared in *al Ahram* of June 20, 1994. The quotations in the text are drawn from these articles. All translations from Arabic-language sources throughout the book are mine.
2. The term "Islamic Awakening" refers to the generalized revitalization of Islam that began in the 1970s as part of the worldwide turn to religion. Many currents and trends benefit from the Awakening, including the *Wassatteyya* or mainstream with its emphasis on gradualism and peaceful change. Within the mainstream, there are those like the New Islamist School who focus on education and culture as the primary arenas within which to work for Islamic renewal. This orientation is sometimes referred to as "civilizational Islam." In contrast, others in the mainstream focus on the political arena. Such groups include the Muslim Brothers, who from the 1970s on, when they returned to public life, made the strategic decision to accommodate the regime and work for peaceful change within the established order. What the New Islamists and the Muslim Brothers have in common is their commitment to peaceful change. One of the most important ways in which they differ is in the definition of the priority areas for attention.

   At times, because of the priority they give to politics, the Muslim Brothers are thought of as advocating political Islam, although they do so while eschewing violence. Others with an orientation that focuses on politics do embrace violence to achieve their political objectives; they include the various extremist and underground violent radicals. Political Islam thus has both moderate and radical adherents. Neither civilizational Islam nor political Islam should be thought of as a specific movement or group. These labels refer instead to broad trends or orientations of activists who all respond to the Islamic Awakening. Both civilizational Islam and political Islam, however, do give rise to particular groups or movements, like the

New Islamist School (civilizational Islam), the Muslim Brothers (mainstream political Islam), and Jihad (extremist political Islam).

3. For a full description of various events of the Cairo Book Fair as well as an assessment of the importance of the fairs in Egyptian public life, see Osama Ibrahim, *Rose al Yusuf,* January 6, 1992.
4. Farag Foda is joined by Muhammad Khallafalah, a founding member of the Tugamu Party and a self-described representative of the "Islamic left."
5. The Islamist camp is represented, as well, by a well-known independent Islamist intellectual, Muhammad Emara, whose views at times come close to Ghazzaly's own, but just as often express a far less open and inclusive spirit.
6. A full account of the debate, from which these summaries are drawn, appeared in *al Musawwar,* January 17, 1992.
7. *Al Musawwar,* January 17, 1992.
8. *Al Ahram,* January 2, 1990.
9. In his remarks, Abul Magd summarized the major themes of the manifesto. For a report on his comments, see *The Book Fair, 1992,* Al Hayaa al Misrya al Amma lil Kitab, Ministry of Culture, January 4, 1992, issue no. 8.
10. These summations and others like them offered at various points in the book owe a great deal to conversations with my colleague and friend Karen Abul Kheir, who worked with me at the American University in Cairo.
11. See Muhammad al Ghazzaly, in *al Wafd,* February 2, 1989.
12. Kamal Abul Magd, *A Contemporary Islamic Vision: Declaration of Principles* (Cairo: Dar al Shuruq, 1991), p. 13.

1. Reforming Education

1. Fahmy Huwaidy, in *al Ahram,* January 13, 1998.
2. The interview from which these quotations are taken was held on Egyptian television, channel 1, on March 27, 1994.
3. *Al Ahram,* April 5, 1994.
4. For a discussion of Ghazzaly's view of the role of women in the Islamic community, see Chapter 3.
5. See the discussion of New Islamist views of violence in Chapter 3.
6. Kamal Abul Magd, *A Contemporary Islamic Vision: Declaration of Principles* (Cairo: Dar al Shuruq, 1991), p. 35.
7. See Fahmy Huwaidy, in *al Ahram,* February 27, 2001.
8. See Huwaidy, ibid., February 6, 2001.
9. *Al Ahram,* November 4, 1997, and a*l Wafd,* November 6, 1997.
10. For a discussion of this reorientation, see Raymond William Baker, *Sadat and After: Struggles for Egypt's Political Soul* (Cambridge, Mass.: Harvard University Press, 1990).
11. The report was prepared by a research and evaluation center in the Ministry of Education under the direction of Dr. Fuad Abu Hattab. See Huwaidy's summary in *al Ahram,* February 27, 2001.
12. *Al Ahram,* February 27, 2001.
13. Ahmed Bahgat, in *al Ahram,* June 15, 1998. See also Salah Montasser in *al Ahram,* July 21, 1998.

14. See Huwaidy, in *al Ahram,* August 18, 1998.
15. *Al Ahram,* February 27, 2001.
16. See representative accounts in *al Musawwar,* April 9, 1993, and in *al Shaab,* April 13, 1993.
17. For an example, see *al Araby,* January 13, 2000.
18. See ibid., January 28, 2000.
19. See Huwaidy, in *al Ahram,* November 4, 1997.
20. See Huwaidy, ibid., April 6, 1993.
21. The influential columnist Salama Ahmed Salama sounded all of these themes, warning against the pitfalls of "searching for a black cat in a dark room," in *al Ahram,* May 1, 1993.
22. See the Minister's speech in *al Wafd,* May 26, 1993.
23. See *al Shaab,* March 31, 1998.
24. See *al Wafd,* December 5, 1997.
25. See *al Ahram,* November 3, 1997.
26. Ibid., February 4, 1997.
27. The best of recent attempts to track the private schools can be found in *al Araby,* January 28, 2000.
28. Ibid.
29. For the most part, press commentary is anecdotal and fragmentary. One of the better reviews at the outset of the experiment can be found in *al Musawwar,* August 9, 1996. The characterization offered above is also based on direct observation and conversations with faculty in the new universities and should be regarded as preliminary.
30. See the quotation from a speech by Abul Magd in *al Shaab,* February 9, 1996.
31. *Al Ahram,* May 10, 1988.
32. Hamed Ammar, in *al Ahram,* June 14, 1996.
33. *Al Usbu,* June 15, 1998.
34. See ibid.
35. Ibid.
36. Ibid.
37. Egypt has been under a system of emergency laws for almost the entire period since 1981. The historian Tareq al Bishry discussed prospects for a youth movement under these repressive conditions in a public forum reported in *al Araby,* May 4, 2000.
38. Kamal Abul Magd, *October,* July 8, 1990.
39. Mahfuz made a similar argument in *al Araby,* February 27, 1995.
40. *October,* July 8, 1990.
41. Ibid.
42. *Al Wafd,* November 6, 1997.
43. See Hamed Ammar, in *al Ahram,* October 13, 1997.
44. For a reliable survey of these official plans and projects, see *al Ahram,* January 2, 2001.
45. This assessment of the work of Tareq al Bishry is based on reviews of all his major works as well as specific articles cited in the notes.
46. See Abul Magd, in *al Musawwar,* July 10, 1987.
47. See Huwaidy's analysis of the outbreak of violence between Copts and Islamist militants in Upper Egypt early in 2000 in *Wehgat Nazar,* February 2000.

48. For an eloquent and passionate statement of this commitment, see Abul Magd, in *al Usbu,* January 15, 1998.
49. A moment of clarification of the profound nature of this debate came with the exchange between Fahmy Huwaidy and Abdul Moneim Said in the summer of 1993. See Fahmy Huwaidy's original article in *al Ahram,* July 13, 1993, and Abdul Moneim Said's response on August 8, 1993.
50. These elaborations provide the substance for the subsequent chapters of this book.
51. See the discussion of the implications of such historical amnesia in Huwaidy, *al Ahram,* March 17, 1998.
52. *Al Shaab,* January 4, 1992.
53. *Al Akhbar,* October 4, 1991.
54. See Muhammad al Ghazzaly, *The Battle of the Musshaf* (Cairo: Nadhat Masr, 1996), p. 184.
55. *Al Shaab,* November 1, 1994.
56. Ibid.
57. Yusuf al Qaradawy, *Fiqh of Priorities: A New Study in the Light of Quran and Sunnah* (Cairo: Dar al Wahba, 1995), pp. 227–228.
58. See Kamal Abul Magd on the link between freedom and creativity as something poorly understood and neglected in contemporary Islamic societies. Abul Magd, *Al Iza'a Wal Television,* March 7, 1992.
59. Yusuf al Qaradawy, *Islam and Secularism Face to Face* (Cairo: Dar al Shawa, 1987), p. 21.
60. Surah 96: 1–5.
61. Qaradawy's address can be found in *al Wafd,* September 13, 1996.
62. *Al Shaab,* June 21, 1994.
63. The New Islamist role in encouraging Islamist involvement in these dynamic spheres is discussed in Chapter 3.
64. The emergence of the Wassat Party is discussed in Chapter 5.

2. Embracing the Arts

1. For an important assessment of Muhammad al Ghazzaly's stature by a non-Islamist, see Abdul Halim Kandil, in *al Araby,* December 5, 1994.
2. For Mahfuz's position, see the interviews with him in *al Ahram,* December 8, 1991, and *al Shaab,* October 25, 1994.
3. Quoted in *al Ahaly,* April 26, 1989.
4. *Rose al Yusuf,* April 24, 1989.
5. Ibid., May 1, 1989.
6. See *al Ahaly,* October 26, 1994.
7. Ghazzaly commented that Naguib Mahfuz was a great writer who merited the Nobel Prize, but not, in his view, for *Children of Gebelaawi.* See *al Akhbar,* June 5, 1991.
8. The interview with Mahfuz and Ghazzaly in the hospital after the attempt on Mahfuz's life appeared in *al Musawwar,* December 2, 1994.
9. For Mahfuz's views on relations with Israel, see the interview in *al Wassat,* October 24, 1994.

10. See *al Migalla,* October 2–8, 1994, and *al Araby,* October 24, 1994.
11. *Al Migalla,* October 29, 1994.
12. See also Fahmy Huwaidy in *al Hayat,* October 19, 1994.
13. See the Ghazzaly interview in *al Muslimun,* May 28, 1993.
14. For a mainstream Islamist discussion of these artistic traditions, see the articles of the literary critic Safinaz Qazim, for example in *al Ahram,* February 8, 1993.
15. *See al Musawwar,* May 6, 1988, for a sampling of these extremist views.
16. Video clubs: see the report in *al Wafd,* February 1, 1988. See also the report of an attack on a theater in Assiut in *al Musawwar,* May 6, 1988. Student concerts: one such incident is reported in *al Ahram,* March 9, 1988.
17. For Kamal Abul Magd's authoritative account, see a*l Ahram,* December 29, 1994.
18. *Al Ahram,* December 29, 1994.
19. Selim al Awa declared that an attack on Mahfuz was like an attack on the pyramids in *al Sharq al Awsat,* September 14, 1998.
20. *Al Ahram,* December 29, 1994.
21. For a discussion of Mahfuz's "sociological imagination," see the astute assessment by Sayyid Yassine in *Economic Ahram,* November 21, 1988.
22. Emphasis added.
23. *Al Araby,* February 27, 1995.
24. See the report on the public forum of prominent Islamists discussing art in Islamic civilization in *al Wafd,* December 18, 1992.
25. *Rose al Yusuf,* September 4, 1989.
26. Ibid.
27. *Sabah al Kheir,* April 27, 1989.
28. Ibid.
29. Huwaidy, in *al Ahram,* March 4, 1997; emphasis added.
30. Ibid.
31. Ibid.
32. This theme is emphasized in Ghazzaly's most important theoretical work, *The Prophet's Sunnah between the People of Hadith and People of Fiqh* (Cairo: Dar al Sharuq, 1991).
33. See the discussion of the Prophet's attitude toward the arts in *al Lewa al Islamy,* September 16, 1993.
34. See Ghazzaly in *al Wafd,* December 18, 1992.
35. Cited in *al Musawwar,* April 20, 1990.
36. The general lines of Ghazzaly's position are summarized in *al Musawwar,* April 20, 1999.
37. *Al Akhbar,* October 4, 1991.
38. For a report on the lawsuit by Shakaa, see *al Nur,* June 15, 1988.
39. Mustafa Shakaa, *Literature and the Development of Islamic Civilization* (Cairo: Maktabat al Anglo al Masriyya, 1968).
40. Shakaa, "Introduction" (pages not numbered), *Literature and the Development of Islamic Civilization.*
41. Ibid., p. 129.
42. Ibid., pp. 750–754.
43. *Al Nur,* June 15, 1988.

44. Ibid.
45. *Al Shaab,* August 16, 1988.
46. Ibid.
47. The court added that, since all such programs must be approved by the government censorship with a view to moral and ethical considerations, there was no need to reexamine the contents of the programs. *Al Shaab,* August 16, 1988. See also *al Nur,* March 4, 1991.
48. See, for example, the views of a Nasserist, Mahmud al Saadany, that exactly parallel those of Shakaa. *Al Musawwar,* February 17, 1995.
49. See, for example, Huwaidy, in *al Ahram,* May 10, 1988.
50. This argument provides a major theme for the widely read memoirs of Sarwat Okasha.
51. See Muhammad Salmawy, "Dialogues with Naguib Mahfuz," *al Ahram,* February 1, 1996.
52. Huwaidy, in *al Ahram,* January 12, 1999.
53. See a parallel view expressed by the prominent Islamist journalist Muhammad Abdul Qudus, son of the famous novelist Ihsan Abdul Qudus, in *al Shaab,* February 22, 1994.
54. For a full discussion of the New Islamist position on the place of the Copts and other non-Muslims in Islamic civilization, see Chapter 3.
55. Huwaidy, in *al Ahram,* May 2, 1989, reports the exchange.
56. *Al Musawwar,* July 2, 1993.
57. Ghazzaly, in *al Shaab,* April 5, 1994.
58. See the opening to Chapter 3.
59. Ghazzaly, in *al Shaab,* April 7, 1992.
60. Ibid.
61. See Huwaidy's lengthy discussion in *al Ahram,* February 28, 1989.
62. See the treatment of the incident and discussion of the range of responses it evoked in Huwaidy, *al Ahram,* October 1, 1991.
63. *Al Ahram,* October 1, 1991.
64. For a summary of the ruling of the Council of Islamic Researchers of al Azhar, see *al Wafd,* March 9, 1994.
65. Salah Montasser makes this point in his commentary in *al Ahram,* March 29, 1994.
66. For a discussion of one way in which the official attitude toward the *Wassatteyya* undercut efforts to confront extremism, see *al Shaab,* March 22, 1994.
67. *Al Wafd,* March 14, 1984.
68. For the text of the statement by Hamdy Gheith, see *Rose al Yusuf,* May 9, 1994.
69. Safinaz Qazim, in *al Ahram,* February 8, 1983.
70. See the interview with Mahfuz in *al Ahram,* January 21, 1996, where he confirms the importance of Ghazzaly in his personal religious formation.
71. This concept of Islam's adaptability as a civilizational project to all times and places finds a place in the thinking of all the major New Islamist writers. See, for particularly clear examples, the interview with Kamal Abul Magd in *Izaa wa Television,* March 7, 1992, and Yusuf al Qaradawy, *Elements of Comprehensiveness and Flexibility in the Islamic Sharia* (Cairo: Dar al Sahwa, 1985), passim.
72. See Qaradawy, in *al Hayat,* March 2, 2001.

73. See Huwaidy, in *al Ahram,* March 20, 2001.
74. See Huwaidy, in *al Sharq al Awsat,* March 19, 2001.

3. Building Community

1. The chronology of events is reconstructed from both opposition and government press reports. The *Al Ahram Strategic Report, 1988* (Cairo: Al Ahram Political and Strategic Studies Center, 1989) also provides a summary and analysis.
2. For Muhammad al Ghazzaly's statement, see *al Akhbar,* January 2, 1989.
3. For the text of the al Azhar statement, see *al Ahram,* December 26, 1988.
4. The Muslim Brothers' statement appeared in *Lewa al Islam,* January 9, 1989.
5. Kamal Abul Magd, *A Contemporary Islamic Vision* (Cairo: Dar al Shuruq, 1991), p. 25.
6. Muhammad al Ghazzaly, *The Prophet's Sunnah between the People of Hadith and People of Fiqh* (Cairo: Dar al Shuruq, 1991), p. 8.
7. Muhammad al Ghazzaly, *Women's Issues between Rigid and Alien Traditions* (Cairo: Dar al Shuruq, 1994), p. 174.
8. Ghazzaly, *The Prophet's Sunnah,* p. 7.
9. Ibid., p. 7.
10. Ibid., passim.
11. See Ibrahim Issa, *Rose al Yusuf,* June 28, 1993.
12. The summary and quotations that follow are taken from Abul Magd, *A Contemporary Islamic Vision,* pp. 43–45.
13. Ghazzaly, *The Prophet's Sunnah,* p. 54.
14. See the interview in *Nuss al Dunya,* August 23, 1998.
15. Ghazzaly, *The Prophet's Sunnah,* pp. 91–92.
16. For an effective popularization of Ghazzaly's method, see Fahmy Huwaidy, in *al Ahram,* May 14, 1991.
17. Ghazzaly, *The Prophet's Sunnah,* p. 56.
18. Ibid., p. 57.
19. Ibid.
20. Ibid., p. 59.
21. See Abul Magd, in *al Wafd,* January 28, 1994.
22. See the discussion by Huwaidy in *The Banned Articles* (Cairo: Dar al Shuruq, 1998), p. 107.
23. See Ghazzaly, in *al Shaab,* February 13, 1990.
24. See Ghazzaly, ibid., November 20, 1990.
25. See Al Awa, in *al Usbu,* March 24, 1997.
26. Surah 7: 189.
27. Surah 9: 71.
28. Ghazzaly, *The Prophet's Sunnah,* p. 56.
29. Surah 4: 34.
30. Ghazzaly, *Women's Issues,* p. 175.
31. Ibid., p. 174.
32. Muhammad al Ghazzaly, *Toward a Substantive Interpretation of the Surahs of the Holy Quran* (Cairo: Dar al Shuruq, 1995), p. 5.

33. Kamal Abul Magd, *Dialogue Not Confrontation* (Cairo: Dar al Shuruq, 1988), p. 34.
34. Ghazzaly, *Toward a Substantive Interpretation,* p. 5.
35. Ghazzaly, *The Prophet's Sunnah,* p. 67.
36. Ghazzaly, *Toward a Substantive Interpretation,* p. 70.
37. Surah 2: 228.
38. *Al Usbu,* September 15, 1997.
39. Surah 4: 34.
40. *Al Usbu,* September 15, 1997.
41. Surah 33: 33.
42. *Al Usbu,* September 15, 1997.
43. Abul Magd, *Dialogue,* p. 82; see also pp. 5–12.
44. For Qaradawy's discussion, see *The Islamic Awakening: The Concerns of the Arab and Islamic Homeland* (Cairo: Dar al Sahwa, 1988), pp. 60–62.
45. Ibid, p. 62.
46. Ibid., pp. 78–79.
47. See the discussion by Abul Magd in *al Ahram,* December 11, 1998.
48. Ibid.
49. Ibid.
50. Huwaidy discusses this concept in *al Ahram,* November 26, 1996.
51. Abul Magd, *A Contemporary Islamic Vision,* p. 37.
52. See Yusuf al Qaradawy, *Non-Muslims in Islamic Society,* 2nd ed. (Beirut: Muassasit al Risala, 1983); Fahmy Huwaidy, *Citizens, not Zimmis* (Cairo: Dar al Shuruq, 1985); and Muhammad Selim al Awa, *Copts and Islam* (Cairo: Dar al Shuruq, 1987).
53. *Al Musawwar,* March 23, 1990.
54. Qaradawy, *Non-Muslims,* p. 5.
55. Abul Magd, *Dialogue,* p. 86.
56. Surah 2: 30.
57. Abul Magd, *Dialogue,* p. 87.
58. Ibid., p. 34.
59. Yusuf al Qaradawy, *Elements of Comprehensiveness and Flexibility in the Islamic Sharia* (Cairo: Dar al Sahwa, 1985), p. 62.
60. These adjectives are taken from the title of Qaradawy's indispensable book, *Elements of Comprehensiveness,* 1985.
61. Ibid., p. 11.
62. Ibid., p. 43.
63. Ibid., p. 65.
64. Ibid., p. 44.
65. Abul Magd, *Dialogue,* p. 87.
66. Ibid., pp. 89–90.
67. *October,* July 8, 1990.
68. Qaradawy, *Elements of Comprehensiveness,* pp. 78–113.
69. Abul Magd, *Dialogue,* pp. 88–89.
70. *October,* July 8, 1990.
71. Ibid.
72. Abul Magd, *Dialogue,* p. 175.

73. See the extensive interview with Abul Magd, in *October,* July 8, 1990.
74. Ibid.
75. Abul Magd, *Dialogue,* p. 19.
76. Qaradawy, *Elements of Comprehensiveness,* p. 62.
77. Quran, 11: 118.
78. Quran, 30: 22.
79. Quran, 49: 13.
80. Abul Magd, *A Contemporary Islamic Vision*, p. 12; emphasis added.
81. Ibid.
82. Yusuf al Qaradawy, *Islam and Secularism, Face to Face* (Cairo: Dar al Sahwa, 1987), p. 51.
83. Abul Magd, *Dialogue*, p. 140.
84. Ibid., p. 138.
85. Ibid., pp. 138–139.
86. Ibid., p. 12.
87. Ibid., p. 7.
88. For a particularly clear assessment of this extremist trend by the New Islamists, see Abul Magd, *A Contemporary Islamic Vision,* p. 12.
89. Abul Magd, *Dialogue,* p. 6.
90. Abul Magd, *A Contemporary Islamic Vision,* p. 8.
91. Fahmy Huwaidy, *Falsification of Consciousness* (Dar al Shuruq, 1999), p. 12.
92. *Al Ahram,* April 20, 1993.
93. See Abul Magd, in *al Ahram,* December 11, 1998.
94. See Huwaidy, in *al Ahram,* January 12, 19, and 26, 1999; February 2, 1999; and August 10, 1999.
95. See Huwaidy, in *al Ahram,* January 19, 1999.
96. Ibid.
97. Ibid.
98. Ibid.
99. See Muhammad al Ghazzaly, *The Battle of the Musshaf* (Cairo: Nahdat Masr, 1996), p. 94. See also the related citations by Huwaidy, in *al Ahram,* August 25, 1987.
100. Cited by Huwaidy, in *al Ahram,* February 2, 1999.
101. Ibid.

4. Creating an Economic System

1. See Fahmy Huwaidy, in *al Ahram,* January 24, 1995.
2. See Sayyid Yassine for a sharply critical assessment in *Economic Ahram,* December 15, 1988.
3. See also the appreciative article on the Islamic banks by Ahmed Bahgat, *al Ahram,* January 26, 1995.
4. See the discussion of money in Yusuf al Qaradawy, *The Islamic Awakening: The Concerns of the Arab and Islamic Homeland* (Cairo: Dar al Sahwa, 1988), p. 13.
5. *October,* July 8, 1990.
6. "Survey: Islam and the West," *Economist,* August 6, 1989, p. 9.

7. Huwaidy, in *al Ahram,* January 24, 1995.
8. Sayyid Yassine has written frequently on this issue. In my view, the most cogent of his critical assessments is that in *Economic Ahram,* January 2, 1989.
9. These differences find expression even among the New Islamists. Shaikh Muhammad al Ghazzaly, for example, sided with Shaikh Tantawy, who ruled as Mufti of Egypt that interest offered in the modern banking system differs from the *riba* forbidden in the Quran and is therefore permissible. See *al Ahram,* September 21, 1989. Yusuf al Qaradawy sharply disagrees. For a recent restatement of Qaradawy's views as part of the ongoing debate among New Islamists and the Islamic wave generally in the 1990s, see *al Shaab,* March 21, 1997.
10. "Survey: Islam and the West," *Economist,* August 6, 1989, p. 10.
11. Ibid.
12. Huwaidy, in *al Ahram,* January 24, 1995.
13. Kamal Abul Magd, *A Contemporary Islamic Vision: Declaration of Principles* (Cairo: Dar al Shuruq, 1991), p. 30.
14. Ibid., pp. 31–32.
15. See Huwaidy, in *al Ahram,* September 10, 1996.
16. *Al Ahram,* January 26, 1999.
17. Ibid.
18. Yusuf al Qaradawy, *The Role of Values and Ethics in the Islamic Economy* (Cairo: Maktabit Wahba, 1995), p. 35.
19. Ibid., p. 57.
20. Ibid.
21. Ibid., pp. 68–76.
22. Ibid., p. 50.
23. For example, the *Economist* article reviewing the experiment on Islamic banking provides this incorrect definition of *zakat.* See "Survey: Islam and the West," *Economist,* August 6, 1989, p. 10.
24. Qaradawy, *Role of Values and Ethics,* p. 21.
25. Qaradawy, *The Islamic Awakening,* p. 13.
26. Huwaidy, in *al Ahram,* January 19, 1999.
27. A concise summary of Muhammad al Ghazzaly's ideas on these matters, especially poverty, can be found in Muhammad Emara, *al-Hilal,* January 1990, pp. 166–175.
28. Cited by Huwaidy, in *al Ahram,* January 19, 1999.
29. Abul Magd, *A Contemporary Islamic Vision,* p. 83.
30. Huwaidy, in *al Ahram,* January 26, 1999.
31. Abul Magd, *A Contemporary Islamic Vision,* p. 45.
32. *Al Ahram,* April 29, 1988.
33. See Saad Ibrahim, in *al Jumhuriyyah,* June 4, 1988.
34. See Ahmed Bahaeddine, in *al Ahram,* December 10, 1988.
35. Huwaidy, in *al Ahram,* November 22, 1988. For a parallel early assessment by a highly respected non-Islamist journalist, see also Ahmed Bahaeddine, in *al Ahram,* August 10, 1988.
36. See, in particular, the superlative analysis by Mahmud Abdul Fadil, *The Big Financial Trick: The Political Economy of the Tawzif al Amwal Companies* (Cairo: Dar al Mustaqbal al Arabi, 1989).

37. Huwaidy, *Saut al Arab,* July 5, 1987; see also Huwaidy, in *al Ahram,* December 13, 1988.
38. See Huwaidy's pointed review of the report in *al Ahram,* October 11, 1988.
39. See *al-Nur* newspaper, *Sabah al Kheir,* July 28, 1988.
40. See Abul Magd, in *al Shaab,* March 21, 1997.
41. For an example of this kind of analysis, see Saad Ibrahim, in *al Jumhurriyya,* June 4, 1988.
42. See the interview with Abul Magd in *al Shaab,* March 21, 1997.
43. *Al Shaab,* March 21, 1997.
44. *Al Ahram,* September 25, 1994.
45. Abul Magd, *A Contemporary Islamic Vision,* p. 33.
46. Ibid., p. 32.
47. Ibid., p. 33.
48. Ibid., pp. 32–33.
49. Abul Magd, in *al Ahram,* September 25, 1994.
50. Huwaidy, in *al Ahram,* August 4, 1998.
51. Ibid.
52. Abul Magd makes this general point in *al Nur,* July 28, 1988; Huwaidy cites both Ghazzaly and Qaradawy to the same effect in *al Ahram,* August 25, 1987.
53. Huwaidy adopted this phrase and the thinking behind it from the economist Galal Amin, who has produced an impressive body of work critiquing the Western idea of development and the pitfalls of imitation. See Huwaidy's treatment in *al Ahram,* October 4, 1994.
54. Huwaidy draws on the work of Galal Amin in his summary of this New Islamist position on globalism and development. See *al Ahram,* October 4, 1994.
55. For the main outlines of this assessment, shared by all the major New Islamist thinkers, see Kamal Abul Magd, in *al Ahram,* September 27, 1994.
56. *Al Araby,* June 10, 1996.
57. See Fahmy Huwaidy in *al Ahram,* July 28, 1998.
58. See Galal Amin in *al Ahaly,* February 20, 1995.
59. Huwaidy, in *Al Ahram,* August 4, 1998.
60. Huwaidy, in *al Ahram,* February 27, 2001.
61. Huwaidy, in *al Ahram,* August 4, 1998.
62. Lutfy Abdul Azim, in *Rose al Yusuf,* August 10, 1998.
63. Huwaidy cites an article by Thomas L. Friedman, the *New York Times* columnist, that documents the impressive Israeli progress. See *Al Ahram,* July 28, 1998.
64. Fahmy Huwaidy, in *al Ahram,* June 16, 1998.
65. Ibid.
66. Ibid.
67. This general theme is sounded throughout Qaradawy's *The Islamic Awakening.*
68. Huwaidy, in *al Ahram,* August 18, 1998.
69. Huwaidy, in *al Ahram,* February 2, 1999.
70. Cited by Huwaidy, in *al Ahram,* January 19, 1999.
71. The incident is reported by Huwaidy in *al Ahram,* November 22, 1988.
72. Cited in *al Ahram,* March 17, 1991.
73. *Al Ahram,* January 26, 1999; see also Huwaidy's discussion in *al Wafd,* February 25, 1995.

74. Huwaidy, in *al Ahram,* February 6, 2001.
75. See Huwaidy, in *al Ahram,* June 16, 1998.
76. Huwaidy, *in al Ahram,* February 27, 2001.
77. See Huwaidy, in *al Shaab,* September 3, 1999.
78. Galal Amin makes this point in his insightful analysis of the Marina incident. See Amin, in *al Ahaly,* October 7, 1998.
79. When Huwaidy wrote a lengthy analysis of the incident, it was refused publication in *al Ahram.* Huwaidy eventually published his piece in *al Shaab,* September 3, 1999.
80. *Al Ahaly,* September 23, 1998.
81. *Al Ahram,* June 14, 1997.
82. See Huwaidy's detailed treatment of the history of philanthropy in Egypt in the pre-revolutionary period in *al Ahram,* August 26, 1997.
83. *Al Dustur,* June 18, 1996.
84. *Al Ahram,* July 29, 1997.
85. Ibid.

5. Struggling for Islamic Renewal

1. *Al Ahram* refused to publish the original article as Huwaidy's regular column in that newspaper, as did *al Shaab,* the usual second choice for Huwaidy. Only *al Wafd* saw fit to publish Huwaidy's articulation of the voice of the national political conscience on both occasions. See *Al Wafd,* November 28, 1995; the article was reprinted during the 2000 election campaigns.
2. *Al Wafd,* November 28, 1995.
3. Ibid.
4. Adel Hussein cites the statement in *al Wafd,* November 18, 2000.
5. See *al Wafd,* November 16, 2000.
6. See *al Wafd,* November 16 and 26, 2000.
7. See *al Wafd,* November 26, 2000.
8. See Huwaidy, in *al Ahram,* November 21, 2000.
9. See Sayyid Yassine, in *al Qahira,* November 2, 2000.
10. *Al Ahrar,* March 23, 1992.
11. Fahmy Huwaidy, *Islam and Democracy* (Cairo: Al Ahram Center for Publications and Translations, 1993), p. 122.
12. Ibid., p. 121.
13. Ibid.
14. See, for example, Kamal Abul Magd, *A Contemporary Islamic Vision: Declaration of Principles* (Cairo: Dar al Sharuq, 1991), p. 31.
15. *Al Shaab,* January 24, 1997.
16. Fahmy Huwaidy, *The Quran and the Sultan* (Cairo: Dar al Sharuq, 1999), pp. 20–21.
17. For Iranian developments, see Huwaidy, in *al Sharq al Awsat,* February 28, 2000.
18. Huwaidy, in *al Ahram,* July 30, 1991.
19. See Huwaidy, in *al Migalla,* May 15–21, 1994.
20. Ibid.

21. Huwaidy, *Islam and Democracy,* passim.
22. Ibid., p. 103.
23. Ibid., p. 66.
24. Ibid., p. 113.
25. See Huwaidy, in *al Migalla,* May 15–21, 1994.
26. For a discussion of these three sources, see Huwaidy, in *al Ahram,* January 18, 1996.
27. Muhammad al Ghazzaly, *From Here We Know* (Cairo: Nahdat Masr, 1997), pp. 20–21.
28. Abul Magd, *A Contemporary Islamic Vision,* p. 29; emphasis added.
29. Kamal Abul Magd, *Dialogue Not Confrontation* (Cairo: Dar al Sharuq, 1988), p. 133.
30. Ibid., p. 136.
31. Selim al Awa, in *al Shaab,* November 21, 1995.
32. Al Awa, in *al Usbu,* July 21, 1997.
33. Abul Magd, *A Contemporary Islamic Vision,* p. 29.
34. See, for example, al Awa, in *al Usbu,* August 18, 1997.
35. See Essam Sultan's account in an interview in *al Dustur,* December 10, 1997.
36. See the discussion of the manifesto and its subsequent history in the Introduction.
37. Muhammad Selim al Awa, *The Political and Constitutional Crisis in Egypt* (Cairo: Al Zahraa, 1991).
38. See the discussion of Qaradawy's lecture in a forum in Chapter 6.
39. See Awa's account of the incident in *al Sharq al Awsat,* September 14, 1998.
40. See Bishry's comments in *al Araby,* May 4, 2000.
41. Yusuf al Qaradawy treats all of these themes. See *The Islamic Solution: A Duty and a Necessity,* 3rd ed. (Cairo: Maktabat Wahba, 1977), and *The Islamic Awakening: The Concerns of the Arab and Islamic Homeland* (Cairo: Dar al Sahwa, 1988).
42. For an assessment of the Brothers' success, see *al Usbu,* February 26, 2001.
43. See the discussion of the Ain Shams events in Chapter 3.
44. For a detailed treatment of the complex cases of Farag Foda and the academic Nasr Abu Zeid, see my *Islam in the Moment of Complexity,* forthcoming.
45. Fahmy Huwaidy, in *al Ahram,* July 3, 1993.
46. See Abul Ela Mady in *al Ahram,* February 18, 1998. For a discussion of the composition of the founding group, including a listing of women and Coptic members, see Muhammad Salah, in *al Hayat,* April 6, 1998.
47. See Abul Ela Mady, generally regarded as the Party's leading figure and spokesperson, in *al Wassat,* January 19, 1998.
48. Nabil Abdul Fattah notes of the platform that "it seems to balance the views of the younger generation and the founding generation." See Abdul Fattah, in *al Wafd,* January 18, 1996.
49. For the most insightful of the early reactions to the announcement by non-Islamists, see Abdul Fattah, in *al Wafd,* January 18, 1996. Abdul Fattah correctly understands this development as a reflection of a movement away from the "intellectual rigidity, conservatism, and a fundamentalist vision of the world and man" that had long characterized the Brotherhood. Abdul Fattah's astute assessment of the Wassat program recognizes the influence of such New Islamist figures as al Awa and Abul Magd, as well as other prominent intellectuals.

50. All of the quotations from the platform are from Rafiq Habib, *Al Wassat Party Papers* (Cairo: n.p., 1996).
51. See Abul Ela Mady's comments in *al Araby,* August 29, 1999.
52. For a fascinating treatment of the Wassat break by a Brotherhood figure of the same generation who supports the leadership, see Hamed Abdul Maguid in the Pakistani Arabic-language periodical *Al Gamaia al Islameyya,* no. 371, February 10, 1997.
53. See Rafiq Habib, *Al Wassat Party Papers,* p. 14.
54. Ibid.
55. Ibid., p. 15.
56. Ibid.
57. Ibid., p. 9.
58. Ibid., p. 10.
59. Ibid.
60. Ibid., p. 12.
61. Ibid., p. 11.
62. Ibid., p. 12.
63. Ibid., especially pp. 75–85.
64. Habib in *al Shaab,* April 4, 1996, discusses the government decision.
65. See Ibrahim Khalil, in *Rose al Yusuf,* January 26, 1996.
66. In the wake of Mady's arrest, Habib spoke for the party and provided details of this development in *al Shaab,* April 4, 1996.
67. See Abul Meguid of the Al Ahram Center for Political and Strategic Studies, in *al Hayat,* June 22, 1997, and *al Ahrar,* June 1, 1998.
68. On Brotherhood thinking, see *al Araby,* July 13, 1997. Parallel documentation is provided in *al Wassat,* October 5, 1998. For al Hudaiby's own explanation, see the interviews in the articles by Muhammad Salah, *al Hayat,* February 19 and June 29, 1996.
69. See the report of Qaradawy's reaction in Muhammad Salah, *al Hayat,* September 23, 1996. Later, it was announced that Qaradawy's son had joined the Wassat Party, as reported in Salah, *al Hayat,* November 29, 1996.
70. See the comments by Abul Magd in *al Araby,* July 13, 1997.
71. See al Awa, in *al Usbu,* July 7, 1997.
72. See al Awa, in *al Wassat,* January 13, 1997.
73. Ibid.
74. For details, see the interview with Mady in *al Wassat,* October 5, 1998.
75. For details, see the interview with Mady in *al Ahaly,* May 10, 1998.
76. All quotations from the platform are from Salah Abdul Karim, "Introduction," *Egyptian Wassat Party Platform* (Cairo: n.p., May 1998), pp. 5–11.
77. See Mady's interview in *al Wassat,* January 19, 1998.
78. Abdul Karim, "Introduction," p. 11.
79. *Al Usbu,* May 1, 2000.
80. Al Awa, in *al Usbu,* June 5, 2000.
81. Al Awa, in *al Usbu,* June 12, 2000.
82. All of the quotations and summaries of views from the Cairo University Conference are from the presentations and unpublished papers of Kamal Abul Magd,

Selim al Awa, and Tareq al Bishry, Thirteenth Annual Conference of Cairo University Political Science Research, December 4–6, 1999. A copy of Awa's paper was made available; references to the papers of Bishry and Abul Magd rely on notes taken during the presentations.

83. Hala Mustafa, *Political Islam in Egypt: From Reform Movement to Violent Groups* (Cairo: Al Ahram Center for Political and Strategic Studies, 1992).
84. See Sayyid Yassine on Shawy's work, in *al Ahram,* January 31, 1994.

6. Engaging the World

1. The description and quotations from Qaradawy's address are from my notes taken at the Doctors' Association lecture in Cairo, August 1995.
2. See Yusuf al Qaradawy on the idea of "dialogue" in *Fiqh of Priorities: A New Study in the Light of Quran and Sunnah* (Cairo: Wahba, 1995), especially pp. 168–172.
3. Fahmy Huwaidy, in *al Sharq al Awsat,* February 12, 2001.
4. See Yusuf al Qaradawy, in a*l Ahram,* August 7, 1994.
5. See the series of articles by Fahmy Huwaidy in *al Sharq al Awsat,* January 29, February 12, and February 13, 2001.
6. All quotations in the following paragraphs dealing with the Clinton proposal are from Fahmy Huwaidy's article in *al Ahram,* January 2, 2001.
7. On this claim of historically Jewish neighborhoods, see al Awa, in *al Usbu,* October 16, 2000.
8. Huwaidy cites this assessment by Qaradawy, made five days earlier, in *al Ahram,* August 22, 2000.
9. See Huwaidy's discussion in *al Ahram,* August 22, 2000.
10. See Huwaidy's discussion in *al Ahram,* February 13, 2001.
11. Huwaidy in his series in *al Sharq al Awsat,* January 29, February 12, and February 13, 2001, sums up these general conclusions of the New Islamists. For a more detailed treatment of the peace movement in Israel, see Huwaidy, in *al Ahram,* May 26, 1996.
12. See, for example, Huwaidy's celebration of the Hizbullah resistance and assessment of its lessons for the larger struggle in *al Ahram,* March 30, 1999.
13. Ibid.
14. See Huwaidy, in *al Ahram,* November 7, 2000.
15. See the remarks by Selim al Awa in *Al Usbu,* January 22, 2001.
16. See al Awa, in *al Usbu,* November 27, 2000.
17. Al Awa, in *al Usbu,* December 18, 2000.
18. Huwaidy, in *Sharq al Awsat,* December 11, 2000.
19. Al Awa, in *al Usbu,* November 27, 2000.
20. See Qaradawy's response to Sayyid Yassine in the context of which this observation is made. *Al Ahram,* August 7, 1994.
21. See the report of Ghazzaly's remarks in a*l Wafd,* October 28, 1991.
22. Qaradawy, *Fiqh of Priorities,* pp. 131–132.
23. Tareq al Bishry, "On Jerusalem and Palestine, Its Geographic Container," in Seif Abdul Fatah and Nadia Mustafa, eds., *My Nation and the World* (Cairo: Civilization Center for Political Studies, 1999).

24. Ibid., p. 42.
25. Ibid., p. 44.
26. Huwaidy, in *al Ahram,* October 25, 1988.
27. See Abdul Meguid, *The Decline: From Armed Struggle to Gaza-Jericho* (Cairo: Dar al Karei al Araby, 1994), especially pp. 221–236.
28. See Huwaidy, in *al Ahram,* September 24, 1991.
29. See Huwaidy, in *Al Ahram,* January 1, 1989.
30. For Huwaidy's assessment of Madrid, see *al Ahram,* September 21, 1993.
31. Bishry, "On Jerusalem and Palestine," p. 44.
32. Ibid., p. 41.
33. Ibid., p. 42.
34. Ibid., p. 41.
35. The quotations from Qaradawy are all from the article of January 17, 1995, in *al Shaab.*
36. See also Muhammad al Ghazzaly in an interview with *al Ahrar,* December 19, 1994.
37. The citations are from Awa's article in *al Shaab,* February 25, 1997.
38. Bishry, "On Jerusalem and Palestine," p. 45.
39. These quotations are from the discussion after the lecture at American University in Cairo, November 17, 1993.
40. Huwaidy, in *al Ahram,* October 29, 1996.
41. Qaradawy, *Fiqh of Priorities,* p. 131.
42. Qaradawy discusses these failed efforts in *Nuss al Dunya,* August 23, 1998.
43. Ghazzaly, in *al Shaab,* February 5, 1994.
44. See Huwaidy's treatment of the Taliban in *al Ahram,* October 15, 1996, April 9, 2001, and March 20, 2001.
45. See Qaradawy, in *Nuss al Dunya,* August 23, 1998.
46. Kamal Abul Magd, in *al Ahram,* December 11, 1998.
47. This idea is developed in Chapter 5.
48. See, for example, Abul Magd's assessment of the influence of the work of John Esposito, representing such an alternative trend of thought. *Al Hayat,* March 21, 1997.
49. These general principles are expressed in Kamal Abul Magd, *A Contemporary Islamic Vision: Declaration of Principles* (Cairo: Dar al Sharuq, 1991), pp. 48–50.
50. Ghazzaly frequently registered all of these themes. See, for example, *al Muslimun,* April 3, 1992.
51. Huwaidy regularly makes positive references to the Universal Declaration of Human Rights. See, for example, *al Ahram,* March 29, 1994.
52. Awa made his observation in the context of a public discussion with Naggar and others at the Cairo Center for Human Rights, October 17, 1994.
53. *Al Ahram,* February 28, 1995.
54. See the authoritative statement of this call for such efforts in the human interest in Abul Magd, *A Contemporary Islamic Vision,* pp. 48–50.
55. All of the quotations from Huwaidy on the Conference on Social Justice are from *al Ahram,* February 28, 1995.
56. *Al Ahram,* February 28, 1995.
57. Ibid.

58. All of the following quotations by Abul Magd are from *al Ahram,* September 25, 1994.
59. Muhammad Selim al Awa, *Islamic Fiqh on the Road of Renewal,* 2nd ed. (Beirut: Maktab al Islamy, 1998), p. 208.
60. For a full discussion of the New Islamist interpretations on an array of issues related to the status of women, see Chapter 3.
61. Awa, *Islamic Fiqh,* p. 208.
62. Ibid., p. 212.
63. For a detailed discussion of this concept of *fiqh,* see Chapter 3.
64. *Al Ahram,* September 25, 1994.
65. The complete text, in Arabic and English, of Qaradawy's statement, from which all quotations are taken, was available on Islam Online, September 13, 2001.
66. Surah 5: 32.
67. Surah 2: 30.
68. The compete text, in Arabic and English, of the *fatwa,* from which all quotations are taken, was available on Islam Online, September 27, 2001.
69. See the report on the reaction in *al Qahira,* October 23, 2001.
70. Surah 5: 32–34.
71. Surah 5: 33–34.
72. Surah 5: 2.
73. Surah 64: 16.
74. Tareq al Bishry, *The Arabs in the Face of Aggression* (Cairo: Dar al Sharuq, 2002), p. 33.
75. For an astute discussion that draws on the European critique of the new American century and the Bush strategic doctrine that drives it, see Sayyid Yassine, in *al Ahram,* October 10, 2002.
76. Reported in Islam Online, June 23, 2002.
77. Ibid.
78. Interview in Islam Online, October 10, 2002.
79. Islam Online, February 9, 2003.
80. Ibid.
81. See the article by Selim al Awa in *al Usbu,* March 17, 2003. The Shaikh of al Azhar stated in *al Hayat,* March 17, 2003, that the intent of the statement had been misunderstood and indicated awareness of the opposition to the war by the Egyptian Coptic community and by European states with predominantly Christian populations.
82. The statement of the intellectuals was published in *al Hayat,* March 23, 2003.
83. Abul Magd, *A Contemporary Islamic Vision,* p. 48.
84. Ibid.
85. Surah 49: 13.
86. *A Contemporary Islamic Vision,* p. 49.

Conclusion

1. All quotations from Kamal Abul Magd's intervention are from his article in *Weghat Nazar,* September 1999.

2. See the discussion in Chapter 5.
3. Surah 2: 150.
4. See the report of Qaradawy's speech and interview in *al Hayat,* October 13, 2001.
5. See Huwaidy's revealing discussion of his trip in *al Sharq al Awsat,* November 19, 2001.
6. Ibid.
7. The interview was conducted by Sanaa Mansur for the program "Underscored in Red," March 12, 2002.
8. See Huwaidy, in *al Ahram,* October 8, 1985.

Glossary of Arabic Terms

There are no absolute equivalents in English for the important Islamic concepts and phrases used in this book. The translations provided here should be viewed as only rough approximations to the Arabic terms. They are offered to help non-Arabic readers understand Islamic concepts with which they are unfamiliar. In all cases, the translations follow as closely as possible the meaning given to these terms by the New Islamists in the collective body of their work. Readers should understand that other Islamic scholars might well contest these meanings. The fuller meaning of all these phrases will only become apparent from the contexts in which they are used and the treatment they receive in the body of the book, where the New Islamists' understandings of these phrases are elaborated.

The general system I have used for Arabic terms in the text is that the first time the expression is used in a given chapter, it will appear first in Arabic transliteration in italics followed by an English translation in brackets. Subsequently, only the Arabic transliteration is used. However, for a small group of terms for which an adequate translation is available, the English translation only is used after the term has been introduced with the transliteration. Finally, a handful of Arabic words, now widely used and understood in English, will be treated as English words.

I have simplified the issue of transliteration by avoiding diacritics. Readers of Arabic should still have no trouble recognizing the original, while non-Arabic readers will be spared the cumbersome and distracting symbols necessary to render Arabic letters in English. For plurals, I have simply added an "s" to singular forms, rather than introducing complicated Arabic forms, unless they have already become somewhat familiar. I hope the ease of reading for general readers will compensate for the rightful objections of purists to all of these deviations.

alim (pl. *ulama):* Islamic scholar

amir: leader of Islamist group

faqih (pl. *faqihs):* an Islamic scholar, specially trained and recognized by peers as qualified to contribute to *fiqh;* commonly but misleading translated as "jurisprudent"

fatwa (pl. *fatwas):* religious opinion by a religious scholar *fiqh:* understanding of Quran and *Sunnah,* the work of trained specialists known as *faqihs* (see above); subject to challenge and correction as a fully human endeavor. [*Note:* in Western scholarship, commonly translated as "Islamic jurisprudence." The New Islamists would likely regard this translation as misleading.] Also used with a nontechnical meaning of insight or understanding

gizya: the tax on non-Muslims, provided for by a contract according to which they were exempted from military service and received protection and legal rights

hadith (pl. *hadiths):* sayings of the Prophet that illuminate his thoughts and actions, accompanied by their sources

hajj: pilgrimage to Mecca, held annually and prescribed for all Muslims once in their lifetime

hakemeyya or hakemeyyet Allah: God's rule

halal: religiously permitted

haram: religiously forbidden

hegab: headscarf

hirabah: the Quranic term for waging war against society and civilization

hisbeh: the principle that legal action in defense of the public interest may be taken, even though the individual making the charge has not personally suffered injury or harm

hudud: punishments provided for in *Sharia*

ijtihad: an effort of interpretation of the sacred texts

intifada: uprising

istihlal: considering that which is religiously forbidden to be acceptable because it occurs under conditions of *jahileyya.* Extremist groups used this notion to justify such actions as theft

istikhlaf: Man's calling to act as God's regent on Earth

jahileyya: un-Islamic, atheist, or pagan; originally, the designation for pre-Islamic Arabia

jihad: striving or struggle to uphold and protect the world of Islam; commonly, though misleadingly, translated as "holy war"

khula: divorce initiated by the woman that requires her to return any financial gifts she received from her husband at the time of marriage

mufti: an Islamic scholar qualified to issue a religious opinion or *fatwa*

neqab: face veil

nushuz: an attitude, suggesting unfaithfulness

riba: usury

shaikh: a trained religious teacher or guide, entitled, for example, to give the Friday sermon

Sharia: the provisions from Quran and *Sunnah* to regulate human behavior. [*Note:* in Western scholarship, commonly translated as "Islamic law." The New Islamists would likely regard this translation as misleading.]

shura: consultation

Sunnah: all the deeds and words of the Prophet; the second source of Islam, after the Quran

takfir: declaring Muslims to be unbelievers

talim: formal schooling

tarbeyya: proper upbringing
tarshid: guidance
ulama: see *alim*
ummah: Islamic community
umra: recommended but not prescribed pilgrimage to Mecca at times other than the *hajj*
usul al fiqh: the "roots" or fundamental methods to guide efforts of Islamic scholars to understand the sacred texts
waqf (pl. *awqaf):* Islamic endowment
Wassatteyya: the moderate Islamic mainstream
wilaya: a historical and therefore not binding concept of rule that precludes the rule of women and non-Muslims
zakat: obligatory alms
zimmah: contract of protection of non-Muslims in an Islamic society
zimmi: "protected" non-Muslim people subject to a covenant according to which they were exempted from military service and received protection and legal rights, in return for which they paid a special tax called the *gizya*

Acknowledgments

This book is in every sense the story of a voyage to an intellectual, cultural, and moral world into which I was not born but where I now no longer feel a stranger. It was Karen Aboul Kheir who first brought Islam as a civilization into view for me. She did so at first in conversations with Omar Mahmud, whose wit and sharply critical intelligence disciplined but did not dampen our enthusiasms. Even now, years later, I remember vividly Karen's animated discussion of the latest books of Muhammad al Ghazzaly, Kamal Abul Magd, and especially Yusuf al Qaradawy, who were to number among my principal guides to the Islamic Awakening as experienced and understood in Egypt. We began this book as a joint project, and the ideas and insights we shared in that formative first period are everywhere. Circumstances prevented our professional partnership, though not our friendship, from continuing, and here I can only register my gratitude to a guide and a friend who showed me, in so many ways, how boundaries could be navigated with respect rather than transgressed. I am grateful to Nevine Tewfik, who then worked with me for several years, first as a research assistant and then as a thoughtful colleague at the American University in Cairo. Nevine encouraged me, in particular, to continue to probe the larger philosophical questions that my work on Islam opened.

More recently, three colleagues and fellow travelers helped me to recognize the larger vistas and visions of Islam in more approachable realities. My friend, the late Kamel Attiya, insisted that I attend dawn prayers if I hoped to participate fully in the wonderful religious holidays with his wife Azza, son Mostafa, and daughter Samar. In the narratives of specific occasions and events, the reader should know that for the most part Kamel was with me, commenting, interpreting, and thoroughly enjoying our adventures. He still is. Every time, and there were many, when I felt I was not up to the rigors of the voyage and was ready to abandon the project, my sense that Kamel would be disappointed kept me going. Without Manar Shorbagy and Ramadan, however, even those good intentions would not have been enough. Manar Shorbagy, who teaches political science at the American University in Cairo, is among the most promising scholars of American politics of her generation. At the same time, she is an astute cultural commentator and political analyst of the Egyptian scene. Manar and I have thoroughly enjoyed the complementary character of our intellectual relationship. For all the flaws that may remain, the book is better for our "fights" and endless conversations. Manar did her best to keep me on the straight path, and all the deviations that remain are my fault, not hers. To Ramadan Abdul Aziz, I owe an equal debt of gratitude, though for quite different reasons. When we lost our colleague and friend Berlanti Abdullah, this project seemed in jeopardy. Berlanti brought to her work on our newspaper and journal files the eye of a trained sociologist, not to mention a warm and radiant personality. We marveled at how she mangaged to weave stories of her husband Sami and talented children Rabab and Ahmed into reports on the latest developments in national cultural politics. We thoroughly enjoyed being a part of those lives, too. It is on Ramadan that both Manar and I now rely for greater patience and steadiness than either of us can muster and for a calming, caring, and ordering presence. For the project, Ramadan is our stability and our anchor. He also insists, no matter what else is on the schedule, that I continue to work on my Arabic. And not just for the book—how else to play the important role of "Uncle Raymond" for his children, Muhammad and Sarah, and to side with his wife Nabila on remodeling their apartment and other crucial domestic issues? Islam and Egypt are very much about family, as readers will discover, both the human family in the widest sense and its immediate embodiments in those we love. My daughter Sarah's marriage to Karim Aboul Makarem, that kind and gentle young man she first caught sight of in her high school days in Cairo, and the family life they are lovingly building in Egypt have immeasurably deepened that sense.

Dividing my personal and professional life between Egypt and America has brought me friends and colleagues in three wonderful and diverse academic settings: Williams College where I taught for twenty-five years, Trinity College where I teach now, and the American University in Cairo where I have been both student and professor. So many of my friends at these schools have helped in so many ways with this book that I dare not mention any specific individuals; I thank you all for your support and encouragement. In addition, I note with appreciation that all three institutions provided support for the research for this book. Among other treasures, that support has made it possible to engage the services of Safaa Abdul Masih, who for many years has provided highly competent data entry services and a gracious presence even under pressure. The Egyptian scholars and intellectuals who most influenced my thinking, aside from those who are the subjects of this study, include Galal Amin, Muhammad Sayyid Said, Nabil Abdul Fattah, Sayyid Yassine, and Ahmed Abdullah, most of all for the critical edge of their thinking.

In the last stages of manuscript preparation, Tareq Ismael, Mark Taylor, Khaled Hafzy Abdul Rahman, Jack Waggett, and my brother Don Baker came to my rescue more than once, each with their distinctive talents and insights at just the right moment. I am grateful to each of them. At Harvard University Press, from start to finish, Kathleen McDermott and Kathleen Drummy have been extraordinarily helpful and encouraging, and I appreciate the painstaking and thoughtful editing of Mary Ellen Geer.

Finally and most importantly, I dedicate this book with love to my wife Elaine, with whom I share the values and commitments that inspired this project, and to our children, Sarah, Dorian, Madalyn, and Pamela, with thanks for their tolerance of my absences and other shortcomings, with gratitude for sharing their lives, and with the deepest appreciation for their exemplary openness to the world.

Index